Y0-CXG-111

UNIVERSITY OF NORTH CAROLINA

Library Studies Number 5

WHO'S WHODUNIT

A list of 3218 detective story writers and their 1100 pseudonyms

by

LENORE S. GRIBBIN

Chapel Hill
University of North Carolina Library
1968

UNIVERSITY OF NORTH CAROLINA

LIBRARY STUDIES

No. 1. North Carolina County Histories: A Bibliography, by William S. Powell, 1958.

No. 2. North Carolina Fiction, 1734-1957: An Annotated Bibliography, by a Joint Committee of the North Carolina English Teachers Association and the North Carolina Library Association, 1958.

No. 3. The Graduate School Dissertations and Theses, First Supplement, 1946-1959, compiled by the Humanities Division of the University of North Carolina Library, 1960.

No. 4 A Catalogue of Comedias Sueltas in the Library of the University of North Carolina, by William A. McKnight, with the collaboration of Mabel Barrett Jones, 1965.

No. 5. Who's Whodunit: A list of 3218 Detective Story Writers and Their 1100 Pseudonyms, by Lenore S. Gribbin, 1968.

CONTENTS

INTRODUCTION

This list of detective story writers is designed for the purpose of giving aid and comfort to those interested in the genre—whether for business or pleasure, fun or profit. To readers and writers it may offer unsuspected uses. To librarians it is a name authority list and classification aid, as well as a guide in a field long ignored, and sometimes disdained, and offering little more than the complete enthrallment of a sizeable proportion of the reading public.

It aims to present the names of all American and British authors of book-length detective stories from 1845 through 1961. The meaning of "book-length" is extended to include book collections of short stories by a single author. While it attempts to be a comprehensive list, it is easier to explain what it is not. It is not, of course, complete—completeness always being a bibliographic mirage. The compiler believes it to be complete up to the point of very diminishing returns. It is not critical—all names cited by the sources, unless eliminated for reasons later stated, are given: the author of a single mediocre work finds a place alongside the giants of the field. It is not a list of titles or first editions; those interested in such may refer to the sources indicated for further information.

The period covered is 1845-1961. Why 1845? Accepting the general agreement that Poe's short story, "Murders in the Rue Morgue," 1841, is the first detective story ever written, we proceed to 1845 which marks the first *book* of detective stories—Poe's *Tales,* published by Wiley & Putnam. It contains the three Dupin stories ("Murders in the Rue Morgue," "The Mystery of Marie Rogêt," and "The Purloined Letter") as well as "The Gold-Bug," but not "Thou Art the Man." The year 1961 is an arbitrary cut-off date, bringing the author list into the present decade.

Method

Outstanding bibliographies in the field (see list of Primary Sources) contributed the first group of names. Authors taken from the *United States Catalog* and its supplements, covering 1902-1928, and the *Cumulative Book Index,* 1928-1961, were those listed under the subject headings "Detective stories" and "Mystery stories" (later, in 1949, combined as "Mystery and detective stories"). Further search yielded a few more from sources listed in the bibliography.

All names thus gathered were searched in the *Library of Congress Catalog of Printed Cards* (in more recent years the *National Union Catalog*) for form of name, additional pseudonyms, and any useful information. A number were eliminated in this search—primarily authors of juvenile mysteries, Westerns, and non-fiction crime works. Except for 300 names, all were verified in the Library of Congress book catalogs, and in almost all cases the LC form has been followed. For a few names, the sources gave more recent, complete, or accurate information than LC, and this information is included here. Of the 300 names not found in LC, 200 were further checked in the *British Museum General Catalogue of Printed Books.* As a result, approximately 100 names were not found and were therefore accepted in the form provided by the original source.

Aliases, Pseudonyms, and Cross-References

Following American library practice, the real name of the author is given with references to it from his pseudonyms. Only rarely is the pseudonym listed in preference to the real name, and in most cases when the real name is not known. Occasionally the Library of Congress has desigated as "pseud." a form of the author's real name (e.g. Anne Hocking). In these cases this list gives the cross-reference but does not call it a pseudonym. Other cross-references are provided wherever they appear warranted from maiden name to married name, or married to maiden, if the woman appears to have published under both; from shorter name to full if used, from full form to shorter as needed. In cases of fuller and shorter names where the cross-reference would appear immediately before or after the name referred to, it is omitted.

The sources, as well as the additional search of the LC and BM catalogs, revealed many pseudonyms. It often requires many publications and years to tie together author and pseudonyms, and there are undoubtedly some in the list which bibliographic evidence has thus far failed to reveal. *All* pseudonyms found, including those under which the authors wrote non-detective stories or juvenile mysteries, are given in the list.

Joint pseudonyms, that phenomenal sharing of credit or discredit that seems so prevalent in this genre, are listed with "see also" cross-references to and from the individual authors.

All forms of names for which cross-references are listed are indicated by an "x" at the part referred from, unless the reference would be obvious, as in the pseudonyms.

Exclusions

Wherever possible, and sometimes on flimsy evidence, the following were eliminated: authors of juvenile mysteries, Westerns, ghost stories, supernatural, Gothic horror stories, adventure, non-fiction crime, plays. Anthologies (*i.e.*, editors) are not included—only authors with one or more book-length collections of stories. The nature of the list prohibits inclusion of anonymous works, though a few unidentified presudonyms (*e.g.*, Anonyma) are listed. Elimination of European authors was not difficult because German authors usually have German names and French authors French names; however, slight difficulty was involved because American and British authors sometimes have French and German names. It was with much regret we could not include Gaboriau, Leroux, and Simenon, nor Serner, Groller, and Dostoievsky. Baroness Orczy is included because her works were originally published in English. The period covered excludes any author who published his first detective novel after 1961; it also excludes (again with regret) such interesting precursors as Thomas Gaspey (*Richmond; or, Scenes in the life of a Bow Street Officer*, published 1827).

Sources

Relying heavily upon the comparatively few bibliographies and histories in this field, it was possible to collect names based on the judgment of specialists. It was not possible to read 25,000 books, however enticing, and decide which were "thrillers" or "crime novels" or "suspense" or "spy-with-or-without-detective," as differentiated from true detective novels. Haycraft's definition of the whodunit is closest to our aim: "the term in its widest and commonly accepted generic sense to include all related tales of mystery and crime with a perceptible thread of detection."[1]

Many names are, of course, open to question, and even some of the authors themselves object to being classed in the field (Geoffrey Household, Eric Ambler, James Cain). On such matters we refer to the sources, and cite them for each author—a brief symbol for the Primary Sources, a surname or fuller data for less frequently cited sources in the bibliography. The Primary Sources are those books which contributed the majority of the names in the list. Famous authors cited by many sources have, of course, many symbols after their names. The second part of the bibliography (Secondary Sources) contains those works which added a few new names or were particularly valuable for their guidance in defining the field. Omitted are many references—interesting, hilarious, dull, repetitious—which offered nothing new. For what is perhaps the best bibliography in the field see Haycraft's *Murder for Pleasure.*

Other problems were the borderline cases—length of story (perhaps a novelette which could be eliminated as a short story or included as a book), a collection of stories only part of which are detective, alleged "real-life memoirs" from about 1850 to 1890, usually fiction but occasionally non-fiction. In such dubious instances, it was a great temptation to give the weight of evidence to those authors cited most frequently by the sources; we have usually yielded to the temptation.

For other questions which may arise, attention is again directed to the sources. The James Moffatt cited by Thomson as the translator of the Scriptures is regarded as a different James Moffatt in the *British Museum Catalogue.* Thomson is cited here; any debate is with him.

Great appreciation is due John Dickson Carr, Howard Haycraft, and Frederic Dannay, whose helpful information above and beyond the bibliographic sources is indicated by (JDC), (HH) and (FD) in the column of sources.

This project was initiated at the University of North Carolina Library, Chapel Hill, which is attempting to build a notable detective story collection. The asterisks indicate those authors already represented in its collection as well as those for whom the Library is trying to obtain, as a first step, all first editions. Its ultimate goal is to acquire *all* first editions of *all* American and British detective story authors.

The list was completed by the undersigned in New Orleans. Special thanks are given to Mrs. Suad Jones for information on the University of North Carolina's collection and for searching birth and death dates beyond the Primary and Secondary Sources; to Mrs. Pat Mulligan who typed about 4,000 cards; to the Tulane University Library whose new Director, Dr. John H. Gribbin, helped to search and seize all needed resources; and to Dr. Jerrold Orne, University Librarian, North Carolina, whose importunate insistence led to completion of the task.

Lenore S. Gribbin

1. Haycraft, Howard, *ed. The Art of the Mystery Story.* New York, Simon and Schuster, 1946. p. 536.

PRIMARY SOURCES

Symbols

*	In University of North Carolina Detective Story Collection
**	In University of North Carolina Detective Story Collection with top priority for acquisition of first editions
1	United States Catalog, and supplements. New York, Wilson. 1902-28 (under subject "Detective stories")
	Cumulative book index. New York, Wilson.
2	1928-48 (under subjects "Detective stories" and "Mystery stories")
3	1949-61 (under subject "Mystery and detective stories")
C	Carter, John. Collecting detective fiction. London, Constable; New York, Scribner, 1938.
G	Gilbert, Michael, comp. Crime in good company; essays on criminals and crime-writing. London, Constable, 1959.
H	Haycraft, Howard. Murder for pleasure: the life and times of the detective story. New York, Appleton-Century, 1941.
EQ	Queen, Ellery, *pseud.* The detective short story; a bibliography. Boston, Little, Brown, 1942.
QQ	Queen, Ellery, *pseud.* Queen's quorum. A history of the detective-crime short story, as revealed by the 106 most important books published in this field since 1845. Boston, Little, Brown, 1951.
S	Sandoe, James. "Readers' guide to crime." *In* Haycraft, Howard. The art of the mystery story. New York, Simon and Schuster, 1946. (Revision of his "The detective story and academe," *Wilson Library Bulletin,* XVIII (1944))
St	Stevenson, William Bruce, comp. Detective fiction. Cambridge, National Book League, 1958. (Reader's guide, 3rd series)
Sy	Symons, Julian. The hundred best crime stories. London, The Sunday times, 1959.
W	Wright, Willard Huntington, ed. The great detective stories; a chronological anthology. New York, Scribner, 1939.

SECONDARY SOURCES

Benet, Stephen Vincent. "Bigger and better murders." *Bookman,* May, 1926.

The Book review digest. Minneapolis, New York, Wilson, 1917-26 (under subject "Fiction—Mystery stories")

Bragin, Charles. Bibliography: dime novels 1860-1964. Brooklyn, 1964. (Dime Novel Club issue 63)

Bragin, Charles. Dime novels; bibliography 1860-1928. Brooklyn, 1938.

Cambridge history of English literature. New York, London, Putnam, 1916-17. (Vols. 12-14, "The nineteenth century.")

Carter, John, ed. New paths in book collecting; essays by various hands. London, Constable, 1934.

A Century of thrillers from Poe to Arlen. With a foreword by James Agate. London, Daily Express Publications, 1934.

Chandler, Frank Wadleigh. The literature of roguery. New York, Franklin, 1958. 2 vols.

Chandler, Raymond. "The simple art of murder." *Atlantic Monthly,* Dec. 1944.

Chesterton, Gilbert Keith. A defence of detective stories. (*In his* The defendant. London, Johnson, 1901; New York, Dodd, Mead, 1902)

Crimes, creeps and thrills. London, Samuel, 1936.

Ellery Queen's annual. 1st-12th. 1946-57. New York, Random House. (Title varies: 1946-53, The Queen's awards.—1954-57, Ellery Queen's awards)

Ellery Queen's anthology. 1960-65. New York, Davis Publications.

The Encyclopedia Britannica. 14th ed. London, New York, Encyclopedia Britannica, 1937. ("Mystery stories," by Carolyn Wells, v.16, p.50)

Hardy, T. J. "The romance of crime." (*In his* Books on the shelf. London, Allen, 1934.)

Hawthorne, Julian, ed. The lock and key library. New York, Review of Reviews Co., 1909.

Haycraft, Howard, ed. The art of the mystery story; a collection of critical essays. New York, Simon & Schuster, 1946.

Jeaffreson, John Cordy. Novels and novelists, from Elizabeth to Victoria. London, Hurst and Blackett, 1858. 2 vols.

Johannsen, Albert. The House of Beadle and Adams, and its dime and nickel novels. Norman, University of Oklahoma Press, 1950. 2 vols.

Knox, Ronald Arbuthnott, ed. The best English detective stories of 1928. London, Faber, 1929; New York, Liveright, 1929. (Introduction includes his "decalogue" of detective story commandments.)

Mystery Writers of America. Murder cavalcade, an anthology. New York, Duell, Sloan and Pearce, 1946.

Nicholson, Marjorie. "The professor and the detective." *Atlantic Monthly*, April, 1929.

Pearson, Edmund. Dime novels; or, Following an old trail in popular literature. Boston, Little, Brown, 1929.

Queen, Ellery, *pseud.* ed. Challenge to the reader; an anthology. New York, Stokes, 1936.

Rodell, Marie F. Mystery fiction: theory and technique. New York, Duell, 1943.

Saintsbury, George Edward Bateman. The English novel. London, Dent, 1913.

Sayers, Dorothy Leigh, ed. Great short stories of detection, mystery and horror. London, Gollancz. 1928, 1931, 1934 (Series 1-3) (American editions have title: The omnibus of crime)

Starrett, Vincent. The private life of Sherlock Holmes. New York, Macmillan, 1933; London, Nicholson, 1934.

Symons, Julian. The detective story in Britain. London, Longmans, Green, 1962. British book news: Bibliographical series of supplements, no. 145)

Thomas, Gilbert. How to enjoy detective fiction. London, Rockliff, 1947.

Thomson, H. Douglas. Masters of mystery: a study of the detective story. London, Collins, 1931.

Walker, Hugh. The literature of the Victorian era. Cambridge, University Press, 1921.

Wells, Carolyn. The technique of the mystery story. Rev. ed. Springfield, Mass., Home Correspondence School, 1929.

Wrong, E. M., ed. Crime and detection. London, Oxford University Press, 1926. (World's classics, 301)

ADDITIONAL SOURCES OF DATES AND PSEUDONYMS

The Author's and writer's who's who. 1963. New York, Hafner.

Biography index; a cumulative index to biographical material in books and magazines. Jan. 1946/July 1949-1967. New York, Wilson.

Burke, William Jeremiah. American authors and books, 1640 to the present day [by] W. J. Burke and Will D. Howe. Augm. and rev. by Irving R. Weiss. New York, Crown Publishers, 1962.

Contemporary authors; the international bio-bibliographical guide to current authors and their works. v. 1-16. Detroit, Gale Research, 1962-66.

Dictionary of national biography . . . 1885-1901. Supplement, 1901-1911. Edited by Sir Sidney Lee. London, Oxford University Press, 1920.

Kunitz, Stanley Jasspon, ed. Twentieth century authors, a biographical dictionary of modern literature. First supplement. New York, Wilson, 1955.

The New Century cyclopedia of names, edited by Clarence L. Barnhart . . . New York, Appleton-Century-Crofts, 1954. 3 v.

Thomas, Clara. Canadian novelists, 1920-1945. Toronto, London, New York, Longmans, Green, 1946.

	Sources
A. A. of Punch, *pseud.* *see* Willis, Anthony Armstrong, 1897-	
Aarons, Edward Sidney, 1916- *pseuds.:* Edward Ronns Paul Ayres	2 3
Abby, Kieran, *pseud.* *see* Reilly, Helen (Kieran) 1890?-1962.	
Abbot, Anthony, *pseud.* *see* Oursler, Fulton, 1893-1952.	
Abbott, A. A., *pseud.* *see* Spewack, Samuel, 1899-	
Abbott, Bruce, *pseud.* *see* Reach, James.	
Abrahams, Doris Caroline, 1901- *pseuds.:* Caryl Brahms Oliver Linden	* 2 H S
Abrahams, Robert David, 1905-	2
Absinthe, *Père*, *pseud.* *see* Kelly, George C. 1849-1895.	
Acheson, Edward, 1902- (Full name: Edward Campion Acheson)	2
Acott, J H	2
Acre, Stephen, *pseud* *see* Gruber, Frank, 1904-	
Adair, Cecil, *pseud.* *see* Green, Evelyn Everett-, 1856-1932.	
Adair, Dennis, *pseud.* *see* Cronin, Bernard, 1884-	
Adam, Hargrave Lee, 1867-	2
Adam, Ruth.	2
Adams, Cleve Franklin, 1895-1950. *pseuds.:* Franklin Charles John Spain	* 2 3 H
Adams, Elihu.	2
Adams, Eustace Lane, 1891-	2
Adams, Frank Ramsay, 1883-1963.	2
Adams, Harrison, *pseud.* *see* Rathborne, St. George, 1854-1938.	
Adams, Herbert, 1874- *pseud.:* Jonathan Gray	* 1 2 3
Adams, Leta Zoe.	2
Adams, Samuel Hopkins, 1871-1958. *pseud.:* Warner Fabian	** 1 H EQ QQ
Adams, Shipley.	3
Addams, Julia Cleft- *see* Cleft-Addams, Julia.	
Addis, Eric Elrington. *pseud.:* Peter Drax.	2 H
Addis, Hugh.	3

Sources

Addiscombe, John, *pseud.* *see* Hunter, John, 1891-

Addison, Carol, *pseud.* *see* Clarke, J. Calvitt, 1888-

Addison, Henry Robert, 1805?-1876. EQ

Addison, Hugh, *pseud.* *see* Owen, Harry Collinson, 1882-

Ade, George, 1866-1944. *

Adkins, Cleo. 3

Afford, Max. 2

Aiken, Albert W 1846?-1894. 1 Johannsen
pseuds.: Capt. Frank P. Armstrong
Redmond Blake? (also used by Charles Morris)
Major Lewis W. Carson
A Celebrated Actress
x
Adelaide Davenport
Frances Helen Davenport
Agile Penne
Col. Delle Sara
Lt. Alfred B. Thorne

Aiken, Ralph. 2

Ainsworth, Edward Maddin, 1902- 3

Aintree, *pseuds* *see* Wallace, John

Alan, A. J., *pseud.* *see* Lambert, Leslie Harrison.

Alan, Marjorie, *pseud.* *see* Bumpus, Doris Marjorie, 1905-

Albert, Marvin H 3
pseud.: Anthony Rome

Alderson, James. 3

Aldhouse, Eric. 2

Aldrich, Earl Augustus, 1886- 2
pseud.: A. B. Leonard

Aldrich, Thomas Bailey, 1836-1907. *

Alexander, David, 1907- 3 G

Alexander, Ian. 2

Alexander, John, *pseud.* *see* Vlasto, John Alexander, 1877-1958.

Alexander, Ruth, *pseud.* *see* Rogers, Ruth, 1890-

Alington, Cyril Argentine, 1872- * 1 2
pseud.: S. C. Westerham

Allan, Dennis, *pseud.* *see* Denniston, Elinore, 1900-

Allan, Francis K 2

Allan, Luke, *pseud.* *see* Amy, Lacey.

	Sources
Allan, Mabel Esther, 1915-	3
Allardyce, Paula, *pseud.* *see* Torday, Ursula.	
Allen, Austen, 1887-	* 2
Allen, F	1
Allen, Grace *see* Hogarth, Grace (Allen) 1905-	
Allen, Grant, 1848-1899. *pseuds.:* Cecil Power Olive Pratt Rayner Martin Leach Warborough	** H EQ QQ Sayers 1928
Allen, Herbert Warner, 1881- (Warner Allen) x	H
Allen, Hugh, *pseud.* *see* Morris, Charles, 1833-1922.	
Allen, Marcus.	2
Allen, Warner *see* Allen, Herbert Warner, 1881-	
Allerton, Berridge.	2
Allerton, Mark, *pseud.* *see* Cameron, William Ernest.	
Allerton, Mary, *pseud.* *see* Govan, Christine (Noble) 1898-	
Allingham, Margery, 1904-1966. (Mrs. Philip Youngman Carter)	** 2 3 G H EQ QQ S St Sy Thomas
Allison, William.	1
Allsop, Kenneth, 1920-	3
Alner, James Z	2
Ambler, Eric, 1909- *see also* Reed, Eliot, *pseud.* *of* Eric Ambler and Charles Rodda.	** 2 G H S Sy
Ames, Delano L 1906-	3
Ames, Jennifer, *pseud.* *see* Greig, Maysie, 1902-	
Amos, Alan, *pseud.* *see* Knight, Kathleen Moore.	
Amy, Lacey. (*Full name:* William Lacey Amy) *pseud.:* Luke Allan.	* 2
Anderson, Betty. *pseud.:* Claudia Canyon	3
Anderson, Frederick Irving, 1877-1947.	** 2 H EQ QQ
Anderson, Mary	* EQ
Anderson, Poul, 1926-	3
Anderson, Walter Wadsley, 1904-	2
Andom, R., *pseud.* *see* Barrett, Alfred Walter, 1869-	

	Sources
Andover, Henry.	2
Andrews, Charlton, 1878-1839.	2
Angellotti, Marion Polk, 1912-	1
"Anonyma," *pseud.* (Probably an anonymous syndicate)	** EQ QQ Carter. New paths (Sadleir's essay)
Anson, Lindsay.	2
Anstey, Edgar, 1882- (*Full name:* Edgar Carnegie Anstey)	2
Anthony, Elizabeth.	* 3
Anthony, Peter, *pseud. of* Anthony Shaffer and Peter Shaffer. *see also* Shaffer, Anthony, 1926- Shaffer, Peter, 1926-	* 3
Anthony, Wilder.	2
Antill, Elizabeth.	3
Apery, Helen (Burrell) d' *see* D'Apery, Helen (Burrell) 1842-1915.	
Apple, A E	1 2 Benet
Appleton, George Webb, 1845-1909.	* C
Applin, Arthur, 1883- *pseud.:* Julian Swift	2
Archer, Archie Alexander, *pseud.* *see* Joscelyn, Archie, 1899-	
Archer, Lane, *pseud.* *see* Hauck, Louise (Platt) 1883-1943.	
Archer, Margaret.	2
Archer, Robert.	2
Ard, William, 1922- (*Full name:* William Thomas Ard) *pseuds.:* Ben Kerr Jonas Ward Thomas Wills	3
Aresbys, The, *pseud. of* Raymond S. Bamberger and Helen R. Bamberger. *see also* Bamberger, Helen R 1888- Bamberger, Raymond S	1
Arid, Ben, *pseud.* *see* Barnard, Melville Clemens.	
Arizona Cy, *pseud.* *see* Cowdrick, Jesse C 1859-1899.	
Arkwright, Richard.	C
Arlen, Michael, 1895-1956. (*Name originally:* Dikrān Kuyumjian) x	*
Armat, Mary.	3

	Sources
Armstrong, Anthony, *pseud.* *see* Willis, Anthony Armstrong, 1897-	
Armstrong, Charlotte, 1905- (Mrs. Jack Lewi)	* 2 3 St Sy
Armstrong, *Capt.* Frank P., *pseud,* *see* Aiken, Albert W 1846?-1894.	
Armstrong, Margaret Neilson, 1867-1944.	2 H
Armstrong, Raymond, *pseud.* *see* Lee, Norman, 1905-	
Arnold, Adelaide Victoria (England)	* 2
Arnold, John.	2 Thomson
Arnold, Ralph, 1906- (*Full name:* Ralph Crispian Marshall Arnold)	3
Arre, Helen, *pseud.* *see* Ross, Zola Helen, 1912-	
Arthur, Budd.	3
Arthur, Frank, *pseud.* *see* Ebert, Arthur Frank, 1902-	
Arthur, H. Preston, *pseud.* *see* Hankins, Arthur Preston, 1880-	
Arthur, Harry, *pseud.* *see* Bates, Harry Arthur.	
Asbury, Herbert, 1891-1963.	1 2
Ash, Peter, *pseud.* *see* Hauck, Louise (Platt) 1883-1943.	
Ashbrook, Harriette, 1898-1946. (*Full name:* Harriette Cora Ashbrook) *pseud.:* Susannah Shane.	2 3 H
Ashby, Rubie Constance, 1899-	2 H S
Ashdown, Clifford, *pseud.* (in collaboration with?) *see* Freeman, Richard Austin, 1862-1943.	
Ashe, Douglas, *pseud.*	3
Ashe, Gordon, *pseud.* *see* Creasey, John, 1908-	
Ashenhurst, John.	2
Ashley, Ernest, 1906- (*Full name:* Arthur Ernest Ashley) *pseud.:* Francis Vivian	* 2 3
Ashley, Kenneth H	2
Ashton, Charles, 1884-	2
Ashton, Winifred. *pseud.:* Clemence Dane.	* 2 H
Asquith, *Hon.* Herbert, 1881-1947.	1
"Asterisk", *pseud.* *see* Fletcher, Robert James, 1877-	
Atherton, Gertrude Franklin (Horn) 1857-1948.	1
Atiyah, Edward Selim, 1903-	3

	Sources
Atkey, Bertram.	* 1 2 H EQ
Atkinson, Eleanor Blake *see* Pratt, Eleanor Blake (Atkinson) 1899-	
Atkinson, K	3
Atwater, Mary (Meigs) 1878-1956.	2
Aubrey-Fletcher, *Sir* Henry Lancelot, *bart.*, 1887- *pseud.:* Henry Wade	** 1 2 3 C G H EQ QQ W
Audemars, Pierre. *pseud.:* Peter Hodemart	Thomas
Aumonier, Stacy, 1887-1928.	* EQ Sayers, 1934
Austin, Anne, 1895-	2
Austin, Frederick Britten, 1885-1941.	* EQ Sayers, 1931
Austin, Hugh, *pseud.* *see* Evans, Hugh Austin.	
Austwick, John, *pseud.* *see* Lee, Austin, 1904-1965	
Avallone, Michael. *pseuds.:* Priscilla Dalton Dorothea Nile Edwina Noone	3 (HH)
Averill, H. C., *pseud.* *see* Snow, Charles Horace, 1877-	
Avery, A A 1895-	2
Avery, Robert.	2
Ayres, Paul, *pseud.* *see* Aarons, Edward Sidney, 1916-	
Babcock, Dwight Vincent, 1909-	2
Bachmann, Lawrence Paul, 1912-	2 S
Backhouse, Elizabeth. (*Full name:* Enid Elizabeth Backhouse)	3
Bacon, Josephine Dodge (Daskam) 1876-1961. (Josephine Dodge Daskam) x *pseud.:* Ingraham Lovell	* 1 EQ
Bacon, Peggy, 1895- (*Full name:* Margaret Frances Bacon)	3
Badger, Joseph E 1848-1909. *pseuds.:* Harry Hazard A. H. Post Ralph Roy	Johannsen
Baer, *Mrs.* *pseud.:* Kate F. Hill	1 Johannsen
Bagby, George, *pseud.* *see* Stein, Aaron Marc, 1906-	

	Sources
Baggaley, James.	3
Bailey, Elliot, 1887-	* 2
Bailey, Henry Christopher, 1878-1961.	** 1 2 3 C H EQ QQ S Sy W Thomas Wrong
Bailey, Hilea, *pseud.* *see* Marting, Ruth Lenore, 1907-	
Bailey, Matilda, *pseud.* *see* Radford, Ruby Lorraine, 1891	
Baker, Amy J (Mrs. Maynard Crawford)	2
Baker, Asa, *pseud.* *see* Dresser, Davis, 1904-	
Baker, Howell North *see* Baker, North, 1912-	
Baker, Hugh, *pseud.*	2
Baker, Marceil Genée (Kolstad) 1911- *pseud.:* Marc Miller	3
Baker, North, 1912- (*Full name:* Howell North Baker) x	2
Baker, Richard Merriam, 1896-	* 2
Baker, Sidney J	3
Balchin, Nigel, 1908- (*Full name:* Nigel Marlin Balchin)	MWA
Baldwin, Audry.	EQ Sayers, 1931
Balfour, Eva *see also* Balfour, Hearnden, *pseud. of* Beryl Hearnden and Eva Balfour.	1 2
Balfour, Hearnden, *pseud. of* Beryl Hearnden and Eva Balfour. *see also* Balfour, Eva. Hearnden, Beryl.	1 2
Ball, Doris Bell (Collier) 1897- *pseud.:* Josephine Bell	2 3 G S St
Ball, Eustace Hale, 1881-1931.	2
Ballentine, William, 1812-1887.	*
Ballard, Helen Mabry.	3
Ballard, J. D., *pseud.* *see* Morris, Charles, 1833-1922.	
Ballard, K. G., *pseud.* *see* Roth, Holly, *d.* 1964.	
Ballard, Willis Todhunter, 1903- *pseud.:* Harrison Hunt	2
Ballew, Charles, *pseud.* *see* Snow, Charles Horace, 1877-	
Ballinger, William Sanborn, 1912- *pseud.:* B. X. Sanborn	2 3

	Sources
Balmer, Edwin, 1883-	** 1 2 H EQ QQ S
Bamberger, Helen R 1888- *pseud.:* Helen Berger *see also* Aresbys, The, *pseud. of* Raymond S. Bamberger and Helen R. Bamberger	1 2
Bamberger, Raymond S *see also* Aresbys, The, *pseud. of* Raymond S. Bamberger and Helen R. Bamberger	1 2
Bamburg, Lilian.	* 1 2
Bancroft, George Pleydell *see* Pleydell, George, 1868-	
Bandolier, Stephen.	2
Bangs, John Kendrick, 1862-1922.	EQ
Bankoff, George Alexis, 1903- *pseuds.:* George Borodin George Braddon Peter Conway George Sava	2 3
Bannon, Peter, *pseud.* *see* Durst, Paul, 1921-	
Banzie, Eric de *see* De Banzie, Eric, 1894-	
Barber, Alex.	2 Sayers, 1934
Barber, Willetta Ann, 1911-	2 3
Barbette, Jay, *pseud.* *see* Spicer, Bart, 1918-	
Barbour, Anna Maynard, *d.* 1941.	1 2 Wells
Barbour, Ralph Henry, 1870-1944. *pseud.:* Richard Stillman Powell	2
Barclay, Ann, *pseud.* *see* Greig, Maysie, 1902-	
Barclay, John, 1902-	2
Barclay, Wilson.	2
Bardin, John Franklin.	* 2 G Sy
Bardon, Minna.	2
Barker, Elsa, 1869?-1954.	* 2 EQ
Barker, Leonard Noel, 1882- *pseud.:* L. Noel	1
Barker, Nugent, 1888-	* Crimes, creeps
Barker, Ronald Ernest, 1920- *pseud.:* E. B. Ronald	3
Barling, Muriel, 1912- *pseud.:* Pamela Barrington	3
Barnard, Melville Clemens. *pseud.:* Ben Arid	1
Barnes, Ronald Gorell *see* Gorell, Ronald Gorell Barnes, *Baron*, 1884-	

	Sources
Barnett, Glyn.	2
Barns, Glenn M	3
Baron, Peter, *pseud.* *see* Clyde, Leonard Worswick, 1906-	
Barr, Dennis.	2
Barr, Robert, 1850-1912. *pseud.:* Luke Sharp	** H EQ QQ W
Barrett, Alfred Walter, 1869- *pseud.:* R. Andom	*
Barrett, Monte, 1897?-1949.	2
Barrington, Howard, 1906- *pseud.:* Simon Stone	* 2 3
Barrington, Pamela, *pseud.* *see* Barling, Muriel, 1912-	
Barron, Ann.	3
Barron, Elwyn Alfred, 1855-1929.	1
Barry, Charles, *pseud.* *see* Bryson, Charles, 1877-	
Barry, Jerome, 1894-	2
Barry, Joe, *pseud.* *see* Lake, Joe Barry.	
Barry, John Evarts, 1906-	3
Bartlett, Vernon, 1894- *see also* Oldfeld, Peter, *pseud. of* Vernon Bartlett and P. Jacobsson	2
Barton, Eustace, *pseud.* *see* Rawlins, Eustace, 1854-	
Barton, George, 1866-1940.	* 1 2 EQ
Basil, Don.	2
Basinsky, Earle, 1921-	3
Bass, Charles Beck.	3
Batchelor, Denzil, 1906- (*Full name:* Denzil Stanley Batchelor)	* 2
Bates, Harry Arthur. *pseud.:* Harry Arthur	3
Bates, Herbert Ernest, 1905-	*
Bateson, David, 1921-	3
Baubie, William Edward.	2
Baulsir, Edith.	1
Bawden, Nina, *pseud.* *see* Kark, Nina Mary, 1925-	
Bax, Roger, *pseud.* *see* Winterton, Paul, 1908-	
Baxter, Gregory, *pseud. of* John Ressich and Eric De Banzie. *see also* De Banzie, Eric, 1894-; Ressich, John, 1877-	* 2
Baxter, John, *pseud.* *see* *Hunt,* Howard, 1918-	

Sources

Baxter, Olive, *pseud.* *see* Eastwood, Helen (Baker) 1892-

Baxter, Valerie, *pseud.* *see* Meynell, Laurence Walter, 1899-

Baxter, Young, *pseud.* *see* James, W I

Bayer, Eleanor (Rosenfeld) 2
see also Bayer, Oliver Weld, *pseud. of* Leo G. Bayer and Eleanor (Rosenfeld) Bayer

Bayer, Leo G. 2
see also Bayer, Oliver Weld, *pseud. of* Leo G. Bayer and Eleanor (Rosenfeld) Bayer.

Bayer, Oliver Weld, *pseud. of* Leo G. Bayer and Eleanor (Rosenfeld) Bayer. 2
see also Bayer, Eleanor (Rosenfeld)
Bayer, Leo G

Bayne, Isabella. 3

Bayne, Spencer, *pseud.* 2

Bayne-Powell, Rosamond, 1879- 2 3
x

Beachcroft, Thomas Owen, 1902- *

Beam, Maurice. 2

Beatty, Elizabeth 3

Beaumont, Edgar *see* Halifax, Clifford, *pseud.*

Beck, Henry Charlton. 2

Becke, Louis, 1855-1913. *
(*Full name:* George Louis Becke)

Beckett, Mark, *pseud.* *see* Truman, Marcus George, 1890-

Beckman, Ross, *pseud.* *see* Dey, Frederic van Rensselaer, 1861-1922.

Bedford, Annie North, *pseud.* *see* Watson, Jane (Werner) 1915-

Bedford-Jones, Henry, 1887-1949. BRD, 1921
x
(*Full name:* Henry James O'Brien Bedford-Jones)

Beeding, Francis, *pseud. of* John Leslie Palmer and Hilary Aidan St. George Saunders. * 1 2 H S
see also Palmer, John Leslie, 1885-1944
Saunders, Hilary Aidan St. George, 1898-

Begbie, Garstin. 2

Beith, *Sir* John Hay, 1876-1952. * EQ
pseud.: Ian Hay

Bekker, Jay de, *pseud.* *see* Winchell, Prentice, 1895-

	Sources
Bell, John Joy, 1871-1934.	1 Sayers, 1934
Bell, Josephine, *pseud.* *see* Ball, Doris Bell (Collier) 1897-	
Bell, Neil, *pseud.* *see* Southwold, Stephen, 1887-1964.	
Bell, Vicars Walker, 1904-	3 St
Bellah, James Warner, 1899-	H
Bellairs, George, 1902-	2 3 S St MWA
Bellamann, Henry, 1882-1945.	2
Bellem, Robert Leslie.	2
Belloc, Hilaire, 1870-1953. (*Full name:* Joseph Hilaire Pierre Belloc)	1 2
Belloc-Lowndes, Marie Adelaide *see* Lowndes, Marie Adelaide (Belloc) 1868-1947.	
Bellwood, Herbert, *pseud.* *see* Patten, William George, 1866-1945.	
Belmar, Charles, 1890-	3
Benedict, Gerald.	2
Benét, James Walker, 1914-	3
Benjamin, Edla.	2
Bennet-Thompson, Lilian *see* Thompson, Lilian Bennet-, 1883-	
Bennett, Alfred Gordon.	1
Bennett, Arnold, 1867-1931. (*Full name:* Enoch Arnold Bennett) x	** C EQ QQ S W
Bennett, Dorothy, 1906-	3
Bennett, Enoch Arnold *see* Bennett, Arnold, 1867-1931.	
Bennett, Eric.	2
Bennett, Fred E	1
Bennett, James William, 1891-	2
Bennett, Jay.	3
Bennett, Margot, 1903-	2 3 Sy
Benson, Ben.	3
Benson, Edward Frederic, 1867-1940.	* 1
Benson, Godfrey Rathbone *see* Charnwood, Godfrey Rathbone Benson, *1st Baron*, 1864-1945.	
Benson, Thérèse, *pseud.* *see* Knipe, Emilie (Benson) 1870-1858.	

	Sources
Bentley, Edmund Clerihew, 1875-1956.	** 2 3 C H EQ QQ S Sy W Sayers, 1928 Thomson, Wrong
Bentley, John.	2 3 H
Bentley, Nicolas, 1907- (*Full name:* Nicolas Clerihew Bentley)	3
Benton, John L	2
Berckman, Evelyn.	3
Beresford, John Davys, 1873-1947.	* 2 EQ Sayers, 1928
Beresford, Leslie. *pseud.:* "Pan"	* 2
Beresford, Marcus, 1919- *pseud.:* Marc Brandel	G
Berger, Helen, *pseud.* *see* Bamberger, Helen R 1888-	
Bergquist, Lillian.	2 3
Berkeley, Anthony, *pseud.* *see* Cox, Anthony Berkeley, 1893-	
Berrow, Norman.	2 3
Berry, John Louis.	1
Berton, Guy, *pseud. of* Guy Robert La Coste and Eadfrid A. Bingham. *see also* Bingham, Eadfrid A; La Coste, Guy Robert.	1
Besant, *Sir* Walter, 1836-1901.	Cambridge hist. v. 13 Johannsen Saintsbury
Bessell, J Percival.	1
Bessie, Alvah Cecil, 1904-	3
Bestor, George Clinton. (Clinton Bestor)	2
Bettany, George, 1891-	2
Betteridge, Don, *pseud.* *see* Newman, Bernard, 1897-	
Bevans, Torre, *pseud.* *see* Chanslor, Marjorie Torrey (Hood) 1899-	
Beyer, William Gray.	2
Beynon, Jane, 1915- *pseud.:* Lange Lewis	2 3
Beynon, John, *pseud.* *see* Harris, John Beynon, 1903-	
Bidwell, Margaret.	2

	Sources
Bierce, Ambrose, 1842-1914?	* BRD, 1917
(*Full name:* Ambrose Gwinnett Bierce)	Sayers, 1928
pseud.: Dod Grile	
Bigelow, John Mason.	2
Biggers, Earl Derr, 1884-1933.	* 1 2 H S
Billany, Dan, 1913-	2 MWA
Billett, Mabel Broughton, 1892-	2
Bindloss, Harold, 1866-1945.	BRD, 1917
Bingham, Eadfrid A	1
see also Berton, Guy, *pseud. of* Guy Robert La Coste and Eadfrid A. Bingham	
Bingham, John Michael Ward *see* Clanmorris, John Michael Ward Bingham, *7th Baron,* 1908-	
Binns, Ottwell, 1872-	* 2
pseud.: Ben Bolt	
Bird, Brandon, *pseud. of* George Evans and Kay Evans.	* 3
see also Evans, George, 1906-	
Evans, Kay, 1906-	
Birkley, Dolan, *pseud.* *see* Hitchens, Dolores (Birk) Olsen, 1907-	
Birmingham, George A., *pseud.* *see* Hannay, James Owen, 1865-1950.	
Birney, Hoffman, 1891-	2
(*Full name:* Herman Hoffman Birney)	
pseud.: David Kent	
Birnstingl, Edgar Magnus.	*
Bishop, Morris, 1893-	2 S
(*Full name:* Morris Gilbert Bishop)	
pseud.: W. Bolingbroke Johnson	
Biss, Gerald.	* 1
Black, Elizabeth Best, 1894-	* 2
Black, Gavin, *pseud.* *see* Wynd, Oswald, 1913-	
Black, Ladbroke Lionel Day, 1877-	2
Black, M. Dana, *pseud.* *see* Butler, H M	
Black, Mansell, *pseud.*	3
Black, Peter, *pseud.*	2
Black, Robert Jere, 1892-	2
Black, Thomas B 1910-	* 2
Blackburn, John, 1924-	3
Blackledge, Leonard.	2
Blackmon, Anita *see* Smith, Anita (Blackmon) 1893-	
Blackstock, Charity, *pseud.* *see* Torday, Ursula.	

	Sources
Blackstock, Lee, *pseud.* *see* Torday, Ursula.	
Blackwood, Algernon, 1869-1951.	* 1 H
Blades, J K	2
Blair, Dorothy.	2
see also Scarlett, Roger, *pseud. of* Evelyn Page and Dorothy Blair.	
Blair, E P	2
Blair, H L	2
Blake, E. A., *pseud.* *see* Pratt, Eleanor Blake (Atkinson) 1899-	
Blake, Eleanor, *pseud.* *see* Pratt, Eleanor Blake (Atkinson) 1899-	
Blake, Nicholas, *pseud.* *see* Day Lewis, Cecil, 1904-	
Blake, Redmond, *pseud.?* *see* Aiken, Albert W 1846?-1894. Morris, Charles, 1833-1922.	
Blaker, Richard, 1893-	2
Blakeston, Oswell, 1907-	2 3
see also Simon, *pseud. of* Roger d'Este Burford and Oswell Blakeston.	Crimes, creeps
Blanc, Suzanne.	3
Bland, E A	*
D., E.A.B. x	
E. A. B. D. x	
Blane, Fergus, *pseud.*	2
Blau, Ernest E	2
Blayn, Hugo.	2 3
Bleackley, Horace William, 1868-1931.	2
Bliss, Adam, *pseud. of* Robert Ferdinand Burkhardt and Eve Burkhardt.	2
see also Burkhardt, Eve, 1899- Burkhardt, Robert Ferdinand, 1892-1947.	
Bliss, Tip.	2
Blizard, Marie.	2 3
Bloch, Blanche (Bloch) 1890-	2
Bloch, Robert, 1917-	3
Blochman, Lawrence Goldtree, 1900-	** 2 3 QQ
Blom, Eric Walter.	2
pseud.: Sebastian Farr	

	Sources
Blood, Matthew, *pseud.* *see* Dresser, Davis, 1904-	
Bloomfield, Robert, *pseud.* *see* Edgley, Leslie, 1912-	
Blow, Lynton.	* 2
Blundell, Peter, *pseud.* *see* Butterworth, Frank Nestle.	
Bocca, Al, *pseud.* *see* Winter, Bevis, 1918-	
Bodington, Nancy, 1912- *pseud.:* Shelley Smith	* 2 3 Sy
Bodkin, Matthias McDonnell, 1850-1933. *pseud.:* Crom a Boo x	** 1 2 C H EQ QQ
Bogar, Jeff, *pseud.* *see* Thomas, Ronald Wills, 1910-	
Bogart, William.	2
Boggs, Winifred.	2
Bogue, Hogan.	2
Boland, John, 1913-	3
Boldrewood, Rolf, *pseud.* *see* Browne, Thomas Alexander, 1826-1915.	
Bolt,Ben, *pseud.* *see* Binns, Ottwell, 1872-	
Bolton, George G	*
Bolton, John	2
Bolton, William.	2
Bond, Florence Demarest (Foos) *pseud.:* Ann Demarest	2
Bond, Noreen.	2
Bonett, Emery, *pseud.* *see* Carter, Felicity Winifred, 1907-	
Bonett, John, *pseud.* *see* Coulson, John, 1906-	
Boniface, Marjorie.	2
Bonnamy, Francis, *pseud.* *see* Walz, Audrey.	
Bonnell, James Francis.	2
Bonner, Geraldine, 1870-1930. *pseud.:* Hard Pan x	1
Bonner, Margerie. (Mrs. Malcolm Lowry)	2
Bonney, Joseph L	2
Booth, Charles Gordon, 1896-	* 1 2
Booth, Christopher B	* 1 2 EQ
Booth, Edwin, 1906-	3

	Sources			
Booth, Eliza Margaret J (Gollan) Humphreys *see* Humphreys, Eliza Margaret J (Gollan)				
Booth, Louis F	2			
Boothby, Guy Newell, 1867-1905.	*	1		
Booton, Kage.	3			
Borden, Lowell Mason.	3			
Borgenicht, Miriam, 1915-	3			
Borland, William Armstrong, 1893- *pseud.:* Bingham Dixon	2			
Borneman, Ernest, 1915- (*Full name:* Ernst Wilhelm Julius Bornemann) *pseud.:* Cameron McCabe	*			
Bornemann, Ernst Wilhelm Julius *see* Borneman, Ernest, 1915-				
Borodin, George, *pseud.* *see* Bankoff, George Alexis, 1903-				
Borth, Willan G., *pseud.* *see* Bosworth, Willan George, 1904-				
Bortner, Norman Stanley.	2			
Boston, Charles K., *pseud.* *see* Gruber, Frank, 1904-				
Bosworth, Allan Rucker, 1901-	2	3		
Bosworth, Willan George, 1904- *pseuds.:* Willan G. Borth Leonid	2			
Bottome, Phyllis, 1884- (Mrs. Ernan Forbes-Dennis)	*			
Boucher, Anthony, *pseud.* *see* White, William Anthony Parker, 1911-				
Bourne, Lawrence R	2			
Bourne, Peter, *pseud.* *see* Jeffries, Graham Montague, 1900-				
Bousfield, Henry Thomas Whishart.	*	EQ		
Boutell, Anita.	2	H	S	
Bowden, Jean, 1920- *pseuds.:* Avon Curry Belinda Dell	3			
Bowen, Joseph.	2			
Bowen, Marjorie, *pseud.* *see* Long, Gabrielle Margaret Vere (Campbell) 1886-1952.				
Bowen, Robert Sidney, 1900-	2			
Bowers, Dorothy.	*	2	H	S
Box, Edgar, *pseud.* *see* Vidal, Gore, 1925-				

	Sources
Boyd, Aubrey.	2
Boyd, Catherine Bradshaw.	3
Boyd, Eunice (Mays)	2
Boyd, Hamish.	3
Boyd, Jane, *pseud.*	3
Boyd, Marion Margaret *see* Havighurst, Marion Margaret (Boyd)	
Boyer, Columbia, *pseud.* *see* Martin, Nell Columbia Boyer, 1890-	
Boyers, Audrey.	2
Boyers, Bettina.	2
Boyle, Constance Antonina, 1865-	1 2 BRD, 1922
Boyle, Denis.	3
Boyle, Jack.	* EQ
Boynton, Howard M., *pseud.*	Johannsen
Boz, *pseud.* *see* Dickens, Charles, 1812-1870.	
Brace, Timothy, *pseud.* *see* Pratt, Theodore, 1901-	
Brackeen, Steve.	3
Brackett, Leigh.	2
Braddon, George, *pseud.* *see* Bankoff, George Alexis, 1903-	
Braddon, Mary Elizabeth *see* Maxwell, Mary Elizabeth (Braddon) 1837-1915.	
Bradley, Mary (Hastings) (*Full name:* Mary Wilhelmina (Hastings) Bradley)	2 3
Bradley, Muriel.	3
Bradshaw, Annie (Cropper)	2
Brady, Nicholas, *pseud.* *see* Turner, John Victor, 1900-1945.	
Braha, George, *pseud.* *see* Robinson, Lewis George, 1886-	
Brahms, Caryl, *pseud.* *see* Abrahams, Doris Caroline, 1901-	
Brainerd, Chauncey Corey. *see also* Rath, E. J., *pseud. of* Chauncey Corey Brainerd and Edith Rathbone (Jabobs) Brainerd.	1
Brainerd, Edith Rathbone (Jacobs) *see also* Rath, E. J., *pseud. of* Chauncey Brainerd and Edith Rathbone (Jacobs) Brainerd.	1
Bramah, Ernest, *pseud.* *see* Smith, Ernest Bramah, *d.* 1942.	

	Sources
Bramhall, Marion.	2 3
Brampton, James, *pseud.?* *see* Williams, John Babington.	
Bramwell, James Guy, 1911- *pseud.:* James Byrom	3
Branch, Pamela Jean, 1920-	3
Brand, Charles Neville, 1895- (Neville Brand) x *pseud.:* Charles Lorne	2
Brand, Christianna, *pseud.* *see* Lewis, Mary Christianna (Milne) 1907-	
Brand, Neville, *see* Brand, Charles Neville, 1895-	
Brande, Dorothea (Thompson) 1893- (Mrs. Seward Bishop Collins)	2
Brandel, Marc, *pseud.* *see* Beresford, Marcus, 1919-	
Brandon, Gordon.	3
Brandon, John Gordon, 1879-	* 1 2 3
Brandon, William.	2
Branson, Henry C	2 3 S
Braun, Reinhard A	3
Brean, Herbert.	* 2 3 St
Brebner, Arthur.	*
Brebner, Percy James, 1864-1922. *pseud.:* Christian Lys	* 1 EQ
Bremer, Ward, *pseud.* *see* Reach, James.	
Bremner, Marjorie, 1916-	3
Brenn, George J	1
Brennan, Robert, 1881-	3
Brenning, L. H., *pseud.* *see* Hunter, John, 1891-	
Brent, Carl, *pseud.* *see* Willett, Edward, 1830-1889.	
Brent, Loring, *pseud.* *see* Worts, George Frank, 1892-	
Brent, Nigel, *pseud.* *see* Wimhurst, Cecil Gordon.	
Brett, George Ira, *pseud.?* *see* Crawfurd, Oswald John Frederick, 1834-1909.	
Brett, Martin, *pseud.* *see* Sanderson, Douglas, 1922-	
Brewster, Eugene Valentine, 1869-	2
Bridges, Roy, 1885-	2
Bridges, Thomas Charles, 1868-	* EQ
Bridges, Victor.	* 1 2 3

	Sources
Bridgmont, Leslie, 1901- (*Full name:* James Leslie Bridgmont)	3
Brillant, J Maurice.	3
Brinton, Henry, 1901- *pseud.:* Alex Fraser	3
Bristow, Gwen, 1903	* 2
Britt, Sappho Henderson, *pseud.* *see* Woolfolk, Josiah Pitts, 1894-	
Britton, Sumner, 1902-	2
Broad, Peter.	3
Brock, Alan Francis Clutton- *see* Clutton-Brock, Alan Francis.	
Brock, Alan St. Hill, 1886- *pseud.:* Peter Dewdney	2 3
Brock, Lynn, *pseud.* *see* McAllister, Alister, 1877-	
Brock, Stuart, *pseud.* *see* Trimble, Louis, 1917-	
Brode, Robert.	2
Brodie, Julian Paul. *see also* Denbie, Roger, *pseud. of* Alan Baer Green and Julian Paul Brodie.	2
Brodie-Innes, John William, 1848-	BRD, 1919
Broemel, Rose. *pseud.:* Rose d'Evelyn	2
Brogan, Colm, 1902-	2
Bronson, Francis Woolsey, 1901-1966.	2 3 MWA (HH)
Bronson-Howard, George Fitzalan *see* Howard, George Fitzalan Bronson-, 1883-1922.	
Broocks, Schuyler.	2
Brook, Barnaby, *pseud.* *see* Brooks, Collin, 1893-	
Brooke, Essex.	*
Brooker, Bertram, 1888-1955. *pseuds.:* Huxley Herne Richard Surrey	2
Brooks, Collin, 1893- (*Full name:* William Collin Brooks) *pseud.:* Barnaby Brook	2
Brooks, Edwy Searles, 1889- *pseuds.:* Robert W. Comrade Berkeley Gray	2 3
Brooks, James J	* EQ
Brooks, Vivian Collin *pseud.:* Osmington Mills	3
Brooks, William Collin *see* Brooks, Collin, 1893-	

	Sources
Broome, Adam, *pseud.* *see* James, Godfrey Warden, 1888-	
Brown, Alice, 1857-1948. *pseud.:* Martin Redfield	1 2 BRD, 1925
Brown, Andrew Cassels, 1875-	1 2
Brown, Carnaby.	3
Brown, Dorothy Foster.	2
Brown, Elwood S	3
Brown, Fredric, 1906-	* 2 3
Brown, Gerald.	2
Brown, Morna Doris (MacTaggart) 1907- *pseuds.:* E. X. Ferrars Elizabeth Ferrars	2 3
Brown, Robert Carlton, 1886-1959.	* EQ
Brown, Walter C	2 Wells
Brown, Wenzell, 1912-	2
Brown, William Perry, 1847-1923. *pseud.:* *Captain* William B. Perry	Johannsen
Brown, Zenith (Jones) 1898- *pseuds.:* Leslie Ford David Frome	** 2 3 H EQ S
Browne, Barum, *pseud.*	* 2
Browne, Douglas Gordon, 1884-	2 3
Browne, Eleanore.	2
Browne, Howard, 1908- *pseud.:* John Evans	2 3
Browne, Robert Gore- *see* Gore-Browne, Robert.	
Browne, Thomas Alexander, 1826-1915. *pseud.:* Rolf Boldrewood	*
Browning, Sterry, *pseud.* *see* Gribble, Leonard Reginald, 1908-	
Bruce, George, 1898-	* 2
Bruce, Kennedy.	2
Bruce, Leo, *pseud.* *see* Croft-Cooke, Rupert, 1903-	
Brucker, Margaretta.	2
Brussel, James Arnold, 1905-	3
Bruton, Eric, 1915- (*Full name:* Eric Moore Bruton)	3
Bryan, Michael.	3
Bryant, Marguerite. (Mrs. P. W. Munn)	1 BRD, 1925
Bryant, Matt.	3
Bryce, *Mrs.* Charles.	1

	Sources
Bryce, Ronald, *pseud.* *see* Rockey, Howard, 1886-1934.	
Bryson, Charles, 1877- *pseud.:* Charles Barry	* 1 2 W
Bryson, Leigh, *pseud.* *see* Rutledge, Nancy.	
Buchan, John, 1875-1940. (Baron John Buchan Tweedsmuir) x	** 3 H EQ S Sy Thomson Wrong
Buchanan, B J *pseud.:* Joan Shepherd	3
Buchanan, Madeleine (Sharps)	1 2
Buck, Charles Neville, 1879-	1 2
Buckingham, Bruce, *pseud. of* Peter Lilley and Anthony Stansfeld. *see also* Lilley, Peter. Stansfeld, Anthony.	3
Budd, Jackson, *pseud.* *see* Budd, William John, 1898-	
Budd, William John, 1898- *pseuds.:* Jackson Budd Wallace Jackson	2 3
Bude, John.	* 2 3
Bull, Lois, 1900- *pseuds.:* Melville Burt Judith Grovner Wright	2
Bullett, Gerald William, 1894-1958. *pseud.:* Sebastian Fox	* 3
Bullivant, Cecil Henry.	* EQ
Bumpus, Doris Marjorie, 1905- *pseud.:* Marjorie Alan	2 3
Bunce, Frank, 1907- (*Full name:* Frank David Bunce)	3
Bunce, Sydney.	3
Burbridge, Edith Joan *see* Macintosh, Edith Joan (Burbridge) 1919-	
Burdick, Austin C., *pseud.* *see* Cobb, Sylvanus, 1823-1887.	*
Burford, Eleanor Alice *see* Hibbert, Eleanor, 1906-	
Burford, Roger d'Este, 1904- x *pseud.:* Roger East *see also* Simon, *pseud. of* Roger d'Este Burford and Oswell Blakeston.	* 2
Burge, Milward Rodon Kennedy, 1894- *pseuds.:* Milward Kennedy Robert Milward Kennedy	* 2 3 H W Sayers, 1931

	Sources
Burgess, Gelett, 1866-1951. (*Full name:* Frank Gelett Burgess)	** 2 H EQ QQ
Burgess, Helen (Steers) (Helen Steers) x	2
Burke, Noel, *pseud.* *see* Hitchens, Dolores (Birk) Olsen, 1907-	
Burke, Richard, 1886-	2
Burke, Thomas, 1887-1945.	** EQ QQ Sy
Burkhardt, Eve, 1899- *see also* Bliss, Adam, *pseud. of* Robert Ferdinand Burkhardt and Eve Burkhardt. Eden, Rob, *pseud. of* Robert Ferdinand Burkhardt and Eve Burkhardt. Jardin, Rex, *pseud. of* Robert Ferdinand Burkhardt and Eve Burkhardt.	* 2
Burkhardt, Robert Ferdinand, 1892-1947. *see also* Bliss, Adam, *pseud. of* Robert Ferdinand Burkhardt and Eve Burkhardt. Eden, Rob, *pseud. of* Robert Ferdinand Burkhardt and Eve Burkhardt. Jardin, Rex, *pseud. of* Robert Ferdinand Burkhardt and Eve Burkhardt.	* 2
Burks, Allison L	2
Burland, John Burland Harris- *see* Harris-Burland, John Burland, 1870-	
Burleigh, Donald Quimby, 1894-	2
Burleigh, Hilary.	2
Burnaby, Nigel, *pseud.* *see* Ellett, Harold Pincton, 1882-	
Burne, Glen, *pseud. of* Alan Baer Green and Gladys Elizabeth (Blun) Green. *see also* Green, Alan Baer, 1906- Green, Gladys Elizabeth (Blun) 1908-	2
Burnes, Ed. Gaines, *pseud.*	Johannsen
Burnett, William Riley, 1899-	Sy
Burnham, Clara Louise (Root) 1854-1927. *pseud.:* Edith Douglas	1
Burnham, David, 1907-	2
Burnham, Helen.	2

	Sources
Burning, Michael.	3
Burns, Mary Loveland.	2
Burr, Aaron Ainsworth, *pseud.* *see* Dey, Frederic van Rensselaer, 1861-1922.	
Burr, Anna Robeson (Brown) 1873-1941.	1
Burr, Dangerfield, *pseud.* *see* Ingraham, Prentiss, 1843-1904.	
Burt, Katharine (Newlin) 1882-	* 1
Burt, Melville, *pseud.* *see* Bull, Lois, 1900-	
Burt, Michael.	* 2
Burton, Andy, *pseud.* *see* Rathborne, St. George, 1854-1938.	
Burton, Edmund.	*
Burton, Miles, *pseud.* *see* Street, Cecil John Charles, 1884-	(JDC)
Burton, Thomas, *pseud.* *see* Longstreet, Stephen, 1907-	
Bush, Christopher, 1885- *pseud.:* Michael Home	** 2 3 H
Butler, Ellis Parker, 1869-1937.	** 1 2 EQ QQ
Butler, George Frank, 1857-1921.	* 1 EQ
Butler, Gwendoline.	3
Butler, H B *pseud.:* M. Dana Black	2
Butterworth, Frank Nestle. *pseud.:* Peter Blundell	*
Byers, Charles Alma, 1879-	2
Byrne, Donn, 1889-1928. (*Full name:* Brian Oswald Donn-Byrne)	*
Byrne, Mary.	2
Byrom, James, *pseud.* *see* Bramwell, James Guy, 1911-	
C., WAA, *pseud.* *see* WAAC, *pseud.*	
Cade, Paul.	2
Cadel, James, *pseud.* *see* Thomas, Ronald Wills, 1910-	
Cadett, Herbert.	** EQ QQ
Cagney, Peter, *pseud.* *see* Winter, Bevis, 1918-	
Cain, James Mallahan, 1892-	** G Sy
Caire, Edwin de, *pseud.* *see* Williams, Edwin Alfred.	
Cairns, Cicely.	3
Caldwell, Alfred Betts.	2

	Sources
Calin, Hal Jason.	3
Callaway, Sloane.	2
Callender, Julian, *pseud.* *see* Lee, Austin, 1904-1965.	
Cameron, Courtney Owen *see* Cameron, Owen, 1905-	
Cameron, Donald Clough.	2
Cameron, Evelyn.	2
Cameron, John, *pseud.* *see* Macdonell, Archibald Gordon, 1895-1941.	
Cameron, Margaret, *pseud.* *see* Lindsay, Kathleen, 1903-	
Cameron, Owen, 1905- (*Full name:* Courtney Owen Cameron)	3
Cameron, William Ernest. *pseud.:* Mark Allerton.	W
Camp, Charles Wadsworth, 1879-1936. (Wadsworth Camp)	* 1 EQ
Campbell, Alice (Ormond) 1887-	2 H
Campbell, Colin, *pseud.* *see* Christie, Douglas, 1894-	
Campbell, Donald Frederick, 1906-	2
Campbell, *Sir* Gilbert Edward, *bart.*, 1838-	* EQ
Campbell, Harriette (Russell) 1883-	2 H
Campbell, Hazel.	2
Campbell, Keith, *pseud.* *see* West-Watson, Keith Campbell.	
Campbell, *Sir* Malcolm, 1885-1948.	2
Campbell, Mary Elizabeth, 1903-	2
Campbell, R T	* 2
Campbell, Reginald, 1894-1950. (*Full name:* Reginald Wilfred Campbell)	3
Campbell, Scott, *pseud.* *see* Davis, Frederick William, 1858-1933.	
Campbell, Walter Stanley, *pseud.* *see* Vestal, Stanley, 1887-	
Campbell, William Edward March, 1894-1954. *pseud.:* William March	*
Campion, Peter.	3
Canaday, John Edwin, 1907- *pseud.:* Matthew Head	* 2 3 S St MWA
Candy, Edward, *pseud.* *see* Neville Alison.	
Cane, Bevis.	*
Cannan, Joanna, 1898- (Mrs. J. J. Pullein-Thompson)	2 3 S St

	Sources
Cannell, Charles, *pseud.* *see* Vivian, Evelyn Charles H	
Cannell, John Clucas.	* 2
Canning, Victor, 1911-	3 Sy
Canyon, Claudia, *pseud.* *see* Anderson, Betty.	
Capes, Bernard Edward Joseph, *d.* 1918.	* 1 EQ Sayers, 1928
Capeto, Isabel.	3
Capon, Paul, 1912-	2 3
Capstan, *pseud.* *see* Hardinge, Rex, 1904-	
Cardwell, Ann, *pseud.* *see* Powley, Jean (Makins)	
Carew, Dudley, 1903-	*
Carew, Jean, *pseud.* *see* Corby, Jane, 1899-	
Carey, Basil.	2 3
Carey, Charles, *pseud.* *see* Waddel, Charles Carey, 1868-1930.	
Carey, Elisabeth. *see also* Magoon, Carey, *pseud. of* Elisabeth Carey and Marian Austin (Waite) Magoon.	2
Cargill, Leslie.	2
Carle, C E *see also* Morgan, Michael, *pseud. of* C. E. Carle and Dean M. Dorn.	2
Carleton, Marjorie (Chalmers) 1897-1964.	1 3
Carleton, S., *pseud.* *see* Jones, Susan Carleton, 1869-	
Carlton, Gerald, *fl.* 1883-1903.	Johannsen
Carlyle, Anthony, *pseud.* *see* Milton, Gladys Alexandra.	
Carmack, Jesse.	2
Carmichael, Archibald.	Chandler, F. W.
Carmichael, Harry, *pseud.* *see* Ognall, Leopold Horace, 1908-	
Carnac, Carol, *pseud.* *see* Rivett, Edith Caroline, 1894-1958.	
Carpenter, Margaret.	S MWA
Carr, Antony. (*Full name:* Antony John Edwin Carr)	3
Carr, Glyn, *pseud.* *see* Styles, Showell, 1908-	
Carr, John Dickson, 1906- *pseuds.:* Carr Dickson Carter Dickson	** 2 3 G H EQ QQ S Sy (JDC)
Carr, Jolyon.	*
Carr, Joseph Baker.	2

	Sources
Carrington, Elaine (Sterne) 1892-1958.	2
Carryl, Charles Edward, 1841-1920.	* EQ
Carson, Bart.	3
Carson, *Major* Lewis W., *pseud.* *see* Aiken, Albert W 1846?-1894.	
Carstairs, Henry.	* 2 3
Carter, Felicity Winifred, 1907- (*Full name:* Felicity Winifred (Carter) Coulson) x *pseud.:* Emery Bonett	2
Carter, Herbert, *pseud.* *see* Rathborne, St. George, 1854-1938.	
Carter, John Franklin, 1897- *pseuds.:* Diplomat, Jay Franklin, Unofficial Observer x	2 H
Carter, Nicholas, *pseud.* As in the Old Cap Collier stories, the name of the detective-hero, Nicholas Carter (or Nick Carter) became the pseudonym used by the numerous writers of the many books published 1889 to about 1910 by Street and Smith, John Russell Coryell planned the series, and Frederic van Rensselaer Dey wrote most of the stories. Authorship of many is difficult to determine. *see also* Coryell, John Russell, *d.* 1924. Davis, Frederick William, 1858-1933. Dey, Frederic van Rensselaer, 1861-1922. Jenks, George Charles, 1850-1929. Sawyer, Eugene T 1846-1924.	1 C EQ QQ Bragin (two titles) Pearson
Cartlidge, Alice.	2
Cartrell, Pierre.	2
Carver, Stewart.	3
Cary, Falkland Litton. (*Full name:* Thomas Falkland Litton Cary)	*
Caryer, Nellie.	2
Caseleyr, Camille Auguste Marie, 1909- *pseud.:* Jack Danvers	3
Casey, Robert Joseph, 1890-1962.	* 2
Caspary, Vera, 1904-	* Sy MWA
Cassells, John, *pseud.* *see* Duncan, William Murdoch, 1909-	

	Sources
Cassiday, Bruce, 1920- (*Full name:* Bruce Bingham Cassiday) *pseud.:* Max Day	3
Casson, Stanley, 1889-1944.	* 2
Castier, Jules.	* EQ
Castleton, Charles, *pseud.* *see* Cobb, Sylvanus, 1823-1887.	
Caudwell, Christopher, *pseud.* *see* Sprigg, Christopher St. John, 1907-1937.	
Causey, James O	3
Cavendish, Peter, *pseud.* *see* Horler, Sidney, 1888-1954.	
Caverhill, William Melville, 1910- *pseud.:* Alan Melville	2
Cecil, Henry, *pseud.* *see* Leon, Henry Cecil.	
Cecil, Olive.	2
A Celebrated Actress, *pseud.* *see* Aiken, Albert W 1846?-1894.	
Chaber, M. E., *pseud.* *see* Crossen, Kendell Foster, 1910-	
Chadwick, Charles, 1874-1953.	1
Chadwick, William.	*
Chalmers, Stephen, 1880-1935.	2
Chamberlain, Elinor, 1901-	* 2
Chamberlain, Esther, *d.* 1908.	1
Chamberlain, George Agnew, 1879-	1 2
Chamberlain, Lucia.	1
Chambers, Dana, *pseud.* *see* Leffingwell, Albert, 1895-1946.	
Chambers, Elwyn Whitman, 1896- (Whitman Chambers) x	2 II
Chambers, Mary (Strother) 1899-	2
Chambers, Robert William, 1865-1933.	* 1 EQ
Chambers, Whitman *see* Chambers, Elwyn Whitman, 1896-	
Champion, Jessie.	BRD, 1917
Champion, Joan.	*
Champion de Crespigny, Rose (Key) *d.* 1935.	2
Chance, John Newton, 1911-	2 3
Chance, Simon.	2
Chancellor, John, *pseud.* *see* Rideaux, Charles de Balzac, 1900-	
Chandler, Raymond, 1888-1959.	** 2 3 G H QQ S Sy

	Sources
Chandos, Fay, *pseud.* *see* Tempest, Jan.	
Channing, Mark.	2
Channon, Ethel Mary, 1875-	2
Chanslor, Marjorie Torrey (Hood) 1899- (Torrey Hood) (Torrey Chanslor) x *pseuds.:* Torre Bevans Marjorie Torrey	2
Chapin, Carl Mattison, 1879-	2
Chapman, George Warren Vernon, 1925- *pseud.:* Vernon Warren	3
Chapman, H E	2
Chapman, Robert, 1916- (*Full name:* Robert Alec Mark Chapman)	3
Charles, Ernest F	2
Charles, Franklin, *pseud.* *see* Adams, Cleve Franklin, 1895-1950.	
Charles, Theresa, *pseud of* Charles Swatridge and Irene Swatridge. *see also* Swatridge, Charles Swatridge, Irene.	3
Charlton, Marjory.	* 2
Charnwood, Godfrey Rathbone Benson, *1st Baron,* 1864-1945. (Godfrey Rathbone Benson) x	2 H Nicholson
Charteris, Leslie, 1907-	** 2 3 H EQ QQ
Chase, Arthur Minturn, 1875-1947.	2
Chase, James Hadley, *pseud.* *see* Raymond, René, 1906-	
Chesney, Weatherby, *pseud.* *see* Hyne, Charles John Cutcliffe Wright, 1865-1944.	
Chester, Ann.	3
Chester, George Randolph, 1869-1924.	** EQ QQ
Chester, Peter.	3
Chesterton, Gilbert Keith, 1874-1936.	** 1 2 C H EQ QQ S Sy W Sayers, 1928 Thomson Wrong
Chestor, Rui, *pseud.* *see* Courtier, Sidney Hobson.	
Chetwynd, Bridget.	3
Cheyney, Peter, 1896-1951.	* 2 3 G H S
Chichester, John Jay.	* 1 2
Chidsey, Donald Barr, 1902-	2

	Sources
Child, Nellise	2
Child, Richard Washburn, 1881-1935.	* EQ
Childerness, George.	2
Childers, James Saxon, 1899-	2
Chipperfield, Robert Orr, *pseud.* *see* Ostrander, Isabel Egenton, 1883-1924.	
Chittenden, Frank Albert, 1910-	3
Chitty, *Sir* Thomas Willes, *Bart.*, 1926- *pseud.*: Thomas Hinde	(HH)
Cholmondeley, Mary, 1859-1925.	*
Christian, Kit, *pseud of* Delos Russell Thorson and Sara Winfree Thorson. *see also* Thorson, Delos Russell, 1906- Thorson, Sara Winfree, 1906-	2
Christie, Agatha (Miller) 1891- (Mrs. Max Mallowan) *pseud.*: Mary Westmacott	** 1 2 3 C G H EQ QQ S Sy W Chandler, R. Sayers, 1928 Thomas Thomson Wrong
Christie, Douglas, 1894- *pseuds.*: Colin Campbell Lynn Durie	2
Christopher, Matthew F 1917-	3
Church, Granville, *pseud.* *see* People, Granville Church.	
Churchill, Edward.	2
Chute, Mary Grace, 1907-	* EQ
Chute, Verne.	2
The City-Items Scribe, *pseud.* *see* Cowdrick, Jesse C 1859-1899.	
Clandon, Henrietta, *pseud.* *see* Vahey, John George Haslette, 1881-	
Clanmorris, John Michael Ward Bingham, *7th Baron*, 1908- (John Michael Ward Bingham) x	* 3 St Sy
Clare, Marguerite, *pseud.* *see* Heppell, Mary.	
Clark, Alfred Alexander Gordon, 1900-1958. *pseud.*: Cyril Hare	** 2 3 G S Sy MWA
Clark, Dale, *pseud.* *see* Kayser, Ronal.	
Clark, Dorothy (Park) 1899- *see also* McMeekin, Clark, *pseud. of* Dorothy (Park) Clark and Isabel (McLennan) McMeekin.	2 3

	Sources
Clark, Edward C	2
Clark, Marian Buxton.	2
Clark, Philip.	2 3
Clark, Wesley Clarke, 1907-	2
Clark, Winifred, 1909- *pseud.:* Scott Finley	3
Clarke, J Calvitt, 1888- *pseuds.:* Carol Addison Richard Grant	3
Clarke, Josephine Fitzgerald (Moylan) *Lady* *pseud.:* Erroll Fitzgerald	*
Clarke, William James, 1872- *pseud.:* G. F. Monkshood	*
Clason, Clyde B	2 H S
Clausen, Carl.	2 Sayers, 1934
Clay, Bertha M., *pseud.* *see* Dey, Frederic van Rensselaer, 1861-1922.	
Clay, Robert Keating.	1 2
Claymore, Tod, *pseud.* *see* Clevely, Hugh.	
Cleft-Addams, Julia. x	1
Clemens, Nancy.	2
Clemens, Samuel Langhorne, 1835-1910. *pseud.:* Mark Twain	** 1 H EQ QQ
Clement, Frank A	* 2
Clements, Colin Campbell, 1894-	*
Clements, Eileen Helen, 1905-	2 3 H S
Clements, Florence (Willard) Ryerson *see* Ryerson, Florence.	
Cleveland, John, *pseud.* *see* McElfresh, Adeline.	
Clevely, Hugh. *pseud.:* Tod Claymore	* 2 3 St
Clifford, Charles L	2
Clift, Dennison Halley, 1885-	2
Clifton, Oliver Lee, *pseud.* *see* Rathborne, St. George, 1854-1938.	
Clive, Caroline (Wigley) 1801-1873.	Cambr. hist.v.13 Saintsbury
Clouston, Joseph Storer, 1870-	** 1 EQ QQ
Clutton-Brock, Alan Francis.	2
Clyde, Leonard Worswick, 1906- *pseud.:* Peter Baron	2
Coates, John, 1912-	3
Coates, Robert Myron, 1897-	* 2

	Sources
Cobb, Belton, 1892- (*Full name:* Geoffrey Belton Cobb)	* 2 3
Cobb, Irvin Shrewsbury, 1876-1944.	** 2 EQ QQ
Cobb, Sylvanus, 1823-1887. *pseuds.:* Austin C. Burdick Charles Castleton Walter B. Dunlap Enoch Fitzwhistler Symus, the Pilgrim Amos Winslow, Jr.	1 Johannsen
Cobb, Thomas, 1854-1932.	* 2
Cobb, Weldon J *fl.* 1866-1895. *pseud.:* Genevieve Ulmar	Johannsen
Cobden, Guy.	3
Cobnor, John.	2
Cockin, Joan, *pseud.* *see* Macintosh, Edith Joan (Burbridge) 1919-	
Cocking, Ronald.	3
Cockrell, Francis Marion. (Frank Cockrell)	2
Cockrell, Marian, 1909-	2
Cody, C. S., *pseud.* *see* Waller, Leslie, 1923-	
Cody, Hiram Alfred.	*
Coe, Charles Francis, 1890-1956.	* 2
Coffin, Carlyn.	2
Coffin, Geoffrey, *pseud.* *see* Mason, Francis van Wyck, 1901-	
Coffin, Peter, *pseud.*	2
Cofyn, Cornelius.	*
Coggin, Joan.	3
Coghlan, Lida Lavinia, 1860-	1
Cohen, Octavus Roy, 1891-1959.	** 1 2 3 H EQ QQ W
Colbron, Grace Isabel, 1869-1948. *pseud.:* Romano Isabel Marchant	* 1 2 EQ
Cole, Diane.	3
Cole, George Douglas Howard, 1889-1959	** 1 2 C G H EQ QQ S Sayers, 1928 (HH)
Cole, Jackson, *pseud.* *see* Schisgall, Oscar, 1901-	
Cole, Katharine S	2
Cole, Margaret Isabel (Postgate) 1893-	** 1 2 G H EQ QQ S Sayers, 1928

	Sources
Coles, Cyril Henry, 1898-1965. *see also* Coles, Manning, *pseud. of* Adelaide Frances Oke Manning and Cyril Henry Coles. Gaite, Francis, *pseud. of* Adelaide Frances Oke Manning and Cyril Henry Coles.	2 3 (HH)
Coles, Manning, *pseud. of* Adelaide Frances Oke Manning and Cyril Henry Coles. *see also* Coles, Cyril Henry, 1898-1965. Manning, Adelaide Frances Oke.	2 3 G H S
Collans, Dev, *pseud.* *see* Winchell, Prentice, 1895-	
Collier, Douglas, *pseud.* *see* Fellowes-Gordon, Ian, 1921-	
Collier, John, 1901-	*
Collier, Old Cap *see* Old Cap Collier, *pseud.*	
Collins, Charles, *pseud.? of* Charles Dickens and Wilkie Collins? *see also* Collins, Wilkie, 1824-1889. Dickens, Charles, 1812-1870.	EQ
Collins, Gilbert, 1890-	1 2
Collins, Hunt, *pseud.* *see* Hunter, Evan, 1926-	
Collins, Mary (Garden)	2 3 MWA
Collins, Norman, 1907- (*Full name:* Norman Richard Collins)	3
Collins, Wilkie, 1824-1889. (*Full name:* William Wilkie Collins) *see also* Collins, Charles, *pseud.?* of Charles Dickens and Wilkie Collins?	** 1 2 C G H EQ QQ S Sy W Sayers, 1928 Wrong
Collinson, Peter, *pseud.* *see* Hammett, Dashiell, 1894-1961.	
Collison, Wilson, 1893- *pseud.:* Willis Kent	2
Colson, Percy, 1873-1952.	2
Colter, Eli.	2
Coltman, Ernest Vivian, *pseud.* *see* Dudley, Ernest, 1908-	
Colton, A. J., *pseud.* *see* Hook, Alfred Samuel.	
Colton, Mel. *pseud.:* Merrill Trask	3
Colver, Anne, 1908- (*Full name:* Polly Anne (Colver) Harris) x *pseud.:* Colver Harris	2
Comley, Gertrude.	2

	Sources
Compton-Rickett, Arthur, 1869-1937. x	* 2
Comrade, Robert W., *pseud.* *see* Brooks, Edwy Searles, 1889-	
Comstock, Caroline.	3
Conant, Paul.	3
Connell, Richard Edward, 1893-	* 2 EQ
Connington, J. J., *pseud.* *see* Stewart, Alfred Walter, 1880-1947.	
Connington, John Jervis, *pseud.* *see* Stewart, Alfred Walter, 1880-1947.	
Conrad, Clive, *pseud.* *see* King, Frank, 1892-1958.	
Constellano, Illion, *pseud.* *see* Lewis, Julius Warren, 1833-1920.	
Constiner, Merle. (*Full name:* Francis Merle Constiner)	3
Converse, Anita Marie (Stewart) *see* Stewart, Anita, 1901-	
Converse, Florence, 1871-	* 1
Conway, Peter, *pseud.* *see* Bankoff, George Alexis, 1903-	
Conyn, Cornelius.	3
Cook, Douglas, 1927-	3
Cook, Theodore Kenyon, 1897-	2
Cooke, Joseph Cottin.	2
Cooke, Rupert Croft- *see* Croft-Cooke, Rupert, 1903-	
Cookson, Gathorne.	2
Coolidge, Erwin L	* 1
Coolidge-Rask, Marie. x	* 2
Coombs, Murdo, *pseud.* *see* Davis, Frederick Clyde, 1902-	
Cooper, Charles, *pseud.* *see* Lock, Arnold Charles Cooper.	
Cooper, John Murray, 1908- *pseud.:* William Sutherland	2
Cooper, Leonard.	*
Cooper, Monte.	2
Copp, A E	* 2
Coppard, Alfred Edgar, 1878-1957.	*
Coppel, Alec.	* 2
Copplestone, Bennet, *pseud.* *see* Kitchin, Frederick Harcourt, 1867-1932.	

	Sources
Corbett, Elizabeth Burgoyne.	* EQ
Corbett, James.	* 2 3
Corby, Jane, 1899- *pseuds.:* Jean Carew Joanne Holden	3
Cores, Lucy Michaella, 1914-	2 S MWA
Corey, Herbert, 1872-1954.	2
Corkill, Louis.	3
Corne, Molly E	2
Cornell, Louis.	2
Cornish, Constance.	3
Cornwell, David John Moore, 1931- *pseud.:* John Le Carré x	(HH)
Correll, A Boyd.	3
Corrigan, Mark, *pseud.* *see* Lee, Norman, 1905-	
Corson, Geoffrey, *pseud.* *see* Sholl, Anna McClure.	
Cory, Desmond, *pseud.* *see* MacCarthy, John Lloyd.	
Coryell, John Russell, *d.* 1924 . *pseuds.:* Julia Edwards Geraldine Fleming Margaret Grant *see also* Carter, Nicholas, *pseud.*	*
Costello, Paul.	3
Couch, *Sir* Arthur Thomas Quiller- *see* Quiller-Couch, *Sir* Arthur Thomas, 1863-1944.	
Coulson, Felicity Winifred (Carter) *see* Carter, Felicity Winifred, 1907-	
Coulson, John, 1906- (Full name: John Hubert Arthur Coulson) *pseud.:* John Bonett	3
Coulter, H G	2
Courage, John, *pseud.* *see* Goyne, Richard.	
Cournos, John, 1881-1966. *pseuds.:* John Courtney Mark Gawlt	2
Courtier, Sidney Hobson. *pseud.:* Rui Chestor	3
Courtney, John, *pseud.* *see* Cournos, John, 1881-1966.	
Courtney, Robert, *pseud.* *see* King, Charles Daly, 1895-	
Cousins, Edmund George, 1893-	3

	Sources
Coverack, Gilbert, *pseud.* *see* Warren, John Russell, 1886-	
Coverdale, Harry.	1
Cowan, G K	2
Cowan, Sada.	2
Cowdrick, Jesse C 1859-1899.	Johannsen
pseuds.: Arizona Cy x The City-Items Scribe x	Pearson
Cowdroy, Joan Agnes.	2
Cox, Anthony Berkeley, 1893-	** 1 2 C
pseuds.: Anthony Berkeley Francis Iles	G H S Sy
Cox, *Sir* Edmund Charles, *bart.*, 1856-	* EQ
Cox, Irving E	3
Coxe, George Harmon, 1901-	* 2 3 H
Coxe, Kathleen Buddington, *pseud. of* Amelia Reynolds Long and Edna McHugh.	2
see also Long, Amelia Reynolds, 1904- McHugh, Edna.	
Cozzens, James Gould, 1903-	EQ's anthology, 1965
Crabb, Arthur, *pseud.*	* 1 EQ
Craddock, Irving.	1
Cragg, E H	* C
Craig, Peter, *pseud.* *see* MacClure, Victor, 1887-	
Crane, Frances (Kirkwood)	2 3
Cranston, Claudia, 1886-1947.	2
Cranston, Maurice William, 1920-	*
Crauford, William Harold Lane, 1886-	2 3
Crawford, Jack Randall, 1878-	2
Crawfurd, Oswald John Frederick, 1834-1909.	* 1 EQ
pseuds.: George Ira Brett? John Daingerfield John Latouche	
Crawley, J Cooper, *pseud.*	3
Crawley, Rayburn.	2
Crawshay-Williams, Eliot, 1879- x	*

	Sources
Creasey, John, 1908-	** 2 3
pseuds.: Gordon Ashe	G H (HH)
Norman Deane	
Michael Halliday	
Kyle Hunt	
Peter Manton	
J. J. Marric	
Richard Martin	
Anthony Morton	
Ken Ranger	
William K. Reilly	
Tex Riley	
Jeremy York	
Creed, Sibyl.	1
Créspigny, *Capt.* Charles de, *pseud. of* Charles Norris Williamson and Alice Muriel (Livingston) Williamson.	1 2
see also Williamson, Alice Muriel (Livingston) 1869-1933.	
Williamson, Charles Norris, 1859-1920.	
Crespigny, Rose (Key) Champion de *see* Champion de Crespigny, Rose (Key) *d.* 1935.	
Crispin, Edmunds, *pseud.* *see* Montgomery, Robert Bruce, 1921-	
Crockett, James, *pseud. of* Cornelia Warriner and James A. MacPhail.	2
see also MacPhail, James A	
Warriner, Cornelia.	
Croft, Desmond Warrick, 1894-	1
Croft, Taylor, *pseud.* *see* Croft-Cooke, Rupert, 1903-	
Croft-Cooke, Rupert, 1903- x	* 2 3 H Thomas
pseuds.: Leo Bruce	
Taylor Croft	
Crofts, Freeman Wills, 1879-1957.	** 1 2 3 C G H S Sy W Chandler, R. Sayers, 1928 Thomson Wrong
Crom a Boo, *pseud.* *see* Bodkin, Matthias McDonnell, 1850-1933.	
Cromarty, Noel.	3
Cromie, Robert, 1856-1907.	*

	Sources
Cronin, Bernard, 1884- (*Full name:* Bernard Charles Cronin) *pseuds.:* Dennis Adair Wallace Dixon Eric North	2
Cronin, Brendon Leo. *pseud.:* Michael Cronin	3
Cronin, Michael, *pseud.* *see* Cronin, Brendon Leo.	
Crooker, Herbert.	2
Crosby, John.	2
Crosby, Lee, *pseud.* *see* Torrey, Ware, 1905-	
Cross, James, *pseud.* *see* Parry, Hugh Jones, 1916-	
Cross, John Keir, 1914- *pseud.:* Stephen MacFarlane	*
Cross, Mark, *pseud.* *see* Pechey, Archibald Thomas, 1876-1961.	
Crossen, Kendell Foster, 1910- *pseuds.:* M. E. Chaber Christopher Monig Clay Richards	3
Crouse, Russell, 1893-	*
Crozier, John.	2
Crozier, Kathleen Muriel (Eyles) *see* Eyles, Kathleen Muriel, 1913-	
Crunden, Allan B 1878-	3
Crunden, Robert Morse.	3
Cullingford, Guy, *pseud.* *see* Taylor, Constance Lindsay, 1907-	
Culver, Kathryn, *pseud.* *see* Dresser, Davis, 1904-	
Cumberland, Marten, 1892- *pseuds.:* R. Laugier Kevin O'Hara	* 2 3
Cunningham, Albert Benjamin, 1888- *pseud.:* Garth Hale	2 3 H S
Curle, Richard, 1883- (*Full name:* Richard Henry Parnell Curle)	* 2
Currier, Jay L., *pseud.* *see* Henderson, James Leal, 1913-	
Curry, Avon, *pseud.* *see* Bowden, Jean, 1920-	
Curties, Henry, 1860-	1
Curtis, David A 1846-1923.	*
Curtis, Peter, *pseud.* *see* Lofts, Norah (Robinson) 1904-	
Curtis, Robert.	* C EQ
Curtis, Robert G	2

	Sources
Curtis, Tom, *pseud.* *see* Pendower, Jacques, 1899-	
Curtis, Wardon Allan, 1867-	* EQ
Curtiss, Elizabeth (Mangam)	2
Curtiss, Philip Everett, 1885-	1
Curtiss, Ursula (Reilly)	2 3 St
Curzon, Sam, *pseud.* *see* Krasney, Samuel A 1922-	
Curzon, Virginia, *pseud.* *see* Hawton, Hector, 1901-	
Cushing, Enid Louise.	3
Cushman, Clarissa (Fairchild) 1889- (*Full name:* Clarissa White (Fairchild) Cushman)	3 H
D., E.A.B. *see* Bland, E A	
Dahl, Roald.	*
Daiger, Katherine S	* 2
Daingerfield, Foxhall, 1887-1933. (*Full name:* Foxhall Alexander Daingerfield)	1 2
Daingerfield, John, *pseud.* *see* Crawfurd, Oswald John Frederick, 1834-1909.	
Dale, Dash, *pseud.* *see* Rathborne, St. George, 1854-1938.	
Dale, William.	2
Dallas, Duncan.	* EQ
Dalman, Max.	* 2
Dalton, Moray.	* 2 3
Dalton, Priscilla, *pseud.* *see* Avallone, Michael.	
Daly, Carroll John, 1889-1958.	1 2 3
Daly, Elizabeth, 1878-	2 3 H S St
Damer, Anne.	2
Dana, Freeman.	2
Dana, Marvin, 1867-	1
Danby, Frank, *pseud.* *see* Frankau, Julia (Davis) 1864-1916.	
Dane, Clemence, *pseud.* *see* Ashton, Winifred.	
Dane, Joel Y., *pseud.* *see* Delany, Joseph Francis, 1905-	
Dane, Mary, *pseud.* *see* Morland, Nigel, 1905-	
Dangerfield, Harry, *pseud.* *see* Patten, William George, 1866-1945.	
Daniel, Glyn Edmund, 1914- *pseud.:* Dilwyn Rees	* 2

	Sources
Daniel, Roland.	** 2 3
Daniels, Harold R	3
Daniels, Norman A	2
Dannay, Frederic, 1905-	* 2 3 H EQ QQ Sy
see also Queen, Ellery, *pseud. of* Frederic Dannay and Manfred Bennington Lee.	
Queen, Ellery, Jr., *pseud. of* Frederic Dannay and Manfred Bennington Lee.	
Ross, Barnaby, *pseud. of* Frederic Dannay and Manfred Bennington Lee.	
Danning, Melrod, *pseud.* *see* Gluck, Sinclair, 1887-	
Danvers, Jack, *pseud.* *see* Caseleyr, Camille Auguste Marie, 1909-	
Danvers, Milton.	* C
D'Apery, Helen (Burrell) 1842-1915.	1
x	
pseud.: Olive Harper	
Darby, J. N., *pseud.* *see* Govan, Christine (Noble) 1898-	
Darby, Ruth.	2
Dare, Alan, *pseud.* *see* Goodchild, George, 1888-	
Dare, Michael.	* 2
Dare, Roland, *pseud.* *see* Morris, Charles, 1833-1922.	
Dark, Rex.	2
Darlington, William Aubrey, 1890-	* 2
Darwent, George.	2
Daskam, Josephine Dodge *see* Bacon, Josephine Dodge (Daskam) 1876-1961.	
Davenport, Adelaide, *pseud.* *see* Aiken, Albert W 1846?-1894.	
Davenport, Frances Helen, *pseud.* *see* Aiken, Albert W 1846?-1894.	
Davey, Jocelyn, *pseud.* *see* Raphael, Chaim, 1908-	
Davidson, T L	2
Davies, Arthur Charles Fox- *see* Fox-Davies, Arthur Charles, 1871-1928.	
Davies, Betty Evelyn.	2
pseud.: Pauline Warwick	

	Sources
Davies, Ernest, 1873- *pseud.:* Oliver Martin	* 1
Davies, N E	2
Davies, Rhys, 1903-	*
Daviot, Gordon, *pseud.* *see* Mackintosh, Elizabeth, 1896-1952.	
Davis, Burton, 1893- *see also* Saunders, Lawrence, *pseud.* of Burton Davis and Claire (Ogden) Davis.	2
Davis, Clare (Ogden) 1892- (*Full name:* Clarisy Musadore (Ogden) Davis) *see also* Saunders, Lawrence, *pseud. of* Burton Davis and Clare (Ogden) Davis.	2
Davis, Don, *pseud.* *see* Dresser, Davis, 1904-	
Davis, Dorothy (Salisbury) 1916-	3 St
Davis, Frederick Clyde, 1902- *pseuds.:* Murdo Coombs Stephen Ransome	* 2 3 H
Davis, Frederick William, 1858-1933. *pseud.:* Scott Campbell *see also* Carter, Nicholas, *pseud.*	1 EQ
Davis, Gordon, *pseud.* *see* Hunt, Howard, 1918-	
Davis, Harry, *pseud.* *see* Hill, Roberta.	
Davis, Howard Charles.	3
Davis, Lavinia (Riker) 1909-1961. *pseud.:* Wendell Farmer	* 2 3
Davis, Martha (Wirt) *pseud.:* Wirt Van Arsdale	3
Davis, Means.	2
Davis, Mildred B	2
Davis, Norbert.	2
Davis, Reginald.	* 2
Davis, Richard Harding, 1864-1916.	** 1 EQ QQ
Davis, Stratford, 1915-	3
Davis, Tech.	* 2
Davis, Yorke, *pseud.*	1
Davis, Zeke.	3
Davison, Gilderoy, 1892-	* 2
Dawe, William Carlton Lanyon, 1865-1935.	* 2
Dawson, Carolyn Byrd.	2
Dawson, Coningsby William, 1883-1959.	1

	Sources
Dawson, Francis Warrington, 1878- (Warrington Dawson) x	2
Dawson, Helen.	3
Dawson, Warrington *see* Dawson, Francis Warrington, 1878-	
Dawson, William James, 1854-1928.	BRD, 1920
Dawson-Scott, Catharine Amy *see* Scott, Catharine Amy (Dawson)	
Day, Anthony, *pseud.* *see* Hunter, John, 1891-	
Day, Lillian (Abrams) 1893-	2
Day, Max, *pseud.* *see* Cassiday, Bruce, 1920-	
Day Lewis, Cecil, 1904- x *pseud.:* Nicholas Blake	** 2 3 H S Sy (JDC)
Deakin, Hilda L	2
Deal, Mason, *pseud.* *see* Eliot, Henry Ware, 1879-	
Dean, Amber, 1902-	2 3
Dean, Dennis.	2
Dean, Elizabeth.	2
Dean, Gregory, *pseud.* *see* Posner, Jacob D 1883-	
Dean, Robert George. *pseud.:* George Griswold	2 3 H
Dean, Spencer, *pseud.* *see* Winchell, Prentice, 1895-	
Deane, Donald.	2
Deane, Norman, *pseud.* *see* Creasey, John, 1908-	
De Banzie, Eric, 1894- x *see also* Baxter, Gregory, *pseud.* *of* John Ressich and Eric De Banzie.	2
De Bra, Lemuel.	*
Debrett, Hal, *pseud.* *of* Davis Dresser and Kathleen Rollins. *see also* Dresser, Davis, 1904- Rollins, Kathleen.	3
De Forbes, *pseud.* *see* Forbes, DeLoris (Stanton) 1923-	
De Hamel, Felix John. (*Name originally:* Felix John Hamel) x *pseud.:* Lionel J. F. Hexham	*
De Hamel, Herbert.	* 3
Dehan, Richard, *pseud.* *see* Graves, Clotilde Inez Mary, 1863-	

	Sources
Dejeans, Elizabeth (Janes) (Mrs. Sidney Budgett)	1
De Laguna, Frederica, 1906-	2
De La Mare, Walter John, 1873-1956.	*
Delancey, Roger.	2
Delaney, Denis, *pseud.* *see* Green, Peter, 1924-	
Delannoy, Burford.	* C EQ
Delany, Joseph Francis, 1905- *pseud.:* Joel Y. Dane	2
De La Torre, Lillian, 1902- (*Full name:* Lillian (De La Torre Bueno) McCue) x x	* S
De La Torre Bueno, Lillian *see* De La Torre, Lillian, 1902-	
Delf, Thomas, 1810-1865. *pseud.:* Charles Martel	* C EQ
Dell, Amen.	2
Dell, Belinda, *pseud.* *see* Bowden, Jean, 1920-	
Dell, Ethel May, *d.* 1939. (Mrs. Gerald Tabourdin Savage)	*
Dellbridge, John, 1887- *pseud.:* Plummy	* 2 3
Delta, *pseud.* *see* Wentworth, Patricia, *pseud.* d. 1961.	
De Mar, Paul, *pseud.* *see* Foley, Pearl.	
Demarest, Ann, *pseud.* *see* Bond, Florence Demarest (Foos)	
De Mille, James, 1837-1880.	Wells
Deming, Richard, 1915- *pseud.:* Max Franklin	3
De Morgan, William Frend, 1839-1917.	BRD, 1919
Denbie, Roger, *pseud. of* Alan Baer Green and Julian Paul Brodie. *see also* Brodie, Julian Paul. Green, Alan Baer, 1906-	2
Denison, Frank.	EQ
Denniston, Elinore, 1900- *pseuds.:* Dennis Allan Rae Foley	2 3
Dent, Lester, 1904-	2 3
De Pue, Edward Spence *see* De Puy, Edward Spence, 1872-	

	Sources
De Puy, Edward Spence, 1872- x (Edward Spence De Pue) x	1 2
Derby, Mark, *pseud.* *see* Wilcox, Harry.	
Derleth, August William, 1909- *pseud.:* Tally Mason	* 2 3
De Saix, Tyler. x	1
Desmond, Hugh.	2 3
Despard, Leslie, *pseud.* *see* Howitt, John Leslie Despard.	
Dessart, Gina, 1912-	3
De Steiguer, Walter George, 1884- x	3
Detzer, Karl William, 1891-	* 2 EQ
Devine, Stewart. (*Full name:* Virginia Stewart Devine)	3
Dewdney, Peter, *pseud.* *see* Brock, Alan St. Hill, 1886-	
Dewes, Simon, *pseud.* *see* Muriel, John Saint Clair, 1909-	
Dewey, Thomas Blanchard, 1915-	2 3
Dey, Frederic van Rensselaer, 1861-1922. *pseuds.:* Ross Beckman Aaron Ainsworth Burr Bertha M. Clay (also used by others) Marmaduke Dey Marian Gilmore (also used by others) Frederic Ormond Varick Vanardy Dirck Van Doren *see also* Carter, Nicholas, *pseud.*	1 Bragin (2 titles) Johannsen Pearson
Dey, Marmaduke, *pseud.* *see* Dey, Frederic van Rensselaer, 1861-1922.	
Diamond, Frank.	2
Dick, Alexandra, *pseud.* *see* Erickson, Sibyl Alexandra.	
Dickens, Charles, 1812-1870. *pseud.:* Boz *see also* Collins, Charles, *pseud.? of* Charles Dickens and Wilkie Collins?	** C G H EQ QQ S Sy W Wrong
Dickenson, Fred.	3
Dickinson, Weed.	2
Dickson, Carr, *pseud.* *see* Carr, John Dickson, 1906-	

	Sources
Dickson, Carter, *pseud.* *see* Carr, John Dickson, 1906-	
Dickson, Grierson.	3
Dietrich, Robert, *pseud.* *see* Hunt, Howard, 1918-	
Dignam, C B	2
Dillon, Dora Amy *see* Wentworth, Patricia, *pseud.* *d.* 1961.	
Dillon, Eilís, 1920-	3 St
Dilnot, George, 1883-	* 1 2 EQ
Dingwall, Peter, *pseud.* *see* Forsythe, Robin, 1879-	
Diplomat, *pseud.* *see* Carter, John Franklin, 1897-	
Disney, Doris (Miles) 1907-	* 3 MWA
Disney, Dorothy Cameron.	2 3 H
Divine, Arthur Durham, 1904- *pseuds.:* David Divine; David Rame	2
Divine, David, *pseud.* *see* Divine, Arthur Durham, 1904-	
Dix, Maurice Buxton, 1889-	* 2
Dixon, Bingham, *pseud.* *see* Borland, William Armstrong, 1893-	
Dixon, Charles.	3
Dixon, J Earle.	3
Dixon, Wallace, *pseud.* *see* Cronin, Bernard, 1884-	
Dobbins, Paul H 1916-	3
Dobbs, Frank.	3
Dobie, Charles Caldwell, 1881-1943.	*
Dobson, Kenneth Austin.	* 2
Docherty, James, *pseud.* *see* Raymond, René, 1906-	
Dodge, David.	* 2 3 St MWA
Dodge, Langdon, *pseud.* *see* Wolfson, Victor, 1910-	
Dodge, Louis, 1870-	1 W
Doe, John, *pseud.* *see* Thayer, Tiffany, 1902-	
Doherty, Edward Joseph, 1890-	2
Dollond, John.	2
Dolph, Jack, 1894-	2 3
Donavan, John, *pseud.* *see* Morland, Nigel, 1905-	

	Sources
Donn-Byrne, Brian Oswald *see* Byrne, Donn, 1889-1928.	
Donnel, C Philip.	2
Donovan, Dick, *pseud.* *see* Muddock, Joyce Emmerson Preston, 1843-1934.	
Dorn, Dean M *see also* Morgan, Michael, *pseud. of* C. E. Carle and Dean M. Dorn.	2
Dorrington, Albert.	*
Dory, John, *pseud.*	2
Doubleday, Roman, *pseud.* *see* Long, Lily Augusta, *d.* 1927.	
Dougall, Bernard.	2
Doughty, Francis Worcester, *d.* 1917. (Supposed author of Old King Brady stories)	EQ Pearson
Douglas, Dayle.	2
Douglas, Donald.	BRD, 1925
Douglas, Edith, *pseud.* *see* Burnham, Clara Louise (Root) 1854-1927.	
Douglas, Laura W	3
Douglas, Malcolm, *pseud.* *see* Sanderson, Douglas, 1922-	
Douglass, Alexander, *pseud.*	Johannsen
Douglass, Donald McNutt.	3
Douie, Marjorie.	1
Douthwaite, Louis Charles, 1878-	2 Wells
Dow, John.	2
Dowers, Penn, *pseud.* *see* Pendower, Jacques, 1899-	
Downes, Quentin, *pseud.* *see* Harrison, Michael, 1907-	
Downing, Todd, 1902- (*Full name:* George Todd Downing)	2
Doyle, *Sir* Arthur Conan, 1859-1930.	** 1 2 3 G H EQ QQ S Sy W Chandler, R. Sayers, 1928 Wrong
Doyle, Charles William.	*
Draco, F., *pseud.*	3
Drake, Maurice, 1875-1924.	2
Drax, Peter, *pseud.* *see* Addis, Eric Elrington.	
Dreiser, Theodore, 1871-1945.	* EQ's anthology, 1965

	Sources
Drennen, Raymond.	3
Dresser, Davis, 1904- *pseuds.:* Asa Baker Matthew Blood Kathryn Culver Don Davis Brett Halliday Anthony Scott Peter Shelley Anderson Wayne *see also* Debrett, Hal, *pseud. of* Davis Dresser and Kathleen Rollins.	** 2 3 G
Drewe, Marcus.	2
Druce, Hubert.	*
Drummond, Anthony, *pseud.* *see* Hunter, John, 1891-	
Drury, C W C	2
Dubois, Alan, *pseud.* *see* Wood, Clement, 1888-1950.	
Du Bois, Theodora (McCormick) 1890-	2 3 H
Du Bois, William, 1903-	2 H
Du Cann, Charles Garfield Lott, 1889-	2
Dudley, Dorothy, 1884- (*Full name:* Helen Dorothy Dudley) x	2
Dudley, Ernest, 1908- *pseud.:* Ernest Vivian Coltman	* 2 3
Dudley, Frank, *pseud.* *see* Greene, Ward, 1892-1956.	
Dudley, Helen Dorothy *see* Dudley, Dorothy, 1884-	
Dudley-Smith, Trevor *see* Trevor, Elleston, 1920-	
Düring, Stella M	Wells
Duff, Beldon.	2
Duff, David, 1912- (*Full name:* David Skene Duff)	3
Duff, James P	3
Dugdale, Giles.	2
Duke, Winifred.	2 S Thomas
Du Maurier, Daphne, 1907-	** Sy
Dun, Marie de Nervaud. (Nervaud Dun)	3
Dunbar, Noel, *pseud.* *see* Ingraham, Prentiss, 1843-1904.	

	Sources
Duncan, Actea, 1913- *pseud.:* Carolyn Thomas	3
Duncan, David, 1913-	2
Duncan, Duke, *pseud.* *see* Rathborne, St. George, 1854-1938.	
Duncan, Francis.	2 3
Duncan, William Murdoch, 1909- *pseuds.:* John Cassells Neill Graham Martin Locke Peter Malloch Lovat Marshall	* 2 3
Duncombe, Frances.	3
Dunkerley, William Arthur *see* Oxenham, John, *d.* 1941.	
Dunlap, Walter B., *pseud.* *see* Cobb, Sylvanus, 1823-1887.	
Dunn, *Detective.*	*
Dunn, Dorothy, 1913-	3
Dunning, Dan, *pseud?*	Johannsen
Dunsany, Edward John Moreton Drax Plunkett, *Lord*, 1878-1957. (Edward John Moreton Drax Plunkett) x	* EQ
Dunton, James Gerald.	1
Dupree, Morrison, *pseud.*	2
DuPuy, William Atherton, 1876-1941.	* EQ
Durbridge, Francis, 1912- *see also* Temple, Paul, *pseud. of* Francis Durbridge and James Douglas Rutherford McConnell	2 3 (JDC)
Durham, David.	2
Durham, Mary.	2 3
Durie, Lynn, *pseud.* *see* Christie, Douglas, 1894-	
Durrant, Theo, *pseud.*	3
Durst, Paul, 1921- *pseud.:* Peter Bannon	3
Dutton, Charles Judson, 1888-	* 1 2
Dwight, Olivia.	3
Dyar, Harrison Gray, 1866-1929.	1
Dyce, Gilbert, *pseud.* *see* Fitzgerald, Percy Hetherington, 1834-1925.	
Dye, William H	3
Dyer, George, 1903- (*Full name:* George Bell Dyer)	2 H

	Sources
E.A.B.D. *see* Bland, E A	
Eades, Maude L	2
Eadie, Arlton.	2
East, Roger, *pseud.* *see* Burford, Roger d'Este, 1904-	
Easterling, Narena. *pseud.:* René Easterling	3
Easterling, René, *pseud.* *see* Easterling, Narena.	
Eastman, Roy O 1883-	3
Easton, Nat.	3
Eastwood, Helen (Baker) 1892- *pseud.:* Olive Baxter	3
Eberhard, Frederick George, 1889-	2
Eberhardt, Walter F *d.* 1935.	2
Eberhart, Mignon (Good) 1899-	** 2 3 G H EQ QQ S
Ebert, Arthur Frank, 1902- *pseud.:* Frank Arthur	2 3
Eby, Lois Christine, 1908-	2 3
Echard, Margaret.	2
Eddy, John Percy, 1881-	*
Edelstein, Mortimer S	2
Eden, Dorothy, 1912- (*Full name:* Dorothy Enid Eden)	3
Eden, Rob, *pseud. of* Robert Ferdinand Burkhardt and Eve Burkhardt. *see also* Burkhardt, Eve, 1899- Burkhardt, Robert Ferdinand, 1892-1947.	* 2
Edginton, Helen Marion, 1883- (May Edginton)	* EQ
Edgley, Leslie, 1912- *pseud.:* Robert Bloomfield *see also* Hastings, Brook, *pseud. of* Leslie and Mary Edgley.	* 2 3
Edgley, Mary. *see also* Hastings, Brook, *pseud. of* Leslie and Mary Edgley.	3
Edington, Arlo Channing, 1890-1953.	2
Edington, Carmen Ballen, 1894-	2
Edmiston, Helen Jean Mary, 1913- *pseud.:* Helen Robertson	3
Edmonds, Harry.	2
Edmunds, Brent.	3

	Sources			
Edwards, Charman, *pseud.* *see* Edwards, Frederick Anthony, 1896-				
Edwards, Frederick Anthony, 1896- *pseuds.:* Charman Edwards, J. Van Dyke	*	2		
Edwards, Harry Stillwell, 1855-1938.	1			
Edwards, James G., *pseud.* *see* MacQueen, James William, 1900-				
Edwards, Julia, *pseud.* *see* Coryell, John Russell, *d.* 1924.				
Edward, Ward, *pseud.* *see* Rathborne, St. George, 1854-1938.				
Edwin, Maribel (Thomson)	2			
Egan, Lesley, *pseud.* *see* Linington, Elizabeth, 1921-				
Ehrlich, Max Simon, 1909-	3			
Eichler, Alfred, 1908-	2			
Eiker, Mathilde, 1893- *pseud.:* March Evermay	2	H		
Eisinger, Jo.	2			
Elder, Evelyn.	2			
Eldredge, Gilbert.	2			
Eldridge, George Dyre, 1848-	*	1		
Elias, David.	3			
Eliot, George Fielding, 1894-	2			
Eliot, Henry Ware, 1879- *pseud.:* Mason Deal	2			
Ellett, Harold Pincton, 1882- *pseud.:* Nigel Burnaby	2			
Ellin, Stanley, 1916-	3	G	St	Sy
Ellinger, Geoffrey.	2			
Ellington, Richard.	2	3		
Elliott, Robin.	*			
Elliott, William James, 1886-	3			
Ellis, John Breckenridge, 1870-1956.	2			
Ellis, N. A. Temple-, *pseud.* *see* Holdaway, Neville Aldridge, 1894-				
Ellsworth, Elmer, Jr., *pseud.* *see* Thayer, Tiffany, 1902-				
Ellsworth, Paul, *pseud.* *see* Triem, Paul Ellsworth, 1882-				
Elsworthy, Alexander Lockhart.	2			
Elton, John, *pseud.* *see* Marsh, John, 1907-				
Elwin, Malcolm, 1902-	3			

	Sources	
Emery, J Inman.	1	BRD,1925
Emery, Russell Guy, 1908-	2	
Emery, Samuel.	2	
Emery, Steuart Mackie, 1891-	1	
England, George Allan, 1877-1936.	*	
Englis, Golden Lorraine.	3	
English, Richard.	2	
Enright, Richard Edward, 1871-1953.	1	
Ensor, David.	3	
Ephesian, *pseud.* *see* Roberts, Carl Eric Bechhofer, 1894-1949.		
Eppley, Louise.	2	
Erikson, Charlotte, *pseud.* *see* Erikson, Sibyl Alexandra.		
Erikson, Sibyl Alexandra. (*Full name:* Cicely Sibyl Alexandra Erikson) *pseuds.:* Alexandra Dick Charlotte Erikson Frances Hay	2	
Ernst, Paul.	3	
Erskine, Firth, *pseud. of* Gladys Shaw Erskine and Ivan Eustace Firth. *see also* Erskine, Gladys (Shaw) 1895- Firth, Ivan Eustace, 1891-	2	
Erskine, Gladys (Shaw) 1895- *see also* Erskine, Firth, *pseud. of* Gladys Shaw Erskine and Ivan Eustace Firth.	2	
Erskine, Margaret, *pseud.* *see* Williams, Wetherby.		
Erwin, Howard W., *pseud.* *see* Ingraham, Prentiss, 1843-1904.		
Eshleman, John Morton.	3	
Esmond, Sidney.	3	
Essex, Richard, *pseud.* *see* Starr, Richard Harry, 1878-		
Este Burford, Roger d' *see* Burford, Roger d'Este, 1904-		
Estes, Carroll Cox.	3	
Esteven, John, *pseud.* *see* Shellabarger, Samuel, 1888-1954.		
Ethan, John B	3	
Etheridge, A I	2	

Sources

Eton, Robert, *pseud.* *see* Meynell, Laurence Walter, 1899-

Eustace, Robert, *pseud.* *see* Rawlins, Eustace, 1854-

Eustis, Helen, 1916- — 2 Sy

Evans, Alfred John, 1889- — 3

Evans, Dean. — 3

Evans, George, 1906- — 3
(*Full name:* George Bird Evans)
see also Bird, Brandon, *pseud. of* George Evans and Kay Evans.
Evans, Harris, *pseud. of* George Evans and Kay Evans.

Evans, Gwyn. — 2

Evans, Harris, *pseud. of* George Evans and Kay Evans. — 3
see also Evans, George, 1906-
Evans, Kay, 1906-

Evans, Howel. — * 1

Evans, Hugh Austin — * 2 3 H
pseud.: Hugh Austin

Evans, John, *pseud.* *see* Browne, Howard, 1908-

Evans, Kay, 1906- — 3
(*Full name:* Kay Harris Evans)
see also Bird, Brandon, *pseud. of* George Evans and Kay Evans.
Evans, Harris, *pseud. of* George Evans and Kay Evans.

Evelyn, John Michael, 1916- — 3
pseud.: Michael Underwood

Evelyn, Rose d', *pseud.* *see* Broemel, Rose.

Evens, Glyn Kinnaird. — 3
pseud.: Raq

Everett-Green, Evelyn *see* Green, Evelyn Everett-, 1856-1932.

Evermay, March, *pseud.* *see* Eiker, Mathilde, 1893-

Everton, Francis, *pseud.* *see* Stokes, Francis William, 1883-

Eyles, Alfred W — 2

Eyles, Kathleen Muriel, 1913- — 3
(*Full name:* Kathleen Muriel (Eyles) Crozier)
x
pseuds.: Merle Eyles
Catherine Tennant

	Sources
Eyles, Margaret Leonora (Pitcairn) 1890- (Mrs. David Leslie Murray)	2
Eyles, Merle, *pseud.* *see* Eyles, Kathleen Muriel, 1913-	
Eyster, William Reynolds, 1841-1918. *pseud.:* R. Hunt Wilby	Johannsen
F., *Inspector, pseud.* *see* Russell, William.	
F.O.O., *pseud.* *see* Street, Cecil John Charles, 1884-	
Fabian, Warner, *pseud.* *see* Adams, Samuel Hopkins, 1871-1958.	
Fahrenkopf, Anne. *see also* Irving, Alexander, *pseud. of* Ruth Fox and Anne Fahrenkopf.	2
Fair, A. A., *pseud.* *see* Gardner, Erle Stanley, 1889-	
Fairfax, Dennis.	2
Fairlie, Gerard, 1899-	* 2 3 H
Falkner, John Meade.	S
Falkner, Leonard.	2
Fane, Anthony.	2
Farjeon, Benjamin Leopold, 1838-1903.	1 C Johannsen
Farjeon, Joseph Jefferson, 1883-1955. *pseud.:* Anthony Swift	** 1 2 3 H EQ
Farmer, Bernard James, 1902- *pseud.:* Owen Fox	3
Farmer, Lucy.	* EQ
Farmer, Wendell, *pseud.* *see* Davis, Lavinia (Riker) 1909-1961.	
Farndale, John, *pseud.* *see* Harvey, John Wilfred.	
Farnol, Jeffery, 1878-1952. (*Full name:* John Jeffery Farnol)	1 2
Farr, John, *pseud.* *see* Webb, Jack, 1920-	
Farr, Sebastian, *pseud.* *see* Blom, Eric Walter.	
Farrar, Helen.	2
Farrar, Stewart.	3
Farrer, Katharine (Newton) 1911- (*Full name:* Katharine Dorothy Farrer)	3 St
Fast, Julius, 1918-	2
Faulkner, William, 1897-1962.	** G QQ Sy
Fay, Dorothy, *pseud.* *see* Lindholm, Anna Chandler, 1870-	

	Sources
Feagles, Anita (MacRae) 1926- *pseud.:* Travis Macrae	3
Fearing, Kenneth, 1902-	3 St Sy Chandler, R.
Fearnley, John Blakeway.	2
Fearon, Diana.	3
Feilding, Dorothy, 1884- (Works erroneously attributed to Archibald E. Fielding) x *pseud.:* A. Fielding	1 2 H W
Fellowes-Gordon, Ian, 1921- (*Full name:* Ian Douglas Fellowes- Gordon) *pseuds.:* Douglas Collier Ian Gordon	3
Fenisong, Ruth.	*2 3 MWA
Fenn, Caroline K *see also* McGrew, Fenn, *pseud. of* Caroline K. Fenn and Julia McGrew.	3
Fenn, George Manville, 1831-1909.	1 Johannsen Sayers, 1928 Wells
Fenn, Louis Anderson.	2
Fenwick, E P	2
Ferguson, John Alexander, 1873-	* 2 H W
Ferguson, William Blair Morton, 1882- *pseud.:* William Morton	* 1 2
Fernald, Chester Bailey, 1869-1938.	*
Ferrars, E. X., *pseud.* *see* Brown, Morna Doris (MacTaggart) 1907-	
Ferrars, Elizabeth, *pseud.* *see* Brown, Morna Doris (MacTaggart) 1907-	
Fethaland, John.	2
Fetta, Emma Lou.	2
Fetter, Elizabeth (Head) 1904- *pseud.:* Hannah Lees	2 S
Fidler, Henry J	* EQ
Field, Herbert N	2
Field, Julian Osgood. *pseud.:* X. L. (L., X.) x x	*
Field, Medora *see Perkerson,* Medora (Field)	
Field, Temple.	2
Fielding, A., *pseud.* *see* Feilding, Dorothy, 1884-	
Fielding, Archibald E 1900- *see* Feilding, Dorothy, 1884-	

	Sources
Fielding, Howard, *pseud.* *see* Hooke, Charles Witherle, 1861-1929.	
Findley, Ferguson, *pseud.* *see* Frey, Charles Weiser, 1910-	
Finley, Glenna.	3
Finley, Scott, *pseud.* *see* Clark, Winifred, 1909-	
Finnegan, Robert, *pseud.* *see* Ryan, Paul William, 1906-1947.	
Finney, Jack, 1911-	* St
Firth, Ivan Eustace, 1891- *see also* Erskine, Firth, *pseud. of* Gladys Shaw Erskine and Ivan Eustace Firth.	2
Fischer, Bruno, 1908-	* 2 3 MWA
Fisher, Douglas.	3
Fisher, Gerard.	3
Fisher, Rudolph, 1897-	2
Fisher, Stephen Gould, 1912- *pseuds.:* Stephen Gould; Grant Lane	2 3
Fishter, Jacob Franz, 1904-	2
Fitt, Mary, *pseud.* *see* Freeman, Kathleen, 1897-	
Fitts, James Franklin, 1840-1890.	1
Fitzgerald, Errol, *pseud.* *see* Clarke, Josephine Fitzgerald (Moylan) *Lady*	
FitzGerald, Kevin, 1902- (*Full name:* Kevin Columba FitzGerald)	3
FitzGerald, Nigel.	3 St
Fitzgerald, Percy Hetherington, 1834-1925. *pseud.:* Gilbert Dyce	* Chandler, F.W.
Fitzsimmons, Cortland, 1893-	2 H
Fitzwhistler, Enoch, *pseud.* *see* Cobb, Sylvanus, 1823-1887.	
Flanagan, Dorothy Bell *see* Hughes, Dorothy Belle(Flanagan) 1904-	
Flanagan, T. J., *pseud.?*	1 Johannsen
Fleischman, Albert Sidney, 1920-	3
Fleming, Brandon, 1889-	1
Fleming, Ethel.	2
Fleming, Geraldine, *pseud.* *see* Coryell, John Russell, *d.* 1924.	
Fleming, Ian, 1908-1964.	* Sy
Fleming, Joan Margaret.	* 3
Fleming, John Chester, 1906-	2 3
Fleming, Oliver, *pseud.* *see* MacDonald, Philip.	

	Sources
Fleming, Peter, 1907- (*Full name:* Robert Peter Fleming) *pseuds.:* Moth Strix	*
Fleming, Rudd, 1908-	2
Fletcher, Harry Lutf Verne, 1902- *pseuds.:* John Garden John Hereford	3
Fletcher, *Sir* Henry Lancelot Aubrey- *see* Aubrey-Fletcher, *Sir* Henry Lancelot, *Bart.*, 1887-	
Fletcher, Joseph Smith, 1863-1935.	** 1 2 H EQ QQ S W Thomson
Fletcher, Robert James, 1877- *pseud.:* "Asterisk"	2
Flower, Elliott, 1863-1920.	*
Flower, Pat.	3
Flowerdew, Herbert.	Wells
Floyd, Louise McKnight.	3
Flynn, Brian, 1885-	* 2 3
Flynn, J M	3
Flynn, William James, 1867-1952.	1
Flynt, Josiah, *pseud.* *see* Willard, Josiah Flynt, 1869-1907.	
Foley, Charles, 1908-	*
Foley, Pearl. *pseud.:* Paul De Mar x x	2
Foley, Rae, *pseud.* *see* Denniston, Elinore, 1900-	
Fonseca, Esther Haven.	2
Footman, David John, 1895-	2
Footner, Hulbert, 1879-1944.	** 1 2 H EQ
Forbes, Aleck, *pseud.* *see* Rathborne, St. George, 1854-1938.	
Forbes, DeLoris (Stanton) 1923- *pseuds.:* De Forbes x Stanton Forbes *see also* Rydell, Forbes, *pseud. of* DeLoris (Stanton) Forbes and Helen B. Rydell.	3
Forbes, Donald.	3
Forbes, Robert Erstone.	* EQ

	Sources
Forbes, Stanton, *pseud.* *see* Forbes, DeLoris (Stanton) 1923-	
Ford, Bryant.	2
Ford, Corey, 1902- *pseud.:* John Riddell	* EQ
Ford, Elbur, *pseud.* *see* Hibbert, Eleanor, 1906-	
Ford, Ford Maddox, 1873-1939. (*Name originally:* Ford Maddox Hueffer) x	2
Ford, Jeremy.	3
Ford, Leslie, *pseud.* *see* Brown, Zenith (Jones) 1898-	
Ford, Lillian Cummings, 1881-	2
Ford, Marcia, *pseud.* *see* Radford, Ruby Lorraine, 1891-	
Forester, Cecil Scott, 1899-	** 2 S Sy
Forgione, Louis.	2
Forman, Henry James, 1879-	1 2 W
Forrest, Alfred Edgar, 1863-	1
Forrest, Mark, *pseud.* *see* Morton, Guy Mainwaring, 1896-	
Forrest, Norman, *pseud.* *see* Morland, Nigel, 1905-	
Forrester, Andrew.	* C EQ
Forrester, Izola Louise, 1878- (Mrs. Reuben Roberts Merrifield)	1
Forsyte, Charles.	3
Forsyth, Gideon.	Wrong
Forsythe, Robin, 1879- *pseud.:* Peter Dingwall	2
Fort, Frank, *pseud.?*	Johannsen
Foss, John, *pseud.* *see* Gordon, James, 1912-	
Foster, Francis *see* Foster, Reginald Francis, 1896-	
Foster, George Cecil, 1893- *pseud.:* "Seaforth"	* 2
Foster, Maximilian, 1872-1956.	1
Foster, Reginald Francis, 1896- (Francis Foster) x	* 1 2 EQ
Foulis, Hugh, *pseud.* *see* Munro, Neil, 1864-1930.	
Fouts, Edward Lee, 1902- *pseud.:* Edward Lee	2 3
Fowler, Marie Louise.	2

	Sources
Fowler, Sydney, *pseud.* *see* Wright, Sydney Fowler, 1874-	
Fox, David, *pseud.* *see* Ostrander, Isabel Egenton, 1883-1924.	
Fox, George R	BRD, 1924
Fox, James M., *pseud.* *see* Knipscheer, James M W	
Fox, Marion.	BRD, 1919
Fox, Owen, *pseud.* *see* Farmer, Bernard James, 1902-	
Fox, Ruth.	2
see also Irving, Alexander, *pseud. of* Ruth Fox and Anne Fahrenkopf.	
Fox, Sebastian, *pseud.* *see* Bullett, Gerald William, 1894-1958.	
Fox-Davies, Arthur Charles, 1871-1928.	* 1 C
x	EQ
pseud.: 'X'	
Francis, Basil, 1906-	* 2
(*Full name:* Basil Hoskins Francis)	
pseud.: Austen Rhode	
Francis, C. D. E., *pseud.* *see* Howarth, Patrick.	
Francis, Caroline.	2
Francis, William, *pseud.* *see* Urell, William Francis.	
Frank, Theodore, *pseud.* *see* Gardiner, Dorothea Frances.	
Frank, Waldo David, 1889-	1
pseud.: Search-light	
Frank, Walter I	3
Frankau, Gilbert, 1884-1952.	* 2 EQ
Frankau, Julia (Davis) 1864-1916.	* 1 EQ
pseud.: Frank Danby	
Frankish, H	EQ
Franklin, Charles, *pseud.* *see* Usher, Frank Hugh, 1909-	
Franklin, Cynthia.	*
pseud.: C. J. Neville	
Franklin, Jay, *pseud.* *see* Carter, John Franklin, 1897-	
Franklin, Max, *pseud.* *see* Deming, Richard, 1915-	
Franklin, Miles.	2
Fraser, Alex, *pseud.* *see* Brinton, Henry, 1901-	
Fraser, Ferrin L	2

	Sources
Fraser, Hermia Harris.	3
Fraser, John A *pseud.:* Hawkshaw	1
Fraser, Robert	1
Fraser, William Alexander, 1859-1933.	*
Fraser-Simson, Cicely (Devenish) x	1 2
Fray, Al.	3
Frazer, Martin.	2
Frazier, S. M., *pseud.* *see* Morris, Charles, 1833-1922.	
Fredericks, Arnold, *pseud.* *see* Kummer, Frederic Arnold, 1873-1943.	
Fredericks, Ernest Jason.	3
Freedgood, Morton. *pseud.:* John Godey	2 3
Freeman, Kathleen, 1897- *pseud.:* Mary Fitt	* 2 G St
Freeman, Martin Joseph, 1899-	2
Freeman, Mary Eleanor (Wilkins) 1852-1930.	H
Freeman, Richard Austin, 1862-1943. *pseud.* (*in collaboration with ?*): Clifford Ashdown	** 1 2 C G H EQ QQ S Sy W Sayers, 1928
French, Allen, 1870-1946.	BRD, 1917
Frey, Charles Weiser, 1910- *pseud.:* Ferguson Findley	3
Freyer, Frederic, *pseud.*	3
Friedman, Stuart, 1913-	3
Friend, Oscar Jerome, 1897- *pseuds.:* Owen Fox Jerome Ford Smith	1 2
Froest, Frank.	1 EQ
Frome, David, *pseud.* *see* Brown, Zenith (Jones) 1898-	
Frost, Barbara.	2 3
Frost, Frederick.	*
Frost, Lesley.	2
Frost, Walter Archer, 1876-1964.	2
Fry, Pamela, 1917-	3
Fry, Pete, *pseud.* *see* King, Clifford, 1914-	
Fuller, Anne.	2
Fuller, Lester, 1908-	2
Fuller, Roy Broadbent, 1912-	3 St Sy
Fuller, Timothy, 1914-	* 2 3 S Thomas

	Sources
Fuller, Vincent, *pseud.*	1
Fuller, William Oliver, 1856-1941.	EQ
Furber, Douglas, 1885-1961.	3
Furniss, Averil Dorothy Sanderson. (Averil Dorothy Sanderson) x	2
Futrelle, Jacques, 1875-1912.	** 1 C H EQ QQ Sy W
Gabriel, H Wilhelm.	3
Gaines, Audrey.	2 3
Gainham, Sarah.	3
Gair, Malcolm.	3
Gaite, Francis, *pseud. of* Adelaide Frances Oke Manning and Cyril Henry Coles. *see also* Coles, Cyril Henry, 1898-1965. Manning, Adelaide Frances Oke.	3
Gale, John, 1917-	3
Gallagher, Gale, *pseud.*	2
Gallimore, F A	2
Galsworthy, John, 1867-1933.	*
Galwey, Geoffrey Valentine.	* 2 3
Gambier, Kenyon, *pseud.* *see* Lathrop, Lorin Andrews, 1858-	
Gamble, Frederick, 1904- (*Full name:* Frederick John Gamble)	3
Ganachilly, Alfred.	1
Gannett, James.	3
Gannett, Joy King.	3
"Ganpat," *pseud.* *see* Gompertz, Martin Louis Alan, 1886-	
Gard, Oliver.	3
Garden, John, *pseud.* *see* Fletcher, Harry Lutf Verne, 1902-	
Gardenhire, Samuel Major, 1855-	* 1 EQ
Gardiner, Dorothea Frances. *pseud.:* Theodore Frank	2
Gardiner, Dorothy, 1894-	2 3
Gardiner, Gordon, 1874-1937. (*Full name:* Theodore James Gordon Gardiner) x	* 2
Gardiner, Heather.	3
Gardiner, Stephen.	3

	Sources
Gardiner, Theodore James Gordon *see* Gardiner, Gordon, 1874-1937.	
Gardner, Curtiss T	2
Gardner, Erle Stanley, 1889- *pseuds.:* Charles M. Green Carleton Kendrake Charles J. Kenny	** 2 3 G H S Sy
Garland, Isabel, 1903- (*Full name:* Mary Isabel Garland) *see also* Lord, Garland, *pseud. of* Isabel Garland and Mindret Lord.	2
Garnett, *Captain* Mayn Clew, *pseud.* *see* Hains, Thornton Jenkins, 1866-	
Garnett, Roger, *pseud.* *see* Morland, Nigel, 1905-	
Garrett, Truman, *pseud.* *see* Judd, Margaret Haddican, 1906-	
Garrett, William A 1890-	1 2 **Benet**
Garth, Will, *pseud.* *see* Kuttner, Henry, 1914-1958.	
Gartland, Hannah.	1
Garve, Andrew, *pseud.* *see* Winterton, Paul, 1908-	
Gask, Arthur.	2 3
Gaskell, Elizabeth Cleghorn (Stevenson) 1810-1865.	A century of thrillers Johannsen
Gates, Henry Leyford, 1880-	2
Gault, Mark, *pseud.* *see* Cournos, John, 1881-1966.	
Gault, William Campbell.	3 G
Gaunt, Mary Eliza Bakewell, 1872-1942. (Mrs. Hubert Lindsay Miller)	* 1 2
Gay, Amelia, *pseud.* *see* Hogarth, Grace (Allen) 1905-	
Gay, Greer, *pseud.* *see* Payne, Hazel Belle (Saulisberry) 1892-	
Gaye, Phoebe Fenwick, 1905- (Mrs. F.L.S. Pickard)	3
Gayle, Newton, *pseud. of* Muna Lee de Munoz Marin and Maurice C. Guinness. *see also* Guinness, Maurice C Lee de Munoz Marin, Muna, 1895-	* 2
Gayton, Rebecca.	2
Gearon, John.	2
Geller, Eli.	3
Geoghegan, Laurence.	2
George, Ethel.	2

	Sources
George, Peter, 1924-1966.	3
(*Full name:* Peter Bryan George)	
pseud.: Bryan Peters	
Gerahty, Digby George.	*
pseud.: Robert Standish	
Gérard, Francis, 1905-	* 2 3 H
Gerard, Morice, *pseud.* *see* Teague, John Jessop, 1856-1929.	
Gerould, Gordon Hall, 1877-1953.	1
Gerrare, Wirt, *pseud.* *see* Greener, William Oliver, 1862-	
Gibbons, Cromwell, 1893-	2
Gibbs, Angelica.	2
Gibbs, George Fort, 1870-1942.	1 2
Gibbs, Henry.	3
pseud.: Simon Harvester	
Gielgud, Val Henry, 1900-	* 2 3
Gilbert, Anthony, *pseud.* *see* Malleson, Lucy Beatrice, 1899-	
Gilbert, Michael Francis, 1912-	* 3 G St Sy
Gilbert, *Sir* William Schwenck, 1836-1911.	* EQ
pseud.: F. Tomline	
Giles, Guy Elwyn, 1904-	2
Giles, Kris, *pseud.* *see* Nielsen, Helen, 1918-	
Gill, Elizabeth.	* 2
Gill, Herbert J	2
Gill, Josephine Eckert.	3
Gilla, Esker N	3
Gillette, William Hooker, 1855-1937.	* 1 2
Gillian, Michael.	3
Gillmore, Rufus Hamilton, 1879-1935.	* 2
Gilmore, Marian, *pseud.* *see* Dey, Frederic van Rensselaer, 1861-1922.	
Gilruth, Susan, 1911-	3
(*Full name:* Susannah Margaret Gilruth)	
Givens, Charles G	2
Glanville, Alec, *pseud.* *see* Grieve, Alexander Haig Glanville, 1902-	
Glaspell, Susan, 1882-1948.	* QQ
Glass, Montague Marsden, 1877-1934.	*
Glen, Elsa.	2
Glew, Doris Muriel, 1899-	2

	Sources
Glick, Carl, 1890- (*Full name:* Carl Cannon Glick)	2
Glidden, Minna (Wesselhoft)	2
Gloag, John, 1896- (*Full name:* John Edwards Gloag)	* 2
Glover, Robert, 1913-	3
Gluck, Sinclair, 1887- *pseud.:* Melrod Danning	1 2
Godey, John, *pseud.* *see* Freedgood, Morton.	
Godfrey, Peter.	3
Godley, Robert, 1908- *pseud.:* Franklin James	2
Goldie, Bertha Barré, 1871-	*
Goldie, Valentine Francis Taubman- *see* Taubman-Goldie, Valentine Francis.	
Golding, Louis, 1895-	** QQ
Goldman, Lawrence.	2 3
Goldman, Raymond Leslie, 1895-	2
Goldsmith, Frederic.	3
Goldsmith, Gene.	2 3
Goldsmith, Norman.	2
Goldsmith, Peter, *pseud.* *see* Priestley, John Boynton, 1894-	
Goldstone, Lawrence Arthur *see* Treat, Lawrence, 1903-	
Goldthwaite, Eaton Kenneth, 1907-	2 3
Gollomb, Joseph, 1881-1950.	1 2 Wells
Gompertz, Martin Louis Alan, 1886- *pseud.:* "Ganpat"	2
Goodchild, George, 1888- *pseuds.:* Alan Dare Wallace Q. Reid Jesse Templeton	** 2 3 EQ
Goode, George W	1
Goodis, David, 1917-1967.	2 3 (HH)
Goodridge Roberts, Theodore, 1877-1953. x (*Full name:* George Edward Theodore Roberts, x *surname after 1911*, Goodridge Roberts)	1
Goodspeed, Edgar Johnson, 1871-1962.	2
Goodwin, John, *pseud.* *see* Gowing, Sidney Floyd, 1878-	
Gordon, Alex.	3

	Sources
Gordon, Gordon, 1912-	3
Gordon, Ian, *pseud.* *see* Fellowes-Gordon, Ian, 1921-	
Gordon, James, 1912- *pseud.:* John Foss	3
Gordon, Jan, 1882-1944. *pseud.:* William Gore	2
Gordon, Mildred, 1912-	2 3
Gordon, Neil, *pseud.* *see* Macdonell, Archibald Gordon, 1895-1941.	
Gordon, Russell.	2
Gore, William, *pseud.* *see* Gordon, Jan, 1882-1944.	
Gore-Browne, Robert. x	* 2
Gorell, Ronald Gorell Barnes, *Baron,* 1884- (Ronald Gorell Barnes) x	1 2 H Sayers, 1928
Gough, Barbara Worsley- *see* Worsley-Gough, Barbara.	
Gould, Stephen, *pseud.* *see* Fisher, Stephen Gould, 1912-	
Govan, Christine (Noble) 1898- (*Full name:* Mary Christine Noble Govan) *pseuds.:* Mary Allerton J. N. Darby	2
Gowing, Sidney Floyd, 1878- *pseud.:* John Goodwin	1 2
Goyder, Margot, 1903- *see also* Neville Margot, *pseud. of* Margot Goyder and Neville (Goyder) Joske.	2 3
Goyne, Richard. *pseud.:* John Courage	* 2 3
Graaf, Peter.	3 St
Grady, Tex, *pseud.* *see* Webb, Jack, 1920-	
Graeme, Bruce, *pseud.* *see* Jeffries, Graham Montague, 1900-	
Graeme, David, *pseud.* *see* Jeffries, Graham Montague, 1900-	
Graeme, Roderic, *pseud.* *see* Jeffries, Graham Montague, 1900-	
Graeme-Holder, W *see* Holder, W Graeme-	
Grafton, Cornelius Warren, 1909-	* 2 MWA Thomas

	Sources			
Graham, Anthony.	3			
Graham, Nancy.	3			
Graham, Neill, *pseud.* *see* Duncan, William Murdoch, 1909-				
Graham, Peter.	2			
Graham, *Lieut.* Preston, *pseud.* *see* Ingraham, Prentiss 1843-1904.				
Graham, Winston. (*Full name:* Winston Mawdsley Graham)	2	G		
Grainger, Francis Edward, 1857- *pseud.:* Headon Hill	*	1	C	EQ
Granby, George.	2			
Granger, Henry Francis.	1			
Grant, *Major* A. F., *pseud.* *see* Harbaugh, Thomas Chalmers, 1849-1924.				
Grant, Alan, *pseud.* *see* Kennington, Alan, 1906-				
Grant, Ambrose, *pseud.* *see* Raymond, René, 1906-				
Grant, Douglas, *pseud.* *see* Ostrander, Isabel Egenton, 1883-1924.				
Grant, Douglas Allen.	2			
Grant, Ethel (Watts) Mumford, 1878- (Ethel (Watts) Mumford) x	1			
Grant, James Edward.	2			
Grant, Landon, *pseud.* *see* Gribble, Leonard Reginald, 1908-				
Grant, Margaret, *pseud.* *see* Coryell, John Russell, *d.* 1924.				
Grant, Richard, *pseud.* *see* Clarke, J Calvitt, 1888-				
Grantham, Gerald, *pseud.* *see* Wallace, John.				
Graves, Clothilde Inez Mary, 1863-1932. *pseud.:* Richard Dehan	*			
Gray, Althea.	3			
Gray, Berkeley, *pseud.* *see* Brooks, Edwy Searles, 1889-				
Gray, Charles Edward.	3			
Gray, Dulcie, 1920-	3			
Gray, Hilary.	3			
Gray, Jonathan, *pseud.* *see* Adams, Herbert, 1874-				
Gray, Oscar.	2			
Grayson, *Capt.* J. J., *pseud.* *see* Wright, Elsie N 1907-				

	Sources
Grayson, Richard, *pseud.* *see* Grindal, Richard.	
Graystone, John.	2
Green, Alan Baer, 1906- *see also* Burne, Glen, *pseud. of* Alan Baer Green and Gladys Elizabeth (Blun) Green. Denbie, Roger, *pseud. of* Alan Baer Green and Julian Paul Brodie.	* 3
Green, Anna Katharine *see* Rohlfs, Anna Katharine (Green) 1846-1935.	
Green, Charles M., *pseud.* *see* Gardner, Erle Stanley, 1889-	
Green, Evelyn Everett-, 1856-1932. x *pseud.:* Cecil Adair	*
Green, Gladys Elizabeth (Blun) 1908- *see also* Burne, Glen, *pseud. of* Alan Baer Green and Gladys Elizabeth (Blun) Green.	3
Green, Glint, *pseud.* *see* Peterson, Margaret, 1883-1933.	
Green, Helen, 1882-	*
Green, Janet.	3
Green, Peter, 1924- (*Full name:* Peter Morris Green) *pseud.:* Denis Delaney	3
Greene, Elizabeth (Russell) 1899-	2
Greene, Frances Nimmo.	BRD, 1918
Greene, Graham, 1904-	** G H S Sy
Greene, Josiah E 1911-	2
Greene, L Patrick. (Name originally: Louis Montague Greene) x	*
Greene, Louis Montague *see* Greene, L Patrick.	
Greene, Richard, 1901- (*Full name:* Richard George Hubert Plunket Greene)	2
Greene, Ward, 1892-1956. *pseud.:* Frank Dudley	2 S
Greener, William Oliver, 1862- *pseud.:* Wirt Gerrare	*
Greenham, George Hepburn.	* EQ
Greenleaves, Winifred.	2
Greenwood, Edwin.	2

	Sources
Gregg, Cecil Freeman, 1898-	2 3 H
Gregory, Franklin Long, 1905-	2
Gregory, Jackson, 1882-1943.	1 2
Gregory, Mason, *pseud. of* Doris Meek and Adrienne Jones. *see also* Jones, Adrienne. Meek, Doris.	3
Gregory, Sacha, *pseud.*	*
Greig, Ian.	* 2
Greig, Maysie, 1902- (*Full name:* Maysie (Greig) Murray) x *pseuds.:* Jennifer Ames Ann Barclay Madeline Thompson Mary Douglas Warren	3
Grenvil, William, *pseud.* *see* Martyn, Wyndham, 1875-	
Gresham, Elizabeth F *pseud.:* Robin Grey	2
Grex, Leo, *pseud.* *see* Gribble, Leonard Reginald, 1908-	
Grey, A. F., *pseud.* *see* Neal, Adeline Phyllis, 1894-	
Grey, Donald, *pseud.* *see* Thomas, Eugene, 1894-	
Grey, Douglas.	1
Grey, Louis, *pseud.* *see* Gribble, Leonard Reginald, 1908-	
Grey, Robin, *pseud.* *see* Gresham, Elizabeth F	
Gribble, Leonard Reginald, 1908- *pseuds.:* Sterry Browning Landon Grant Leo Grex Louis Grey Dexter Muir	** 2 3 H
Grierson, Edward, 1914-	* Sy
Grierson, Francis Durham, 1888-	* 1 2 3 H
Grierson, Jane, *pseud.* *see* Woodward, Edward.	
Grieve, Alexander Haig Glanville, 1902- *pseud.:* Alec Glanville	* 2
Griffin, Aceituna, 1876- (*Full name:* Editha Aceituna Griffin)	2
Griffin, Frank.	3

	Sources
Griffith, E G (*Mr. and Mrs.*) *see also* Griffith, Jason, *pseud. of* Mr. and Mrs. E. G. Griffith.	2
Griffith, George Chetwynd. (*Name originally:* George Chetwynd Griffith Jones) x *pseud.:* Lara	*
Griffith, Jason, *pseud. of* Mr. and Mrs. E. G. Griffith. *see also* Griffith, E G (*Mr. and Mrs.*)	2
Griffiths, Arthur George Frederick, 1838-1908.	* 1 C EQ Chandler, F.W.
Grile, Dod, *pseud.* *see* Bierce, Ambrose, 1842-1914?	
Grimshaw Beatrice Ethel.	2
Grindal, Richard. *pseud.:* Richard Grayson	3
Griswold George, *pseud.* *see* Dean, Robert George.	
Griswold, Latta, 1876-1931.	1
Groom, Kathleen Clarice.	*
Gropper, Milton Herbert, 1897-	2
Gruber, Frank, 1904- *pseuds.:* Stephen Acre Charles K. Boston John K. Vedder	* 2 3 G H S
Gubbins, Nathaniel, *pseud.* *see* Mott, Edward Spencer, 1844-1910.	
Guest, Francis Narold, 1901- *pseud.:* James Spenser	*
Guigo, Ernest Philip. *pseud.:* E. Carleton Holt	3
Guildford, John, *pseud.* *see* Hunter, Bluebell Matilda, 1887-	
Guinness, Katherine Doris.	3
Guinness, Maurice C *see also* Gayle, Newton, *pseud. of* Muna Lee de Munoz Marin and Maurice C. Guinness.	* 2
Guise, Stanley.	2
Gulik, Robert Hans van, 1910- x	* 3
Gull, Cyril Arthur Edward Ranger, 1876-1923. *pseud.:* Guy Thorne	* 1

Sources

Hannay, James Owen, 1865-1950. — 2
pseud.: George A. Birmingham

Hanshew, Hazel Phillips, *pseud. of* Mary E. and Thomas W. Hanshew. — 2
see also Hanshew, Mary E
Hanshew, Thomas W 1857-1914.

Hanshew, Mary E — * 1
see also Hanshew, Hazel Phillips, *pseud. of* Mary E. and Thomas W. Hanshew.
Kingsley, Anna, *pseud. of* Mary E. and Thomas W. Hanshew.

Hanshew, Thomas W 1857-1914. — ** 1 2 C H EQ QQ
pseud.: Charlotte May Kingsley
see also Hanshew, Hazel Phillips, *pseud. of* Mary E. and Thomas W. Hanshew.
Kingsley, Anna, *pseud. of* Mary E. and Thomas W. Hanshew.

Hansom, Mark. — 2

Hanson, Virginia. — 2

Harbage, Alfred, 1901- — 2 3
pseud.: Thomas Kyd.

Harbaugh, Thomas Chalmers, 1849-1924. — 1 Johannsen Pearson
pseuds.: *Major* A. F. Grant
Capt. Howard Holmes
Charles Howard
Robert Randolph Inman? (also used by Prentiss Ingraham, W. H. Manning, and Charles Morris)
Howard Lincoln
Major S. S. Scott
(and 12 unconfirmed pseuds.)
see also Old Cap Collier, *pseud.*

Hard Pan, *pseud.* *see* Bonner, Geraldine, 1870-1930.

Hardie, David William Ferguson, 1906- — 3

Hardin, Peter, *pseud.* *see* Vaczek, Louis Charles.

Harding, Albert. — 3

Hardinge, George. — 3
pseud.: George Milner

Hardinge, Rex, 1904- — 3
pseud.: Capstan

Hardy, Arthur Sherburne, 1847-1930. — ** 1 QQ

Hardy, Lindsay. — 3

	Sources
Hardy, Robert, 1917-	3
Hardy, Russ, *pseud.* *see* Snow, Charles Horace, 1877-	
Hardy, Stuart, *pseud.* *see* Schisgall, Oscar, 1901-	
Hardy, William Marion, 1922-	3
Hare, Cyril, *pseud.* *see* Clark, Alfred Alexander Gordon, 1900-1958.	
Hare, Robert, *pseud.* *see* Hutchinson, Robert Hare, 1887-	
Harley, John, *pseud.* *see* March, John, 1907-	
Harman, Neal.	3
Harnan, Terry.	2
Harper, Olive, *pseud.* *see* D'Apery, Helen (Burrell) 1842-1915.	
Harris, Charles, 1913- (*Full name:* Charles Stanley Henry Frederick Harris)	* 2
Harris, Colver, *pseud.* *see* Colver, Anne, 1908-	
Harris, John Beynon, 1903- *pseuds.:* John Beynon John Wyndham	2
Harris, Kathleen, *pseud.* *see* Humphries, Adelaide.	
Harris, Larry M 1933-	3
Harris, Polly Anne (Colver) *see* Colver, Anne, 1908-	
Harris-Burland, John Burland, 1870- x	* BRD, 1919
Harrison, Bruce.	2
Harrison, Michael, 1907- *pseud.:* Quentin Downes	3
Harrison, Richard, 1901- *pseud.:* Peter Motte	* 2 3
Hart, Frances (Noyes) 1890-1943. (*Full name:* Frances Newbold (Noyes) Hart)	** 1 2 C H S Sy
Hart, Innes Ruth Gray, 1889-	2
Harte, Bret, 1836-1902. (*Full name:* Francis Bret Harte)	** EQ QQ
Hartley, Leslie Poles, 1895-	*
Hartley, Olga.	1
Hartman, Lee Foster, 1879-1941.	1
Hartmann, Helmut. *pseud.:* H. Seymour	3
Harvester, Simon, *pseud.* *see* Gibbs, Henry.	

Sources

Harvey, Annie Jane (Tennant) *d.* 1898. *
pseud.: Andrée Hope

Harvey, Jack. 2

Harvey, John Wilfred. 2
pseud.: John Farndale

Harvey, Marion. 1 2 W

Harvey, William Clunie, 1900- 2

Harvey, William Fryer, 1885- * 2 EQ

Harwell, King M 3

Haslette, John, *pseud.* *see* Vahey, John George Haslette, 1881-

Hastings, Brook, *pseud. of* Leslie and Mary Edgley. 3
see also Edgley, Leslie, 1912-
Edgley, Mary.

Hastings, Dorothy Grace, 1911- 2

Hastings, Graham. 3

Hastings, Harrington, *pseud.* *see* Marsh, John, 1907-

Hastings, Macdonald. 3

Hastings, Roslyn S 3

Hastings, Wells Southworth, 1879- 1

Hasty, John Eugene. 3

Hatch, Mary R (Platt) 1848- 2

Hauck, Darby. 1

Hauck, Louise (Platt) 1883-1943. 1
pseuds.: Lane Archer
Peter Ash
Louise Landon

Havighurst, Marion Margaret (Boyd) 2
(Marion Margaret Boyd)
x

Hawk, John, 1893- 1 2

Hawkins, Dean. 2

Hawkins, John, 1910- 3

Hawkins, Ward, 1912- 3

Hawkins, Willard E 1887- 2

Hawkshaw, *pseud.* *see* Fraser, John A

Hawthorne, Julian, 1846-1934. * 1 C H
EQ

Hawton, Hector, 1901- * 3
pseud.: Virginia Curzon

Hay, Frances, *pseud.* *see* Erikson, Sibyl Alexandra.

	Sources
Hay, Ian, *pseud.* *see* Beith, *Sir* John Hay, 1876-1952.	
Hay, James, 1881-1936.	1 2 H W
Hay, Mavis Doriel.	2
Hay, William Laing, 1892-	2
Hayes, Milton.	BRD, 1926
Hayes, William Edward, 1897-	2
Haynes, Annie, *d.* 1929.	* 1 2
Hays, Hoffman Reynolds, 1904-	MWA Haycraft, Art
Hays, Sue Brown.	2
Hayward, William Stephens.	EQ
Hazard, Forrester.	2
Hazard, Harry, *pseud.* *see* Badger, Joseph E 1848-1909.	
Hazard, Laurence.	3
Hazeltine, Horace.	1
Head, Helen Smith.	3
Head, Matthew, *pseud.* *see* Canaday, John Edwin, 1907-	
Healey, Evelyn.	3
Healy, Eugene P	2
Heard, Gerald, 1889- (*Full name:* Henry FitzGerald Heard)	* 2 3 S MWA
Hearnden, Beryl. *see also* Balfour, Hearnden, *pseud. of* Beryl Hearnden and Eva Balfour.	1 2
Heath, Elizabeth Alden, *pseud.* *see* Holton, Edith Austin, 1881-	
Heath, Eric.	2
Heberden, Mary Violet, 1906- *pseuds.:* Charles L. Leonard	2 3
Hecht, Ben, 1894-1964.	* 1 2 EQ
Heckstall-Smith, Anthony, 1904- x	3
Hedges, Sidney George, 1897-	2
Hedley, Frank.	*
Heed, Rufus.	3
Heffernan, Dean.	2
Heitner, Iris. *pseud.:* Robert James	3
Held, Peter.	3
Heller, Lorenz.	2
Helm, Jeannette.	1

	Sources
Helm, Peter, 1916-	3
Hemingway, Kenneth.	3
Hemyng, Bracebridge, 1841-1901. (*Full name:* Samuel Bracebridge Hemyng)	* EQ Johannsen Pearson
Henderson, *Col.*	*
Henderson, Donald Landels, 1905- *pseud.:* D. H. Landels	Chandler, R. MWA
Henderson, J. Stanley, *pseud.* *see* Willett, Edward, 1830-1889.	
Henderson, James Leal, 1913- *pseud.:* Jay L. Currier	2
Henderson, William.	* C EQ
Hendryx, James Beardsley, 1880-	* 3 EQ
Henry, Jack.	3
Henry, O., *pseud.* *see* Porter, William Sydney, 1862-1910.	
Henshaw, Nancy Ely.	3
Heppell, Mary. *pseud.:* Marguerite Clare	3
Herber, William.	3
Hereford, John, *pseud.* *see* Fletcher, Harry Lutf Verne, 1902-	
Hering, Henry A	*
Heritage, Martin, *pseud.* *see* Horler, Sidney, 1888-1954.	
Herman, Lewis, 1905-	2
Herne, Huxley, *pseud.* *see* Brooker, Bertram, 1888-1955.	
Heron, E., *pseud.* *see* Prichard, Kate O'Brien Hesketh-	
Heron, H., *pseud.* *see* Prichard, Hesketh Vernon Hesketh-, 1876-1922.	
Herring, Paul.	2
Herrington, Lee.	3
Hervey, Harry, 1900- (*Full name:* Harry Clay Hervey)	BRD, 1923
Hervey, Maurice H	*
Hesketh-Prichard, Hesketh Vernon *see* Prichard, Hesketh Vernon Hesketh-, 1876-1922.	
Hesketh-Prichard, Kate O'Brien *see* Prichard Kate O'Brien Hesketh-	
Hewitt, Kathleen Douglas, 1893- *pseud.:* Dorothea Martin	3

	Sources
Hewlett, William.	2
Hexham, Lionel J. F., *pseud.* *see* De Hamel, Felix John.	
Hext, Harrington, *pseud.* *see* Phillpotts, Eden, 1862-1960.	
Heyer, Georgette, 1902- (Mrs. George R. Rougier) *pseud.:* Stella Martin	2 3 S St
Heyes, Douglas.	3
Heyward, Dorothy Hartzell (Kuhns)	2
Hibbert, Eleanor, 1906- (*Full name:* Eleanor Alice (Burford) Hibbert) *pseuds.:* Elbur Ford Kathleen Kellow Jean Plaidy Ellalice Tate	*
Hichens, Robert Smythe, 1864-1950.	*
Hickok, Frances.	2
Higginson, Harold Wynyard, 1887-	2
Highsmith, Patricia, 1921- (*Full name:* Mary Patricia Highsmith) *pseud.:* Claire Morgan	3 Sy
Hill, Amy Hoskin.	3
Hill, Brian, 1896- *pseud.:* Marcus Magill	2
Hill, Frederick Trevor, 1866-1930.	*
Hill, H. Haverstock, *pseud.* *see* Walsh, James Morgan, 1897-1952.	
Hill, Headon, *pseud.* *see* Grainger, Francis Edward, 1857-	
Hill, John.	* 2
Hill, Kate F., *pseud.* *see* Baer, *Mrs.*	
Hill, Katharine.	2
Hill, Lawrence.	2
Hill, Monica, *pseud.* *see* Watson, Jane (Werner) 1915-	
Hill, Roberta. *pseud.:* Harry Davis	3
Hill, Vincent.	3
Hill, Warren.	2
Hilliard, Alec Rowley, 1908-	2 MWA
Hillyard, William Heard.	EQ

	Sources
Hilton, James, 1900-1954.	* 2 S
pseud.: Glen Trevor	EQ's anthology, 1965
Himes, Chester B 1909-	(HH)
Hinde, Thomas, *pseud.* *see* Chitty, *Sir* Thomas Willes, *Bart.*, 1926-	
Hinds, Roy W	2
Hingston, William Edward, 1851-	* 1
Hipkins, Charles Hammond, 1893- *pseud.:* Carl Talbot	2
Hird, Frank, 1873-	2
Hirsch, Leon David, 1881- (Lee Hirsch)	2
Hiscock, Leslie, 1902- *pseud.:* Patrick Marsh	*
Hitchens, Dolores (Birk) Olsen, 1907- (D. B. Olsen) x *pseuds.:* Dolan Birkley Noel Burke	* 2 3
Hitchens, Hubert.	* 3
Hoare, Douglas.	2
Hobart, Donald Bayne.	2
Hobart, Robertson, *pseud.*	3
Hobhouse, Adam.	2
Hobson, Coralie (von Werner) 1891- *pseud.:* Sarah Salt	*
Hobson, Harry, 1908- (Hank Hobson) *pseud.:* Hank Janson	3
Hockaby, Stephen, *pseud.* *see* Mitchell, Gladys, 1901-	
Hocking, Anne *see* Messer, Mona Naomi Anne (Hocking)	
Hodder, Alfred, 1866-1907. *pseud.:* Francis Walton	* EQ
Hodemart, Peter, *pseud.* *see* Audemars, Pierre.	
Hodges, A Noel.	2
Hodges, Arthur, 1864-	2
Hodgkins, Marion Rous.	3
Hodgson, Anthony.	3
Hodgson, William Hope, 1877-1918.	** EQ QQ
Hoffecker, Douglas Meade.	2

	Sources
Hogarth, Emmett, *pseud. of* Mitchell A. Wilson and Abraham Polonsky.	2
see also Polonsky, Abraham.	
Wilson, Mitchell A 1913-	
Hogarth, Grace (Allen) 1905-	3
pseud.: Amelia Gay	
see also Weston, Allen, *pseud. of* Grace (Allen) Hogarth and Alice Mary Norton.	
Hogg, Daniel.	3
Hogue, Dock, *pseud.* *see* Hogue, Wilbur Owings.	
Hogue, Wilbur Owings.	2 3
pseuds.: Dock Hogue	
Carl Shannon	
Holbrook, Marion.	2 3
Holdaway, Neville Aldridge, 1894-	2
pseud.: N. A. Temple-Ellis	
x x	
Holden, Genevieve, *pseud.* *see* Pou, Genevieve (Long) 1919-	
Holden, Inez, 1906-	*
Holden, J Railton.	2
(Railton Holden)	
x	
Holden, Joanne, *pseud.* *see* Corby, Jane, 1899-	
Holden, Railton *see* Holden, J Railton.	
Holden, Raymond Peckham, 1894-	2
pseud.: Richard Peckham	
Holder, W Graeme-	2
x	
Holding, Elisabeth (Sanxay) 1889-1955.	2 3 H S
Holland, Marty.	2
Holland, Rupert Sargent, 1878-1952.	1 2
Holley, Helen (Mullen)	2
Hollingworth, Leonard.	2
Holloway, Elizabeth Hughes.	2
Holman, Clarence Hugh, 1914-	2 3
(Hugh Holman)	
pseud.: Clarence Hunt	
Holmes, David Charles, 1919-	3
Holmes, Gordon, *pseud. of* Louis Tracy alone and with Matthew Phipps Shiel.	C H
see also Shiel, Matthew Phipps, 1865-1947.	
Tracy, Louis, 1863-1928.	
Holmes, Grant, *pseud.* *see* Knipscheer, James M W	

	Sources
Holmes, H. H., *pseud.* *see* White, William Anthony Parker, 1911-	
Holmes, *Capt.* Howard, *pseud.* *see* Harbaugh, Thomas Chalmers, 1849-1924.	
Holmes, Paul Allen, 1901-	3
Holmes, Robert.	2
Holt, Allison.	2
Holt, Barry.	2
Holt, Deben, *pseud.*	3
Holt, E. Carleton, *pseud.* *see* Guigo, Ernest Philip.	
Holt, Gavin, *pseud.* *see* Rodda, Charles, 1891-	
Holt, Harrison Jewell.	1 Wells
Holt, Henry.	* 2 3
Holton, Edith Austin, 1881- *pseud.:* Elizabeth Alden Heath	2
Holton, Leonard, *pseud.* *see* Wibberley, Leonard Patrick O'Connor, 1915-	
Home, Michael, *pseud.* *see* Bush, Christopher, 1885-	
Homersham, Basil Henry, 1902- *pseud.:* Basil Manningham	2
Homes, Geoffrey, *pseud.* *see* Mainwaring, Daniel, 1902-	
Honeyman, William C *see* M'Govan, James, *pseud.*	
Honeywell, E L *pseud.:* Olin Stanley	3
Hood, Margaret Page, 1892-	3
Hood, Torrey *see* Chanslor, Marjorie Torrey (Hood) 1899-	
Hook, Alfred Samuel. *pseud.:* A. J. Colton	3
Hooke, Charles Witherle, 1861-1929. *pseud.:* Howard Fielding	1 2
Hooke, Nina Warner, 1907-	3
Hooker, Brian, 1880-1946. (*Full name:* William Bryan Hooker)	1
Hope, Andrée, *pseud.* *see* Harvey, Annie Jane (Tennant) *d.* 1898.	
Hope, Colin.	* 2
Hope, Essex. (*Full name:* Frances Essex Theodora Hope) *pseud.:* Essex Smith x	2
Hope, Fielding, 1897-	2

	Sources
Hope, Frances Essex Theodora *see* Hope, Essex.	
Hopkins, A. T., *pseud.* *see* Turngren, Annette, 1902-	
Hopkins, Kenneth, 1914-	* 3
Hopkins, Linton C 1872-	2
Hopkins, Nevil Monroe, 1873-1945.	* 1 EQ
Hopkins, Stanley, *Jr., pseud.*	2 MWA
Hopley, George, *pseud.* *see* Hopley-Woolrich, Cornell George, 1903-	
Hopley-Woolrich, Cornell George, 1903- *pseuds.:* George Hopley William Irish Cornell Woolrich	** 2 3 H QQ S Sy
Hopwood, Avery, 1884-1928.	1
Horler, Sidney, 1888-1954. *pseuds.:* Peter Cavendish Martin Heritage	** 1 2 3 H
Horn, Holloway, 1886- *pseud.:* H. L. Waghorn	2
Horne, Geoffrey, 1916- *pseud.:* Gil North	3
Hornung, Ernest William, 1866-1921.	** 1 C H EQ QQ S Sy W
Hosken, Clifford James Wheeler, 1882- *pseud.:* Richard Keverne	* 2 H EQ
Hoskins, Bertha Ladd.	1
Hoster, Grace.	2 3
Houghton, Claude, *pseud.* *see* Oldfield, Claude Houghton, 1889-	
Hoult, Norah, 1901-	3
Household, Geoffrey, 1900- (*Full name:* Geoffrey Edward West Household)	** 3 G EQ S Sy
Hovick, Rose Louise *see,* Lee, Gypsy Rose, 1914-	
Howard, Charles, *pseud.* *see* Harbaugh, Thomas Chalmers, 1849-1924.	
Howard, George Fitzalan Bronson-, 1883-1922. x	* 1 EQ
Howard, Harety, *pseud.* *see* Ognall, Leopold Horace, 1908-	
Howard, Herbert Edmund, 1900- *pseud.:* R. Philmore	* 2
Howard, Jack, *pseud.* *see* Rathborne, St. George, 1854-1938.	
Howard, James Arch, 1922-	3

	Sources
Howard, Leigh. *pseud.:* Alexander Krislov	3
Howard, Louis G Redmond- *see* Redmond-Howard, Louis G 1884-	
Howard, Mark, *pseud.* *see* Rigsby, Howard, 1909-	
Howard, Vechel, *pseud.* *see* Rigsby, Howard, 1909-	
Howarth, Caroline M	3
Howarth, David Armine, 1912-	3
Howarth, Patrick. (*Full name:* Patrick John Fielding Howarth) *pseud.:* C. D. E. Francis	3
Howes, Royce.	2
Howie, Edith.	2
Howitt, John Leslie Despard. *pseuds.:* Leslie Despard; John Leslie	* 2
Hubbard, George, 1884-	2
Hubbard, Margaret Ann, 1909-	3
Huber, Bertrand.	2
Hudson, William Cadwalader, 1843-1915. *pseud.:* Barclay North	Chandler, F. W.
Hueffer, Ford Maddox, *see* Ford, Ford Maddox, 1873-1939.	
Huggins, Roy, 1914-	2 3
Hughes, Alfred.	Haycraft, Art
Hughes, Babette (Plechner) 1906-	2
Hughes, Dorothy Belle (Flanagan) 1904- (Dorothy Belle Flanagan) x	* 2 3 H S
Hughes, M. Alison, *pseud.* *see* Steed, Mabel A 1894-	
Hughes, Rupert, 1872-1956.	* 1 2 EQ
Hull, Richard, *pseud.* *see* Sampson, Richard Henry, 1896-	
Hultman, Helen Joan.	2
Hume, David, *pseud.* *see* Turner, John Victor, 1900-1945.	
Hume, Fergus, 1859-1932. (*Full name*: Ferguson Wright Hume)	** 1 2 C H EQ Sy W
Humphreys, Eliza Margaret J (Gollan) (*Full name:* Eliza Margaret J (Gollan) Humphreys Booth) *pseud.:* Rita x	* 1

	Sources	
Humphries, Adelaide. *pseuds.:* Kathleen Harris Wayne May Token West	3	
Hunt, Clarence, *pseud.* *see* Holman, Clarence Hugh, 1914-		
Hunt, Harrison, *pseud.* *see* Ballard, Willis Todhunter, 1903-		
Hunt, Howard, 1918- *pseuds.:* John Baxter Gordon Davis Robert Dietrich	3	
Hunt, Joseph Wray Angus *see* Hunt, Wray, 1899-		
Hunt, Katherine Chandler. *pseud.:* Chandler Nash	3	
Hunt, Kyle, *pseud.* *see* Creasey, John, 1908-		
Hunt, Peter, *pseud. of* Charles Hunt Marshall and George Worthing Yates. *see also* Marshall, Charles Hunt. Yates, George Worthing.	2	
Hunt, Violet, 1866-1942.	*	Sayers, 1928
Hunt, Wray, 1899- (*Full name:* Joseph Wray Angus Hunt)	2	
Hunter, Alan, 1922- (*Full name:* Alan James Herbert Hunter)	*	3
Hunter, Bluebell Matilda, 1887- *pseud.:* John Guildford	2	
Hunter, Clementine, *pseud.* *see* Keynes, Helen Mary.		
Hunter, Evan, 1926- *pseuds.:* Hunt Collins Ed McBain Richard Marsten	3	
Hunter, John, 1891- *pseuds.:* John Addiscombe L. H. Brenning Anthony Dax Anthony Drummond Peter Meriton	*	2
Huntingdon, John, *pseud.* *see* Phillips, Gerald William, 1884-		
Huntsberry, William Emery, 1916-	3	
Hurlbut, Edward H	*	EQ
Hurley, Gene.	2	
Hurst, Norman.	C	

	Sources			
Hurt, Freda Mary Elizabeth, 1911-	3			
Huston, Howard Chauncey.	3			
Hutchison, Arthur Stuart-Menteth, 1880-	*			
Hutchinson, Horatio Gordon, 1859-1932.	*	1	2	
Hutchinson, Robert Hare, 1887-	2			
pseud.: Robert Hare				
Hutchison, Graham Seton, 1890-	*	2		
pseud.: Graham Seton				
Hutton, Joy Ferris.	2			
Huxley, Aldous Leonard, 1894-	*	EQ		
Huxley, Elspeth Josceline (Grant) 1907-	*	2	H	S
Hyatt, Stanley Portal, 1877-1914.	1	2		
Hyde, Theodore, *pseud.*	2			
Hyland, Henry Stanley, 1914-	3			
Hyne, Charles John Cutcliffe Wright, 1865-1944. (Cutcliffe Hyne) x	*	EQ		
pseud.: Weatherby Chesney				
Hyne, Cutcliffe *see* Hyne, Charles John Cutcliffe Wright, 1865-1944.				
Hythe, Gabriel, *pseud.*	3			
Iams, Jack, 1910-	*	2	3	St
Iconoclast, *pseud.* *see* Hamilton, Mary Agnes (Adamson) 1883-				
Iles, Bert, *pseud.* *see* Ross, Zola Helen, 1912-				
Iles, Francis, *pseud.* *see* Cox, Anthony Berkeley, 1893-				
Imbert-Terry, *Sir* Henry Machu, *Bart.*, 1854-1938. (Henry Machu Terry) x	2			
Ingraham, Prentiss, 1843-1904.	Johannsen			
pseuds.: Dangerfield Burr				
Noel Dunbar				
Howard W. Erwin				
Lieut. Preston Graham				
Midshipman Tom W. Hall				
Robert Randolph Inman? (also used by T. C. Harbaugh, W. H. Manning, and Charles Morris)				
T. W. King				
Colonel Leon Lafitte				
Harry Dennies Perry				
Frank Powell				
Major Henry B. Stoddard				
Capt. Alfred B. Taylor				

	Sources	
Ingram, Eleanor Marie, 1886-1921.	1	
Ingram, Kenneth, 1882-	2	
Inman, Robert Randolph, *pseud.?* *see* Harbaugh, Thomas Chalmers, 1849-1924.		
see also Ingraham, Prentiss, 1843-1904.		
Manning, William Henry, 1852-1929.		
Morris, Charles, 1833-1922.		
Innes, Hammond, 1913-	3	
(*Full name:* Ralph Hammond Innes) x x		
pseud.: Ralph Hammond		
Innes, John William Brodie- *see* Brodie-Innes, John William, 1848-		
Innes, Michael, *pseud.* *see* Stewart, John Innes Mackintosh, 1906-		
Innes, Ralph Hammond *see* Innes, Hammond, 1913-		
Irish, William, *pseud.* *see* Hopley-Woolrich, Cornell George, 1903-		
Ironside, John, *pseud.* *see* Tait, Euphemia Margaret.		
Irving, Alexander, *pseud. of* Ruth Fox and Anne Fahrenkopf.	2	
see also Fahrenkopf, Anne.		
Fox, Ruth.		
Irving, Peter, 1914-	3	
Irwin, Inez (Haynes) 1873-	2	
Irwin, William Henry, 1873-1948.	1	EQ
Jackson, Charles Ross, 1867-1915.	1	
Jackson, Giles, *pseud.* *see* Leffingwell, Albert, 1895-1946.		
Jackson, Marr.	2	
Jackson, Wallace, *pseud.* *see* Budd, William John, 1898-		
Jackson, Wilfrid Scarborough, 1871-	*	
Jacobs, Thomas Curtis Hicks, *pseud.* *see* Pendower, Jacques, 1899-		
Jacobs, William Wymark, 1863-	*	EQ
Jacobsson, P	2	
see also Oldfeld, Peter, *pseud. of* Vernon Bartlett and P. Jacobsson.		
Jaediker, Kermit.	2	
Jaffe, Michael.	2	
Jakes, John W 1932-	3	

	Sources
James, Brèni.	3
James, Florence Alice (Price) 1857-1929. *pseud.:* Florence Warden	Wells
James, Franklin, *pseud.* *see* Godley, Robert, 1908-	
James, Godfrey Warden, 1888- *pseud.:* Adam Broome	2
James, Robert, *pseud.* *see* Heitner, Iris.	
James, Stuart.	3
James, W I *pseud.:* Young Baxter x *see also* Old Cap Collier, *pseud.*	Bragin Pearson
Janson, Hank, *pseud.* *see* Hobson, Harry, 1908-	
Jardin, Rex, *pseud. of* Robert Ferdinand Burkhardt and Eve Burkhardt *see also* Burkhardt, Eve, 1899- Burkhardt, Robert Ferdinand, 1892-1947.	2
Jarrett, Cora (Hardy) 1877- *pseud.:* Faraday Keene	* 2 H S
Jarvie, Clodagh Gibson, 1923-	3
Jay, Charlotte, *pseud.* *see* Jay, Geraldine, 1919-	
Jay, Geraldine, 1919- (*Full name:* Geraldine Mary Jay) *pseud.:* Charlotte Jay	3 St
Jaye, Peter.	3
Jefferson, Beatrice W	2
Jeffries, Graham Montague, 1900- *pseuds.:* Peter Bourne Bruce Graeme David Graeme Roderic Graeme	** 1 2 H EQ
Jenkins, Cecil.	3
Jenkins, Herbert George, 1876-1923.	* 1 EQ W
Jenkins, William Fitzgerald, 1896- *pseud.:* Murray Leinster	2
Jenks, George Charles, 1850-1929. *pseud.:* W. B. Lawson (also used by St. George Rathborne) *see also* Carter, Nicholas, *pseud.*	Johannsen
Jepson, Edgar, 1863-1938.	* 1 2 EQ
Jepson, Selwyn, 1899-	* 2 3 H S
Jerome, Owen Fox, *pseud.* *see* Friend, Oscar Jerome, 1897-	

	Sources
Jesse, Fryniwyd Tennyson, 1889?-1958. (Mrs. Harold Marsh Harwood)	** 2 G H EQ QQ Sy
John, Katherine (Gower)	2
John, Romilly.	2
Johns, Foster, *pseud.* *see* Seldes, Gilbert Vivian, 1893-	
Johns, Veronica Parker, 1907-	2 S
Johns, William Earl, 1893-	2 3
Johnson, Evelyn Davies, 1904-	2 EQ
Johnson, Gladys Etta, 1891-	1
Johnson, Maurice C	2
Johnson, Owen McMahon, 1878-1952.	* EQ
Johnson, Pamela Hansford, 1912- (Lady C. P. Snow) *see also* Lombard, Nap, *pseud. of* Neil Stewart and Pamela Hansford Johnson.	2
Johnson, Philip, 1911- (*Full name:* Philip Edward Johnson)	2
Johnson, W. Bolingbroke, *pseud.* *see* Bishop, Morris, 1893-	
Johnson, Zoë.	2
Johnston, Christopher Nicholson *see* Sands, Christopher Nicholson Johnston, *Lord,* 1857-1934.	
Johnston, Frank, 1900- (*Full name:* Frank Norman Howard Johnston)	2
Johnston, George Henry, 1912-	* 3
Johnston, Madeleine.	2
Johnston, William Andrew, 1871-1929.	1 2
Jones, Adrienne. *see also* Gregory, Mason, *pseud. of* Doris Meek and Adrienne Jones. Mason, Gregory, *pseud. of* Doris Meek and Adrienne Jones.	3
Jones, Arthur E	3
Jones, Charles Reed, 1910-	2
Jones, Eugene.	2
Jones, G Wayman.	2
Jones, George Chetwynd Griffith *see* Griffith, George Chetwynd.	
Jones, Henry Bedford- *see* Bedford-Jones, Henry, 1887-	
Jones, Inigo, *pseud.*	2
Jones, J L T E	2

	Sources
Jones, Jennifer.	2
Jones, Lucy M *pseud.:* Lux	EQ's annual, 1946
Jones, Nard, 1904- (*Full name:* Maynard Benedict Jones)	2
Jones, Susan Carleton, 1869- *pseud.:* S. Carleton	1
Jordan, Elizabeth Garver, 1867-1947.	1 2
Jorgenson, George E	2
Jorgenson, Nora.	2
Joscelyn, Archie, 1899- (*Full name:* Archie Lynn Joscelyn) *pseuds.:* Archie Alexander Archer Evelyn McKenna Lynn Westland	2
Joseph, George, Sept. 19, 1912-	* 3
Joske, Neville (Goyder) 1893- *see also* Neville, Margot, *pseud. of* Margot Goyder and Neville (Goyder) Joske.	2 3
Judd, Margaret Haddican, 1906- *pseud.:* Truman Garrett	3
Judge, James P	*
Jughston, Josephine.	2
Junor, Charles.	EQ's annual, 1946
Kagey, Rudolf, 1904- (*Full name:* Rudolph Hornaday Steel) *pseud.:* Kurt Steel	2 H S
Kaine, George S., *pseud.* *see* Morris, Charles, 1833-1922.	
Kaledin, Victor K 1887-	*
Kampf, Harold, 1916- *pseud.:* Harold B. Kaye	3
Kane, Frank, 1912-	2 3
Kane, Henry.	* 2 3
Kane, William Reno, 1885-	2
Karig, Walter, 1898-1956. *pseud.:* Keats Patrick	2
Kark, Nina Mary, 1925- *pseud.:* Nina Bawden	* 3
Karlova, Irina.	2
Kauffman, Reginald Wright, 1877-	* 1 Chandler, F. W

	Sources
Kauffman, Ruth (Hammitt) *d.* 1952. *pseud.:* Ruth Wright	2
Kauffmann, Lane, 1921-	3
Kaufman, Louis, 1916- *pseud.:* Dan Keller	3
Kaufman, Wolfe.	2
Kay, Kenneth, 1915- (*Full name:* Kenneth Edmond Kay)	3
Kaye, Harold B., *pseud.* *see* Kampf, Harold, 1916-	
Kaye, Mary Margaret, 1911- (Mrs. G. Howard)	3
Kayser, Ronal. *pseud.:* Dale Clark	2
Keate, Edith Murray.	2
Keating, Joseph, 1871-	2
Keator, Maude C	2
Keck, Maud. see also Orbison, Keck, *pseud. of* Maud Keck and Olive Orbison.	2
Keeler, Harry Stephen, 1890-1967.	** 1 2 3 H EQ (HH)
Keene, Faraday, *pseud.* *see* Jarrett, Cora (Hardy) 1877-	
Keirstead, Burton Seely, 1907-	2
Keith, Carlton, *pseud.* *see* Robertson, Keith, 1914-	
Keith, David, *pseud.* *see* Steegmüller, Francis, 1906-	
Keith, J. Kilmeny, *pseud.* *see* Malleson, Lucy Beatrice, 1899-	
Kelland, Clarence Budington, 1881-1964.	* 3
Keller, Dan, *pseud.* *see* Kaufman, Louis, 1916-	
Keller, Harry A 1894-	2
Kellett, G	3
Kelley, Audrey *see* Roos, Audrey (Kelley) 1912-	
Kelley, Martha Mott. *see also* Patrick, Q., *pseud.*	2
Kelliher, Dan T *see also* Secrist, Kelliher, *pseud. of* Dan T. Kelliher and W. G. Secrist.	2
Kellow, Kathleen, *pseud.* *see* Hibbert, Eleanor, 1906-	

	Sources
Kelley, George C 1849-1895. *pseuds.:* Père Absinthe Harold Payne	Johannsen
Kelly, Mary, 1927-	3 G
Kelly, William Patrick, 1848-	*
Kelsey, Vera.	2
Kemp, Harold Curry, 1896-	2 3
Kendall, Carol, 1917-	2 3
Kendall, Kathrya.	3
Kendall, Ralph Selwood, 1878-	1
Kendrake, Carleton, *pseud.* *see* Gardner, Erle Stanley, 1889-	
Kendrick, Baynard Hardwick, 1894-	* 2 3
Kennedy, Harvey J	3
Kennedy, Howard, *pseud.* *see* Woolfolk, Josiah Pitts, 1894-	
Kennedy, Howard Angus, 1861-1938.	2
Kennedy, John, 1921- (*Full name:* John Boyd Kennedy)	3
Kennedy, Milward, *pseud.* *see* Burge, Milward Rodon Kennedy, 1894-	
Kennedy, Robert Milward, *pseud.* *see* Burge, Milward Rodon Kennedy, 1894-	
Kennington, Alan, 1906- (*Full name:* Gilbert Alan Kennington) *pseud.:* Alan Grant	2 3
Kenny, Charles J., *pseud.* *see* Gardner, Erle Stanley, 1889-	
Kent, David, *pseud.* *see* Birney, Hoffman, 1891-	
Kent, Elizabeth, *pseud.*	1 Wells
Kent, Mary.	2
Kent, Michael.	2
Kent, Willis, *pseud.* *see* Collison, Wilson, 1893-	
Kenyon, Camilla.	2
Kerkow, Herbert.	2
Kernahan, Coulson, 1858-1943.	* EQ
Kerner, Ben.	2
Kerr, Ben, *pseud.* *see* Ard, William, 1922-	
Kersh, Gerald, 1909-	*
Ketchum, Philip, 1902- *pseud.:* Carl McK. Saunders	2
Ketterer, Bernadine.	2
Keverne, Richard, *pseud.* *see* Hosken, Clifford James Wheeler, 1882-	

	Sources
Keyes, Michael.	2
Keynes, Helen Mary. *pseud.:* Clementine Hunter	2
Keystone, Oliver, *pseud.* *see* Mantinband, James H	
Kiddy, Maurice George, 1894-	2
Kilpatrick, Florence Antoinette (Wharton) 1888-	2
Kilvington, Edwin.	2
Kimberley, Hugh.	3
Kimmins, Anthony Martin.	3
Kindon, Thomas.	2
King, Basil, 1859-1928. (*Full name:* William Benjamin Basil King)	2
King, Charles Daly, 1895- *pseud.:* Robert Courtney	** 2 EQ QQ
King, Clifford, 1914- (*Full name:* James Clifford King) *pseud.:* Pete Fry	3
King, Frank, 1892-1958. *pseud.:* Clive Conrad	* 2 3
King, James Clifford *see* King, Clifford, 1914-	
King, R Raleigh.	2
King, Raymond Sherwood, 1904- (Sherwood King) x *pseud.:* Sherry King	2
King, Rufus, 1893-	* 1 2 3 H EQ S
King, Sherry, *pseud.* *see* King, Raymond Sherwood, 1904-	
King, Sherwood *see* King, Raymond Sherwood, 1904-	
King, T. W., *pseud.* *see* Ingraham, Prentiss, 1843-1904.	
King, William Benjamin Basil *see* King, Basil, 1859-1928.	
King of the Black Isles, *pseud.* *see* Nicolson, John Urban, 1885-	
Kingsley, Anna, *pseud. of* Mary E. and Thomas W. Hanshew. *see also* Hanshew, Mary E Hanshew, Thomas W 1857-1914.	1
Kingsley, Charlotte May, *pseud.* *see* Hanshew, Thomas W 1857-1914.	

	Sources
Kingsley, Florence (Morse) 1859-1937. (Florence Morse) x	2
Kingston, Charles.	* 2
Kinney, Thomas, *pseud.* *see* Thomas, Curtis.	
Kinsburn, Emart, *pseud.* *see* Hankins, Arthur Preston, 1880-	
Kipley, Joseph.	1
Kipling, Rudyard, 1865-1936.	* Sayers,1928
Kippax, Peter.	* 2
Kirk, Laurence, *pseud.* *see* Simson, Eric Andrew, 1895-	
Kitchin, Clifford Henry Benn, 1895-	2 3 Thomas Thomson
Kitchin, Frederick Harcourt, 1867-1932. *pseud.:* Bennet Copplestone	* H EQ W
Klein, Kate.	3
Klein, Norman.	2
Kline, Otis Adelbert.	*
Klingsberg, Harry M	* EQ
Knapp, George Leonard, 1872-	Wells
Knevels, Gertrude, 1881-	1 2
Knight, Adam, *pseud.* *see* Lariar, Lawrence, 1908-	
Knight, Clayton, 1891-	*
Knight, Clifford, 1886-	* 2 3 H
Knight, David, *pseud.* *see* Prather, Richard Scott, 1921-	
Knight, Kathleen Moore. *pseud.:* Alan Amos	2 3 H
Knight, Leonard A	* 2
Knipe, Emilie (Benson) 1870-1958. *pseud.:* Thérèse Benson	2
Knipscheer, James M W *pseuds.:* James M. Fox Grant Holmes	2 3 St
Knoblock, Kenneth Thomas, 1898-	2
Knotts, Raymond, *pseud.* *see* Volk, Gordon, 1885-	
Knowland, Helen Davis (Herrick)	3
Knowles, Vernon, 1899-	*
Knowlton, Robert Almy, 1914-	3
Knox, Bill, 1928-	3
Knox, Jackson, *pseud.?*	Johannsen

	Sources
Knox, Ronald Arbuthnott, 1888-1957.	1 2 C H S W Sayers, 1928 Thomson Wrong
Knox, Timothy.	2
Knox, Winifred Frances *see* Peck, Winifred, *Lady*.	
Koehler, Robert Portner, 1905-	2
Koonce, Charles.	2
Kootz, Samuel Melvin, 1898-	2
Krasner, William, 1917-	3
Krasney, Samuel A 1922- *pseud.:* Sam Curzon	3
Krepps, Robert Wilson, 1919-	3
Krislov, Alexander, *pseud.* *see* Howard, Leigh.	
Krumgold, Joseph, 1906-	2
Kummer, Frederic Arnold, 1873-1943. *pseud.:* Arnold Fredericks	1 2
Kurnitz, Harry. *pseud.:* Marco Page	2 3 H S
Kutak, Rosemary.	2 MWA
Kuttner, Henry, 1914-1958. *pseuds.:* Will Garth Lewis Padgett Jack Vance	2
Kuyumjian, Dikran *see* Arlen, Michael, 1895-1956.	
Kyd, Thomas, *pseud.* *see* Harbage, Alfred, 1901-	
Kyle, Ella Jane.	2
Kyle, Sefton.	2
L., X., *pseud.* *see* Field, Julian Osgood.	
La Coste, Guy Robert. *see also* Berton, Guy, *pseud. of* Guy Robert La Coste and Eadfrid A. Bingham.	1
Lacy, Ed.	3
Ladline, Robert.	2
Lady, Frederick.	2
Lafitte, *Colonel* Leon, *pseud.* *see* Ingraham, Prentiss, 1843-1904.	
LaFrance, Marston.	3
Laing, Alexander Kinnan, 1903-	2 H
Laing, Kenneth.	3

	Sources		
Laing, Patrick, *pseud.* *see* Long, Amelia Reynolds, 1904-			
Lake, Joe Barry. *pseud.:* Joe Barry	2		
Lakin, Richard.	*	2	
La Marre, Joseph.	2		
La Master, Slater, 1890-	2		
Lambert, Dudley.	2		
Lambert, Elisabeth.	3		
Lambert, Gerard Barnes, 1886-	2		
Lambert, Leslie Harrison. *pseud.:* A. J. Alan	*	EQ	
Lambert, Rosa.	2		
Lancaster, Paul.	2		
Landels, D. H., *pseud.* *see* Henderson, Donald Landels, 1905-			
Landon, Christopher, 1911- (*Full name:* Christopher Guy Landon)	3		
Landon, Herman, 1882-	*	1	2
Landon, Louise, *pseud.* *see* Hauck, Louise (Platt) 1883-1943.			
Lane, Grant, *pseud.* *see* Fisher, Stephen Gould, 1912-			
Lane, Gret.	*	2	3
Lane, Jeremy, 1893-	2	3	
Lane, Kenneth Westmacott, 1893- *pseud.:* Keith West	*	2	
Lang, Andrew, 1844-1912.	*	EQ	
Lang, Anthony, *pseud.* *see* Vahey, John George Haslette, 1881-			
Lang, Harry.	2		
Lang, Theo. (*Name originally:* Theo Langbehn) *pseud.:* Peter Piper x	*	3	
Langbehn, Theo *see* Lang, Theo.			
Langham, James R	2		
Langley, John Prentice, *pseud.* *see* Rathborne, St. George, 1854-1938.			
Langslow, Jane.	2		
Lanham, Edwin Moultrie, 1904-	2	3	
Lansdowne, Andrew.	*		
Lanza, Clara (Hammond) 1859-	EQ		
Lara, *pseud.* *see* Griffith, George Chetwynd.			

	Sources
Larbalestier, Philip George. *pseud.:* Archer G. Scott	* 3
Lariar, Lawrence, 1908- *pseuds.:* Adam Knight Michael Lawrence Michael Stark	2 3
Larminie, Margaret Rivers *see* Tragett, Margaret Rivers (Larminie)	
LaRoche, K Alison.	2
Larson, Russell W	3
Lathen, Emma, *pseud.*	3
Lathrop, Cornelia (Penfield) 1892-1938. (*Full name:* Cornelia Sterrett (Penfield) Lathrop) (Cornelia Penfield) x	2
Lathrop, Francis, *pseud.* *see* Leiber, Fritz, 1910-	
Lathrop, Lorin Andrews, 1858- *pseuds.:* Kenyon Gambier Andrew Loring	1
Latimer, Jonathan, 1906-	** 2 H S Sy
Latimer, Rupert, *pseud.* *see* Mills, Algernon Victor, 1905-	
Latouche, John, *pseud.* *see* Crawfurd, Oswald John Frederick, 1834-1909.	
Latta, Gordon, 1904-	* 2
Lauer, Harry C	3
Lauferty, Lillian, 1887- (Mrs. James Wolfe)	2
Laugier, R., *pseud.* *see* Cumberland, Marten, 1892-	
Launay, Andrew Joseph. (Droo Launay) x	3
Launay, Droo *see* Launay, Andrew Joseph.	
Laurence, John, *pseud.* *see* Pritchard, John Laurence, 1885-	
Laurenson, R M	3
Lauriston, Victor, 1881-	BRD, 1923
Lawless, Anthony, *pseud.* *see* MacDonald, Philip.	
Lawrence, David.	3
Lawrence, Hilda.	2 3 S St MWA
Lawrence, Margery H	*

	Sources
Lawrence, Michael, *pseud.* *see* Lariar, Lawrence, 1908-	
Lawrence, Robert Jackson.	3
Lawson, W. B., *pseud.* *see* Jenks, George Charles, 1850-1929. Rathborne, St. George, 1854-1938.	
Layhew, Jane.	2
Lea, Hugh.	2
Leacroft, Eric ,*pseud.* *see* Young, Eric Brett.	
Leaderman, George, *pseud.* *see* Robinson, Richard Blundell, 1905-	
Leaman, Adele.	2
Le Carré, John *pseud.* *see* Cornwell, David John Moore, 1931-	
Lederer, Norbert, 1888-1955.	2
Lee, Austin, 1904-1965. *pseuds.:* John Austwick Julian Callender	3 (HH)
Lee, Babs, *pseud.* *see* Lee, Marion (Van der Veer) 1914-	
Lee, Edward, *pseud.* *see* Fouts, Edward Lee, 1902-	
Lee, Elizabeth.	2
Lee, Emma Redington *see* Thayer, Lee, 1874-	
Lee, Gerald.	3
Lee, Gypsy Rose, 1914- (*Name originally:* Rose Louise Hovick)	* 2 S
Lee, Jennette Barbour (Perry) 1860-1951.	1 W
Lee, Leonard.	2
Lee, Manfred Bennington, 1905- *see also* Queen, Ellery, *pseud. of* Frederic Dannay and Manfred Bennington Lee. Queen, Ellery, *Jr.*, *pseud. of* Frederic Dannay and Manfred Bennington Lee. Ross, Barnaby, *pseud. of* Frederic Dannay and Manfred Bennington Lee.	** 2 3 H EQ QQ Sy
Lee, Marion (Van der Veer) 1914- *pseud.:* Babs Lee	2
Lee, Norman, 1905- *pseuds.:* Raymond Armstrong Mark Corrigan	3
Lee, Ranger, *pseud.* *see* Snow, Charles Horace, 1877-	

	Sources
Lee, Thorne.	3
Lee de Munoz Marin, Muna, 1895- *see also* Gayle, Newton, *pseud. of* Muna Lee de Munoz Marin and Maurice C. Guinness.	* 2
Lees, Hannah, *pseud.* *see* Fetter, Elizabeth (Head) 1904-	
Le Fanu, Joseph Sheridan, 1814-1873.	** 1 G Sy Johannsen Sayers,1928
Leffingwell, Albert, 1895-1946. *pseuds.:* Dana Chambers Giles Jackson	2 3
Lehmann, Rudolph Chambers, 1856-1929.	* EQ
Leiber, Fritz, 1910- *pseud.:* Francis Lathrop	*
Leigh, Johanna, *pseud.* *see* Sayers, Dorothy Leigh, 1893-1957.	
Leighton, Alexander, 1800-1874.	*
Leighton, Florence, *pseud.* *see* Pfalzgraf, Florence Leighton, 1902-	
Leighton, Marie (Connor)	* C
Leighton, Robert, 1859-	* C H
Leighton, Wing.	2
Leinster, Murray, *pseud.* *see* Jenkins, William Fitzgerald, 1896-	
Leite, George Thurston, 1920- *see also* Scott, Thurston, *pseud. of* George Thurston Leite and Jody Scott.	3
Leitfred, Robert H	2
Lejeune, Anthony.	3
Le May, Alan, 1899-	2
Lemmon, Laura Elizabeth, 1917- *pseud.:* Lee Wilson	2
Lemon, Mark, 1809-1870.	* EQ
Lemuel, George, *pseud.?*	Johannsen
Lenehan, John Christopher.	2
Leon, Henry Cecil. *pseud.:* Henry Cecil	* 3
Leonard, A. B., *pseud.* *see* Aldrich, Earl Augustus, 1886-	
Leonard, Charles L., *pseud.* *see* Heberden, Mary Violet, 1906-	
Leonard, Henry.	*
Leonid, *pseud.* *see* Bosworth, Willan George, 1904-	

	Sources
L'Epine, Charles, *pseud.*	*
Le Queux, William, 1864-1927. (*Full name:* William Tufnell Le Queux)	** 1 2 H EQ QQ W Sayers, 1928
Leslie, Francis.	* 2
Leslie, Jean.	* 2 3
Leslie, John, *pseud.* *see* Howitt, John Leslie Despard.	
Leslie, Lawrence, *pseud.* *see* Rathborne, St. George, 1854-1938.	
Leslie, Norman.	2
Leslie, O. H., *pseud.* *see* Slesar, Henry, 1927-	
Lesser, Milton, 1928- *pseuds.:* Stephen Marlowe C. H. Thames	3
Lester, Edward Castellain.	2
Lester, Frank, *pseud.* *see* Usher, Frank Hugh, 1909-	
Lester, Vincent.	2
Letherby, Jack.	3
Levene, Philip, 1926-	3
Leverage, Henry, 1885-	1 BRD, 1918
Levin, Ira, 1929-	Sy
Levin, Meyer, 1905-	G Sy
Levine, William, 1881- *pseud.:* Will Levinrew	2
Levinrew, Will, *pseud.* *see* Levine, William, 1881-	
Levinson, Eric.	1
Levon, Fred.	3
Lewis, Alfred Henry, 1857-1914. *pseud.:* Dan Quin	** 1 EQ QQ
Lewis, Cecil Day- *see* Day Lewis, Cecil, 1904-	
Lewis, Gita.	3
Lewis, Julius Warren, 1833-1920. *pseuds.:* Illion Constellano Leon Lewis	Johannsen
Lewis, Lange, *pseud.* *see* Beynon, Jane, 1915-	
Lewis, Leon, *pseud.* *see* Lewis, Julius Warren, 1833-1920.	
Lewis, Mary Christianna (Milne) 1907- *pseuds.:* Christianna Brand Mary Roland	* 2 3 St Sy
Lewis, Michael Arthur, 1890-	1 2
Lewis, Phyllis.	*

	Sources
Lewis, Walter Reginald Sunderland *see* Sunderland Lewis, Walter Reginald, 1861-	
Leyford, Henry, *pseud.*	2
Leyton, Patrick.	* 1 2
Liddon, Eloise S 1897- (Mrs. George Albert Soper)	2
Liebeler, Jean (Mayer) *pseud.:* Virginia Mather	2
Lilley, Peter. *see also* Buckingham, Bruce, *pseud. of* Peter Lilley and Anthony Stansfeld.	3
Lilly, Jean.	2
Limnelius, George, *pseud.* *see* Robinson, Lewis George, 1886-	
Lincoln, Howard, *pseud.* *see* Harbaugh, Thomas Chalmers, 1849-1924.	
Lincoln, Natalie Sumner, 1881-1935.	* 1 2 H
Lincoln, Victoria, 1904- (*Full name:* Victoria Endicott (Lincoln) Watkins Lowe) x x	2
Linden, Oliver, *pseud.* *see* Abrahams, Doris Caroline, 1901-	
Lindholm, Anna Chandler, 1870- *pseud.:* Dorothy Fay	2
Lindsay, David T	2
Lindsay, John, *pseud.* *see* Muriel, John Saint Clair, 1909-	
Lindsay, Kathleen, 1903- *pseuds.:* Margaret Cameron Mary Richmond	2 3
Lindsay, Robert Howard, 1910-	2
Lingo, Ada E	2
Linington, Elizabeth, 1921- *pseuds.:* Lesley Egan Egan O'Neill Dell Shannon	3
Linklater, J. Lane, *pseud.* *see* Watkins, Alex.	
Linsingen, Frederick William Berry von, 1901- (Von Linsingen, Frederick William Berry) x	2
Lippencott, Norman.	2
Lipsky, Eleazar.	2 3
Litsey, Edwin Carlisle, 1874-	3
Little, Constance.	* 2 3 H

	Sources
Little, Gwenyth.	2 3
Littlechild, John George.	* EQ
Littlefield, Anne.	3
Livingston, Armstrong.	1 2
Livingston, Kenneth, *pseud.* *see* Stewart, Kenneth Livingston, 1894-	
Livingston, Walter, 1895-	2
Lloyd, Herbert.	EQ
Loban, Ethel H	2
Lobaugh, Elma K 1907- *pseud.:* Kenneth Lowe	2
Lobell, Griselda G	3
Lobell, Nathan David, 1911-	3
Lock, Arnold Charles Cooper. *pseud.:* Charles Cooper	2
Locke, Dorothy Mary.	3
Locke, Gladys Edson, 1887-	1 2
Locke, Martin, *pseud.* *see* Duncan, William Murdoch, 1909-	
Lockridge, Frances Louise (Davis) *see also* Richards, Francis, *pseud. of* Frances and Richard Lockridge.	* 2 3 H S
Lockridge, Richard, 1898- (*Full name:* Richard Orson Lockridge) *see also* Richards, Francis, *pseud. of* Frances and Richard Lockridge.	* 2 3 H S
Lockwood, David.	3
Loder, Vernon, *pseud.* *see* Vahey, John George Haslette, 1881-	
Lodwick, John, 1916-	3
Lofts, Norah (Robinson) 1904- (*Full name:* Norah Ethel (Robinson) Lofts Jorisch) *pseud.:* Peter Curtis	3
Logan, Carolynne (Chitwood) 1902-	2
Logan, Malcolm Roderick, 1901-	2
Lomas, John E W	1
Lombard, Nap, *pseud. of* Neil Stewart and Pamela Hansford Johnson. *see also* Johnson, Pamela Hansford, 1912- Stewart, Neil.	2
Lombardi, Cynthia, *pseud.* (*Real name:* Georgina M (Richmond) Lombardi)	1

	Sources
Lombardi, Georgina M (Richmond) *see* Lombardi, Cynthia, *pseud.*	
London, Jack, 1876-1916.	* G EQ
Long, Amelia Reynolds, 1904- *pseuds.:* Patrick Laing Adrian Reynolds Peter Reynolds *see also* Coxe, Kathleen Buddington, *pseud.* *of* Amelia Reynolds Long and Edna McHugh.	2 3
Long, Ernest Laurie, 1886-	3
Long, Gabrielle Margaret Vere (Campbell) 1886- 1952. *pseuds.:* Marjorie Bowen Robert Paye George Preedy Joseph Shearing John Winch	* 2 3 H EQ S
Long, Harman.	*
Long, Julius.	2
Long, Lily Augusta, *d.* 1927. *pseud.:* Roman Doubleday	1 Wells
Long, Manning, 1906- (Mrs. Peter Williams)	2 3
Long, Max. (*Full name:* Max Freedom Long)	* 2
Longman, M E	*
Longmate, Norman, 1925- *Full name:* Norman Richard Longmate)	3
Longstreet, Stephen, 1907- *pseuds.:* Thomas Burton Paul Haggard David Ormsbee Henri Weiner	2
Longstreth, Thomas Morris, 1886-	* 2
Lookabee, Emmitt, *pseud.*	3
Lorac, E. C. R., *pseud.* *see* Rivett, Edith Caroline, 1894-1958.	
Loraine, Philip, *pseud.*	3
Lord, Garland, *pseud. of* Isabel Garland and Mindret Lord. *see also* Garland, Isabel, 1903- Lord, Mindret.	2
Lord, Jeremy, *pseud.*	2
Lord, Mindret. *see also* Lord, Garland, *pseud. of* Isabel Garland and Mindret Lord.	2

	Sources
Loring, Andrew, *pseud.* *see* Lathrop, Lorin Andrews, 1858-	
Loring, Emilie (Baker) *d.* 1951. *pseud.:* Josephine Story	3
Loring, Peter, *pseud.* *see* Shellabarger, Samuel, 1888-1954.	
Lorne, Charles, *pseud.* *see* Brand, Charles Neville, 1895-	
Lovell, B E 1920-	3
Lovell, Ingraham, *pseud.* *see* Bacon, Josephine Dodge (Daskam) 1876-1961.	
Low, Gardner, *pseud.* *see* Rodda, Charles, 1891-	
Lowe, Kenneth, *pseud.* *see* Lobaugh, Elma K 1907-	
Lowe, Victoria Endicott (Lincoln) Watkins *see* Lincoln, Victoria, 1904-	
Lowis, Cecil Champain, 1866-	1
Lowndes, Marie Adelaide (Belloc) 1868-1947. (Marie Adelaide Belloc-Lowndes) x	* 1 2 3 H S W Sayers, 1928
Lucas, Norman.	3
Luck, Peter.	2
Ludlow, Geoffrey, *pseud.* *see* Meynell, Laurence Walter, 1899-	
Ludwell, Bernice, *pseud.* *see* Stokes, Manning Lee.	
Luehrmann, Adele.	1
Luhrs, Victor, 1912-	2 H
Lustgarten, Edgar Marcus, 1907-	* Sy
Luther, Mark Lee, 1872-	2
Lux, *pseud.* *see* Jones, Lucy M	
Lyall, David, *pseud.* *see* Reeves, Helen Buckingham (Mathers) 1853-1920.	
Lyell, William Darling, 1860-	1
Lynch, Lawrence L., *pseud.* *see* Van Deventer, Emma Murdoch.	
Lynch, Miriam.	3
Lynch, Terry Wayman, 1940-	3
Lynde, Francis, 1856-1930.	* 1 EQ
Lynwood, Leslie J	* EQ
Lyon, Dana.	2
Lyon, Edna Wright.	2
Lyon, Harris Merton, *d.* 1916.	*
Lyon, Mabel Dana, 1897-	2

	Sources
Lys, Christian, *pseud.* *see* Brebner, Percy James, 1864-1922.	
Lytton, Edward, *pseud.* *see* Morris, Charles, 1833-1922. Wheeler, Edward Lytton, 1854 or 1855-1885.	
Maartens, Maarten, *pseud.* *see* Schwartz, Jozua Marius Willem van der Poorten, 1858-1915	
McAllister, Alister, 1877- *pseuds.:* Lynn Brock, Anthony Wharton	* 1 2 C H S W Sayers, 1928
Macaulay, Rose	1
McBain, Ed, *pseud.* *see* Hunter, Evan, 1926-	
McCabe, Cameron, *pseud.* *see* Borneman, Ernest, 1915-	
McCarthy, David.	3
MacCarthy, John Lloyd. *pseud.:* Desmond Cory	* 3
McChesney, Mary F *pseud.:* Joe Rayter	3
McCloy, Helen, 1904- (*Full name:* Helen Worrell Clarkson McCloy)	2 3 S St
MacClure, Victor, 1887- *pseud.:* Peter Craig	* 2
McComb, Katherine.	3
McCombs, R L F	2
McConnell, James Douglas Rutherford, 1915- *pseud.:* Douglas Rutherford *see also* Temple, Paul, *pseud. of* Francis Durbridge and James Douglas Rutherford McConnell.	3
McCoy, Trent.	*
McCready, Jack, *pseud.* *see* Powell, Talmage, 1920-	
McCue, Lillian (De La Torre Beuno) *see* De La Torre, Lillian, 1902-	
McCulley, Johnston, 1883-1958.	1 2
McCully, Walbridge.	2
McCutcheon, George Barr, 1866-1928.	* EQ BRD, 1917
McCutcheon, Hugh.	3
McDermid, Finlay.	2

	Sources
MacDonald, Allan William Colt *see* MacDonald, William Colt, 1891-	
Macdonald, Charles B	3
McDonald, Hugh C	2 3
Macdonald, John, *pseud.* *see* Millar, Kenneth, 1915-	
MacDonald, John Dann, 1916-	(HH)
Macdonald, John Ross, *pseud.* *see* Millar, Kenneth, 1915-	
MacDonald, Philip. *pseuds.:* Oliver Fleming Anthony Lawless Martin Porlock	** 1 2 3 C G H S Sy W
Macdonald, Ross, *pseud.* *see* Millar, Kenneth, 1915-	
MacDonald, William Colt, 1891- (*Full name:* Allan William Colt MacDonald) x	3
Macdonell, Archibald Gordon, 1895-1941. *pseuds.:* John Cameron Neil Gordon	2
McDonell, Gordon, 1905-	2 3
McDonell, Margaret.	3
McDougald, Roman, 1907?-1960.	2 3
MacDuff, David, 1905-	* 2
McDuff, Eileen May.	2
Mace, Helen.	3
Mace, Merlda.	2
McElfresh, Adeline. *pseuds.:* John Cleveland Jane Scott Elizabeth Wesley	3
McElroy, Hugh Francis.	2
McElwain, Miranda.	3
MacFadyen, Virginia.	1
MacFall, Haldane, 1860-1928.	*
McFarlane, Arthur Emerson, 1876-	* 1 W
MacFarlane, Leslie.	2
MacFarlane, Stephen, *pseud.* *see* Cross, John Keir, 1914-	
McGerr, Patricia.	* 2 3 St
McGibeny, Donald.	1 BRD,1920
McGivern, William P	* 2 3 St
McGloin, Joseph T *pseud.:* Thaddeus O'Finn	3

	Sources
M'Govan, James, *pseud.* (*Real name:* William C. Honeyman) x	** C EQ QQ
MacGowan, Alice, 1858-	1 2
MacGrath, Harold, 1871-1932.	* 1 2
McGrew, Fenn, *pseud. of* Caroline K. Fenn and Julia McGrew. *see also* Fenn, Caroline K McGrew, Julia.	3
McGrew, Julia. *see also* McGrew, Fenn, *pseud. of* Caroline K. Fenn and Julia McGrew.	3
McGuffin, William.	EQ's annual, 1946
McGuire, Paul, 1905- (*Full name:* Dominic Paul McGuire)	2 S St
MacHarg, William Briggs, 1872-1951.	** 1 2 H EQ QQ S
MacHaye, Eric, *pseud.* *see* Roche, Arthur Somers, 1883-1935.	
Machen, Arthur, 1863-1947.	** 1 Sy
McHugh, Edna. *see also* Coxe, Kathleen Buddington, *pseud. of* Amelia Reynolds Long and Edna McHugh.	2
McHugh, Jay, *pseud.* *see* MacQueen, James William, 1900-	
Macintosh, Edith Joan (Burbridge) 1919- (Edith Joan Burbridge) x *pseud.:* Joan Cockin	3
McIntyre, John Thomas, 1871-1951. *pseud.:* Kerry O'Neil	* 1 2 C H W
MacIsaac, Frederick John, 1886-	2
Mack, Evalina, *pseud.* *see* McNamara, Lena (Brooke) 1891-	
Mackail, Denis George, 1892-	1
McKay, Randle.	2 EQ Thomson
McKechnie, Neil Kenneth, 1873-	2
McKenna, Evelyn, *pseud.* *see* Joscelyn, Archie, 1899-	
MacKenzie, Adelbert Roland, 1907-	2
MacKenzie, Andrew. (*Full name:* Andrew Carr MacKenzie)	3

	Sources
Mackenzie, Compton, 1882- (*Full name:* Edward Montagu Compton Mackenzie) x	2
MacKenzie, Donald, 1908-	3
Mackenzie, Edward Montagu Compton *see* Mackenzie Compton, 1882-	
Mackenzie, Nigel.	3
McKinley, Frances (Burks) 1907- (*Full name:* Mary Frances (Burks) McKinley)	2
McKinney, Alice Jean Chandler (Webster) *see* Webster, Jean, 1876-1916.	
MacKinnon, Allan.	2 3 St
Mackintosh, Elizabeth, 1896-1952. *pseuds.:* Gordon Daviot Josephine Tey	** 3 Sy
MacKnutt M G	3
Mackworth, John Dolben, 1887-	BRD, 1925
MacLaren, Gordon, *pseud.* *see* Patten, William George, 1866-1945.	
Maclaren-Ross, Julian. x	3
McLean, Allan Campbell, 1922-	3
MacLean, Robinson, 1910-	2 3
MacLeod, Adam Gordon, 1883-	* 1 2
MacLeod, Angus, 1906-	3
M'Levy, James.	* C EQ
McMeekin, Clark, *pseud. of* Dorothy (Park) Clark and Isabel (McLennan) McMeekin. *see also* Clark, Dorothy (Park) 1899- McMeekin, Isabel (McLennan) 1895-	2 3
McMeekin, Isabel (McLennan) 1895- *see also* McMeekin, Clark, *pseud. of* Dorothy (Park) Clark and Isabel (McLennan) McMeekin.	2 3
McMorrow, Thomas, 1886-1957.	* 2
McMullen, Mary, 1920-	*
MacNalty, *Sir* Arthur Salusbury, 1880-	*
McNamara, Ed, 1911- (*Full name:* Edward Francis McNamara)	3
McNamara, Lena (Brooke) 1891- (*Full name:* Lena Randolph (Brooke) McNamara) *pseud.:* Evalina Mack	3

	Sources
Macnaughtan, Richard.	2
McNeile, Herman Cyril, 1888-1937. *pseud.:* Sapper	** 1 2 3 G H EQ Sy Thomson
Maconechy, Joanna.	*
MacPhail, James A *see also* Crockett, James, *pseud. of* Cornelia Warriner and James A. MacPhail.	2
MacQueen, James William, 1900- *pseuds.:* James G. Edwards Jay McHugh	2 H
Macrae, Travis, *pseud.* *see* Feagles, Anita (MacRae) 1926-	
McRoyd, Allan.	2
McShane, Mark, 1930-	3
MacVeigh, Sue, *pseud.*	2
MacVicar, Angus, 1908-	2
McWatters, George S	Chandler, F. W.
Maddock, Lucy (Lacoste)	1
Maddock, Stephen.	2
Madeley, Joan.	3
Magarshack, David, 1899-	* 2
Magill, Marcus, *pseud.* *see* Hill, Brian, 1896-	
Magoon, Carey, *pseud. of* Elisabeth Carey and Marian Austin (Waite) Magoon. *see also* Carey, Elisabeth. Magoon, Marian Austin (Waite) 1885-	2
Magoon, Marian Austin (Waite) 1885- *see also* Magoon, Carey, *pseud. of* Elisabeth Carey and Marian Austin (Waite) Magoon.	2
Mahannah, Floyd.	3
Mainwaring, Daniel, 1902- *pseud.:* Geoffrey Homes	2 H S
Mainwaring, Marion.	3 St
Mair, John, 1914- (*Full name:* John Dunbar Mair)	Sy
Makepeace, Ann.	3
Makin, William James, 1894-	2
Malcolm-Smith, George, 1901- x	3
Malim, Barbara.	2
Malina, Fred.	3

	Sources
Malleson, Lucy Beatrice, 1899-	** 1 2 3
pseuds.: Anthony Gilbert J. Kilmeny Keith Anne Meredith	S
Malloch, George Reston, 1875-	Crimes, creeps Sayers, 1934
Malloch, Peter, *pseud.* *see* Duncan, William Murdoch, 1909-	
Mallory, Arthur.	1 2
Melmar, McKnight.	* 2
Manhood, Harold Alfred, 1904-	* Sayers, 1934
Manly, Marline, *pseud.* *see* Rathborne, St. George, 1854-1938.	
Mann, Ernest L	2
Mann, Jack.	2
Manners, David X	2
Manners, Gordon.	2
Manning, Adelaide Frances Oke. *see also* Coles, Manning, *pseud. of* Adelaide Frances Oke Manning and Cyril Henry Coles. Gaite, Francis, *pseud. of* Adelaide Frances Oke Manning and Cyril Henry Coles.	2 3
Manning, Bruce, *pseud.*	* 2
Manning, Hilda, *pseud.* *see* Reach, James.	
Manning, William Henry, 1852-1929. *pseuds.:* Ben Halliday Robert Randolph Inman? (also used by Charles Morris, T. C. Harbaugh, and Prentiss Ingraham) Jo Pierce (also used by Charles Morris) *Major* E. L. St. Vrain Marcus H. Waring *Capt.* Mark Wilton (and 9 unconfirmed pseuds.)	Johannsen
Manningham, Basil, *pseud.* *see* Homersham, Basil Henry, 1902-	
Mannon, M. M., *pseud. of* Mary Ellen Mannon and Martha Mannon. *see also* Mannon, Martha, 1909- Mannon, Mary Ellen, 1913-	2

	Sources
Mannon, Martha, 1909- *see also* Mannon, M. M., *pseud. of* Mary Ellen Mannon and Martha Mannon.	2
Mannon, Mary Ellen, 1913- *see also* Mannon, M. M., *pseud of* Mary Ellen Mannon and Martha Mannon.	2
Manor, Jason, *pseud.* *see* Hall, Oakley Maxwell, 1920-	
Mansfield, Paul H 1922-	3
Mantinband, James H *pseud.:* Oliver Keystone	3
Manton, Peter, *pseud.* *see* Creasey, John, 1908-	
Mar, Paul De, *pseud.* *see* Foley, Pearl.	
Marble, Margaret Sharp, 1913-	2
March, Jermyn, *pseud.* *see* Webb, Dorothy Anna Maria.	
March, Maxwell.	2
March, William, *pseud.* *see* Campbell, William Edward March, 1894-1954.	
Marchant, Ronano Isabel, *pseud.* *see* Colbron, Grace Isabel, 1869-1948.	
Marchmont, Arthur Williams, 1852-1923.	1 C W
Marcus, Arthur A	2
Marfield, Dwight.	2
Marino, Nick, *pseud.*	3
Mario, Queena, 1896-1951.	2
Markham, Virgil, 1899-	* 2
Marlett, Melba Balmat (Grimes) 1909-	* 2 3
Marlowe, Francis.	*
Marlowe, Piers.	*
Marlowe, Stephen, *pseud.* *see* Lesser, Milton, 1928-	
Marquand, John Phillips, 1893-1960. *pseud.:* John Phillips	3 H Thomas
Marric, J. J., *pseud.* *see* Creasey, John, 1908-	
Marsden, Antony.	2
Marsh, Jean, 1898- (Mrs. Gerald E. Marshall)	2 3
Marsh, John, 1907- *pseuds.:* John Elton John Harley Harrington Hastings Grace Richmond Lilian Woodward	3

	Sources
Marsh, Ngaio, 1899-	** 2 3 G H S Sy
Marsh, Patrick, *pseud.* *see* Hiscock, Leslie, 1902-	
Marsh, Richard, 1857-1915.	* 1 2 C EQ Sayers, 1928
Marshall, Archibald, 1866-1934.	* 1 EQ
Marshall, Charles Hunt. *see also* Hunt, Peter, *pseud. of* Charles Hunt Marshall and George Worthing Yates.	2
Marshall, Edison, 1894-	2
Marshall, Gary, *pseud.* *see* Snow, Charles Horace, 1877-	
Marshall, Herbert.	* 1
Marshall, Hurst.	2
Marshall, Lovatt, *pseud.* *see* Duncan, William Murdoch, 1909-	
Marshall, Raymond, *pseud.* *see* Raymond, René, 1906-	
Marshall, Sidney.	2
Marsten, Richard, *pseud.* *see* Hunter, Evan, 1926-	
Martel, Charles, *pseud.* *see* Delf, Thomas, 1810-1865.	
Marten, Jon Chisholm.	3
Martens, Paul, *pseud.* *see* Southwold, Stephen, 1887-1964.	
Martin, A Richard.	* 2
Martin, Absalom.	1
Martin, Archibald Edward, 1885-	2 3 MWA
Martin, Dorothea, *pseud.* *see* Hewitt, Kathleen Douglas, 1893-	
Martin, Hector Paulin.	2
Martin, Henriette.	3
Martin, Nell Columbia Boyer, 1890- *pseud.:* Columbia Boyer	2
Martin, Oliver, *pseud.* *see* Davies, Ernest, 1873-	
Martin, Richard, *pseud.* *see* Creasey, John, 1908-	
Martin, Robert Bernard, 1918-	* 3
Martin, Robert Lee, 1908-	* 3
Martin, Stella, *pseud.* *see* Heyer, Georgette, 1902-	
Martin, Stuart, 1882-	* 2 EQ
Marting, Ruth Lenore, 1907- *pseud.:* Hilea Bailey	2

	Sources
Martyn, Oliver, *pseud.* *see* White, Herbert Oliver, 1885-	
Martyn, Wyndham, 1875- *pseud.:* William Grenvil	* 1 2 3 EQ W
Marvell, Holt, *pseud.* *see* Maschwitz, Eric, 1901-	
Maschwitz, Eric, 1901- *pseud.:* Holt Marvell	* 3
Maske, John.	2
Mason, Alexander Campbell, 1901?-	2
Mason, Alfred Edward Woodley, 1865-1948.	** 1 2 C G H EQ QQ S Sy W Sayers, 1928 Wrong
Mason, Charles. *pseud.:* S. C. Mason	2
Mason, Francis van Wyck, 1901- (Van Wyck Mason) x *pseuds.:* Geoffrey Coffin Frank W. Mason Ward Weaver	* 2 H
Mason, Frank W., *pseud.* *see* Mason, Francis van Wyck, 1901-	
Mason, Gregory, *pseud. of* Doris Meek and Adrienne Jones. *see also* Jones, Adrienne. Meek, Doris.	3
Mason, Howard, *pseud.* *see* Ramage, Jennifer.	
Mason, S. C., *pseud.* *see* Mason, Charles.	
Mason, Sara Elizabeth.	2
Mason, Tally, *pseud.* *see* Derleth, August William, 1909-	
Mason, Van Wyck *see* Mason, Francis van Wyck, 1901-	
Massey, Morrell.	2
Massey, Ruth.	2
Massie, Chris, 1880-	Haycraft, Art MWA
Masterman, John Cecil, 1891-	2
Masterman, Margaret, 1910- (Mrs. Richard Bevan Braithwaite)	2
Masterman, Walter S	1 2 C H W

	Sources
Masterson, Whit, *pseud. of* Bob Wade and Bill Miller.	2 3
see also Miller, Bill, 1920-	
Wade, Bob, 1920-	
Masur, Harold Q 1912-	2 3 G
Mather, Virginia, *pseud.* *see* Liebeler, Jean (Mayer)	
Matheson, Jean.	3
(*Full name:* Jean Chisholm Matheson)	
Mathews, Donna L 1922-	3
Mathews, Nieves (de Madariaga) 1917-	3
Matschat, Cecile (Hulse)	* 2
Matthews, Brander, 1852-1929.	* H EQ
Maugham, William Somerset, 1874-1965.	** G EQ QQ S Sy Sayers, 1928
Maurice, Michael, *pseud.* *see* Skinner, Conrad Arthur, 1889-	
Mavity, Nancy (Barr) 1890-	2
Maxon, P B	2
Maxwell, Brigid, 1916-	3
Maxwell, Mary Elizabeth (Braddon) 1837-1915. (Mary Elizabeth Braddon) x	* EQ Johannsen
Maxwell, William Babington, 1866-1938.	*
May, Henry Bak.	3
May, Wayne, *pseud.* *see* Humphries, Adelaide.	
Maylon, B J	2
Mayne, Ethel Colburn, 187-?-1941.	*
Mayo, James.	3
Mayor, Dorothy.	2
Meade, Dorothy Cole.	2
Meade, Lillie Thomas, *pseud.* *see* Smith, Elizabeth Thomasina (Meade) 1854-1914.	
Means, Mary.	2
see also Scott, Denis, *pseud. of* Mary Means and Theodore Saunders.	
Mearson, Lyon, 1888-1966.	1 2
Mechem, Kirke, 1889-	2
(*Full name:* Kirke Field Mechem)	
Mechem, Philip, 1892-	2
Meek, Doris.	3
see also Gregory, Mason, *pseud of* Doris Meek and Adrienne Jones.	
Mason, Gregory, *pseud. of* Doris Meek and Adrienne Jones.	

	Sources		
Megaw, Arthur Stanley, 1872-	*		
Meik, Vivian Bernard, 1895-	2		
Melville, Alan, *pseud.* *see* Caverhill, William Melville, 1910-			
Melville, Annabelle (McConnell) 1910-	3		
Mercer, Cecil William, 1885-1960. *pseud.:* Dornford Yates	*	2	G
Mercer, Ian.	2		
Meredith, Anne, *pseud.* *see* Malleson, Lucy Beatrice, 1899-			
Meredith, David William, *pseud.* *see* Miers, Earl Schenck, 1910-			
Meredith, Peter, *pseud.* *see* Worthington-Stuart, Brian Arthur.			
Meriton, Peter, *pseud.* *see* Hunter, John, 1891-			
Merlini, *pseud.* *see* Rawson, Clayton, 1906-			
Merrett, Charles Henry.	2		
Merrick, Mark, *pseud.* *see* Rathborne, St. George, 1854-1938.			
Merrick, Mollie.	2		
Merrill, P. J. *pseud.* *see* Roth, Holly, *d.* 1964.			
Merritt, Abraham, 1884-1943.	2		
Mersereau, John, 1898-	2		
Merwin, Samuel, 1910-	2	3	
Messenger, Elizabeth (Esson) 1908- (*Full name:* Elizabeth Margery (Esson) Messenger)	3		
Messer, Mona Naomi Anne (Hocking) (Anne Hocking) x	2	3	H
Metcalfe, Whitaker.	3		
Methley, Violet M	2		
Meyer, Charles	*		
Meyers, Alfred.	2		
Meynell, Laurence Walter, 1899- *pseuds.:* Valerie Baxter; Robert Eton; Geoffrey Ludlow; A. Stephen Tring	2	3	
Meyrick, Gordon.	2		
Michel, Milton Scott, 1916-	2		
Michelson, Miriam, 1870-1942.	*		
Miers, Earl Schenck, 1910- *pseud.:* David William Meredith	3		
Milbrook, John.	2		

Sources

"Miles," *pseud.* *see* Southwold, Stephen, 1887-1964.

Miles, Stella. — 3

Millar, Kenneth, 1915- — 2 3 Sy
pseuds.: John Macdonald
John Ross Macdonald
Ross Macdonald

Millar, Margaret (Sturm) 1915- — 2 3 G Sy

Millar, R — * 2

Miller, Agnes. — * 1

Miller, Alice (Duer) 1874-1942. — *

Miller, Bill, 1920- — 2
see also Masterson, Whit, *pseud. of* Bob Wade and Bill Miller.
Miller, Wade, *pseud. of* Bob Wade and Bill Miller.

Miller, John, 1906- — 2

Miller, Marc, *pseud.* *see* Baker, Marceil Genée (Kolstad) 1911-

Miller, Nathan. — 3

Miller, Wade, *pseud. of* Bob Wade and Bill Miller. — 2 St
see also Miller, Bill, 1920-
Wade, Bob, 1920-

Miller, Warne, *pseud.* *see* Rathborne, St. George, 1854-1938.

Millet, Francis Davis, 1846-1912. — * EQ

Millhauser, Bertram. — 2

Millington, Frances. — 2

Mills, Algernon Victor, 1905- — 2
pseud.: Rupert Latimer

Mills, Arthur Hobart, 1887- — * 2 3
(*Full name:* Arthur Frederick Hobart Mills)

Mills, Harry. — 1

Mills, Harry Roland Woosnam *see* Mills, Woosnam.

Mills, Osmington, *pseud.* *see* Brooks, Vivian Collin.

Mills, Woosnam. — *
(*Full name:* Harry Roland Woosnam Mills)

Millward, Edward J — 2

Milne, Alan Alexander, 1882-1956. — ** 1 2 C H S Sy W Chandler, R. Sayers, 1928 Wrong

Milner, George, *pseud.* *see* Hardinge, George.

	Sources
Milton, Gladys Alexandra. *pseud.:* Anthony Carlyle	1
Minot, George E	*
Mitcham, Gilroy, 1923-	3
Mitchell, Gladys, 1901- (*Full name:* Gladys Maude Winifred Mitchell) *pseud.:* Stephen Hockaby	* 2 3 H S St
Mitchell, Hutton.	2
Mitchell, Lebbeus, 1879- (*Full name:* Lebbeus Horatio Mitchell)	2
Mitchell, Silas Weir, 1829-1914.	*
Mitford, C Guise.	*
Modell, Merriam, 1908- *pseud.:* Evelyn Piper	* 3
Moffatt, James, 1870-1944.	Thomson
Moffett, Cleveland, 1863-1926.	* 1 2 H EQ
Mole, William, *pseud.* *see* Younger, William Antony, 1917-	
Molnar, Louis.	2
Monig, Christopher, *pseud.* *see* Crossen, Kendell Foster, 1910-	
Monkshood, G. F., *pseud.* *see* Clarke, William James, 1872-	
Monroe, Roy, *pseud.*, 1913-	3
Montgomery, Ione.	2
Montgomery, Mary.	3
Montgomery, Robert Bruce, 1921- *pseud.:* Edmund Crispin	* 2 3 G Sy
Moodey, Martha Livingston.	*
Moody, Alan B	1
Moore, Austin, *pseud.* *see* Muir, Augustus, 1892-	
Moore, Harry F S	2
Moore, Irving.	2 3
Moore, Winnie (Fields)	2
Moorhouse, Herbert Joseph, 1882- *pseud.* Hopkins Moorhouse	1 Sayers,1928
Moorhouse, Hopkins, *pseud.* *see* Moorhouse, Herbert Joseph, 1882-	
Mordaunt, Eleanor, *pseud.* *see* Mordaunt, Evelyn May, 1877?-1942.	
Mordaunt, Elinor, *pseud.* *see* Mordaunt, Evelyn May, 1877?-1942.	

	Sources
Mordaunt, Evelyn May, 1877?-1942 (Evelyn May (Clowes) Wiehe) x *pseuds.:* Eleanor Mordaunt Elinor Mordaunt A. Riposte	*
Morden, T R	2
Morgan, Claire, *pseud.* *see* Highsmith, Patricia, 1921-	
Morgan, Geoffrey.	2
Morgan, Lorna Nicholl.	* 2
Morgan, Michael, *pseud. of* C. E. Carle and Dean M. Dorn. *see also* Carle, C E Dorn, Dean M	2
Morgan, Murray Cromwell, 1916- *pseud.:* Cromwell Murray	2
Morgan, Thomas Christopher. *pseud.:* John Muir	3
Morland, Nigel, 1905- *pseuds.:* Mary Dane John Donavan Norman Forrest Roger Garnett Neal Shepherd	** 2 3 H
Morley, Christopher Darlington, 1890-1957.	* H
Moroso, John Antonio, 1874-1957.	* 1 EQ
Morrah, Dermot Macgregor, 1896- (*Full name:* Dermot Michael Macgregor Morrah)	2
Morris, Anthony Paschal, *b.* 1849. *pseud.:* Nat Newton?	1 Johannsen
Morris, Arthur.	* EQ
Morris, Charles, 1833-1922. (*Full name:* Charles Smith Morris) *pseuds.:* Hugh Allen J. D. Ballard Redmond Blake? (also used by Albert W. Aiken) Roland Dare S. M. Frazier Robert Randolph Inman? (also used by Thomas C. Harbaugh, Prentiss Ingraham, and William H. Manning) George S. Kaine Edward Lytton (also used by Edward Lytton Wheeler)	1 Johannsen

	Sources
William Murry Paul Pastnor Jo Pierce (also used by William H. Manning) Paul Preston J. H. Southard C. E. Tripp E. L. Vincent	
Morris, Thomas Baden, 1900-	3
Morris, Walter Frederick, 1892-	2
Morrison, Arthur, 1863-1945.	** 1 C H EQ QQ S W Sayers, 1928 Wrong
Morrison, Hugo.	2
Morrison, Woods.	1
Morrissey, James Lawrence.	2
Morrow, Susan.	3
Morse, Florence *see* Kingsley, Florence (Morse) 1859-1937.	
Morse, Florence Vorpe, 1887-	2
Morse, George Henry, *pseud.?*	Johannsen
Mortimer, Peter.	2
Morton, Anthony, *pseud.* *see* Creasey, John, 1908-	
Morton, Guy Eugene, 1884-	1 2
Morton, Guy Mainwaring, 1896- *pseuds.:* Mark Forrest Peter Traill	* 2
Morton, William, *pseud.* *see* Ferguson, William Blair Morton, 1882-	
Moseley, Dana.	3
Moser, Maurice.	* 2 C EQ
Moth, *pseud.* *see* Fleming, Peter, 1907-	
Mott, Edward Spencer, 1844-1910. *pseuds.:* Nathaniel Gubbins Edward Spencer	*
Motte, Peter, *pseud.* *see* Harrison, Richard, 1901-	
Moulton, *Hon.* Hugh Fletcher, 1876- (*Full name:* Hugh Lawrence Fletcher Moulton)	2
Mountford, Alexander Macdonald.	3
Mountjoy, Henry.	1
Mowbray, John, *pseud.* *see* Vahey, John George Haslette, 1881-	

	Sources
Moyes, Patricia.	3
Muddock, Joyce Emmerson Preston, 1843-1934. *pseud.:* Dick Donovan	** 1 2 C H EQ QQ
Muir, Augustus, 1892- (*Name originally:* Charles Augustus Muir) *pseud.:* Austin Moore	* 1 2 EQ
Muir, Denis.	2
Muir, Dexter, *pseud.* *see* Gribble, Leonard Reginald, 1908-	
Muir, John, *pseud.* *see* Morgan, Thomas Christopher.	
Muir, Thomas.	* 2 3
Mullen, Clarence, 1907-	2 3
Mumford, Ethel (Watts) *see* Grant, Ethel (Watts) Mumford, 1878-	
Mundy, Talbot, 1879-1940.	1 2
Munro, Hugh. (*Full name:* Hugh Macfarlane Munro)	3
Munro, Neil, 1864-1930. *pseud.:* Hugh Foulis	* EQ
Muriel, John Saint Clair, 1909- *pseuds.:* Simon Dewes, John Lindsay	2 Crimes, creeps
Murphy, Marguerite.	3
Murphy, Robert William, 1902-	2
Murray, *Inspector, pseud.*	1
Murray, Cromwell, *pseud.* *see* Morgan, Murray Cromwell, 1916-	
Murray, David Christie, 1847-1907.	C EQ
Murray, Edward.	2
Murray, Max, 1901-	* 2 3
Murray, Maysie (Greig) *see* Grieg, Maysie, 1902-	
Murray, Sinclair, *pseud.* *see* Sullivan, Alan, 1868-1947.	
Murry, William, *pseud.* *see* Morris, Charles, 1833-1922.	
Myers, Isabel Briggs.	2 Haycraft, Art
Myers, Phineas Barton, 1888-	3
Nakagawa, Karl S	2
Napier, N K S	2
Nash, Anne, 1890-	2 3
Nash, Chandler, *pseud.* *see* Hunt, Katherine Chandler.	

	Sources
Nash, Frank, 1912-	3
Nason, Leonard Hastings, 1895- *pseud.:* Steamer	2
Nast, Elsa Ruth, *pseud.* *see* Watson, Jane (Werner) 1915-	
Neal, Adeline Phyllis, 1894- *pseud.:* A. F. Grey	S
Neeley, Deta Petersen.	2
Neidig, William Jonathan.	BRD, 1919
Nelms, Henning. *pseud.:* Hake Talbot	2 S
Nelson, Cholmondeley M 1903-	3
Nelson, Lawrence, 1907- (*Full name:* Hugh Lawrence Nelson) *pseud.:* Peter Trent	* 2 3
Neville, Alison. *pseud.:* Edward Candy	3 St
Neville, C. J., *pseud.* *see* Franklin, Cynthia.	
Neville, Margot, *pseud.* *of* Margot Goyder and Neville (Goyder) Joske. *see also* Goyder, Margot, 1903- Joske, Neville (Goyder) 1893-	* 2 3
New, Clarence Herbert, 1862-	* EQ W BRD, 1918
Newberry, Perry, 1870-1938.	2 BRD, 1926
Newell, Audrey.	* 2
Newland, N M	3
Newman, Bernard, 1897- (*Full name:* Bernard Charles Newman) *pseud.:* Don Betteridge	* 2 3
Newton, Nat, *pseud.*? *see* Morris, Anthony Paschal, *b.* 1849.	
Newton, Wilfrid Douglas, 1884-	1
Nicholas, Jerome.	*
Nicholas, Robert.	3
Nichols, Beverley, 1899-	3
Nichols, Fan, *pseud.* *see* Hanna, Frances (Nichols)	
Nicolai, Charles.	3
Nicolet, Charles Cathcart, 1900-	2
Nicolson, John Urban, 1885- *pseud.:* King of the Black Isles	2
Nielsen, Helen, 1918- *pseud.:* Kris Giles	* 3 St
Nielsen, Virginia, 1909-	3

	Sources
Nile, Dorothea, *pseud.* *see* Avallone, Michael.	
Nisbet, Hume, 1849-1921?	*
Nisot, Mavis Elizabeth (Hocking) 1893- *pseud.:* William Penmare	2
Noel, L., *pseud.* *see* Barker, Leonard Noel, 1882-	
Noel, Sterling, 1903-	3
Nolan, Jeannette (Covert) 1896-	2
Nonweiler, Arville.	2
Noone, Edwina, *pseud.* *see* Avallone, Michael.	
Norman, Bruce.	1 2
Norman, James, *pseud.* *see* Schmidt, James Norman, 1912-	
Norris, William Edward, 1847-1925.	BRD, 1919 Johannsen
Norsworthy, George.	2
North, Andrew, *pseud.* *see* Norton, Alice Mary.	
North, Barclay, *pseud.* *see* Hudson, William Cadwalader, 1843-1915.	
North, Eric, *pseud.* *see* Cronin, Bernard, 1884-	
North, Gil, *pseud.* *see* Horne, Geoffrey 1916-	
North, William 1869- *pseuds.:* Ralph Rodd John Vanner	2
Norton Alice Mary. *pseuds.:* Andrew North Andre Norton *see also* Weston, Allen, *pseud. of* Grace (Allen) Hogarth and Alice Mary Norton.	3
Norton, Andre, *pseud.* *see* Norton, Alice Mary.	
Norwood, Hayden.	2
Norwood, John, *pseud.* *see* Stark, Raymond.	
Notley, John Franke, 1911-	2
Nuraini, *pseud.* *see* Sim, Katharine, 1913-	
Nyland, Gentry.	2
O., F. O., *pseud.* *see* Street, Cecil John Charles, 1884-	
O'Brien, Fitz James, 1828-1862.	Hawthorne, J. Wells
O'Brien, Howard Vincent, 1888-1947. *pseud.:* Clyde Perrin	2
O'Brine, Manning, 1915- (*Full name:* Padriac Manning O'Brine)	3

	Sources
O'Connor, John Marshall, 1909-	2
O'Connor, Patrick, *pseud.* *see* Wibberley, Leonard Patrick O'Connor, 1915-	
O'Connor, Ramoncita Sayer.	3
Odlum, Jerome, 1905-	2
O'Donnell, Elliot, 1872-	2
O'Donnell, Lillian (Udvardy)	3
O'Donnell, Simon.	1
O'Duffy, Eimar, 1893-1935. (*Full name:* Eimar Ultan O'Duffy)	2 Crimes, creeps
Oellrichs, Inez Hildagard, 1907-	* 2 3 H
O'Farrell, William, 1904-	2 3
Offord, Lenore (Glen) 1905-	2 3 S St
O'Finn, Thaddeus, *pseud.* *see* McGloin, Joseph T	
Ogburn, Dorothy, 1890-	2
Ogle, Richard.	2
Ognall, Leopold Horace, 1908- *pseuds.:* Harry Carmichael Harety Howard	3
O'Hanlon, James D	2
O'Hara, Kevin, *pseud.* *see* Cumberland, Marten, 1892-	
O'Higgins, Harvey Jerrold, 1876-1929.	** 1 2 H EQ QQ
Old Cap Collier, *pseud.* x Like Nick Carter, Old Cap Collier, the name of the detective-hero, became also the pseudonym used by various authors of the stories. W. I. James was author of the first of the series; others are Bernard Wayde and Thomas C. Harbaugh. *see also* Harbaugh, Thomas Chalmers, 1849-1924. James, W I Wayde, Bernard.	Bragin, Bibl Pearson
Old King Brady *see* Doughty, Francis Worcester, *d.* 1917.	
Old Sleuth, *pseud.* *see* Halsey, Harlan Page, 1837-1898.	
Olde, Nicholas.	EQ
Oldfeld, Peter, *pseud. of* Vernon Bartlett and P. Jacobsson. *see also* Bartlett, Vernon, 1894- Jacobsson, P	2

	Sources
Oldfield, Claude Houghton, 1889- *pseud.:* Claude Houghton	2
Olesker, Harry.	3
Oliver, Amy Roberta (Ruck) *see* Ruck, Berta, 1878-	
Oliver, Edwin.	*
Oliver, Gail, *pseud.* *see* Scott, Marian (Gallagher)	
Oliver, George *see* Onions, Oliver, pseud.	
Oliver, John.	2
Olmsted, Lorena Ann.	3
Olsen, D. B. *see* Hitchens, Dolores (Birk) Olsen, 1907-	
O'Malley, Frank, *pseud.* *see* O'Rourke, Frank, 1916-	
O'Neil, Kerry, *pseud.* *see* McIntyre, John Thomas, 1871-1951.	
O'Neil, Wolf, *pseud.* *see* Halsey, Harlan Page, 1837-1898.	
O'Neill, Desmond.	3
O'Neill, Egan, *pseud.* *see* Linington, Elizabeth, 1921-	
Onions, Oliver, *pseud.* (*Real name:* George Oliver) x	* 1
Oppenheim, Edward Phillips, 1866-1946. *pseud.:* Anthony Partridge	** 1 2 3 H EQ S W
Orbison, Keck, *pseud. of* Maud Keck and Olive Orbison. *see also* Keck, Maud. Orbison, Olive.	2
Orbison, Olive. *see also* Orbison, Keck, *pseud. of* Maud Keck and Olive Orbison.	2
Orcutt, William Dana, 1870-1952.	1
Orczy, Emmuska, *Baroness,* 1865-1947. (Mrs. Montagu Barstow)	** 1 2 C H EQ QQ Sy W Sayers, 1928
Orde-Powlett, *Hon.* Nigel, 1900- x (*Full name:* Hon. Nigel Amyas Orde-Powlett)	2
Ormond, Frederic, *pseud.* *see* Dey, Frederic van Rensselaer, 1861-1922.	
Ormsbee, David, *pseud.* *see* Longstreet, Stephen, 1907-	

	Sources
O'Rourke, Frank, 1916- *pseud.:* Frank O'Malley	3
Orpet, Fred.	3
Orr, Clifford, 1899-	2
Orr, Myron David.	2
Osbourne, Lloyd, 1868-1947.	2 C S
Osgood, Lucian Austin.	2
Ostrander, Isabel Egenton, 1883-1924. *pseuds.:* Robert Orr Chipperfield David Fox Douglas Grant	* 1 2 C H Sayers, 1928
O'Sullivan, James Brendan, 1919-	* 3
Ottolengui, Rodrigues, 1861?-1937.	** 1 EQ QQ
Oursler, Fulton, 1893-1952. (*Full name:* Charles Fulton Oursler) *pseud.:* Anthony Abbot	* 2 H EQ
Oursler, William Charles, 1913-	* 2 3
Owen, Harry Collinson, 1882- (Collinson Owen) *pseud.:* Hugh Addison	* 2
Oxenham, John, *d* 1941. (*Name originally:* William Arthur Dunkerley) x	Sayers, 1928
Ozaki, Milton K *pseud.:* Robert O. Saber	2
Packard, Frank Lucius, 1877-1942.	* 1 2 EQ
Paddon, Wreford, 1917- (*Full name:* William Wreford Paddon)	3
Padgett, Lewis, *pseud.* *see* Kuttner, Henry, 1914- 1958.	
Page, Evelyn, 1902- *see also* Scarlett, Roger, *pseud. of* Evelyn Page and Dorothy Blair.	2
Page, Marco, *pseud.* *see* Kurnitz, Harry.	
Page, Stanley Hart.	2
Pahlow, Gertrude Curtis (Brown) 1881-	2
Pain, Barry, 1864-1928. (*Full name:* Barry Eric Odell Pain)	* H EQ W Wrong
Palmer, Gretta.	2 EQ

Sources

Palmer, John Leslie, 1885-1944. 2
pseud.: Christopher Haddon
see also Beeding, Francis, *pseud. of* John Leslie Palmer and Hilary Aidan St. George Saunders.
Pilgrim, David, *pseud. of* John Leslie Palmer and Hilary Aidan St. George Saunders.

Palmer, Stuart, 1905- ** 2 3 H
pseud.: Jay Stewart QQ S

"Pam," *pseud.* *see* Beresford, Leslie.

Panbourne, Oliver, *pseud.* *see* Rockey, Howard, 1886-1934.

Paradise, Viola. 2

Pargeter, Edith, 1913- * 3

Parke, F. G., *pseud.* 2

Parker, Ellis 1871- * EQ
(*Full name:* Ellis Howard Parker)

Parker, Maude, *d.* 1959. 3
(Mrs. William Pavenstedt)

Parker, Richard. 1

Parker, Richard, 1915- 3

Parker, Robert B 1906- * 3

Parmer, Charles B 2

Parrish, Randall, 1858-1923. 1

Parry, Hugh Jones, 1916- 3
pseud.: James Cross

Parsons, Anthony. 3 Sayers, 1934

Parsons, Luke. 2

Partridge, Anthony, *pseud.* *see* Oppenheim, Edward Phillips, 1866-1946.

Pastnor, Paul, *pseud.* *see* Morris, Charles, 1833-1922.

Pastor, Tony, *pseud.* *see* Halsey, Harlan Page, 1837-1898.

Paternoster, George Sidney, 1866- * 1
(Sidney Paternoster)

Patrick, Keats, *pseud.* *see* Karig, Walter, 1898-1956.

Patrick, Q., *pseud.* 2 S
Originally used by Richard Wilson Webb in collaboration with Martha Mott Kelley; later by Webb alone, and subsequently by Webb with Hugh Callingham Wheeler.
see also Kelley, Martha Mott.
Webb, Richard Wilson.
Wheeler, Hugh Callingham, 1913-

	Sources
Patrick, Victor.	2
Patten, Gilbert, *pseud.* *see* Patten, William George, 1866-1945.	
Patten, William George, 1866-1945. *pseuds.:* Herbert Bellwood Harry Dangerfield Gilbert Patten Gordon MacLaren Julian St. Dare Burt L. Standish William West Wilder	Johannsen
Patterson, Innis. (*Full name:* Isabella Innis Patterson)	2
Patton, David Knox.	2
Paul, Elliot Harold, 1891-1958. *pseud.:* Brett Rutledge	2 3 H
Paul, John.	3
Paye, Robert, *pseud.* *see* Long, Gabrielle Margaret Vere (Campbell) 1886-1952.	
Payes, Rachel C	3
Payn, James, 1830-1898.	*
Payne, Evelyn.	3
Payne, Harold, *pseud.* *see* Kelly, George C 1849-1895.	
Payne, Hazel Belle (Saulisberry) 1892- *pseud.:* Greer Gay	3
Payne, Laurence, 1919-	3
Payne, Will, 1865-1954.	1
Pearson, D A G	2
Pearson, William, 1922-	3
Pease, Howard, 1894-	* 2
Pechey, Archibald Thomas, 1876-1961. *pseuds.:* Mark Cross Valentine	** 3 EQ Sayers, 1928
Peck, Winifred, *Lady.* (*Full name:* Lady Winifred Frances (Knox) Peck) (Winifred Frances Knox) x	2 3
Peckham, Richard, *pseud.* *see* Holden, Raymond Peckham, 1894-	
Peel, Frederick, 1888- *see also* Slingsby, Rufus, *pseud. of* Frederick Peel and Charles Siddle.	2
Pell, Franklyn, *pseud.* *see* Pelligrin, Frank E	

	Sources		
Pelligrin, Frank E *pseud.:* Franklyn Pell	2		
Pemberton, *Sir* Max, 1863-1950.	*	C	EQ
Pender, Lex, *pseud.* *see* Pendower, Jacques, 1899-			
Penders, Marilyn, *pseud.* *see* Pendower, Jacques, 1899-			
Pendower, Jacques, 1899- *pseuds.:* Tom Curtis Penn Dowers Thomas Curtis Hicks Jacobs Lex Pender Marilyn Penders Anne Penn	2	3	
Penfield, Cornelia *see* Lathrop, Cornelia (Penfield) 1892-1938.			
Penmare, William, *pseud.* *see* Nisot, Mavis Elizabeth (Hocking) 1893-			
Penn, Anne, *pseud.* *see* Pendower, Jacques, 1899-			
Penne, Agile, *pseud.* *see* Aiken, Albert W 1846?-1894.			
Penny, Fanny Emily (Farr)	2		
Penny, Rupert.	2		
Pentecost, Hugh, *pseud.* *see* Philips, Judson Pentecost, 1903-			
People, Granville Church. *pseud.:* Granville Church	2		
Percy, Catherine, *pseud.*	3		
Perdue, Virginia.	2	3	MWA
Perkerson, Medora (Field) (Medora Field) x	2	3	H
Perkins, Kenneth, 1890-	*	2	
Perowne, Barry.	*	2	
Perrin, Clyde, *pseud.* *see* O'Brien, Howard Vincent, 1888-1947.			
Perry, Frank.	2		
Perry, George Sessions, 1910-	3		
Perry, Harry Dennies, *pseud.* *see* Ingraham, Prentiss, 1843-1904.			
Perry, James DeWolf, 1895-	2		
Perry, Tyline.	2		
Perry, *Captain* William B.,, *pseud.* *see* Brown, William Perry, 1847-1923.			
Pertwee, Roland, 1885-1963.	*	2	EQ
Perutz, Leo, 1884-	*	1	2

	Sources
Peskett, S John, 1906-	2
Peters, Alan.	2
Peters, Bryan, *pseud.* *see* George, Peter, 1924-1966.	
Peters, Ellis, *pseud.*	3
Peters, William, 1921-	3
Petersen, Herman, 1893-	2
Peterson Margaret, 1883-1933. (Mrs. A. O. Fisher) *pseud.:* Glint Green	2
Pettee, Florence Mae, 1888-	1 2
Peverett, Allan.	3
Pfalzgraf, Florence Leighton, 1902- *pseud.:* Florence Leighton	2
Philips, Austin, 1875-	2
Philips, Judson Pentecost, 1903- *pseud.:* Hugh Pentecost	* 2 3 H
Phillips, Conrad.	* 3
Phillips, Gerald William, 1884- *pseud.:* John Huntingdon	2
Phillips, Henry Lawrence, 1868-	2
Phillips, James Atlee.	2 3
Phillips, John, *pseud.* *see* Marquand, John Phillips, 1893-1960.	
Phillips, Russell R	2
Phillpotts, Eden, 1862-1960. *pseud.:* Harrington Hext	** 1 2 3 C G H EQ QQ W
Philmore, R., *pseud.* *see* Howard, Herbert Edmund, 1900-	
Pickering, Edith.	2
Pidgin, Charles Felton, 1844-1923.	* 1 EQ
Pierce, Jo, *pseud.* *see* Manning, William Henry, 1852-1929. Morris, Charles, 1833-1922.	
Pierson, Eleanor.	2
Pilgrim, Chad.	3
Pilgrim, David, *pseud. of* John Leslie Palmer and Hilary Aidan St. George Saunders. *see also* Palmer, John Leslie, 1885-1944. Saunders, Hilary Aidan St. George, 1898-	2
Pim, Sheila.	* 3
Pinkerton, A Frank. (Frank Pinkerton) x	* 1

	Sources
Pinkerton, Allan, 1819-1884.	* 1 C EQ
Pinkerton, Frank *see* Pinkerton, A Frank.	
Piper, Evelyn, *pseud.* *see* Modell, Merriam, 1908-	
Piper, H Beam, 1904-	3
Piper, Peter, *pseud.* *see* Lang, Theo.	
Pirkis, Catharine Louisa.	* H EQ
Pitman, William Dent.	1
Plaidy, Jean, *pseud.* *see* Hibbert, Eleanor, 1906-	
Plain, Josephine.	2
Platt, Robert, 1894-	2
Player, Robert.	* 2
Pleasants, W Shepard.	* 2
Pleydell, George, 1868- (*Name originally:* George Pleydell Bancroft) x	* 1 W Sayers, 1928 Thomson
Pliny the Youngest, *pseud.* *see* Wilson, Stanley Kidder, 1879-	
Plum, Mary.	* 2 3
Plummer, Thomas Arthur. *pseud.:* Michael Sarne	** 2 3
Plummy, *pseud.* *see* Dellbridge, John, 1887-	
Plunkett, Edward John Moreton Drax *see* Dunsany, Edward John Moreton Drax Plunkett, *Lord,* 1878-1957.	
Poate, Ernest M	* 1 2 H EQ W
Poe, Edgar Allan, 1809-1849.	** 1 2 C G H EQ QQ S Sy W Sayers, 1928 Wrong
Poe, Edgar Allan, 1871- "A collateral descendant . . . but the mantle of great Edgar Allen Poe has not fallen upon the shoulders of the present bearer of the name."	2 (HH)
Pollard, Alfred Oliver, 1893-	* 2 3
Pollard, Percival, 1869-1911.	** EQ QQ
Pollock, Channing, 1880-1946.	2
Polonsky, Abraham. *see also* Hogarth, Emmett, *pseud. of* Mitchell A. Wilson and Abraham Polonsky.	2
Polsky, Thomas.	2 3
Ponder, Zita Inez.	2

	Sources
Poole, Michael, *pseud.* *see* Poole, Reginald Heber, 1885-	
Poole, Reginald Heber, 1885- *pseud.:* Michael Poole	* 2
Poorten Schwartz, Jozua Marius Willem van der *see* Schwartz, Jozua Marius Willem van der Poorten, 1858-1915.	
Popkin, Zelda, 1898-	2 3
Porcelain, Sidney E	2
Porlock, Martin, *pseud.* *see* MacDonald, Philip.	
Porter, Harold Everett, 1887-1936. *pseud.:* Holworthy Hall	BRD, 1917
Porter, Rebecca Newman, 1883-	1
Porter, William Sydney, 1862-1910. *pseud.:* O. Henry	** EQ QQ
Posner, Jacob D 1883- *pseud.:* Gregory Dean	2
Post, A. H., *pseud.* *see* Badger, Joseph E 1848-1909.	
Post, Melville Davisson, 1871-1930.	** 1 2 C H EQ QQ S W Sayers, 1928 Thomas
Post, Mortimer.	2
Post, Roy.	2 EQ
Postgate, John W	1
Postgate, Raymond William, 1896-	** 2 H S Sy Chandler, R.
Potter, George William, 1930- *pseud.:* E. L. Withers	3
Potts, Jean, 1910-	* 3 St
Pou, Genevieve (Long) 1919- *pseud.:* Genevieve Holden	3
Powell, Frank, *pseud.* *see* Ingraham, Prentiss, 1843-1904.	
Powell, Lester.	3
Powell, Percival Henry.	3
Powell, Richard Pitts, 1908?-	2 3
Powell, Richard Stillman, *pseud.* *see* Barbour, Ralph Henry, 1870-1944.	
Powell, Rosamond Bayne- *see* Bayne-Powell, Rosamond, 1879-	
Powell, Talmage, 1920- *pseud.:* Jack McCready	3

	Sources
Power, Cecil, *pseud.* *see* Allen, Grant, 1848-1899	
Powlett, Nigel Orde- *see* Orde-Powlett, *Hon.* Nigel, 1900-	
Powley, Jean (Makins) *pseud.:* Ann Cardwell	2
Poynter, Beulah.	1 2
Poyntz, Launce, *pseud.* *see* Whittaker, Frederick, 1838-1889.	
Prather, Richard Scott, 1921- *pseuds.:* David Knight Douglas Ring	3
Pratt, Eleanor Blake (Atkinson) 1899- (Eleanor Blake Atkinson) x *pseuds.:* E. A. Blake Eleanor Blake	2
Pratt, Theodore, 1901- *pseud.:* Timothy Brace	2
Preedy, George, *pseud.* *see* Long, Gabrielle Margaret Vere (Campbell) 1886-1952.	
Prentis, John Harcourt, 1878-	1
Prescott, Hilda Frances Margaret, 1896-	2
Prescott, S C	EQ
Presnell, Frank G 1906-	2 3
Preston, Arthur, *pseud.* *see* Hankins, Arthur Preston, 1880-	
Preston, Paul, *pseud.* *See* Morris, Charles, 1833-1922	
Price, Evadne, *pseud.* *see* Smith, Helen Zenna.	
Price, Frank J *Jr.*	* 2 EQ
Price, Wesley.	2
Prichard, Hesketh Vernon Hesketh-, 1876-1922. *pseud.:* H. Heron x	** 1 H EQ QQ
Prichard, Kate O'Brien Hesketh- *pseud.:* E. Heron x	** 1 EQ
Pridham, Sylvia Sandys.	3
Priestley, Clive Ryland, 1892- *pseud.:* Clive Ryland	2 3
Priestley, John Boynton, 1894- *pseud.:* Peter Goldsmith	2
Priestley, Lee, 1904- (*Full name:* Lee Shore Priestley)	3
Pritchard, John Laurence, 1885- *pseud.:* John Laurence	* 2
Procter, Arthur Wyman, 1889-1961.	2

	Sources
Procter, Maurice, 1906-	3 G St
Propper, Milton Morris, 1906-	* 2 3 H
Prosper, John.	1
Proudfoot, Walter, *pseud.* *see* Vahey, John George Haslette, 1881-	
Prout, Geoffrey, 1894-	2
Pruitt, Alan, *pseud.* *see* Rose, Alvin Emanuel.	
Pryde, Anthony, *pseud.* *see* Weekes, Agnes Russell.	
Pullein-Thompson, Josephine. x	3
Pulsford, Norman George, 1902- *pseud.:* A. C. Trevor	2
Punnett, Ivar. *see also* Simons, Roger, *pseud. of* Ivar Punnett and Margaret Punnett.	3
Punnett, Margaret. *see also* Simons, Roger, *pseud. of* Ivar Punnett and Margaret Punnett.	3
Punshon, Ernest Robertson, 1872-	* 1 2 3 H St
Purcell, Mary, 1906-	*
Purdy, Claire Lee.	2
Purtell, Joseph.	2
Putnam, Xeno.	1
Puy, Edward Spence De *see* De Puy, Edward Spence, 1872-	
Q, *pseud.* *see* Quiller-Couch, *Sir* Arthur Thomas, 1863-1944.	
Queen, Ellery, *pseud. of* Frederic Dannay and Manfred Bennington Lee. *see also* Dannay, Frederic, 1905- ; Lee, Manfred Bennington, 1905-	** 2 3 C G H EQ QQ S Sy
Queen, Ellery, Jr., *pseud. of* Frederic Dannay and Manfred Bennington Lee. *see also* Dannay, Frederic, 1905- ; Lee, Manfred Bennington, 1905-	2 3
Quentin, Patrick, *pseud. of* Richard Wilson Webb and Hugh Callingham Wheeler. *see also* Webb, Richard Wilson. ; Wheeler, Hugh Callingham, 1913-	** S
Quick, Dorothy, 1900-	2
Quiller-Couch, *Sir* Arthur Thomas, 1863-1944. *pseud.:* Q	* 2
Quin, Basil Godfrey.	* 2

	Sources
Quin, Dan, *pseud.* *see* Lewis, Alfred Henry, 1857-1914.	
Quin, Mike, *pseud.* *see* Ryan, Paul William, 1906-1947.	
Quinn, Eleanor Baker.	2
Quirk, Leslie W 1882-	2
Rabe, Peter.	3
Radcliffe, Garnett, 1899-	2
(*Full name:* Henry Garnett Radcliffe)	Sayers, 1934
pseud.: Stephen Travers	
Radford, Edwin, 1891-	2 3
(*Full name:* Edwin Isaac Radford)	
Radford, Mona Augusta (Mangan)	3
Radford, Ruby Lorraine, 1891-	2
pseuds.: Matilda Bailey	
Marcia Ford	
Ragg, Thomas Murray, 1897-	2
pseud.: Murray Thomas	
Raimond, C. E., *pseud.* *see* Robins, Elizabeth, 1862-1952.	
Raine, William MacLeod, 1871-1954.	1 2
Raison, Milton Michael, 1903-	2 3
Ramage, Jennifer.	* 3
pseud.: Howard Mason	
Rame, David, *pseud.* *see* Divine, Arthur Durham, 1904-	
Ramsey, Guy, 1900-	3
Rand, John, *pseud.* *see* Reach, James.	
Randall, William, *pseud.* *see* Gwinn, William R.	
Randall, William R	2
Randau, Carl, 1893-	2
Randolph, Marion, *pseud.* *see* Rodell, Marie (Freid) 1912-	
Randolph, Vance, 1892-	2
Ranger, Ken, *pseud.* *see* Creasey, John, 1908-	
Ransome, Stephen,, *pseud.* *see* Davis, Frederick Clyde, 1902-	
Raphael, Chaim, 1908-	3
pseud.: Jocelyn Davey	
Raq, *pseud.* *see* Evens, Glyn Kinnaird.	
Rask, Marie Coolidge- *see* Coolidge-Rask, Marie.	

	Sources
Rath, E. J., *pseud. of* Chauncey Corey Brainerd and Edith Rathbone (Jacobs) Brainerd.	1
see also Brainerd, Chauncey Corey.	
Brainerd, Edith Rathbone (Jacobs)	
Rath, Virginia, 1905-	2
(*Full name:* Virginia Anne Rath)	
Rathbone, Cornelia Kane.	1
Rathbone, Richard Adams.	3
Rathborne, St. George, 1854-1938.	* 1
pseuds.: Harrison Adams	Johannsen
Andy Burton	
Herbert Carter	
Oliver Lee Clifton	
Dash Dale	
Duke Duncan	
Ward Edwards	
Aleck Forbes	
Jack Howard	
John Prentice Langley	
W. B. Lawson (also used by George C. Jenks)	
Lawrence Leslie	
Marline Manly	
Mark Merrick	
Warne Miller	
Alex Robertson	
Harry St. George	
Jack Sharpe	
Gordon Stewart	
Rattray, Simon, *pseud.* *see* Trevor, Elleston, 1920-	
Raven, Simon, 1927-	3
Rawlings, Frank.	2
Rawlins, Eustace, 1854-	* H EQ QQ
pseuds.: Eustace Barton	Sayers, 1928
Robert Eustace	
Rawson, Clayton, 1906-	2 H S
pseuds.: Merlini	
Stuart Towne	
Raymond, Clifford Samuel, 1875-	1 2
Raymond, Ernest, 1888-	** Sy
Raymond, René, 1906-	* 2 3
pseuds.: James Hadley Chase	Thomas
James Docherty	
Ambrose Grant	
Raymond Marshall	
Rayner, Augustus Alfred, 1894-	2
pseud.: Whyte Hall	

	Sources
Rayner, Olive Pratt, *pseud.* *see* Allen, Grant, 1848-1899.	
Rayter, Joe, *pseud.* *see* McChesney, Mary F	
Rea, Margaret Lucile Paine.	2
Reach, James. *pseuds.:* Bruce Abbott Ward Bremer Hilda Manning John Rand George Ressieb Thomas Sutton Tom West Pete Williams Richard Williams	* 3
Redfield, Martin, *pseud.* *see* Brown, Alice, 1857-1948.	
Redmond-Howard, Louis G 1884- x	2
Reed, Blair. *pseud.:* Adam Ring	2
Reed, Edward Charles.	* 2
Reed, *Sir* Edward James, 1830-1906.	C
Reed, Eliot, *pseud. of* Eric Ambler and Charles Rodda. *see also* Ambler, Eric, 1909- Rodda, Charles, 1891-	* 3
Reed, Howard, 1885-	2
Reed, Wallace.	2
Rees, Arthur John, 1872-	* 1 2 H Sayers, 1928
Rees, Dilwyn, *pseud.* *see* Daniel, Glyn Edmund, 1914-	
Rees, Olwen.	*
Reeve, Arthur Benjamin, 1880-1936.	** 1 2 C H EQ QQ W Sayers, 1928 Thomson
Reeve, Christopher.	2 3
Reeves, Helen Buckingham (Mathers) 1853-1920. *pseud.:* David Lyall	1
Reeves, Robert, *pseud.?*	2 3
Regis, Julius.	* 1
Reid, Eleanor, *pseud.* *see* Smith, Constance Isabel, 1894-	
Reid, Wallace Q., *pseud.* *see* Goodchild, George, 1888-	

	Sources
Reilly, Helen (Kieran) 1890?-1962. *pseud.:* Kieran Abbey	2 3 H EQ's annual, 1946
Reilly, William K., *pseud.* *see* Creasey, John, 1908-	
Reisner, Mary.	2
Remenham, John, *pseud.* *see* Vlasto, John Alexander, 1877-1958.	
Rendall, Vernon Horace, 1869-	* 1 C EQ
Renwick, Peter.	*
Ressich, John, 1877- (*Full name:* John Sellar Matheson Ressich) *see also* Baxter, Gregory, *pseud. of* John Ressich and Eric De Banzie.	2
Ressieb, George, *pseud.* *see* Reach, James.	
Revell, Louisa.	2 3
Revere, M. P., *pseud.* *see* Williamson, Alice Muriel (Livingston) 1869-1933.	
Reynolds, Adrian, *pseud.* *see* Long, Amelia Reynolds, 1904-	
Reynolds, *Mrs.* Baillie see Reynolds, Gertrude M (Robins)	
Reynolds, Barbara Leonard.	3
Reynolds, Gertrude M (Robins) (Mrs. Baillie Reynolds) x	1 2
Reynolds, Liggett, *pseud.* *see* Simon, Robert Alfred, 1897-	
Reynolds, Peter, *pseud.* *see* Long, Amelia Reynolds, 1904-	
Reywall, John, *pseud.*	2
Rhoades, Knight.	2
Rhode, Austen, *pseud.* *see* Francis, Basil, 1906-	
Rhode, John, *pseud.* *see* Street, Cecil John Charles, 1884-	
Rice, Craig, 1908-1957. (Mrs. Lawrence Lipton) *pseuds.:* Daphne Sanders Michael Venning	* 2 3 H S St
Rice, Laverne.	2
Rice, Louise (Guest) 1880-	2
Rich, Willard, *pseud.*	2
Richards, Allen, *pseud.* *see* Rosenthal, Richard, 1925-	
Richards, Clay, *pseud.* *see* Crossen, Kendell Foster, 1910-	

Sources

Richards, Francis, *pseud. of* Frances and Richard Lockridge. — 2 3
see also Lockridge, Frances Louise (Davis)
Lockridge, Richard, 1898-

Richardson, Anthony, 1899- — St
(*Full name:* Anthony Thomas Stewart Currie Richardson)

Richardson, Norval, 1877-1940. — 2

Richart, Mary. — 2

Richmond, Grace, *pseud.* *see* Marsh, John, 1907-

Richmond, Mary, *pseud.* *see* Lindsay, Kathleen, 1903-

Rickard, Jessie Louisa, 1879- — 1 2

[illegible] — Sayers, 1928

Rickett, Arthur Compton- *see* Compton-Rickett, Arthur, 1869-1937.

Riddell, Charlotte Eliza Lawson (Cowan) 1832-1906. — C
pseud.: F. G. Trafford

Riddell, John, *pseud.* *see* Ford, Corey, 1902-

Rideal, Charles Frederick, 1858- — 2 EQ

Rideaux, Charles de Balzac, 1900- — * 1 2
pseud.: John Chancellor

Rideout, Henry Milner, 1877-1927. — 1

Rider, Sarah. — 2

Ridley, Nat, *Jr.* — 1

Rigsby, Howard, 1909- — 3
pseuds.: Mark Howard
Vechel Howard

Riley, Tex, *pseud.* *see* Creasey, John, 1908-

Rimel, Duane W — 2

Rinehart, Mary (Roberts) 1876-1958. — * 1 2 3 C H EQ S

Ring, Adam, *pseud.* *see* Reed, Blair.

Ring, Douglas, *pseud.* *see* Prather, Richard Scott, 1921-

Ripley, Clements, 1892-1954. — 2

Ripley, Harold Austin, 1896- — 2 EQ

Riposte, A., *pseud.* *see* Mordaunt, Evelyn May, 1877?-1942.

Rising, Lawrence. — BRD, 1920

Rita, *pseud.* *see* Humphreys, Eliza Margaret J (Gollan)

Rivers, Ronald. — 1

	Sources
Rivett, Edith Caroline, 1894-1958. *pseuds.:* Carol Carnac E. C. R. Lorac	** 2 3 H S
Robbins, Clarence Aaron, 1888-1949. *pseud.:* Tod Robbins	* 2
Robbins, Clifton, 1890-	* 2
Robbins, Tod, *pseud.* *see* Robbins, Clarence Aaron, 1888-1949.	
Roberts, Carl Eric Bechhofer, 1894-1949. (Bechhofer Roberts) *pseud.:* Ephesian	* 2
Roberts, George Edward Theodore *see* Goodridge Roberts Theodore, 1877-	
Roberts, Katharine.	Rodell MWA
Roberts, Theodore Goodridge *see* Goodridge Roberts Theodore, 1877-	
Roberts, Walter Adolphe, 1886-1962.	1 2
Roberts, Willo Davis.	3
Robertson, Alex, *pseud.* *see* Rathborne, St. George, 1854-1938.	
Robertson, Colin, 1906-	* 2 3
Robertson, Constance (Noyes) 1897- *pseud.:* Dana Scott	2
Robertson, Helen, *pseud.* *see* Edmiston, Helen Jean Mary, 1913-	
Robertson, Keith, 1914- (*Full name:* Keith Carlton Robertson) *pseud.:* Carlton Keith	3
Robertson, Wilfrid, 1892-	3
Robins, Elizabeth, 1862-1952. (Mrs. George Richmond Parks) *pseud.:* C. E. Raimond	1
Robins, Raymond, 1900-	2
Robinson, Bertram Fletcher.	** EQ QQ
Robinson, Eliot Harlowe, 1884-	1 2
Robinson, Ethelbert McKennon.	3
Robinson, Frederick William, 1830-1901.	* Johannsen
Robinson, Lewis George, 1886- *pseuds.:* George Braha George Limnelius	2
Robinson, Richard Blundell, 1905- *pseud.:* George Leaderman	2
Robinson, Robert Henry, 1927-	3
Robison, Gerda.	3

	Sources
Roche, Arthur Somers, 1883-1935. *pseud.:* Eric MacHaye	1 2 H
Roche, Kay.	3
Rochester, George E	* 2
Rockey, Howard, 1886-1934. *pseud.:* Ronald Bryce Oliver Panbourne	BRD, 1926
Rockwood, Harry, *pseud.* *see* Young, Ernest A	
Rodd, Ralph, *pseud.* *see* North, William, 1869-	
Rodda, Charles, 1891- *pseuds.:* Gavin Holt Gardner Low *see also* Reed, Eliot, *pseud. of* Eric Ambler and Charles Rodda.	* 2 3
Rodell, Marie (Freid)1912- *pseud.:* Marion Randolph	2
Rodell, Vic.	3
Roden, Henry Wisdom, 1895-	2 3
Roeburt, John.	2 3
Rogers, Joel Townsley.	2 MWA
Rogers, Ruth, 1890- *pseud.:* Ruth Alexander	*
Rogers, Samuel, 1894- (*Full name:* Samuel Greene Arnold Rogers)	2 MWA
Rohde, Robert H	2
Rohlfs, Anna Katharine (Green) 1846-1935. (Anna Katharine Green) x	** 1 2 C H EQ QQ S W Sayers, 1928 Wrong
Rohmer, Elizabeth Sax.	3
Rohmer, Sax, *pseud.* *see* Ward, Arthur Sarsfield, 1883-1959.	
Roland, Mary, *pseud.* *see* Lewis, Mary Christianna (Milne) 1907-	
Rolfe, Edwin, 1909-	2
Rollins, Kathleen. *see also* Debrett, Hal, *pseud. of* Davis Dresser and Kathleen Rollins.	3
Rollins, William, 1897- *pseud.:* O'Connor Stacy	2
Rolls, Anthony, *pseud.* *see* Vulliamy, Colwyn Edward, 1886-	
Rome, Anthony, *pseud.* *see* Albert, Marvin H.	
Romsey, Peter.	3
Ronald, E. B., *pseud.* *see* Barker, Ronald Ernest, 1920-	

	Sources
Ronald, James, 1905-	2 3
Ronns, Edward, *pseud.* *see* Aarons, Edward Sidney, 1916-	
Roof, Katharine Metcalf.	2
Rook, Clarence.	*
Roos, Audrey (Kelley) 1912- (Audrey Kelley) x	3
see also Roos, Kelley, *pseud. of* Audrey (Kelley) Roos and William Roos.	
Roos, Kelley, *pseud. of* Audrey (Kelley) Roos and William Roos.	* 2 3
see also Roos, Audrey (Kelley) 1912-	
Roos, William, 1911-	
Roos, William, 1911-	3
see also Roos, Kelley, *pseud. of* Audrey (Kelley) Roos and William Roos.	
Root, Pat.	* 3
Roscoe, John, 1921-	3
see also Roscoe, Mike, *pseud. of* Michael Ruso and John Roscoe.	
Roscoe, Mike, *pseud. of* Michael Ruso and John Roscoe.	3
see also Roscoe, John, 1921-	
Ruso, Michael.	
Roscoe, Theodore.	2 3
Rose, Alvin Emanuel.	2
pseud.: Alan Pruitt	
Rosenbach, Abraham Simon Wolf, 1876-1952.	* EQ
Rosenberg, Elizabeth (King)	3
Rosenberg, John, 1931-	3
Rosenhayn, Paul, 1877-1929.	* 2 EQ
Rosenthal, Richard, 1925-	3
pseud.: Allen Richards	
Roser, Val.	3
Rosmanith, Olga.	2
Ross, Barnaby, *pseud. of* Frederic Dannay and Manfred Bennington Lee.	2
see also Dannay, Frederic, 1905-	
Lee, Manfred Bennington, 1905-	
Ross, Carlton.	*
Ross, Frances Moyer *see* Stevens, Frances Moyer (Ross) 1895-	
Ross, Ivan T., *pseud.*	3

	Sources
Ross, John.	*
Ross, Julian Maclaren- *see* Maclaren-Ross, Julian.	
Ross, Mander.	2
Ross, Zola Helen, 1912- *pseuds.:* Helen Arre Bert Iles	2
Ross Williamson, Hugh, 1901-	3
Roth, Holly, *d.* 1964. *pseuds.:* K. G. Ballard P. J. Merrill	3 St
Rowe, Anne (von Meibom)	2
Rowland, Henry Cottrell, 1874-1933.	1
Rowland, John, 1907-	* 2 3 Crimes, creeps
Roy, Ralph, *pseud.* *see* Badger, Joseph E 1848-1909.	
Royce, Kenneth, 1920-	3
Ruck, Berta, 1878- (*Full name:* Amy Roberta (Ruck) Oliver) x	1
Rud, Anthony Melville, 1893-	2
Ruegg, Alfred Henry, 1854-	2
Runyon, Damon, 1880-1946.	** QQ
Rushton, Charles, *pseud.* *see* Shortt, Charles Rushton, 1904-	
Ruso, Michael. *see also* Roscoe, Mike, *pseud. of* Michael Ruso and John Roscoe.	3
Russell, Charles Edmund, 1878-	*
Russell, Charlotte Murray.	* 2 3 H
Russell, Donn.	3
Russell, Fox.	* EQ
Russell, John, 1885-1956. *pseud.:* Luke Thrice	** EQ QQ
Russell, William. *pseuds.:* Inspector F. x "Waters" Thomas Waters?	** C EQ QQ
Russell, William Clark, 1844-1911.	* C
Rutherford, Douglas, *pseud.* *see* McConnell, James Douglas Rutherford, 1915-	
Rutland, Harriet.	3 H
Rutledge, Brett, *pseud.* *See* Paul, Elliot Harold, 1891-1958.	

Sources

Rutledge, Nancy. — 2 3
pseud.: Leigh Bryson

Rutter, Amanda. — 3

Ryan, Jessica. — 2

Ryan, Paul William, 1906-1947. — 2 3 St
pseuds.: Robert Finnegan
Mike Quin

Rydell, Forbes, *pseud. of* DeLoris (Stanton) Forbes and Helen B. Rydell. — 3
see also Forbes DeLoris (Stanton) 1923-
Rydell, Helen B

Rydell, Helen B — 3
see also Rydell, Forbes, *pseud. of* DeLoris (Stanton) Forbes and Helen B. Rydell.

Ryerson, Florence. — * 2
(*Full name:* Florence (Willard) Ryerson Clements)
x

Ryerson, Lowell, *pseud.* *see* Van Atta, Winfred, 1910-

Ryland, Clive, *pseud.* *see* Priestley, Clive Ryland, 1892-

Ryland, John Knox. — 2

Sabatini, Rafael, 1875-1950. — * QQ

Saber, Robert O., *pseud.* *see* Ozaki, Milton K

Sabre, Dirk. — 3

Sage, Dana. — 2 3

Saint Aubyn, Frank. — *

St. Clair, Ian. — 2

St. Dare, Julian, *pseud.* *see* Patten, William George, 1866-1945.

St. Dennis, Madelon. — 2

St. George, Harry, *pseud.* *see* Rathborne, St. George, 1854-1938.

St. James, Andrew, *pseud.* *see* Stern, James, 1904-

St. John, *Miss* Darby. — 2

St. Meyer, Ned, *pseud.?* — Johannsen

St. Vrain, *Major* E. L. *pseud.* *see* Manning, William Henry, 1852-1929.

Saix, Tyler De *see* De Saix, Tyler.

Sale, Richard, 1911- — 2 S Chandler, R. MWA
(*Full name:* Richard Bernard Sale)

Sources

Salmon, Geraldine Gordon, 1897- 2
pseud.: J. G. Sarasin

Salt, Sarah, *pseud.* *see* Hobson, Coralie (von Werner) 1891-

Salter, Elizabeth, 1918- 3
(*Full Name:* Elizabeth Fulton Salter)

Salter, Marion Armour. 3

Saltmarsh, Max. 2

Saltus, Edgar Evertson, 1855-1921. * EQ

Sampson, Richard Henry, 1896- 2 3 H S
pseud.: Richard Hull

Sampson, Victor, 1855- 2

Sanborn, B. X., *pseud.* *see* Ballinger, William Sanborn, 1912-

Sanborn, Ruth Burr, 1894- 2

Sandberg, H W 2

Sanders, Bruce. * 3

Sanders, Daphne, *pseud.* *see* Rice, Craig, 1908-1957.

Sanders, George, 1906- 2

Sanders, Marion K 2

Sanderson, Averil Dorothy *see* Furniss, Averil Dorothy Sanderson.

Sanderson, Douglas, 1922- 3
(*Full name:* Ronald Douglas Sanderson)
pseuds.: Martin Brett
Malcolm Douglas

Sanderson, Ronald Douglas *see* Sanderson, Douglas, 1922-

Sands, Christopher Nicholson Johnston, *Lord,* 1857-1934. *
(Christopher Nicholson Johnston)
x

Sandys, James. *

Sanger, Joan. 2

Sapper, *pseud.* *see* McNeile, Herman Cyril, 1888-1937.

Sara, *Col.* Delle, *pseud.* *see* Aiken, Albert W 1846?-1894.

Sarasin, J. G., *pseud.* *see* Salmon, Geraldine Gordon, 1897-

Sargeant, Adeline. 1
(*Full name:* Emily Frances Adeline Sargeant)

Sarmiento, Dorothy. 3

	Sources
Sarne, Michael, *pseud.* *see* Plummer, Thomas Arthur.	
Sarsfield, Maureen.	2
Satchell, William.	*
Saunders, Carl McK., *pseud.* *see* Ketchum, Philip, 1902-	
Saunders, Clare Castler.	2
Saunders, Hilary Aidan St. George, 1898- *see also* Beeding, Francis, *pseud. of* John Leslie Palmer and Hilary Aidan St. George Saunders. Pilgrim, David, *pseud. of* John Leslie Palmer and Hilary Aidan St. George Saunders.	*
Saunders, Lawrence, *pseud. of* Burton Davis and Clare (Ogden) Davis. *see also* Davis, Burton 1893- Davis, Clare (Ogden) 1892-	2
Saunders, Montagu.	*
Saunders, Theodore. *see also* Scott, Denis, *pseud. of* Mary Means and Theodore Saunders.	2
Sava, George, *pseud.* *see* Bankoff, George Alexis, 1903-	
Savage, Richard, 1913-	* 2 3
Savage, Richard Henry, 1846-1903.	* 1
Savallo Teresa de, *Marquesa d' Alpens, pseud.* *see* Williamson, Alice Muriel (Livingston) 1869-1933.	
Sawyer, Eugene T 1846-1924. *see also* Carter, Nicholas, *pseud.*	Bragin (2) Pearson
Saxby, Charles.	2
Saxon, John A 1886 or 7-1947.	2 3
Sayers, Dorothy Leigh, 1893-1957. (Mrs. Atherton Fleming) *pseud.:* Johanna Leigh	** 1 2 3 C G H EQ QQ S Sy W Chandler, R. Thomas
Sayre, Gordon, *pseud.* *see* Woolfolk, Josiah Pitts, 1894-	
Scarlett, Roger, *pseud. of* Evelyn Page and Dorothy Blair. *see also* Blair, Dorothy. Page, Evelyn, 1902-	2
Schabelitz, Rudolf Frederick, 1884-	2 3
Scherf, Margaret, 1908-	* 2 3

	Sources
Schisgall Oscar, 1901- *pseuds.:* Jackson Cole Stuart Hardy	* 2 EQ
Schley, Sturges Mason.	2 3
Schmalz, Flora.	*
Schmidt, James Norman, 1912- *pseud.:* James Norman	* 2
Scholey, Eric.	3
Scholey, Jean.	3
Schriber, Ione Sandberg.	*
Schurr, Cathleen.	3
Schwartz, Jozua Marius Willem van der Poorten, 1858-1915. x *pseud.:* Maarten Maartens	C Wells
Scobie, Alastair, 1918- (*Full name:* Alastair Gordon Scobie)	3
Scotland, Jay.	3
Scott, Anthony, *pseud.* *see* Dresser, Davis, 1904-	
Scott, Archer G., *pseud.* *see* Larbalestier, Philip George.	
Scott, Catharine Amy (Dawson) (Catherine Amy Dawson-Scott) x	*
Scott, Dana, *pseud.* *see* Robertson, Constance (Noyes) 1897-	
Scott, Denis, *pseud. of* Mary Means and Theodore Saunders. *see also* Means, Mary. Saunders, Theodore.	2
Scott, Evelyn, 1893- (Mrs. John Metcalfe) *pseud.:* Ernest Souza	2
Scott, Jack Denton, 1915-	2
Scott, Jane, *pseud.* *see* McElfresh, Adeline.	
Scott, Jody, 1923- *see also* Scott, Thurston, *pseud. of* George Thurston Leite and Jody Scott.	3
Scott, John Reed, 1869-	1 BRD, 1917
Scott, Leroy, 1875-1929.	* 1 2 EQ
Scott, Mansfield.	* 1 2
Scott, Marian (Gallagher) *pseuds.:* Gail Oliver Katherine Wolffe	2
Scott, Marion.	2
Scott, Mary Semple.	2

	Sources
Scott, Reginald Thomas Maitland, 1882-	* 1 2 EQ
Scott, *Major* S. S., *pseud.* *see* Harbaugh, Thomas Chalmers, 1849-1924.	
Scott, Sutherland.	* 2 3
Scott, Thurston, *pseud. of* George Thurston Leite and Jody Scott. *see also* Leite, George Thurston, 1920- Scott, Jody, 1923-	3
Scott, Warwick, *pseud.* *see* Trevor, Elleston, 1920-	
Scott, Will.	1 2
Scudder, Antoinette Quinby, 1898-	2
Seabrooke, John Paul.	1
"Seaforth," *pseud.* *see* Foster, George Cecil, 1893-	
Seamark, *pseud.* *see* Small, Austin J *d.* 1929.	
Search-light, *pseud.* *see* Frank, Waldo David, 1889-	
Seaton, Stuart.	3
Secrist, Kelliher, *pseud. of* Dan T. Kelliher and W. G. Secrist. *see also* Kelliher, Dan T. Secrist, W G	2
Secrist, W G *see also* Secrist, Kelliher, *pseud. of* Dan T. Kelliher and W. G. Secrist.	2
Seeley, Mabel (Hodnefield) 1903-	2 3 H S St
Seibert, Elizabeth.	3
Seifert, Adele.	2
Seifert, Shirley, 1889- (*Full name:* Shirley Louise Seifert)	2
Selborne, John.	1
Seldes, Gilbert Vivian, 1893- *pseud.:* Foster Johns	* 1 2
Sellars, Eleanore Kelly.	2
Selman, Robert.	* 2 3
Sennocke, T J R	2
Serrester, Leonard.	3
Service, Robert William, 1874-1958.	1 Thomson
Seton, Georgina.	2
Seton, Graham, *pseud.* *see* Hutchison, Graham Seton, 1890-	
Severy, Melvin Linwood, 1863-	* 1

Sources

Seymour, H., *pseud.* *see* Hartmann, Helmut.

Shaffer, Anthony, 1926- * 3
(*Full name:* Anthony Joshua Shaffer)
see also Anthony, Peter, *pseud. of* Anthony Shaffer and Peter Shaffer.

Shaffer, Peter, 1926- *
see ailso Anthony, Peter, *pseud. of* Anthony Shaffer and Peter Shaffer.

Shallit, Joseph. 2 3

Shand, William. 3

Shane, Susannah, *pseud.* *see* Ashbrook, Harriette, 1898-1946.

Shanks, Edward, 1892- 2

Shannon, Carl, *pseud.* *see* Hogue, Wilbur Owings.

Shannon, Dell, *pseud.* *see* Linington, Elizabeth, 1921-

Shannon, Jimmy, *pseud.* 3

Sharkey, John Michael, 1931- 3
(Jack Sharkey)

Sharp, David. * 2

Sharp, Luke, *pseud.* *see* Barr, Robert, 1850-1912.

Sharp, Robert George. 3

Sharp, Willoughby. * 2

Sharpe, Jack, *pseud.* *see* Rathborne, St. George, 1854-1938.

Shattuck, Richard. 2

Shaw, Charles, 1900- 3
pseud.: Bant Singer

Shaw, Frank H 1878- 2

Shaw, Joseph Thompson, 1874-1952. 2

Shay, Frank, 1888-1954. 2

Shayne, Gordon, *pseud.* *see* Winter, Bevis, 1918-

Sheahan, K M 2

Shearing, Joseph, *pseud.* *see* Long, Gabrielle Margaret Vere (Campbell) 1886-1952.

Shedd, George Clifford, 1877-1937. BRD, 1918

Sheehan, Perley Poore, 1875- 2

Shefler, Harry F 3

Sheldon, Richard. 3

Shellabarger, Samuel, 1888-1954. * 2
pseuds.: John Esteven
Peter Loring

Shelley, Peter, *pseud.* *see* Dresser, Davis, 1904-

Shenkin, Elizabeth. 3

	Sources
Shepherd, Eric.	3 H
Shepherd, Joan, *pseud.* *see* Buchanan, B J	
Shepherd, Neal, *pseud.* *see* Morland, Nigel, 1905-	
Sheridan, Juanita.	3
Sherry, Edna, *d.* 1967.	2 3 (HH)
Sherwood, John, 1913- (*Full name:* John Herman Mulso Sherwood)	" 3
Shiel, Matthew Phipps, 1865-1947. *see also* Holmes, Gordon, *pseud. of* Louis Tracy alone and with Matthew Phipps Shiel.	** 2 C H EQ QQ Carter, New Sayers, 1928
Sholl, Anna McClure. *pseud.:* Geoffrey Corson	1
Shore, Julian.	2
Shore, P R	2
Shore, Viola (Brothers) 1895- (Mrs. Harry Braxton)	2
Short, Ernest Henry, 1875-	* 2
Shortell, Leslie T	*
Shortt, Charles Rushton, 1904- *pseud.:* Charles Rushton	2 3
Shoubridge, Donald.	2
Shriber, Ione (Sandberg) 1911-	2 3
Shurman, Ida.	2
Sibley, Celestine.	3
Siddall, Roger Beard, 1896-	3
Siddle, Charles, 1892- *see also* Slingsby, Rufus, *pseud. of* Frederick Peel and Charles Siddle.	2
Siegel, Doris. *pseud.:* Susan Wells	3
Sieveking, Lancelot de Giberne, 1896-	* 2
Siller, Van, *pseud.* *see* Van Siller, Hilda.	
Silliman, Vera.	2
Silverman, Marguerite Ruth.	* 2 3
Sim, Katharine, 1913- *pseud.:* Nuraini.	3
Simmons, Addison, 1902-	2
Simmons, Denis.	1
Simon, *pseud. of* Roger d'Este Burford and Oswell Blakeston. *see also* Blakeston, Oswell, 1907- Burford, Roger d'Este, 1904-	Crimes, creeps
Simon, Robert Alfred, 1897- *pseud.:* Liggett Reynolds	* 1

	Sources
Simon, S. J., *pseud.* *see* Skidelsky, Simon Jasha.	
Simons, Roger, *pseud. of* Ivar Punnett and Margaret Punnett. *see also* Punnett, Ivar. Punnett, Margaret.	3
Simpson, Helen De Guerry, 1897-1940.	* H
Simpson, Spencer.	2
Sims, George Robert, 1847-1922.	** C H EQ QQ W Sayers, 1928
Simson, Cicely (Devenish) Fraser- *see* Fraser-Simson, Cicely (Devenish)	
Simson, Eric Andrew, 1895- *pseud.:* Laurence Kirk	2
Sinclair, Fiona.	2 3
Sinclair, May, 1865?-1946.	* EQ
Sinclair, Robert Bruce, 1905-	* 3
Sinclair, Sally.	3
Singer, Bant, *pseud.* *see* Shaw, Charles, 1900-	
Skene, Anthony.	2
Skidelsky, Simon Jasha. *pseud.:* S. J. Simon	* H S
Skinner, Conrad Arthur, 1889- *pseud.:* Michael Maurice	1
Skinner, John.	2
Slaney, George Wilson, 1884- *pseud.:* George Woden	* 2 3
Slate, John.	2 3
Slater, Will.	EQ
Slesar, Henry, 1927- *pseud.:* O. H. Leslie	3
Slingsby, Rufus, *pseud. of* Frederick Peel and Charles Siddle. *see also* Peel, Frederick, 1888- Siddle, Charles, 1892-	2
Sloane, William Milligan, 1906-	H
Small, Austin J d. 1929. *pseud.:* Seamark	* 1 2
Smith, Alexander Clark *see* Smith, Clark, 1919-	
Smith, Anita (Blackmon) 1893- (Anita Blackmon) x	2 H
Smith, Anthony Heckstall- *see* Heckstall-Smith, Anthony, 1904-	
Smith, C I D	2

	Sources
Smith, Chester Alfred, 1920-	3
Smith, Clare Breton.	3
Smith, Clark, 1919- (*Full name:* Alexander Clark Smith)	3
Smith, Constance Isabel, 1894- *pseud.:* Eleanor Reid	*
Smith, David Fredrick *see* Smith, Fred, 1888-	
Smith, Elizabeth Thomasina (Meade) 1854-1914. *pseud.:* Lillie Thomas Meade	** C H EQ QQ Sayers, 1928
Smith, Ernest Bramah, *d.* 1942. *pseud.:* Ernest Bramah	** 1 2 C H EQ QQ S Sy W Thomas Wrong
Smith, Essex, *pseud.* *see* Hope, Essex.	
Smith, Ford, *pseud.* *see* Friend, Oscar Jerome, 1897-	
Smith, Francis Hopkinson, 1838-1915.	*
Smith, Fred, 1888- (*Full name:* David Fredrick Smith)	2
Smith, Garret.	2
Smith, George Malcolm- *see* Malcolm-Smith, George, 1901-	
Smith, Helen Zenna. *pseud.:* Evadne Price	*
Smith, Herbert Maynard, 1869-	* 2
Smith, Johnston.	2
Smith, Laurence Dwight.	2
Smith, Shelley, *pseud.* *see* Bodington, Nancy, 1912-	
Smith, Trevor Dudley- *see* Trevor, Elleston, 1920-	
Smith, Wade, *pseud.* *see* Snow, Charles Horace, 1877-	
Smith, Willard K	2 Thomson
Smith, York.	3
Snaith, John Collis, 1876-1936.	* 2
Snell, Edmund.	1 2

	Sources		
Snow, Charles Horace, 1877-	2	3	
pseuds.: H. C. Averill			
Charles Ballew			
Russ Hardy			
Ranger Lee			
Gary Marshall			
Wade Smith			
Dan Wardle			
Chester Wills			
Snow, Charles Percy, 1905-	2		
Snow, Jack, 1907-1956.	*		
Sohl, Jerry.	3		
Somers, Paul, *pseud.* *see* Winterton, Paul, 1908-			
Sonin, Ray, 1907-	2		
Soutar, Andrew, 1879-	*	2	
Southard, J. H., *pseud.* *see* Morris, Charles, 1833-1922.			
Southwold, Stephen, 1887-1964.	*	2	
pseuds.: Neil Bell			
Paul Martens			
"Miles"			
Souza, Ernest, *pseud.* *see* Scott, Evelyn, 1893-			
Spain, John, *pseud.* *see* Adams, Cleve Franklin, 1895-1950.			
Spain, Nancy, 1917-	*	3	
Sparroy, Massicks, *pseud.*	1		
Spatz, H. Donald, 1913-	2		
Spears, Raymond Smiley, 1876-1950.	1		
Speight, Thomas Wilkinson, 1830-	2		
Spencer, Edward *see* Mott, Edward Spencer, 1844-1910.			
Spencer, Erle.	2		
Spencer, Geoffrey, *pseud.* *see* Wilson, Alexander, 1893-			
Spencer, John, *pseud.* *see* Vickers, Roy, 1899-			
Spencer, Lee.	*	3	
Spencer, Philip Herbert, 1924-	3		
Spender, Jean Maude.	2		
Spenser, James, *pseud.* *see* Guest, Francis Narold, 1901-			
Sperduti, Dominick Rocke.	3		
Spewack, Samuel, 1899-	2		
pseud.: A. A. Abbott			
Spicer, Bart, 1918-	*	3	St
pseud.: Jay Barbette			

	Sources			
Spillane, Frank Morrison, 1918- *pseud.:* Mickey Spillane	2	3	G	
Spillane, Mickey, *pseud.* *see* Spillane, Frank Morrison, 1918-				
Spiller, Andrew.	*	2	3	
Sprigg, Christopher St. John, 1907-1937. *pseud.:* Christopher Caudwell	2			
Sproul, Kathleen.	2			
Spurgeon, Douglas W	*	2		
Stacpoole, Henry De Vere, 1863-1951.	*	2	EQ	
Stacy, O'Connor, *pseud.* *see* Rollins, William, 1897-				
Stafford, Muriel, 1903-	2			
Stagg, Clinton Holland, 1890-1916.	*	1	EQ	W
Stagge, Jonathan, *pseud. of* Richard Wilson Webb and Hugh Callingham Wheeler. *see also* Webb, Richard Wilson. Wheeler, Hugh Callingham, 1913-	S			
Standish, Burt L., *pseud.* *see* Patten, William George, 1866-1945.				
Standish, Robert, *pseud.* *see* Gerahty, Digby George.				
Stanley, Arthur, *pseud.* *see* Megaw, Arthur Stanley, 1872-				
Stanley, Fay Grissom.	3			
Stanley, George.	2			
Stanley, Olin, *pseud.* *see* Honeywell, E L				
Stanners, Harold, 1894-	2			
Stansfeld, Anthony. *see also* Buckingham, Bruce, *pseud. of* Peter Lilley and Anthony Stansfeld.	3			
Stapleton, D., *pseud. of* Douglas and Dorothy Stapleton. *see also* Stapleton, Dorothy. Stapleton, Douglas.	*	3		
Stapleton, Dorothy. *see also* Stapleton, D., *pseud. of* Douglas and Dorothy Stapleton.	3			
Stapleton, Douglas. *see also* Stapleton, D., *pseud. of* Douglas and Dorothy Stapleton.	3			
Stark, Delbert Raymond *see* Stark, Raymond.				
Stark, Michael, *pseud.* *see* Lariar, Lawrence, 1908-				

	Sources
Stark, Raymond. (*Full name:* Delbert Raymond Stark) *pseud.:* John Norwood x	3
Starnes, Richard, 1922-	3
Starr, Jimmy, 1904-	2 3
Starr, Jonathan.	2
Starr, Richard Harry, 1878- *pseud.:* Richard Essex	* 2
Starrett, Vincent, 1886- (*Full name:* Charles Vincent Emerson Starrett)	** 2 H EQ QQ S
Stead, Robert James Campbell, 1880-1959.	2
Steamer, *pseud.* *see* Nason, Leonard Hastings, 1895-	
Sted, Richard.	3
Steed, Mabel A 1894- *pseud.:* M. Alison Hughes	3
Steegmüller, Francis, 1906- *pseuds.:* David Keith Byron Steel	2 3 H MWA
Steel, Byron, *pseud.* *see* Steegmüller, Francis, 1906-	
Steel, Kurt, *pseud.* *see* Kagey, Rudolf, 1904-	
Steele, Chester K	1 2
Steele, De Forest C	3
Steers, Helen *see* Burgess, Helen (Steers)	
Steeves, Harrison Ross, 1881-	2 H S
Steiguer, Walter George De *see* De Steiguer, Walter George, 1884-	
Stein, Aaron Marc, 1906- *pseuds.:* George Bagby Hampton Stone	** 2 3
Stephens, DeVere Ashmore.	3
Stephens, Robert Neilson, 1867-1906-	* 1
Stephenson, Humphrey Meigh, 1882-	2
Sterling, Stewart, *pseud.* *see* Winchell, Prentice, 1895-	
Sterling, Thomas L 1921-	3
Stern, David, 1909- *pseud.:* Peter Stirling	2
Stern, James, 1904- (*Full name:* James Andrew Stern) pseud.: Andrew St. James	*
Stern, Philip Van Doren, 1900- *pseud.:* Peter Storme	2

	Sources
Stern, Richard Martin, 1915-	*
Sterne, Ashley, *pseud.*	*
Steven, E E	2
Stevens, Frances Moyer (Ross) 1895- *pseud.:* Christopher Hale	2 3 H
Stevens, Frank, 1909- (*Full name:* Frank Edmund Stevens)	3
Stevens, K M	3
Stevenson, Burton Egbert, 1872-1962.	* 1 2 H W
Stevenson, Fanny (Van de Grift) 1840-1914.	EQ
Stevenson, Robert Louis, 1850-1894.	** C H EQ QQ S Sy Sayers, 1928 Wrong
Stevenson, Traill.	2
Steward, Paull.	*
Stewart, Alfred Walter, 1880-1947. *pseuds.:* J. J. Connington John Jervis Connington	* 1 2 G H S Sayers, 1928
Stewart, Anita, 1901- (*Full name:* Anita Marie (Stewart) Converse) x	2
Stewart, Frances, *pseud.* *see* Wilmot, James Reginald, 1897-	
Stewart, Gordon, *pseud.* *see* Rathborne, St. George, 1854-1938.	
Stewart, Jay, *pseud.* *see* Palmer, Stuart, 1905-	
Stewart, John Innes Mackintosh, 1906- *pseud.:* Michael Innes	** 2 3 H S Sy Thomas
Stewart, Kenneth Livingston, 1894- *pseud.:* Kenneth Livingston	* 2 EQ
Stewart, Mary, 1916-	3
Stewart, Neil. *see also* Lombard, Nap, *pseud. of* Neil Stewart and Pamela Hansford Johnson.	2
Stilson, Charles Billings.	1 2
Stimson, Mary (Sturdivant) 1897- (*Full name:* Mary Drake (Sturdivant) Stimson)	2
Stinson, Hunter.	1
Stirling, Peter, *pseud.* *see* Stern, David, 1909-	
Stockwell, Gail.	* 2

	Sources
Stoddard, *Major* Henry B., *pseud.* *see* Ingraham, Prentiss, 1843-1904.	
Stokes, Donald Hubert, 1913-	3
Stokes, Francis William, 1883- *pseud.:* Francis Everton	* 1 2
Stokes, Manning Lee. *pseud.:* Bernice Ludwell	2 3
Stone, Austin.	* 2
Stone, Hampton, *pseud.* *see* Stein, Aaron Marc, 1906-	
Stone, Simon, *pseud.* *see* Barrington, Howard, 1906-	
Stoneham, Charles Thurley, 1895- *pseud.:* Norgove Thurley	2 3
Storer, Maria (Longworth) 1849-	1
Storm, Joan.	3
Storm, Michael.	3
Storm, Virginia, *pseud.* *see* Tempest, Jan.	
Storme, Peter, *pseud.* *see* Stern, Philip Van Doren, 1900-	
Story, Jack Trevor, 1917-	3
Story, Josephine, *pseud.* *see* Loring, Emilie (Baker) *d.* 1951.	
Stout, Rex, 1886- (*Full name:* Rex Todhunter Stout)	** 2 3 G H S Sy
Stowell, William Averill, 1882-1950.	* 1 2
Strahan, Kay (Cleaver) 1888-	2 H
Straker, John Foster, 1904-	3
Strange, Carlton.	*
Strange, John Stephen, *pseud.* *see* Tillett, Dorothy (Stockbridge) 1896-	
Street, Cecil John Charles, 1884- *pseuds.:* Miles Burton F. O. O. x x John Rhode	** 1 2 3 G H S W (JDC)
Street, James.	* 2
Strevens, Robert.	* 2 3
Stribling, Thomas Sigismund, 1881-1965.	** 2 H EQ QQ S
Stringer, Arthur John Arbuthnott, 1874-1950.	* 1 2 EQ
Strix, *pseud.* *see* Fleming, Peter, 1907-	
Strobel, Marion, 1895- (Mrs. James Herbert Mitchell)	2

	Sources
Strong, Ben, *pseud.*	2
Strong, Harrington.	* 1
Strong, Leonard Alfred George, 1896-	* 2 3 G MWA
Stuart, Brian, *pseud.* *see* Worthington-Stuart, Brian Arthur.	
Stuart, Robert.	2
Stuart, William L	2
Sturt, E M Leader.	EQ
Stutley, S J	* 2
Stuyvesant, Alice, *pseud. of* Charles Norris Williamson and Alice Muriel (Livingston) Williamson. *see also* Williamson, Alice Muriel (Livingston) 1869-1933. Williamson, Charles Norris, 1859-1920.	1
Styles, Showell, 1908- (*Full name:* Frank Showell Styles) *pseud.:* Glyn Carr	3
Sullivan, Alan, 1868-1947. (*Full name:* Edward Alan Sullivan) *pseud.:* Sinclair Murray	1 2
Sunderland, Kaye.	2
Sunderland Lewis, Walter Reginald, 1861- x	1
Surrey, Richard, *pseud.* *see* Brooker, Bertram, 1888-1955.	
Sussex, Gordon, *pseud.* *see* Volk, Gordon, 1885-	
Sutcliffe, Halliwell, 1870-1932.	* 2
Sutherland, William, *pseud.* *see* Cooper, John Murray, 1908-	
Sutphen, William Gilbert Van Tassel, 1861-	1
Sutton, Elisabeth.	1
Sutton, Phyllis.	3
Sutton, Thomas, *pseud.* *see* Reach, James	
Swartwout, Robert Egerton.	2
Swatridge, Charles. *see also* Charles, Theresa, *pseud. of* Charles Swatridge and Irene Swatridge,	3
Swatridge, Irene. *see also* Charles, Theresa, *pseud. of* Charles Swatridge and Irene Swatridge	3
Swem, Charles Lee.	2
Swift, Anthony, *pseud.* *see* Farjeon, Joseph Jefferson, 1883-1955.	

	Sources
Swift, Julian, *pseud.* *see* Applin, Arthur, 1883-	
Swiggett, Howard, 1891-1957.	2
Switzer, Robert.	3
Sykes, William Stanley, 1894- (Stanley Sykes)	* 2
Sylvester, Robert, 1907-	3
Symons, Beryl (Taubman)	* 2
Symons, Julian, 1912- (*Full name:* Julian Gustave Symons)	* 2 3 G St
Symus, the Pilgrim, *pseud.* *see* Cobb, Sylvanus, 1823-1887.	
Tabor, Paul *see* Tabori, Paul, 1908-	
Tabori, Paul, 1908- (Paul Tabor) x	3
Tack, Alfred, 1906-	2 3
Taft, William Nelson.	* 1 EQ
Tait, Euphemia Margaret. *pseud.:* John Ironside	* 1 2
Talbot, Carl, *pseud.* *see* Hipkins, Charles Hammond, 1893-	
Talbot, Hake, *pseud.* *see* Nelms, Henning.	
Talbot, Hayden.	Sayers, 1931
Targ, William, 1907-	2
Tarpey, Jessie Toler Kingsley.	2
Tate, Ellalice, *pseud.* *see* Hibbert, Eleanor, 1906-	
Taubman-Goldie, Valentine Francis. x	1
Taunton, Harold Roby, 1880-	2
Taylor, A Frank.	3
Taylor, *Capt.* Alfred B., *pseud.* *see* Ingraham, Prentiss, 1843-1904.	
Taylor, Constance Lindsay, 1907- *pseud.:* Guy Cullingford	2 3
Taylor, Elizabeth Tebbetts- *see* Tebbetts-Taylor, Elizabeth.	
Taylor, John M 1888-	1 EQ
Taylor, Judson R., *pseud.* *see* Halsey, Harlan Page, 1837-1898.	
Taylor, Philip Neville Walker- *see* Walker-Taylor, Philip Neville, 1903-	
Taylor, Phoebe Atwood, 1909- *pseud.:* Alice Tilton	* 2 3 H

	Sources
Taylor, Sam S	3
Teagle, Mike.	2
Teague, John Jessop, 1856-1929. *pseud.:* Morice Gerard	* 2
Teague, Ruth Townsend (Mills) 1896-	2
Teague, Walter Dorwin, 1883-1960.	2
Tebbetts-Taylor, Elizabeth. x	3
Teed, G Hamilton.	* 2
Teilhet, Darwin L 1901-1964.	* 2 H Thomas (HH)
Tempest, Jan. *pseuds.:* Fay Chandos Virginia Storm	3
Temple, Paul, *pseud. of* Francis Durbridge and James Douglas Rutherford McConnell. *see also* Durbridge, Francis, 1912- McConnell, James Douglas Rutherford, 1915-	3
Temple, Robin, *pseud.* *see* Wood, Samuel Andrew, 1890-	
Temple-Ellis, N. A., *pseud.* *see* Holdaway, Neville, Aldridge, 1894-	
Templer, John.	*
Templeton, Jesse, *pseud.* *see* Goodchild, George, 1888-	
Tennant, Catherine, *pseud.* *see* Eyles, Kathleen Muriel, 1913-	
Terhune, Albert Payson, 1872-1942.	* 1 2
Terrall, Robert.	2
Terry, Henry Machu *see* Imbert-Terry, *Sir* Henry Machu, *Bart.*, 1854-1938.	
Texas Ranger, *pseud.* *see* Wallace, John.	
Tey, Josephine, *pseud.* *see* Mackintosh Elizabeth, 1896-1952.	
Thames, C. H., *pseud.* *see* Lesser, Milton, 1928-	
Thayer, Lee, 1874- (*Full name:* Emma Redington (Lee) Thayer) (Emma Redington Lee) x	** 1 2 3 H
Thayer, Tiffany, 1902- (*Full name:* Tiffany Ellsworth Thayer) *pseud.:* John Doe Elmer Ellsworth, Jr.	* 2
Thielen, Bernard.	3
Thierry, James Francis.	1

	Sources
Thomas, Alan Ernest Wentworth, 1896-	* 2
Thomas, Carolyn, *pseud.* *see* Duncan, Actea, 1913-	
Thomas, Curtis. *pseud.:* Thomas Kinney	2
Thomas, Eugene, 1894- *pseud.:* Donald Grey	2
Thomas, Murray, *pseud.* *see* Ragg, Thomas Murray, 1897-	
Thomas, Ronald Wills, 1910- *pseuds.:* Jeff Bogar James Cadell Ronald Wills	3
Thomey, Tedd.	3
Thompson, Estelle.	3
Thompson, James Meyers, 1906-	3
Thompson, John Burton, 1913-	3
Thompson, Josephine Pullein- *see* Pullein-Thompson, Josephine.	
Thompson, Lilian Bennet-, 1883- x	2
Thompson, Lloyd S	2
Thompson, Madeline, *pseud.* *see* Greig, Maysie, 1902-	
Thompson, Vance, 1863-1925.	* 1 EQ
Thompson, Arthur Alexander Malcolm, 1894-	*
Thomson, *Sir* Basil Home, 1861-1939.	* 1 2 H EQ
Thorndike, Arthur Russell, 1885- (Russell Thorndyke) x	* 2 S
Thorndyke, Russell *see* Thorndike, Arthur Russell, 1885-	
Thorne, *Lt.* Alfred B., *pseud.* *see* Aiken, Albert W 1846?-1894.	
Thorne, E P	* 2
Thorne, Emily.	3
Thorne, Guy, *pseud.* *see* Gull, Cyril Arthur Edward Ranger, 1876-1923.	
Thorne, Mabel.	1 2
Thorne, Paul.	1 2
Thorson, Delos Russell, 1906- *see also* Christian, Kit, *pseud. of* Delos Russell Thorson and Sara Winfree Thorson.	2

	Sources
Thorson, Sara Winfree, 1906-	2
see also Christian, Kit, *pseud. of* Delos Russell Thorson and Sara Winfree Thorson.	
Threlfall, T R	*
Thrice, Luke, *pseud.* *see* Russell, John, 1885-1956.	
Thurley, Norgrove, *pseud.* *see* Stoneham, Charles Thurley, 1895-	
Thynne, Molly.	* 2
Tickell, Jerrard, 1905-	2
Tillett, Dorothy (Stockbridge) 1896-	* 2 3 H S
pseud.: John Stephen Strange	
Tilton, Alice, *pseud.* *see* Taylor, Phoebe Atwood, 1909-	
Timins, Douglas.	2
Timony, Arthur N., *pseud.* *see* Vahey, John George Haslette, 1881-	
Tomline, F., *pseud.* *see* Gilbert, Sir William Schwenck, 1836-1911.	
Torday, Ursula.	3
pseuds.: Paula Allardyce Charity Blackstock Lee Blackstock	
Torgerson, Edwin Dial.	* 2
Torrey, Marjorie, *pseud.* *see* Chanslor, Marjorie Torrey (Hood) 1899-	
Torrey, Roger.	* 2
Torrey, Ware, 1905-	2
pseud.: Lee Crosby	
Tower, Stella Mary (Hodgson) 1891-	2
pseud.: Faith Wolseley	
Towne, Stuart, *pseud.* *see* Rawson, Clayton, 1906-	
Toye, Stanley Percival.	3
Tozer, Basil, 1872-	2
(*Full name:* Basil John Joseph Tozer)	
Tracy, Louis, 1863-1928.	* 1 2 C H W
see also Holmes, Gordon, *pseud. of* Louis Tracy alone and with Matthew Phipps Shiel.	
Tracy, Virginia.	* 2
Trafford, F. G., *pseud.* *see* Riddell, Charlotte Eliza Lawson (Cowan) 1832-1906.	

	Sources
Tragett, Margaret Rivers (Larminie) (Margaret Rivers Larminie) x	2
Traill, Peter, *pseud.* *see* Morton, Guy Mainwaring, 1896-	
Train, Arthur Cheney, 1875-1945.	** EQ QQ
Trask, Keith.	2
Trask, Merrill, *pseud.* *see* Colton, Mel.	
Traubel, Helen.	3
Traver, Robert, *pseud.* *see* Voelker, John Donaldson, 1903-	
Travers, Stephen, *pseud.* *see* Radcliffe, Garnett, 1899-	
Travis, Gerry, *pseud.* *see* Trimble, Louis, 1917-	
Trayde, Marque, *pseud.*	2
Treat, Lawrence, 1903- (*Name originally:* Lawrence Arthur Goldstone) x	2 3
Tree, Gregory, *pseud.*	3
Trench, John, 1920-	3 St
Trent, Paul.	* 2
Trent, Peter, *pseud.* *see* Nelson, Lawrence, 1907-	
Trevor, A. C., *pseud.* *see* Pulsford, Norman George, 1902-	
Trevor, Elleston, 1920- (*Name originally:* Trevor Dudley-Smith) *pseuds.:* Simon Rattray x x Warwick Scott	3
Trevor, Glen, *pseud.* *see* Hilton, James, 1900-1954.	
Trevor, Ralph, *pseud.* *see* Wilmot, James Reginald, 1897-	
Treynor, Albert M	BRD, 1926
Treynor, Blair.	3
Triem, Paul Ellsworth, 1882- *pseud.:* Paul Ellsworth	2
Trimble, Louis, 1917- *pseuds.:* Stuart Brock Gerry Travis	2 3
Tring, A. Stephen, *pseud.* *see* Meynell, Laurence Walter, 1899-	
Tripp, C. E., *pseud.* *see* Morris, Charles, 1833-1922.	
Trott, Nicholas.	2

	Sources
Trotta, Geraldine. (Geri Trotta)	3
Troy, Simon, *pseud.* *see* Warriner, Thurman.	
Truax, Rhoda, 1891- (Mrs. Robert Henry Aldrich)	2
Truesdell, June.	2
Truman, Marcus George, 1890- *pseud.*: Mark Beckett	2
Truss, Seldon, 1892- (*Full name:* Leslie Seldon Truss)	2 3
Tucker, Wilson, 1914- (*Full name:* Arthur Wilson Tucker)	2 3
Turnbull, Dora Amy Dillon *see* Wentworth, Patricia, *pseud.* *d.* 1961.	
Turnbull, Margaret, *d.* 1942.	1 2
Turner, James, 1909-	3
Turner, John Victor, 1900-1945. *pseuds.*: Nicholas Brady David Hume	* 2
Turngren, Annette, 1902- *pseud.*: A. T. Hopkins	3
Tuttle, Wilbur C 1883-	1 2
Twain, Mark, *pseud.* *see* Clemens, Samuel Langhorne, 1835-1910.	
Tweedsmuir, John Buchan, *Baron* *see* Buchan, John, 1875-1940.	
Tyler, Charles Waller, 1841-	1
Tyler, Esther.	2
Tyre, Nedra.	3
Tyrell, Patrick.	1
Tyrer, Walter.	3
Tyrrell, Ross.	BRD, 1920
Tyson, John Aubrey, 1870-1930.	* 1 2 EQ W
Ullman, Allan.	3
Ulmar, Genevieve, *pseud.* *see* Cobb, Weldon J *fl.* 1866-1895.	
Umbstaetter, Herman Daniel, 1851-	* EQ
Underwood, Michael, *pseud.* *see* Evelyn, John Michael, 1916-	
Unofficial Observer, *pseud.* *see* Carter, John Franklin, 1897-	
Upfield, Arthur William, 1888-1964.	2 3 S St MWA (HH)

	Sources
Upward, Allen, 1863-1926.	* 1 2
Urell, William Francis. *pseud.:* William Francis	2 3
Usher, Frank Hugh, 1909- *pseuds.:* Charles Franklin Frank Lester	3
Usher, Gray, 1903-	3
Usher, Jack.	3
Usher, Wilfrid.	2
Vachell, Horace Annesley, 1861-1955.	* 2 EQ
Vaczek, Louis Charles. *pseud.:* Peter Hardin	3
Vahey, John George Haslette, 1881- *pseuds.:* Henrietta Clandon John Haslette Anthony Lang Vernon Loder John Mowbray Walter Proudfoot Arthur N. Timony	** 2
Vail, Laurence, 1891-	2
Vaile, William Newell, 1876-	1
Vale, G B	2
Valentine, *pseud.* *see* Pechey, Archibald Thomas, 1876-1961.	
Valentine, Douglas, *pseud.* *see* Williams, Valentine, 1883-1946.	
Vallings, Gabrielle, 1886- (*Full name:* Gabrielle Francesca Lillian Mary Vallings)	2
Vanardy, Varick, *pseud.* *see* Dey, Frederic van Rensselaer, 1861-1922.	
Van Arsdale, Wirt, *pseud.* *see* Davis, Martha (Wirt)	
Van Atta, Winfred, 1910- (*Full name:* Winfred Lowell Van Atta) *pseud.:* Lowell Ryerson	3
Vance, Jack, *pseud.* *see* Kuttner, Henry, 1914-1958.	
Vance, John Holbrook.	3
Vance, Louis Joseph, 1879-1933.	* 1 2 Thomas
Vandam, Albert Dresden, 1843-1903.	* 1 C EQ
Vandeburg, Millie Bird.	1

	Sources
Vandercook, John Womack, 1902-	* 2 S
Vanderpuije, Nii Akrampahene, 1925-	3
Vanderveer, Stewart.	2
Van Deusen, Delia.	2
Van Deventer, Emma Murdoch. *pseud.:* Lawrence L. Lynch	* 1 C
Van de Water, Frederic Franklyn, 1890-	* 1 2
Van Dine, S. S., *pseud.* *see* Wright, Willard Huntington, 1888-1939.	
Van Doren, Dirck, *pseud.* *see* Dey, Frederic van Rensselaer, 1861-1922.	
Van Dycke, Tom.	2
Van Dyke, J., *pseud.* *see* Edwards, Frederick Anthony, 1896-	
Vane, Derek.	* 1 2
Vane, Phillips, *pseud.* *see* Hambledon, Phyllis, 1892-	
Van Gulik, Robert Hans *see* Gulik, Robert Hans van, 1910-	
Vanner, John, *pseud.* *see* North, William, 1869-	
Van Rensburg, Helen.	3
Van Rensburg, Louwrens.	3
Van Siller, Hilda. *pseud.:* Van Siller	2 3
Van Urk, Virginia (Nellis)	3
Varnado, Donald. (*Full name:* Donald Robert Varnado)	3
Varnam, John.	* 3
Vedder, John K., *pseud.* *see* Gruber, Frank, 1904-	
Vedette, *pseud.* *see* Williams, Valentine, 1883-1946.	
Veiller, Bayard, 1869-1943.	2
Veitch, James.	3
Venning, Michael, *pseud.* *see* Rice, Craig, 1908-1957.	
Verner, Gerald.	* 2
Vernon, Frank, 1876-	*
Vernon, Virginia (Fox-Brooks) 1894-	*
Verron, Robert.	3
Vestal, Stanley, 1887- *pseud.:* Walter Stanley Campbell	2 3
Vickers, Roy, 1899- *pseud.:* John Spencer	** 2 3 G EQ QQ Sy
Vidal, Gore, 1925- *pseud.:* Edgar Box	3

	Sources
Vincent, E. L., *pseud.* *see* Morris, Charles, 1833-1922.	
Vinn, Walger.	3
Vinton, Aldin.	2
Virden, Katharine.	* 2
Visiak, Edward Harold, 1878-	2 Crimes, creeps
Vivian, Evelyn Charles H *pseud.:* Charles Cannell	* 2
Vivian, Francis, *pseud.* *see* Ashley, Ernest, 1906-	
Vlasto, John Alexander, 1877-1958. *pseuds.:* John Alexander John Remenham	2
Voelker, John Donaldson, 1903- *pseud.:* Robert Traver	
Volk, Gordon, 1885- *pseuds.:* Raymond Knotts Gordon Sussex	2
Von Linsingen, Frederick William Berry *see* Linsingen, Frederick William Berry von, 1901-	
Vulliamy, Colwyn Edward, 1886- *pseud.:* Anthony Rolls	* 2 3 H
WAAC, *pseud.* (C., WAA, *pseud.*) x	2
Waddel, Charles Carey, 1868-1930. (Charles Carey Waddell) x *pseud.:* Charles Carey	1 2
Waddell, Charles Carey *see* Waddel, Charles Carey, 1868-1930.	
Waddell, Eleanor Lee.	3
Wade, Alan.	3
Wade, Arthur Sarsfield *see* Ward, Arthur Sarsfield, 1883-1959.	
Wade, Bob, 1920- *see also* Masterson, Whit, *pseud. of* Bob Wade and Bill Miller. Miller, Wade, *pseud. of* Bob Wade and Bill Miller.	2 3
Wade, Henry, *pseud.* *see* Aubrey-Fletcher, *Sir* Henry Lancelot, *Bart.*, 1887-	
Wade, Kathleen.	3
Wadsworth, Leda A 1901-	2 3

	Sources
Waer, Jack.	3
Waghorn, H. L., *pseud.* *see* Horn, Holloway, 1886-	
Wagoner, David, 1926-	3
Wahl, Alberta Elizabeth (Hughes) 1904-	2
Waitt, Isabel Woodman.	2
Wakefield, Herbert Russell, 1888-	* 2
Wakefield, R I	3
Walcott, Earle Ashley, 1859-	1
Walk, Charles Edmonds.	* 1
Walker, Charles Maurice.	2
Walker, Gertrude.	3
Walker, Harry, *pseud.* *see* Waugh, Hillary, 1920-	
Walker, Rowland, 1876-	*
Walker-Taylor, Philip Neville, 1903- x	* 2
Wall, John.	3
Wallace, Carlton.	* 2
Wallace, Edgar, 1875-1932. (*Full name*: Richard Edgar Horatio Wallace) x	** 1 2 3 C H EQ QQ Sy W Sayers, 1928 Thomson Wrong
Wallace, John. *pseuds.*: Aintree Gerald Grantham Texas Ranger x	2
Wallace, Mary.	3
Wallace, Richard Edgar Horatio *see* Wallace, Edgar, 1875-1932.	
Wallace, Robert.	2
Waller, Leslie, 1923- *pseud.*: C. S. Cody	3
Walling, Robert Alfred John, 1869-1949.	2 3 H
Wallis, James Harold, 1885-1958.	2
Wallis, Ruth Otis (Sawtell) 1895-	2 3
Walpole, *Sir* Hugh, 1884-1941.	** EQ Sy
Walsh, Goodwin.	1 2
Walsh, James Morgan, 1897-1952. *pseud.*: H. Haverstock Hill	** 1 2 3 EQ Sayers, 1931
Walsh, Maurice, 1879-	2
Walsh, Thomas, 1908- (*Full name:* Thomas Francis Morgan Walsh)	3 St

	Sources
Walter, Alexia E	2
Walter, Hubert Conrad.	2
Walton, Francis, *pseud.* *see* Hodder, Alfred, 1866-1907.	
Walz, Audrey. *pseud.:* Francis Bonnamy	* 2 3
Warborough, Martin Leach, *pseud.* *see* Allen, Grant, 1848-1899.	
Ward, Arthur Sarsfield, 1883-1959. (Arthur Sarsfield Wade) x *pseud.:* Sax Rohmer	** 1 2 EQ QQ Sayers, 1928
Ward, Colin.	2
Ward, Ernest.	2
Ward, Gerald.	3
Ward, Harold.	2
Ward, Jonas, *pseud.* *see* Ard, William, 1922-	
Warden, Florence, *pseud.* *see* James, Florence Alice (Price) 1857-1929.	
Wardle, Dan, *pseud.* *see* Snow, Charles Horace, 1877-	
Waring, Marcus H., *pseud.* *see* Manning, William Henry, 1852-1929.	
Waring, Molly.	3
Warman, Erik, 1904-	2
Warneford, *Lieut., pseud.* *see* Gunter, Archibald Clavering, 1847-1907.	
Warner, Douglas.	3
Warner, Oliver.	1
Warner, Warren, *esq. of the Inner Temple, pseud.* *see* Warren, Samuel, 1807-1877.	
Warren, Charles Marquis, 1912-	3
Warren, James.	2
Warren, John Russell, 1886- *pseud.:* Gilbert Coverack	2 3 H
Warren, Mary Douglas, *pseud.* *see* Greig, Maysie, 1902-	
Warren, Samuel, 1807-1877. *pseud.:* Warren Warner, *esq. of the Inner Temple*	* EQ
Warren, Vernon, *pseud.* *see* Chapman, George Warren Vernon, 1925-	
Warriner, Cornelia. *see also* Crockett, James, *pseud. of* Cornelia Warriner and James A. MacPhail.	2

	Sources
Warriner, Thurman. *pseud.:* Simon Troy	3
Warwick, Pauline, *pseud.* *see* Davies, Betty Evelyn.	
Waten, Judah Leon.	3
"Waters," *pseud.* *see* Russell, William.	
Waters, Thomas, *pseud.?* *see* Russell, William.	
Watkins, Alex. *pseud.:* J. Lane Linklater	2 3
Watkins, Richard Howells.	1 2
Watkins, Victoria Endicott (Lincoln) *see* Lincoln, Victoria, 1904-	
Watson, Colin, 1920-	3
Watson, Jane (Werner) 1915- *pseuds.:* Annie North Bedford Monica Hill Elsa Ruth Nast	2
Watson, John Reay, 1872-	1 Sayers, 1928 Thomson
Watson, Keith Campbell West- *see* West-Watson, Keith Campbell.	
Watson, Maurice.	3
Watters, Rutherford.	3
Waugh, Hillary, 1920- (*Full name:* Hillary Baldwin Waugh) *pseud.:* Harry Walker	* 2 3 St Sy
Wayde, Bernard. *see also* Old Cap Collier, *pseud.*	Pearson
Waye, Cecil.	2
Wayne, Anderson, *pseud.* *see* Dresser, Davis, 1904-	
Weaver, Ward, *pseud.* *see* Mason, Francis van Wyck, 1901-	
Webb, Anthony, *pseud.*	* 2
Webb, Dorothy Anna Maria. *pseud.:* Jermyn March	2
Webb, Jack, 1920- *pseuds.:* John Farr Tex Grady	3
Webb, Jean Francis, 1910- *pseud.:* Ethel Hamill	2
Webb, L. J., *pseud.*	2

	Sources
Webb, Richard Wilson. *see also* Patrick, Q., *pseud.* Quentin, Patrick, *pseud of* Richard Wilson Webb and Hugh Callingham Wheeler. Stagge, Jonathan, *pseud of* Richard Wilson Webb and Hugh Callingham Wheeler.	** 2 3 H S Sy
Webster, Frederick Annesley Michael, 1886-	* 2 EQ
Webster, H M	* 2 3
Webster, Henry Kitchell, 1875-1932.	* 1 2
Webster, Jean, 1876-1916. (*Full name:* Alice Jean Chandler (Webster) McKinney) x	1
Webster, Leslie.	*
Wedlake, George E C	2
Weekes, Agnes Russell. *pseud.:* Anthony Pryde	* 2
Wees, Frances Shelley (Johnson) 1902-	* 2
Weiner, Henri, *pseud.* *see* Longstreet, Stephen, 1907-	
Weir, Hugh, 1884-1934. (*Full name:* Hugh Cosgro Weir)	* 1 EQ
Wellard, James Howard, 1909-	2 3
Wells, Anna Mary, 1906-	2 3
Wells, Carolyn, 1870-1942. (Mrs. Hadwin Houghton) *pseud.:* Rowland Wright	** 1 2 H Thomas
Wells, Herbert George, 1866-1946.	* EQ
Wells, Susan, *pseud.* *see* Siegel, Doris.	
Welton, Arthur Dorman, 1867-	2
Wentworth, Patricia, *pseud.*, *d.* 1961. (*Real name:* Dora Amy Dillon, *afterwards* Turnbull) x x *other pseud.:* Delta	** 1 2 3 H
Wesley, Elizabeth, *pseud.* *see* McElfresh, Adeline.	
West, Geoffrey Philip.	2
West, Keith, *pseud.* *see* Lane, Kenneth Westmacott, 1893-	
West, Token, *pseud.* *see* Humphries, Adelaide.	
West, Tom, *pseud.* *see* Reach, James.	
West-Watson, Keith Campbell. x *pseud.:* Keith Campbell	3

	Sources
Westall, William, 1835-1903.	*
Westbrook, Perry Dickie, 1916-	2 3
Westerham, S. C., *pseud.* *see* Alington, Cyril Argentine, 1872-	
Westlake, Donald E 1934?-	3
Westland, Lynn, *pseud.* *see* Joscelyn, Archie, 1899-	
Westmacott, Mary, *pseud.* *see* Christie, Agatha (Miller) 1891-	
Weston, Allen, *pseud. of* Grace (Allen) Hogarth and Alice Mary Norton.	3
see also Hogarth, Grace (Allen) 1905-	
Norton, Alice Mary.	
Weston, Garnett.	2 3
Weston, George, 1880-	1 2
Weyman, Stanley John, 1855-1928.	*
Weymouth, Anthony, 1887-	2 EQ
Whalen, William Wilfrid, 1886-	2
Whaley, Charles Norman, 1940-	3
Whaley, Francis John, 1897-	2
Wharton, Anthony, *pseud.* *see* McAllister, Alister, 1877-	
Wheatley, Dennis, 1897-	* 2
Wheeler, Benson.	2
Wheeler, Edward Lytton, 1854 or 5-1885.	1
pseud.: Edward Lytton (also used by Charles Morris)	Johannsen
Wheeler, H E	2
Wheeler, Hugh Callingham, 1913-	** H S
see also Patrick, Q., *pseud.*	
Quentin, Patrick, *pseud of* Richard Wilson Webb and Hugh Callingham Wheeler.	
Stagge, Jonathan, *pseud. of* Richard Wilson Webb and Hugh Callingham Wheeler.	
Wheelock, Dorothy.	2
Whelton, Paul.	2 3
Whipple, Kenneth, 1894-	2
White, Ared.	2
White, Ethel Lina.	** 2 3 H S Sy
White, Fred Merrick, 1859-	* 1 Chandler, F. W.
White, Grace M	2

	Sources
White, Grace (Miller)	1
White, Herbert Oliver, 1885- (*Full name:* Herbert Martyn Oliver White) *pseud.:* Oliver Martyn	2
White, Leslie Turner, 1903-	* 2
White, Lionel.	3
White, Reginald James.	3
White, William Anthony Parker, 1911- *pseuds.:* Anthony Boucher H. H. Holmes	2 H S
Whitechurch, Victor Lorenzo, 1868-1933.	** 1 2 C H EQ QQ Sayers, 1928
Whitehouse, Arch *see* Whitehouse, Arthur George Joseph, 1895-	
Whitehouse, Arthur George Joseph, 1895- (Arch Whitehouse) x	2
Whitelaw, David.	* 2 3
Whitfield, Raoul.	2 H S
Whiting, Clifford.	Thomas
Whitney, Phyllis Ayame, 1903-	2
Whittaker, Frederick, 1838-1889. *pseud.:* Launce Poyntz	1 Johannsen
Whittington, Harry.	3
Wibberley, Leonard Patrick O'Connor, 1915- *pseuds.:* Leonard Holton Patrick O'Connor	3
Wickham, Harvey, 1872-1930.	* 1
Wicks, Frederick, 1840-1910.	*
Wiehe, Evelyn May (Clowes) *see* Mordaunt, Evelyn May, 1877?-1942.	
Wight, Natalie.	2
Wilby, R. Hunt, *pseud.* *see* Eyster, William Reynolds, 1841-1918.	
Wilcox, Harry. *pseud.:* Mark Derby	3
Wilde, Percival, 1887-1953.	** 2 H EQ QQ S Chandler, R.
Wilder, William West, *pseud.* *see* Patten, William George, 1866-1945.	
Wiley, Hugh, 1884-	* EQ
Wilkinson, Ellen Cicely, 1891-	2
Wilkinson, Laurence, 1912-	3
Wilkinson, Roderick, 1917-	* 3

	Sources
Willard, John, 1885-	*
Willard, Joshua.	2
Willard, Josiah Flynt, 1869-1907. *pseud.:* Josiah Flynt	* EQ
Willett, Edward, 1830-1889. *pseuds.:* Carl Brent J. Stanley Henderson	Johannsen
Willett, Ernest Noddall.	2
Willett, Hilda, 1878-	2
William, Peter.	2
Williams, Alexander Hazard, 1894-	2
Williams, Ben Ames, 1889-1953.	1 2 H
Williams, Brad, 1918-	3
Williams, Charles, 1909-	3
Williams, Edwin Alfred. *pseud.:* Edwin de Caire	3
Williams, Eliot Crawshay- *see* Crawshay-Williams, Eliot, 1879-	
Williams, George Valentine *see* Williams, Valentine, 1883-1946.	
Williams, Harper.	1
Williams, Henry Smith, 1863-1943.	1
Williams, J Arthur.	2
Williams, John Babington. *pseud.?* James Brampton	Chandler, F.W Haycraft, Art
Williams, Kirby, *pseud.*	2
Williams, Margaret Wetherby *see* Williams, Wetherby.	
Williams, Pete, *pseud.* *see* Reach, James.	
Williams, Philip Claxton.	2
Williams, Richard, *pseud.* *see* Reach, James.	
Williams, Sidney Clark, 1878-1949.	1 2
Williams, Valentine, 1883-1946. (*Full name:* George Valentine Williams) *pseuds.:* Douglas Valentine x Vedette	* 1 2 H EQ
Williams, Wetherby. (*Full name:* Margaret Wetherby Williams) *pseud.:* Margaret Erskine	2 3

Sources

Williamson, Alice Muriel (Livingston) 1869-1933. * 1 EQ
pseuds.: M. P. Revere
Teresa de Savallo, *marquesa*
x
d'Alpens
Mrs. Harcourt Williamson
see also Créspigny, *Capt.* Charles de, *pseud. of* Charles Norris Williamson and Alice Muriel (Livingston) Williamson.
Stuyvesant, Alice, *pseud. of* Charles Norris Williamson and Alice Muriel (Livingston) Williamson.

Williamson, Charles Norris, 1859-1920. * 1 EQ
see also Créspigny, *Capt.* Charles de, *pseud of* Charles Norris Williamson and Alice Muriel (Livingston) Williamson. BRD, 1919
Stuyvesant, Alice, *pseud. of* Charles Norris Williamson and Alice Muriel (Livingston) Williamson.

Williamson, *Mrs.* Harcourt, *pseud. see* Williamson, Alice Muriel (Livingston) 1869-1933.

Williamson, Hugh Ross *see* Ross Williamson, Hugh, 1901-

Willis, Anthony Armstrong, 1897- 1 2 3
pseuds.: A. A. of Punch
x
Anthony Armstrong

Willock, Colin Dennistoun, 1919- 3

Willoughby, John. 1

Wills, Cecil Melville, 1891- *2 3

Wills, Chester, *pseud. see* Snow, Charles Horace, 1877-

Wills, Helen Newington, 1906- 2
(Mrs. Aidan Roark)

Wills, Ronald, *pseud. see* Thomas, Ronald Wills, 1910-

Wills, Thomas, *pseud. see* Ard, William, 1922-

Wilmot, Eileen. 3

Wilmot, James Reginald, 1897- 2
pseuds.: Frances Stewart
Ralph Trevor

Wilmot, Robert Patrick. 3

	Sources
Wilson, Alexander, 1893- (*Full name:* Alexander Douglas Chesney Wilson) *pseud.:* Geoffrey Spencer	* 2
Wilson, Gertrude Mary (Bryant) 1899-	3
Wilson, Grove, 1883-1954.	2
Wilson, Lee, *pseud.* *see* Lemmon, Laura Elizabeth, 1917-	
Wilson, Mitchell A 1913- *see also* Hogarth, Emmett, *pseud. of* Mitchell A. Wilson and Abraham Polonsky.	2 S MWA
Wilson, Philip Whitwell, 1875-1956.	* 2 MWA
Wilson, Robert McNair, 1882- *pseud.:* Anthony Wynne	** 1 2 3 H EQ QQ W
Wilson, Ruth.	2
Wilson, Stanley Kidder, 1879- *pseud.:* Pliny the Youngest	2
Wilton, *Capt.* Mark, *pseud.* *see* Manning, William Henry, 1852-1929.	
Wimhurst, Cecil Gordon. (*Full name:* Cecil Gordon Eugene Wimhurst) *pseud.:* Nigel Brent	3
Winch, Edgar.	2
Winch, Evelyn M., *pseud.* *see* Winch, Marie Elizabeth Agnes.	
Winch, John, *pseud.* *see* Long, Gabrielle Margaret Vere (Campbell) 1886-1952.	
Winch, Marie Elizabeth Agnes. *pseud.:* Evelyn M. Winch	Sayers, 1934
Winchell, Prentice, 1895- *pseuds.:* Jay de Bekker Dev Collans Spencer Dean Stewart Sterling	* 2 3
Winkley, Arthur H	3
Winslow, Amos, Jr., *pseud.* *see* Cobb, Sylvanus, 1823-1887.	
Winslow, Horatio Gates, 1882-	2
Winsor, George McLeod.	1 2
Winter, Bevis, 1918- *pseuds.:* Al Bocca Peter Cagney Gordon Shayne	3
Winter, William West.	1

	Sources
Winterton, Paul, 1908- *pseuds.:* Roger Bax Andrew Garve Paul Somers	3 G St
Wire, Harold Channing.	2
Wishart, Gertrude. (*Full name:* Nancy Gertrude Wishart)	2
Withers, E. L., *pseud.* *see* Potter, George William, 1930-	
Witting, Clifford, 1907-	* 2 3 St
Woden, George, *pseud.* *see* Slaney, George Wilson, 1884-	
Wogan, Charles.	2 3
Wolff, William Almon, 1885-	2
Wolffe, Katherine, *pseud.* *see* Scott, Marian (Gallagher)	
Wolfson, Victor, 1910- *pseud.:* Langdon Dodge.	3
Wolseley, Faith, *pseud.* *see* Tower, Stella Mary (Hodgson) 1891-	
Wood, Clement, 1888-1950. *pseud.:* Alan Dubois	2
Wood, Ellen (Price) 1814-1887. (Mrs. Henry Wood) x	1 Johannsen Sayers, 1928 Thomson
Wood, Eric.	2
Wood, H Freeman Wiber.	* C
Wood, *Mrs.* Henry *see* Wood, Ellen (Price) 1814-1887.	
Wood, Sally Calkins, 1897-	2
Wood, Samuel Andrew, 1890- *pseud.:* Robin Temple	*
Woodford, Jack, *pseud.* *see* Woolfolk, Josiah Pitts, 1894-	
Woodgate, Mildred Violet, 1904-	2
Woodiwiss, John Cecil.	2 3
Woodrow, Nancy Mann (Waddel) 1875?-1935.	1 2
Woods, Katherine.	2 Haycraft, Art
Woodthorpe, Ralph Carter, 1886-	2 H
Woodward, Edward. (*Full name:* Edward Emberlin Woodward) *pseud.:* Jane Grierson.	2
Woodward, Helen (Rosen) 1882-	2
Woodward, Lilian, *pseud.* *see* Marsh, John, 1907-	

	Sources
Woodward, Sherman Melville, 1871-1953.	2
Woodworth, Herbert Grafton, 1860-	1
Woolfolk, Josiah Pitts, 1894- *pseuds.:* Sappho Henderson Britt Howard Kennedy Gordon Sayre Jack Woodford	2
Woolfolk, William.	3
Woolrich, Cornell, *pseud.* *see* Hopley-Woolrich, Cornell George, 1903-	
Worley, William.	2
Wormser, Richard Edward, 1908-	2 3
Worsley-Gough, Barbara. x	3
Worth, Cedric, 1900-	2 H
Worthington-Stuart, Brian Arthur. *pseuds.:* Peter Meredith Brian Stuart	3
Worts, George Frank, 1892- *pseud.:* Loring Brent	2
Wray, I., *pseud.*	* 2
Wren, Lassiter.	2 EQ Thomson
Wren, Percival Christopher, 1885-1941.	* 1 2 EQ
Wrenn, Harold Albert, 1909-	3
Wright, Elsie N 1907- *pseud.:* *Capt.* J. J. Grayson	2
Wright, Judith Grovner, *pseud.* *see* Bull, Lois, 1900-	
Wright, June.	3
Wright, Mason.	2
Wright, Rowland, *pseud.* *see* Wells, Carolyn, 1870-1942.	
Wright, Ruth, *pseud.* *see* Kauffman, Ruth (Hammitt) *d.* 1952.	
Wright, Sydney Fowler, 1874- *pseud.:* Sydney Fowler	* 2
Wright, Willard Huntington, 1888-1939. *pseud.:* S. S. Van Dine x	** 1 2 3 C G H S Sy W
Wurr, H J	*
Wylie, Noël.	3
Wylie, Philip, 1902-	* 2
Wynd, Oswald, 1913- (*Full name:* Oswald Morris Wynd) *pseud.:* Gavin Black	(HH)

	Sources
Wyndham, John, *pseud.* *see* Harris, John Beynon, 1903-	
Wynne, Anthony, *pseud.* *see* Wilson, Robert McNair, 1882-	
Wynnton, Patrick.	*
'X', *pseud.* *see* Fox-Davies, Arthur Charles 1871-1928.	
X. *Captain, pseud.*	*
X. L., pseud. *see* Field, Julian Osgood.	
Xantippe, *pseud.*	2
Yates, Dornford, *pseud.* *see* Mercer, Cecil William, 1885-1960.	
Yates, Edmund Hodgson, 1831-1894.	Chandler, F.W. Johannsen
Yates, George Worthing. *see also* Hunt, Peter, *pseud. of* Charles Hunt Marshall and George Worthing Yates.	* 2 H
Yates, Margaret Polk, 1915-	2
Yates, Margaret (Tayler) 1887-1952. (*Full name:* Margaret Evelyn (Tayler) Yates)	2
York, Jeremy, *pseud.* *see* Creasey, John, 1908-	
Young, Eric Brett. *pseud.:* Eric Leacroft	2
Young, Ernest A *pseud.:* Harry Rockwood	* 1
Young, Florence Ethel Mills, 1875-	2
Young, Francis Brett, 1884-1954.	* Sayers, 1934
Young, Gordon Ray, 1886-1948.	1 2
Young, Rose Emmet, 1869-	1
Younger, Elizabeth (Hely)	3
Younger, William Antony, 1917- *pseud.:* William Mole	3 St
Zangwill, Israel, 1864-1926.	** H EQ QQ W
Zugsmith, Leane, 1903-	2

The Lure of Danger

The heroes of these true stories faced danger because it was part of their job. Here are men who dared pressure to raise sunken gold; men who walked the ocean floor to rescue trapped submarine sailors; men who tracked animals across veldt or through jungle to stock museums and add to scientific knowledge; men who flew because it was in their blood.

These are stories of danger voluntarily challenged; of men of our day who made danger their business and then came back to write of the adventures into which their jobs took them.

The Lure of Danger

TRUE ADVENTURE STORIES
COLLECTED BY

Margaret C. Scoggin

ALFRED A. KNOPF
New York

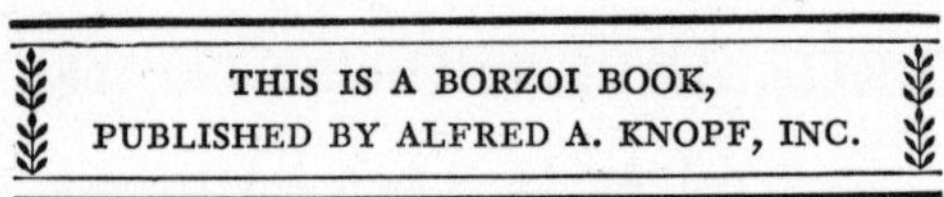
THIS IS A BORZOI BOOK,
PUBLISHED BY ALFRED A. KNOPF, INC.

Published August 21st, 1947
Eighth printing, February 1964

Foreword

The heroes of these true stories faced danger because it was part of the job; they faced it aware of all the risks and with eyes open. Here are men who dared pressure to raise sunken gold; men who walked the ocean floor to rescue trapped submarine sailors; men who tracked animals across veldt or through jungle to stock museums and add to scientific knowledge; men who flew because it was in their blood; men who climbed seemingly impregnable mountain peaks "because they were there."

Someone has said that the more careful the preparations, the less likely the danger. However, since the unknown is always unpredictable, these men—in spite of careful preparations—did meet danger face to face. Because they were skillful and courageous professional men, they lived to tell their tales.

These, then, are stories of danger *voluntarily* challenged, as distinguished from the danger which befalls men through shipwreck, fire or the hazards of war. These are stories of men of our day who made danger their business and came back to write of the adventures into which their jobs took them.

M. C. S.

Contents

The Lure of Danger

The
*Philosophy of Danger**

by John D. Craig

JOHN D. CRAIG's *love of excitement has led him into hair-raising experiences all over the world, from tiger-shooting in India to deep-sea diving and undersea photography off the coast of California. This explanation of why men seek adventure, "The Philosophy of Danger," sums up well the attitude of his fellow adventurers and forms the introduction to his own story,* Danger Is My Business.

* "Philosophy of Danger" from *Danger is My Business* by John D. Craig, reprinted by permission of Simon and Schuster, Inc.

THE BOTTOM of the sea is my workshop, and I like it. It is like a mistress—dangerous, unpredictable—one minute caressing and giving all it has, the next minute furiously trying to destroy with power and cunning and tricks that are endless in variety. But ever since the first day I went down to it, in a rickety diving dress without safety valves or telephone, in fifty feet of water off the coast of Lower California, I have loved it more than any place I have ever been. And before that sunny day in the summer of 1931, I had been in thirty-five countries and had sailed on all of the seven seas and trod on all of the six continents. The bottom of the sea, covering four-fifths of the world, was the continent I finally chose. I was twenty-eight when I found it, and I had looked for many years.

A lot of water has drifted over my head since then, and over the heads of the men who dive with me in my crew. We've been down innumerable times. We've made the pictures you've seen on your local movie screens—the ones you've looked at calmly, and whispered about to your neighbors: "Faked. It's all done in a tank." Some of it has to be faked, of course, especially that part which concerns the hero and heroine, and the villain. But the rest is not faked.

We don't feel that we are taking our lives in our hands every time we dive, any more than a pedestrian feels that he is risking his neck when he crosses a street filled with moving automobiles. We are, of course, just as is the pedestrian, but the feeling is subconscious, as is his, and dulled by faith in our equipment and in our knowledge of the job. We have learned that there is not much danger when we can plot the hazards we are likely to meet. The members of my crew and I have been diving for six years, and we have never had a serious accident that could be blamed on either the equipment or our own negligence. We lost one man, and that was unavoidable—and, if you will believe old Antonio, fated.

When we began we were as ignorant as babes, and the Japs who taught us were little better off. They allowed us to come up as fast as we chose, and we did not know we were risking the bends. They decompressed in hot baths, and taught us to do the same. It wasn't until later that we found out about the dangers of pressure, and got hold of a Navy diving manual with charts of the safe time a diver can remain at each foot of depth, and the safe time for coming up from each foot of depth—decompressing.

The bends are nothing more than internal pressure built up inside the body by nitrogen which has liquefied under pressure. If the diver comes suddenly to the surface, this liquid nitrogen, released of pressure, returns to gaseous form, and lags in its escape, forming bubbles in the blood, in the joints, and along the spine. The pain, of course, is excruciating. Blood vessels may burst, and if one breaks in the brain, it is all over. After effects include paralysis, sometimes permanent, and a mental condition similar to punch drunkenness in fighters.

By decompressing the diver—that is, by bringing him up slowly, holding him stationary at points along the way—the lungs have a chance to gather the gaseous nitrogen from the blood and exhale it. Eventually all the gaseous nitrogen gets around to the lungs by way of the blood stream, and is exhaled. Then a diver can come out of the water into normal atmospheric pressure and suffer no ill effects.

If something goes wrong and a diver has to ascend quickly, either by inflating his dress and ballooning up or being drawn by the men in the boat, he can be put immediately into a recompression chamber, filled with compressed air which is brought to the same pressure at which the diver was working on the bottom. This can be gradually decreased until surface pressure is reached. Then the decompressed diver can be safely taken out. The Navy has recompression chambers but you seldom find them aboard an expedition ship. We've always decompressed in the water.

If something happens which makes it necessary for the diver to remain longer than is safe at his depth, decompression time is increased in ratio to the overtime, and usually everything turns out all right. None of my boys, nor I myself, has ever had a really severe attack of the bends, which is more credit to our luck, I think, than to our skill. Nowadays we take all precautions, but in the beginning we must have been guarded by angels.

There is, I suppose, something that has to do with courage in the business of deep-sea diving, but it never occurs to me that the word which means valor on the battlefield and sacrifice in the wars of peace has anything to do with me or my business. I know that my business is dangerous, but I accept that element much as a speculator in grain or wheat accepts the chances he takes of financial ruin.

Courage, it seems to me, is simply something that keeps logic from working, and allows a recklessness to operate which ordinarily would be termed irrationality. It has been that way with me. I have done things that were dangerous, and while I was doing them I have known that my mind was shutting out and gagging perfectly logical thoughts that strove to tell me I was being a damned fool. When the act is completed, and the logic enters unassailed, I do my trembling. But invariably I get in trouble again, and the curious something enters my mind and shuts out reason until it is over.

There is, of course, another kind of courage—and that, I think, is what is meant by the word. It is the courage which goes forward when logic is operating unhampered, and fright is right there, ruling your emotions. To go forward then is to be truly courageous.

There is also the courage that rises from a religious

principle instilled into men for two thousand years, until it is an instinct—the principle of brotherly love. That causes a man to go to the aid of another man in peril. There is no logic in this kind of courage, for frequently it operates when situations are hopeless. We all have that courage.

And there is still another kind of courage, which all men must have who deal with animals. An animal senses, or smells, fear and confidence and bravery. To win an animal's respect, you must show no fear, either of him or of anything else. That is a curious kind of courage, for it must often be engendered, and then logic must overcome logic and convince the mind that recklessness in this instance is wisdom.

I had to give myself that kind of courage the first time real danger confronted me. I was only seventeen, vacationing in the Ventura Mountains near Los Angeles, and blithely by myself I was taking eleven pack horses from Wheeler's Hot Springs, back of Ventura, up to Lathrop's ranch, eleven miles by a narrow trail up the Sespe watershed.

It was wild and lovely country. The sagebrush was seventeen feet high, for there hadn't been a fire there in thirty years. The trail was narrow, so much so that at turns we were told to whistle, so that anyone coming in the opposite direction would be warned. Except for the wired sagebrush there was nothing to keep horses and men from slipping off two hundred feet into a ravine below.

I was having a grand time, dreaming to myself, when Princess, my white horse, shied. The pack mule behind her immediately got hysterical and started to buck. When I got to the spot I saw a rattlesnake in the path, toward the edge that dropped off, between the first two horses. I had no gun. To get to one I would have to pass by either the rattlesnake or the bucking, pitching mule and the horses, which were shying. I couldn't get by them without being kicked and probably thrown off the trail.

They wanted me to kill the snake, I knew, and they expected it. I was scared. They knew this, too. The whole train was gradually getting into a panic. So I engendered courage by cursing my fright and forcing recklessness on myself.

I had a short rope, that was all, and a stick I had cut so that I could amuse myself by flicking the sagebrush. I tied the rope to the stick and flicked it at the rattler. He struck, his teeth caught, and I flipped him over the side of the trail and let go of the stick.

He was gone, but now the horses wouldn't pass the spot where he had been. I was shaking and quivering, but I had to convince them. Gradually I felt the flow of fear in myself quiet down, and another flow begin—one of confidence. I strutted to the horses, patted them, talked to them, and finally half led and half hauled Princess past the spot where the rattler had been. The first horse, safe beyond it, took up the journey then, the second followed, and the others went trembling by the danger spot while I shouted and laughed at them. Their lost leader,

I was informing them, had been found again. It wasn't a very convincing act, but it worked.

The kind of courage which operates in professional workers in danger, however, is the kind that has a monitor, a sort of censor which throws out logic until the danger is passed. This kind has possessed me more than any other, and I think it is the characteristic that makes a man an adventurer. That and the ability to recover from one close shave and not be affected by it when the next comes along. I have only been able to find that it is something—like blue eyes or red hair or six fingers—which some men have and others do not.

The average man in the shoes of Douglas Campbell, for instance—the lad who has been shooting tigers in India and shooting pictures under the sea—would long ago have retired to a farm to spend the rest of his days protecting his nose. But Campbell goes right on sticking his nose out, and getting it smashed.

He broke his nose first when he fell off a set of parallel bars in the gymnasium of the University of Southern California, where he went to swim and get an education. He smashed it next when he fell into a tiger pit in India and was spiked by a piece of bamboo. He broke it a third time against the cowl of a racing car he was driving around the track at Ascot, California. He smeared it to pulp against the inside of his diving helmet when he came up fast and struck the boat off Cedros Island. He put the finishing touches to it while driving a car through a house as a stunt for the movies. It isn't much of a nose nowadays, but Campbell is still pushing it into trouble.

It is that kind of philosophy, or lack of it—that kind of inability to reason the body into fear, that makes men take up danger as a business. Danger does not become a drug. It is not something that is desired. It is something that certain people are unable to think about, that's all.

To the professional worker in danger, however, there is a compensating factor. We find, as we study conditions under which we work, dangers which are not known to the layman. On the other hand we explode or debunk certain dangers in which the layman believes implicitly. Thus we are often afraid of things into which the average person would walk with the greatest assurance, while to things from which he would run we walk with a smile, knowing there is nothing to fear. We come to have a feeling toward danger which is entirely different from that of a person living a normal life. And we know that we cannot give way to fright. It would chase us out of our jobs.

Fear is a destroying thing. We regard it—my men and I—as a form of nervous shock which increases respiration, perspiration, and pulse count. Living with it we treat it as a problem, a problem which can be overcome by rhythmical breathing and by the application of the logic of comparison. We have known great fears and lesser fears, and by comparison the lesser fears are not important.

But we are not big, brave, fearless men. On the contrary, we often are scared badly. It is only that we have been frightened so often, and can thus grade fear by its intensity and actual threat to our lives, that we endure its constant presence. And we know that fear itself is our greatest danger. Once it succeeds in knocking us down, we aren't apt to get up. We can go back home to the farm then, and swat flies for excitement.

We find it best not to think about fear at all. Yet think about something a diver must, as he wanders around the sea bottom, or as he drifts slowly upward, his head clearing as he stops now and then to let the nitrogen out of his system. What occurs to me most frequently is an idea —an idea that perhaps life, instead of being a reality, is a fantasy, a dream, from which we will wake when we die. Having my mind clouded and partially shut off from me perhaps fathers that thought. I know what it is to watch mind, man's proudest possession, slip from me, leaving an inadequate animal body. It gives me curious ideas about the relative importance of mind and body. It has given me the belief that no matter what happens, there is still danger ahead. The things we do now may be nothing compared to what we will run into some day. And some day any one of us may step off a curb and go down under an automobile.

That is not a fatalistic philosophy. It is based on knowledge. When a man goes into the jungles of India to photograph tigers, the folks in New York City consider that he is deliberately risking his life. But in those jungles live natives who are exposed to these dangers from birth. They do not think they are deliberately risking their lives every day. They would think that of New Yorkers, though, if they could see them scurrying through traffic, riding in elevators in tall buildings, and tearing through underground tunnels on subway trains.

Some places are safer than others, of course. And yet the most alive thing in man, his mind, is at the mercy of his body whether he is in bed in a New England farmhouse or sleeping on a cot in the Indian jungle. The delicate mechanism of a human body can go awry at any moment. Usually it doesn't, so man feels safe. He regards things which may act upon him from without as his greatest menace. Most of these he has created himself: mechanically propelled vehicles, diseases which have arisen from community living, and hatred of one person or one race for another person or race. Nature, except when her own laws break down somewhat, causing a hurricane, an earthquake, or a volcanic eruption, is not a menace. Most animals, when let alone, do not bother man.

In the last analysis, man manufactures his danger. He flies through the air when he knows he is subject to gravity. He walks on the bottom of the sea when he knows he cannot breathe in water. He is constantly taking chances on annihilation. But if that thought had been constantly with him, he would be like a frightened rabbit, hiding still in caves. And he would be in more danger than he is now. He would be the prey of other animals. He would be hunted. In constructing a civilized world he has merely exchanged one danger for another. I say danger is my business, but actually it is every man's business. No matter what he does, death stands at his side. So why worry about it? Death may be, for all we know, a good deal more fun than living.

When I slip below the surface of the water in a diving dress, I do not think that I will die. If it comes I will meet it with whatever weapons are at hand, and do my best to stave it off. I do not believe, somehow, that it will come soon. I have a fanciful idea that I will be fairly long-lived. But one way or another, I already have more than a nodding acquaintance with death. It has only two possible things to offer—the lady and the tiger—sleep or a new adventure. Either might be attractive.

*The Terror of the Deep**

by Henry Wysham Lanier and Victor Berge

For stories of encounters with the giant clam, with sharks, and with octopuses, Pearl Diver *is the book. From the time he ran away from Sweden to go to sea until he found a profession in pearl diving,* Victor Berge *met more than his share of dangers. He admits there are two schools of thought on the viciousness of octopuses but he tells this story "The Terror of the Deep" to give his version.*

* "The Terror of the Deep" from *Pearl Diver* by Henry Wysham Lanier and Victor Berge, reprinted by permission of Doubleday and Company, Inc.

WE WERE OFF, on the Golden Adventure of a life which has had no lack of varied and unusual happenings.

We were Four Musketeers of the Sea, all for each and each for all; young, already devoted to each other, free, with plenty of money and plenty of time and no rules except those we made ourselves; with a trade that is a daily adventure; with a staunch little vessel under our feet for home; sailing away into the stretching wonder of the island world. Something new and memorable every day. The lure of the huge, perfect pearl, waiting for us in some weed-encrusted oyster at the bottom of the sea, which is like the Argonaut tales of the Golden Fleece to every pearler—and taking this perpetual gamble in the holiday mood of four youngsters, doing together just what they want to do.

That's a lot pleasanter calling than

> To be young, handsome, twenty-two,
> With nothing in the world to do
> But sit all day and bill and coo.

Those island maids Ro told of were in our minds, to be sure; but they were a decoration to the life, not the main object.

No wonder we called ourselves the Pearl Vikings and made up songs of oared galleys and raids to southward—though we contemplated no forceful raid except upon the unfortunate flaccid pearl oyster. No wonder we were utterly carefree and happy. We were a gay party as the little lugger slipped along to eastward.

While I had no notion of it, I had some stern and needed education coming to me. I was quite at home now in undersea work; I'd never had any serious accident or misadventure in this first year or more, though I had learned most things by actual experience with no guide; and I assumed unconsciously that I knew it all. I considered myself now a master pearler of the world.

Of course, one heard plenty of stories. I don't mean such ridiculous absurdities as the "first-hand" account of Skipper James Floyd of the *Pearl* (published as fact in Indian newspapers of 1874 and since reprinted in popular works) of how an octopus with a body "like the back of a huge whale" came aboard his 150-ton schooner, capsized her, and pulled her down, with two of the crew! What I'm referring to is the statements made by captains who at least know what another seaman, or diver, might swallow.

A master pearler of the world's fishing grounds is in quite different case from one who works a given locality. A man who spends his working life in fishing one group or region becomes familiar with the growth, the fish, the dangerous creatures of those special waters; he may know nothing whatever about what another man might find who's dived in many waters in widely separated corners of the globe.

It seems to me that is a main reason why there has been so much fiction masquerading as fact about the undersea monsters. That, and a certain tendency of marine biologists to assume that under-water life is the same in all the Southern seas as in those places where they have established stations for marine studies; or that they can make statements about the giant octopus because they have charted the anatomy and habits and strength of the insignificant creatures common in the Mediterranean or West Indies, or even the fossil octopods of Lebanon rocks; or because they have the results of oceanographic sweepings. I have made inquiries of a courteous museum expert in this branch of marine biology. It didn't trouble him in the least that he couldn't give me any reference whatever to scientific studies of cephalopods, or marine life in general, from any part of an island-studded ocean much larger than the continent of North America. No, "an octopus" could do so-and-so. I'm not stingy. I'd gladly give that nice gentleman and excellent naturalist a few moments of one particular experience of my own.

For, after all, what does our knowledge of deep-sea life amount to compared with the area to be explored—a total more than twice as large as the earth's land area—and the difficulties: peaks and mountain ranges and chasms and clefts and caverns beyond anything the land has to show? Just imagine yourself in a airship sailing over the Alps or the Alleghany Mountains for instance, unable to see down more than a hundred feet or so, exploring the life of that region by dredges or nets or traps or cylinders or sounding leads: how long might you be at it without obtaining any evidence, for example, of raccoons, which den up during the day in hollow trees or caves in the ledges? And the octopus is normally a cave-dweller.

Perhaps I shouldn't say it. But I know enough from observation to know how much there may be about which I know nothing. And I know enough to be highly skeptical of some of the positive "Noes" that science has uttered from the laboratory.

When pearlers get together each man naturally tries to make the most of his own experiences; they are fairly sure, after the bottle's been passed once or twice, to begin out-talking each other; some writer overhears these yarns and adds his own literary touches. Often the man who first related the tale wouldn't recognize it when it's printed.

Owing to this urge of mine to see new places and new people and new pearling beds, I have happened, during twenty years, to wander over a vast expanse: from Borneo to Easter Island, from the Marshalls to the lower Paumotus, probably covers twice as much space on the map as the whole of Africa. I've been down in countless places, drifted for miles and miles along the bottom behind my lugger. I feel I have some judgment to bring to bear on the truth of the tales related. I have been told by natives in the eastern Fijis of a big canoe full of men drawn under by an octopus, and of a Jap diver who went down near that spot in a suit—and never came up. I happen to believe that. But it has seemed to me more sensible to speak only of what I have seen with my own eyes—limited as must be the experiences of any one man, however afflicted with wandering feet.

Among all the strange undersea creatures which have interested me the octopus holds first place.

Speaking as a diver—not as a seaman, or a whaler, or anything else—this is the most formidable monster of our working world. He is, without sensationalism, the Terror of the Deep. I almost despair of giving a reader any adequate idea of the extraordinary creature. Still, here's the result of some years of acquaintance.

First of all, it has eight arm-feet, coming off from around a hideous mouth, very long in proportion to its body size, and these eight arms are just like eight boa constrictors all going at the same time, for their swift, flexible movements are precisely those of an active snake. When he stands up to the height of a man and oozes or darts forward, backward, sideways, any way, these eight sinuous arms are all going at the same time; when he climbs swiftly up over a cliff like a spider, or creeps under an overhanging reef, every part of these eight arms in continually doing something. He is horribly, squirmingly, frighteningly alive. And then suddenly he'll stop—and be as horribly dead, turn to any color to match his background, no matter what, mimic the shapes about him, lying in wait for prey. Under water one becomes accustomed to all sorts of startling color changes, as I've said, but there's no animal in all the world who can equal the octopus in imitating anything. The fishes are amateurs beside him: he'll imitate pink, red, purple, blue coral—I've seen him break out with dark stripes. As you study him, you feel the Creator has given him everything.

This "head-foot" mollusk (cephalopod) has along the inside of each of his eight arms a double row of protruding suckers which, when it clamps them firmly against anything, form a vacuum and cling like a monstrous leech; and where these radiating lines of suckers meet, around his voracious belly mouth, there is a perfect mesh of similar gripping suction disks. Any prey forced by these loathsome muscular, grasping arms into that pit of adhesiveness is held fast in the very jaws of destruction. For here gapes a great fleshy mouth, and, just within the opening, a big, hooked beak like an overgrown parrot or toucan. This horny weapon can cut or tear to pieces any soft flesh that reaches this torture chamber; it can rip open the shells of the crabs which seem to be a customary food.

There is a tremendous force back of all this terrible mechanism: the octopus seems to gulp down whole living creatures, or big gobbets ripped out, and somehow get rid of the bones. The size of the mouthfuls he will take in is quite incredible unless one has actually watched him feeding. Likewise the awful swiftness with which he digests it—like some devouring mechanism with fiery acids in its maw which instantly dissolve the ingredients poured into it.

Then his eyes! Fishes' eyes are usually dull, but I believe the octopus does most of its hunting at night. Anyhow, its eyes are quite different in expression from those of any sea creature I know. If any great painter should wish to picture the Devil—even if he specialized on that subject, like those morbid old mediæval artists—let him come down undersea with me and get the vision I have had: he will become famous for portraying the most sinister, terrible eyes that human imagination has ever depicted. They are not round but oval, slanting; not dark or large, but small, intent with that completely terrifying expression of cold malignity toward all other life. The rhinoceros has something of the same look, but he's generally in a childish temper; devilish is the only expression for this beast's alert, steady, evil glance.

The strength of these arms is almost unnatural. I believe some scientific investigators in the West Indies or Bermuda have tested the holding power of the baby specimens taken there, and my museum acquaintance quoted their report as showing that a man's strength could easily pull those suckers loose. That's like frolicking with a newborn lion cub and announcing that a full-grown lion is a nice safe playmate. I am speaking of what we call the giant octopus of Eastern and Southern seas—I haven't been able to learn from scientists whether it is a different species, or simply an extra large variety. As I shall explain, I have captured good-sized octopi alive and watched them for hours in a pool from which they couldn't escape. And I shall relate another even more pertinent experience. In my judgment a big serpent of the same size has nothing like the sheer muscular strength of these arms: the octopus has eight working in partnership, with no brittle backbone like the snake which can be paralyzed with one sharp blow; and it also has the aid of these powerful, gripping suction disks.

Watch one of these octopi standing up on these long, snaky arms, creeping sideways, shooting here and there, fixing his prey with that slant eye, oozing behind a boulder to lie in wait—I'd like to see the man heroic enough to go down and challenge him to a fight! There is no shark, no matter what its size and voracity, that is so repulsive and fearful to every human instinct.

We haven't begun as yet to list his queernesses. As I say, the Creator gave him everything in the way of equipment.

He has a funnel-shaped cavity in his body, opening by a tube below his mouth, with a pair of gill plumes by which he breathes, but having a return valve much like that on a diving helmet; this valve he can close at will. (The biologists declare it a rudimentary hind foot.) This funnel, six inches to a foot long, is the siphon (or midfoot.) He takes in water through the tube, extracts oxygen, and squirts out the liquid from his siphon: you

can follow his slow breathing by these jets like the discharge of an automatic pump.

But the most spectacular function of this siphon is its use to shoot the mollusk swiftly to a distance. For this formidable creature has three distinct methods of locomotion. He can crawl nimbly like a huge spider, on the bottom or over rocks, with these eight flexible arms moving like walking snakes. He can paddle or swim through the water with a kind of rowing motion. But above all, when he is attacking, he can hurl himself to a distance by air-and-water pressure through this siphon. With a powerful, swift effort he can expel the water and air through this funnel and shoot himself backward like a rocket, fifty to a hundred feet, almost faster than the eye can follow him. It seems to be a trick he uses for attack, and it is a tiger's spring—the fastest movement I have seen in the water world. His long arms trail back close to his body; he steers both with them and the siphon, I fancy; and the instant he reaches his mark those snaky arms whip around it, the scores of suckers fasten tight, he drags it down. If it is very large or active he must get hold of an anchoring place with a couple of arms.

Nobody who hasn't seen it could credit the catlike swiftness and savagery of these long-distance assaults.

In addition to all this, masking his movements and for defence, he possesses an ink sac. When he wants to cover up his retreat and prepare for another attack, he can squirt out a cloud of this blue-black liquid, laying his own smoke screen for yards about, while he darts in among the rocks and creeps out for an assault from an unexpected point. He has the cunning of a fox. This ejection is odorless down below, and after some emptyings of the sac the animal must have time to renew it; I have prodded a captive with a bamboo pole: he kept squirting ink for several minutes, then the supply of coloring matter ran dry; but the amount of protective discoloration a large octopus can produce in the water is extraordinary.

It has no proper heart, but a ventricle outside the cœlum cavity, on each side of which is an extension of a vein serving as an auricle. When an arm is cut off, one sees no blood—just a little bluish ooze. And one of these arms of a male is modified at breeding time and is used to fertilize the eggs in the female.

The sacklike body is most elastic, capable of changing shape like a rubber bag; the creature can twist and stretch this fleshy ball till it is like a snake, and it will crawl into holes and crevices which look impossible to its size when normally rounded.

I've read the scientists' theory that the first beasts crawled from under the seas up on the land. This thing must have crawled the other way. Personally, I'm convinced that the chief reason we know so little about him is that his true home is in depths of a hundred fathoms or more. We know just nothing from actual observation of six-hundred-foot depths undersea. He lives down there, this giant octopus, and the only time he comes even to the shallows is during the breeding season. (The adult, that is. The baby octopi swarm in the shallow water at times, even on the beach. They are a standard article of food.)

They are always in pairs when man comes in contact with them; and the time a pearl diver has to be on guard is in this breeding period.

The female, larger than the male, finds a quiet place, some deep crevice or lonely cavern—for this creature is essentially a cave-dweller; and, cunning fox as he is, one might haul drags past his retreat year in and year out without ever bringing up evidence of his presence. In this safe solitude the female lays long strings of eggs, like ropes with knots hanging there in the cavern. It continually siphons these eggs, some of which are the size of a man's thumb, and both parents hang about until they hatch out, the whole process taking apparently a couple of months.

The young octopi go straight to the surface, play around the rocks, lie along the beach; they seem to enjoy sunning themselves. When they are three or four months old they begin to go down. As they reach full size I am sure they are living in the deeps—though, of course, not below the stratum where there is abundant sea life, for, like sharks, they prefer live food.

I have attempted to set down some of the more striking facts as I have been able to observe and learn them; but no description could do justice to the living, prowling, lurking, attacking creature.

I always think of him as the most extraordinary actor in the animal world (or any other world). He can mimic anything. Changing his color through the whole range, he can also push out lumps and knobs on top of his head, on the backs of his arms, to resemble the roughnesses of the coral rock. "Making up" before your eyes, he is one thing now and a completely different thing a moment later. In school I read the Greek myth of Proteus, the old man of the sea, who changed from shape to shape in the hands of anyone who caught hold of him—leopard, snake, bush, fire: it no longer seems impossible when you've watched this mimicking thug of the deeps. You stand there, not believing your own eyes. Then he lurks like a crafty spider; camouflaging himself into invisibility; instead of a web, holding ready these swift, snaky, suckered arms; waiting for his prey to come within range. When a fish touches one of these deadly living strands of the web it often seems stunned as if by an electric shock. Not a kick out of it. One touch and it is food.

I have often wondered why these incredible creatures should have their home down in these deep, dark waters; it must be an entirely different life there; one cannot imagine such a place—the picture of hell cannot begin to equal it: these creeping, darting, vicious monsters dodging about, fighting for supremacy a hundred fathoms below the surface. Who knows what else may live in that fearsome world, never coming up in contact with human activities except possibly, like the octopus, to reproduce and give its young a start before they can stand such pressure?

It seems to me some of the confusion about him is like two people quarrelling over what they know about "cats": one is discussing the house cat, or even the wild cat; the other has had experience with the big cats, say, an African lion. There are many species of octopus. I am talking about the lion of the family, the giant who rises periodically from his deep home caverns to give birth to a new generation. That is my octopus.

While there is almost no danger from them except in the neighborhood of submarine caves, it happens, unfortunately, that shell often grows around just such formations, on the shelves, or on overhanging ledges. Hence the chance for an unpleasant or fatal encounter at these times.

I had listened to plenty of awed tales, by natives and white men, of this monster of the water underworld.

At nineteen, with my own experience, day after day, on many beds, my answer had always been, "Rubbish!"

Then I got my first lesson in this particular sea mystery.

We were coming down from northeast Borneo to Macassar Strait. That is in my opinion the meanest, ugliest, most godforsaken coast in all the world, a succession of dirty rivers and swamps and reefs and real "wild men of Borneo" and fevers. A ghastly country. Even the ocean is discolored far out from these mucky rivers pouring in —none of that crystal clearness of the South Seas or even the Moluccas. We were just above the Equator, perhaps forty miles north of Cape Mangka-Tihat, when we sighted a couple of little islands. Ro found out from one of the crew that the nearest one was called Bilangbilangan, that it was uninhabited, and that there were turtles there. So we put in to get turtle—for that means eggs and fresh meat and tortoise-shell to a rover of Eastern seas.

This island is at the tip of a huge shoal stretching twenty miles from shore, and there's a narrow deep passage between it and Muaras Reef. You can sail for miles over twenty or thirty feet of water, and then suddenly the bottom pitches down to five hundred or a thousand feet.

As is customary with every pearler, I was watching the sea floor while we moved easily over these shallows toward land. I noticed a number of patches here and there: they began to interest me.

"Gee!" said I, "it looks like shell here."

It looked good—these shell, the current, all the signs a diver learns which are so hard to describe. Ro went down after a while, and I tendered him.

Presently he came up with a piece of small shell which we always go by a lot.

"By God!" he said. "I no find. But it look like shell all right."

We grew excited: finding a new and virgin bed is an adventure that never fails to get a pearler keyed up.

"I'll go down and have another look-see," I told him.

Getting into the suit, I started to explore thoroughly, gliding up and down over these patches, drifting along behind the lugger, straining my eyes for the first glimpse of the big pearl oysters which had come to be my special game in my submarine hunting.

The water was fairly deep, about twenty fathoms. To one side of me there was, not exactly a hole, but an open space between masses of coral: I fancied I could distinguish something lying down there suspiciously like real shell. So I worked my way over these boulders down into this flat well.

The object which had drawn me there seemed more than ever what I was seeking so keenly. I stooped down to pick it up. And at that instant I felt something touch me quite lightly on the left arm.

Instinct and under-water training saved my life. Quick as a flash, before I had the least notion of what it was, I whirled about, grabbing the razor-sharp knife from my belt sheath, and slashed three or four times with a full sweep of my arm in the direction of this touch. By luck I severed two of the lassooing arms that were gripping me; in another instant the octopus would have had my two arms pinioned and I should have been helpless.

As I slashed and felt the blade cut through a mass of soft flesh, two more arms laid hold of me, one around each ankle. I felt a vicious jerk at my legs which almost upset me.

It all sounds melodramatic when one recounts it in protected civilization. Yet no description in words could paint the horror of that moment. It was rather murky in this place, but I could see a sort of shapeless mass and wavering, squirmy arms—even one severed stump—ahead there by the rocks; and I knew only too well now that this was the Thing which had produced those fearsome native tales I had pooh-poohed. I had a swift picture of my companions above pulling up severed, dangling life-line and air-hose; of a human being, that was myself, gripped close to the maw of this loathsome monster.

Meanwhile I was fighting automatically. Each time I would bend to try to cut my ankles free, the creature would jerk me so violently that I seemed to be a little boy pulled about at will by a strong man; it was with the greatest difficulty that I kept my footing. The helmet and breastplate banged against my head and chest with punishing force. One jerk dashed me against a rock and left me breathless. The force of the beast was terrific and produced a deathly sense of fear. Also, the cold intelligence with which he appeared to anticipate my actions, and checkmate my every attempt, had a deep effect on nervous resistance.

It was life or death. My body and mind were working as if they had no relation to each other: one was straining, struggling, fighting against these shattering tugs, trying to cut, to stab, to free myself; the other, somewhere, was carefully weighing chances, considering the elements of the situation, attempting to decide whether I dared give the danger signal.

That's the last thing a diver resorts to in an emergency —four pulls, meaning, "Pull until the line breaks." The emergency was there all right; but the trouble was that I feared my air-pipe and life-line might have become tangled in some of these coral projections all about: should they be fouled, such a strain from above might easily cut them off or leave me hopelessly jammed into some crevice. A man working under water always has those two lines of communication in his subconscious mind; it becomes automatic never to take action without making sure neither has been fouled. And little chance I had in this fix to check up on that!

All this time our strange duel was continuing. I was using all my strength to resist the creature's pulls, while striving to cut more of these living fetters which bound me. (There seemed to be a mass of them, twice as many as in reality, coiled, all about.)

To add to my difficulties I found my weights, where I was getting hit, were swinging the wrong way: I had to keep my helmet above my body—otherwise the air there gets into the body and legs of the suit and a man is finished. The outlet valve had to be manipulated, and through all this struggle I must remain erect, righting myself after every jerk at my ankles.

And it was as if that devilish brain in that voracious pulpy creature understood all this perfectly: the instant my hand would stretch down with the big knife he'd give a terrific jerk, sometimes dragging me ten or fifteen feet, jamming the heavy helmet against my jaws and skull, bruising me against the rough, crusted rock wall. All this in a pool now blackened and turbid with the ink the beast had squirted out.

Occasionally I'd get help in righting myself from a strain on the life-line and air-line; and after a while a slight current seemed to set through and carry off some of the thickest discoloration.

When I got a glimpse of that disgusting mass of arms and squirming legs, and especially one look into those diabolical eyes, I stretched up to give the danger signal. Instantly the octopus yanked me a dozen feet, and I had all I could manage just not to topple over.

The thought flashed through my mind: "This is exactly like Hell." For it was all this foul, unnatural, dirty black, and this unbelievable thing had me in its grip, bent on devouring me.

Apparently what I have been telling must have occupied ten to fifteen minutes. At the time it was an eternity to me—there was nothing before or after this nightmare struggle. I began to realize I could not last much longer. The first severe knock with the helmet had cut and bruised and dizzied me; the subsequent rough handling and battering against the coral had worn down my strength, till I perceived I was lost unless something were done quickly. It no longer seemed a desperate measure to take a chance on my air-hose's being clear.

All at once I knew I was going. Just before the wave of fear-freighted unconsciousness swept over me I threw up my arms, caught both lines, gave four frantic pulls. There was an instant when I had the sensation of being pulled in two lengthways. Then I knew nothing.

Up above, Ro had been tending me from the lugger's deck. He could see nothing down there, but his experience and water sense told him something was wrong. All during that eventful quarter of an hour he had been waiting, taut, fearing to destroy me if he acted before receiving some signal, yet certain I was in trouble.

Then my four jerks spelled out extreme peril.

Ro pulled. Nothing budged. He shouted to a man at the pumps. This fellow ran across the heaving deck—there was quite a swell on the surface—and lay to behind him. Still no give. In a frenzy he brought a third man. He was in a quandary now: the life-line is a light affair and would hardly stand three good men's full effort, particularly if caught in the rocks.

The situation seemed desperate: they put forth all their strength. They could not stir whatever was holding me down below.

It was then that Ro's quick thinking saved me from a horrible death. The boat was rising and falling on this swell, which had been getting heavier. He leaped back, took several turns around a stout stanchion, ordered the two men to strain up till my life-line and air-hose were taut and rigid just as the lugger was at the bottom of one of these surges. The ocean swell picked her up, and the full force of the lift came on my two tight lines.

I fancy my captor must have been caught momentarily off balance, or perhaps while shifting those two anchoring arms, by which he had been fastened to a solid support and enabled to shake me as a terrier shakes a rat.

Anyhow, I shot suddenly up to within ten or fifteen feet of the surface.

I do not know why, but it was at this moment I regained consciousness with a jerk.

I knew I must be near the top, from the light above. I woke to that same dream of being pulled in two: looking down, I could see the sea-demon's suckered arms were still fast about my ankles; the loathsome mass of his body was suspended below. It was not a pleasant wakening.

There was nothing I could do. Impossible to stretch down and free my legs with that pull on them and the lines pulling up. The octopus was pulling with all its force, siphoning violently. Fortunately I did not have to do anything.

The instant I was close enough to see what was the matter, Ro yelled at the men to pull hard. Deftly he got a stouter line about my body. Two more men caught this and hauled me upward.

Ro slipped into the water, his big knife ready. In two sure slashes he had cut off those horrible arms.

The two men hauled me to the surface, more dead than alive, with the pieces of suckered feelers still coiled about my legs.

They got me on deck and took off the helmet. I looked, and felt, as if I had been through the worst fight of my life—blood all over my face and neck and shoulders, hands and arms and legs torn from the action of the suckers, bruised from head to foot by the bangings about. I was pretty well all in. My eyes closed. They thought for a moment I was dying.

Someone ran for a glass of brandy and poured it down my throat. The fiery stuff brought me somewhat to my senses. I opened my eyes and looked about.

There they were, my three chums, standing about in the bright sunlight, with anxious faces. But they and the familiar lugger and all those things I knew so intimately looked quite strange. It must be that if a dead man could come back to life he would feel as I did then.

First I laughed, and then I cried. Hysterical, just like a nervous woman. What with their fright and the sight of that beast, my companions were in bad shape themselves. They needed a drink and then another. We did not do much work for the next three days.

The Story of Michels *

by Tom Eadie

Few books of adventure can beat TOM EADIE'S I Like Diving, *the simple and unpretentious but engrossing account of his career as a Navy diver. He went into submarines in 1909 when submarine duty was volunteer duty; he became a diver and later served as a civilian diving instructor; in 1926 he re-enlisted in the Navy as a diver and became one of the outstanding men in the profession. He did his job with quiet skill and was always in demand when danger threatened. "The Story of Michels" from his* I Like Diving *is his account of the S-4 disaster and of the courageous rescue which won him the Medal of Honor.*

* "The Story of Michels" from *I Like Diving* by Tom Eadie, reprinted by permission of Houghton Mifflin Company.

THE PAULDING STRUCK the S-4 at 3:37 on the afternoon of Saturday, December 17, 1927, and I first heard of it through a telephone message from the Newport torpedo station to my home in Newport, at 6:15.

I had been in Fall River with my wife and daughter that afternoon, doing Christmas shopping, and we had just come home and had had our supper.

"Come to the station immediately," was the order on the telephone. "The S-4 has been sunk." I was in civilian clothes, but I changed into uniform, got out, begged a ride to the ferry—which is about a mile from my home—and caught the boat that left at 6:25. I remember that, during that whirl of changing my clothes, my wife was standing by, wildly anxious, and I was trying to tell her what had happened and dress at speed at the same time.

At the station I was met by Commander Causey, the executive officer. He told me the details of the disaster, and asked me what gear would be required. I said, "Hardly any; only men will be needed. The Falcon will undoubtedly have all the gear that is needed."

He said word had been sent to all the station's divers,

but that I was the first to report. They were even then coming in one by one: Michels, Carr, who was a member of the Falcon's crew, but was on leave at his home in Jamestown, Bailey, Burd, Brown, Winters, Anderson, Hawkes—there were about eleven in all.

We left in three machines. Captain Hart lent his; Commander Causey his, and Lieutenant Matthews not only gave his car, but drove it himself. While we were loading up the cars, the Captain called up the State Police and asked them to meet us and clear a way for us. We were met at the Two-Mile Corner outside of Newport, and the motorcycle policeman pulled us along all the way to the outskirts of Fall River.

In the meantime, word had been telephoned ahead to the Massachusetts State Police, and we were met in Pleasant Street, Fall River, by one of their men. He took us as far as his authority would take him, and then said, "You've got a hundred miles straight away now. Good luck to you; I wish I could go with you."

Lieutenant Matthews said, "All right. Now, boys, you can settle back for a sleep." Can you imagine anybody's sleeping with the thought of what we were coming to on our minds?

Of course, we talked a good deal over the possibility that there might be still somebody alive in the submarine, but we were well agreed that there was practically no chance—that it was just another salvage job.

We couldn't see the reason for all the hurry, in fact—and we were certainly hurrying. It was one of the wildest rides in my whole experience. But I think the Navy Department should be given great credit for carrying on when anybody connected with the game and knowing the conditions would have said that there wasn't a chance in a thousand that life still existed in the submarine. You see, she was sunk while still submerged, and that meant that everything would be open below, and if she had sunk she was cut into, and if she was cut into she would have filled with water.

We were going fast, and we didn't know the roads too well. So we had many a quick stop to make sure of our way; once in so often all of us would be piled up in a heap in the car. It was a wonder that with three cars traveling like that we didn't have an accident. We did have a narrow escape in New Bedford from a collision with a trolley car.

We reached Provincetown at 12:30 that night. The Falcon wasn't in; she had been at New London, and on the first unconfirmed report had begun to make ready for a quick start. They were all ready to let go and start when the report was confirmed; she was under way just sixty-eight minutes after the first report reached her. She got in early the next morning.

Lieutenant Matthews went to report our arrival, and returned about 2 A.M. He decided that, as we couldn't get out to the wreck we would better get a little sleep, and he got rooms for us in a lodginghouse.

The town was already swarming with reporters and photographers. They were all over us; they wanted to know who we were, where we came from, how many of us there were, and when we were going out.

Even after we got turned in, one man came into our rooms. He asked so many foolish questions that the crowd began kidding him. I was laughing myself sick, and I'd say after each story they'd tell him, "Tell him another." Later, I realized that when you kid a reporter you are really kidding the public.

A young gale had been blowing all the afternoon and evening, and next morning—Sunday—it was even worse. The only boat safe for us to go out in was a surfboat belonging to the coast guard at Wood End.

They took us out, with a dory towing astern of the surfboat. When we got out to the scene of the wreck, it was so rough we couldn't go alongside the Falcon. So we went to windward of her, and two of us got into the dory. I was one of the two. Then the men in the surfboat slacked her down alongside the Falcon, I threw my suitcase aboard, and when there was a chance I climbed aboard myself.

Captain Hartley met me. "Eadie," said he, "you'll be the first man to go down."

I said, "All right, sir, as soon as I get into my gear."

We were not even sure then that we had the S-4's position. The coast guard had grapneled, and had hooked onto some object on the bottom. But what they had caught onto could not be known until the catch was "proved" by a diver.

The Wandank was already at Provincetown, lying in

the inner harbor. During the day the Bushnell arrived, and she served as a repair ship and machine shop, though she was not nearly so elaborately outfitted as the Vestal, which we had had on the S-51 job. The Mallard also arrived, and tugs from the Boston yard.

The Falcon was anchored right over the submarine, on the mark set by the coast guard. She wasn't moored out, for there was too much sea running to place moorings, and it wasn't yet sure it was the submarine we had found.

I went over the side on the stage. It was bitter cold; the vessel was rolling, and but for the many hands that crowded to hold the stage steady, I should have been smashed against the Falcon's side.

They lowered me quickly, and I was soon below the send of the sea; for you get the forward motion of a sea only so far below the surface as its height above the surface. That is, a wave five feet high will give you a "send" five feet below the surface. When you get deeper than that, the only effect of the sea on the diver is the varying pressure when a wave passes over him. This is a serious effect—and in deep-sea work, where there is always more or less of a swell, it is always present. If a wave two feet high passes over you, you get a sudden increase of pressure amounting to one pound of square inch—really almost a ton on your whole body.

As soon as I was well under the water, I tested everything, telephone, valves, and the suit for leaks, and then left the stage and slid down on the grapnel line. On that dive I wore a suit with gloves on it, and carried nothing but a hammer with me. The hammer was for the purpose of tapping signals on the various compartments of the submarine, though I never for a moment thought there would be such a thing as life aboard of her.

I went down one hundred feet in less than fourteen seconds, and landed between the two periscopes. I had come down so fast that my shoes hit there with a clang that was heard by the six men imprisoned in the torpedo-room. And I thought I heard a signal.

I said at once over the telephone, "It is the submarine." Then I looked round. The visibility was very poor. The current was running thwartships, and stirred up the mud, making the water terribly murky. To make it worse, the day was overcast, and so there was very little light there at all.

I jumped down to the forward deck locker, and this time I heard another signal, and heard it plain. They were pounding, inside of her, and I said, "My God, a signal."

I knew exactly where it came from, and I didn't have to waste my time running around frantically hunting for it, but could run directly to it. I had to climb over the gun, which was slewed round to port, and had its breech up and its muzzle down.

As I walked—or rather, ran—along the narrow deck, I found loose pieces of wreckage lying about—bits of metal that I could pick up and throw overboard. They were bits broken off the Paulding and off the S-4's own superstructure deck. Larger twisted and bent pieces were all snarled up in a heap forward of the gun.

The Paulding had ridden right over her, and I could see where she had cut across the superstructure deck to within four inches of its outboard edge.

I climbed over the gun, and into a tangled mess of wreckage. The way she looked, she was far worse off than the S-51 ever thought of being—that is, going by the open wreckage you could see.

I picked my way over the mess to the place where I knew the sounds were coming from, the torpedo loading hatch. This is the only opening from the deck into the torpedo-room, and the way those men would have had to come out if they came at all. The men were pounding on the torpedo-room hatch, which is just inside the loading hatch. That loading hatch, by the way, has on its inner side two little tracks; it doesn't open all the way back, but is stopped on a slant, and when torpedoes are being loaded, they are cradled in the two little tracks and slid down on the proper slant.

I banged with my hammer a number of times on the hatch, holding my other hand down on it to feel the vibration of any response. I got a response at once, and it seemed to hit right under my hand. They made six taps. Every time they signaled, it was six taps.

The vibration of it was so strong that it was transmitted through my body and to my telephone line. The man tending my telephone told me afterward that before I told him there was life aboard, he already knew it. He said, "I could hear your signal and their answer, and I could tell the difference between them."

As soon as I had their answer, I banged the hatch again a few times as a message of good cheer; I didn't have any Morse, but I just let them know we were on the job. I telephoned to the topside, "Life aboard in forward torpedo-room." Then I headed toward the bow of the boat, telling them over the telephone I was doing so. I found the bow was covered with mud. This showed that the boat had gone to the bottom on a sharp angle and had scooped up the mud with her bow. She was lying on a level keel, both fore and aft and thwartships.

The idea of going to the bow was so that the people on the topside could trace my bubbles and so know the boat's position as she lay on the bottom, and would know how to set the moorings as soon as it was possible to go to work.

I reported every bit of information, as fast as I came to it. I told them, "There is a mess of wreckage—she looks very bad; worse than the 51—I am on the hatch—I am on the bow—her bow is covered with mud—I am now going aft."

All this time the men inside never sent another signal. I figure that they knew what I was doing, and that I would try to signal other compartments. If I did, and they replied, they knew it would only confuse me, and so they kept still.

"Gee, Eadie," I said to myself, "if you never do anything more in your whole life, inspire those men in there with the confidence that we on the topside are onto our job, and doing every last thing we can."

I fully realized their predicament, and that because of the bad weather and heavy sea at the surface we had little chance to work quickly—and only speed could save their lives.

I got aft to the conning tower and tapped on it, but got no answer. Worse than that, you can tell by the sound when you tap a metal plate like that whether the space behind it is full of water or empty so that it sounds hollow. And I knew the conning tower was full.

That one thing alone settled the question of the crew being able to do anything to help us help them. The control-room, or central operating compartment, was right under the conning tower, and I knew it was full of water.

The men forward didn't signal even when I tapped the conning tower. You see, they could figure exactly what I was doing.

Now I ran along the deck, going aft, until I was brought up by a sudden jerk. In my anxiety to cover the ground as fast as I could I had not been as watchful as I should have, and I had run into the boat's tangled radio antenna, which had been carried away by the collision. It was found on one side of my helmet on the spitcock, and on the other side on the exhaust valve.

They noticed on the topside that I had stopped, and that I hadn't traveled the length of the boat.

"Are you in trouble?" the tender asked. "What's happened?"

"I'm foul in the antenna, but I'm all right and can clear myself shortly."

I did get clear, and tried to move farther aft. Still I couldn't; I was held up somehow. I pulled at my hose and life line to get some slack, and it wouldn't come. Then, looking up, I saw that I was foul round the submarine's little yardarm.

"I guess I can't get any farther aft," I told the topside. "I'm foul on the yardarm. But I'll lie down and stretch out as far as I can, and try a tap."

As it was, I just did reach the engine-room hatch, and sent a few signals, without getting any response. And then I was perfectly assured that there was nobody alive inside the boat excepting the men in the forward torpedo-room.

I got back to the conning tower and climbed it to clear my lines from the yardarm, about seven feet above me. When I came down from the tower, knowing that what they would try next would be to blow the ballast tanks from the topside, I went to the side of the cutwater on the conning tower and opened the hatch there, though without any instructions to do so. There is a hatch on each side of the cutwater, containing the external connections to the ballast tanks and the compartments. These hatches and connections are placed there for this very emergency which had occurred.

I told the topside then that I had completed my inspection and opened the hatch, and what did they want me to do. They answered, "You've been down long enough. Stand by to come up; we have another man ready to go over."

This man was Bill Carr, and while I was going up he was coming down; I saw him pass me. He was carrying with him an air hose, to hook onto the external connections, to blow the ballast tanks, and if possible to make her light enough and bring her to the surface. They figured that if the ballast tanks were flooded it would be through the Kingston valves, and they could also be blown through that opening.

There was a chance that the ballast tanks were not flooded, for she was just at the surface and coming up when she was hit. Her tanks might have been already blown. This would not help, however, if the compartments were all flooded and the ballast tanks dry; she would still be held down.

As soon as Carr had hooked up, the Falcon was moved a little away from the position, in the hope that the boat would come up—and so as to be out of the way of her—and started blowing.

After they had given her all the air they could get together, they blew for half an hour. Then a big eruption of air was seen at the surface—and that attempt was a failure. It was readily seen that one of the tanks must have been ruptured by the collision, so it was useless to carry on any further in that respect: there was nothing to be gained, and it wasn't possible to make an external patch on her, except by a long job.

The men in the S-4 didn't signal to Carr at all. I figure they could hear him hitching up to the connection and hear the air going into her. It took him perhaps ten minutes to make his hitch, and it was just an hour and ten minutes from the time we started that the air was going into her. Those men, being experienced, could undoubtedly tell what was happening.

On the topside, as soon as they knew there was life aboard the submarine, they got the oscillator of their submarine signal system overside and sent signals. I think the first signal—they were in Morse—was to ask what the conditions were. The answer was, "There are six in the torpedo-room with fifteen inches of water and a slow leak."

This was close to noon on Sunday, for I had gone down about eleven. Carr came up before the Falcon started to blow the tanks, and nothing else could be done until this plan had been tried and found useless.

The next thing to try was to put air into the compartments. This meant taking the gags off the lines at the connections inside the hatch on the cutwater. The diver, instead of taking off the air hose already set on the tank connection, to save time would take down another hose line and set that onto the connection to the compartments.

By this time, it was getting dark and the sea was getting worse all the time.

Let me say right here that diving has never been attempted before under such desperate conditions as we had, and it never will be tried again unless by a man of the United States Navy. No commercial diver would think of doing it.

Every time you went over the side, it was an attempt at suicide, because of the sudden increase of pressure every time a sea went over you. There was a ten-foot rise and fall of the waves; with one pound pressure to every two feet that meant five pounds additional pressure, suddenly applied and as suddenly taken off again, to the square inch of your body. A man's body is approximately two thousand square inches of surface, and that means five tons of pressure for the five pounds per square inch. It causes intense waves of pain in the ear drums; it may burst them, and it can quite simply kill a man.

It was bitter cold. The seas were by this time coming aboard the Falcon, and the tenders standing along the rail and holding a man's lines, or watching his air or handling his telephone, were hit by the spray and solid water that came over the rail and were rapidly coated with ice.

Before a diver going over the side could get under water, the spray and wind had made him a mass of ice. The cold lets up a little when you actually get under water, but if you have got chilled before that, you never do come back. You stay chilled.

But Captain King said, "We must get air in there to-night. It's to-night or never." So they looked round for the best man to send, and decided on Fred Michels. He went down, taking the second hose.

When he had been down three quarters of an hour, and

they had heard nothing from him for quite a while, they grew anxious. He said he was badly fouled and asked them to send me down. They couldn't understand him very well, but he seemed to be saying, "Send Eadie. Cutters, Eadie, cutters."

They came down for me. I was in my bunk; it was about five and a half hours since I had made my dive, and after an hour below, I had been decompressed on board the Falcon, in the chamber. I had got warm, had something to eat, and turned in and gone to sleep.

Captain Hartley, the commanding officer, came down himself and woke me.

"Mike is foul," he said, "and it looks kind of bad. Will you go after him?"

"Yes, sir," I said. "I'll be up as soon as I can." And I was in such a hurry that, instead of putting on three suits of underwear, as we usually did in that cold weather, I put on only one.

On the topside I asked for a suit without any gloves, for I knew I should need the freedom of my hands.

The temperature of the water that night was thirty-four degrees and putting your hands into it was like putting them into freezing brine, and was extremely painful.

By this time, too, the seas were coming well over the rail and giving everybody a good ducking. In fact, they had to put up a canvas shield to make a lee where I could get dressed without getting sopping wet before I even went over the side.

I got into my outfit, and before putting the helmet on

tried the telephone. It wouldn't work. Of course, it had been tested after it was taken off the last man who used it. But apparently it had been capsized by the roll of the ship and some water had slopped into it and put it out of commission. That meant taking off the breastplate—since the breastplates are fitted to the helmets, and won't fit other helmets—and getting another. It also meant more delay for Michels, down below in the dark, before some one could get to him.

They fetched another breastplate and helmet, and the telephone in this one worked all right.

Captain Hartley said, "We are still talking with Mike, but we can't hear him very well. I can't make it out, but it seems to be cutters, wire cutters, so I'm giving you a heavy pair of wire cutters."

"All right," said I, "but put in a hammer, a chisel, and small crowbar." And I put these tools in the bag on top of the wire cutters.

Carr had shifted the descending line when he went down to a cleat forward, clear of the wreckage, so to save time I went down on Michels' own line, carrying a thousand-watt lamp, and landed close by Mike, who was lying in the wreckage on deck, forward of the gun. He never had made his connection at all.

Mike was lying face down in the wreckage, and there were at least eight turns of his lines woven back and forth across his back. There must have been one hundred and fifty to one hundred and seventy-five feet of his hose and life line laid back and forth across that deck. It was caught in the wreckage on one side, and on the other, on what afterward proved to be a piece of the bow of the Paulding that was sticking in the gash in the hull.

Mike's pickle was due to the storm that was blowing on the surface. The Falcon, lying to an anchor, naturally would yaw. As she went off to one side, Michel's lines would come taut, and the tender had to give him some slack or haul him off the deck of the sub.

When the limit of the yaw came, and the Falcon began to go the other way, the line and hose lying on the bottom promptly became a bight, a long, narrow loop. The tender wouldn't notice any slacking and even if he did, he couldn't have taken it up much without pulling Mike away from his work.

But when the ship had gone over to the other side, the loop would catch on a piece of wreckage. Again the tender had to give slack while the yaw kept up in that direction; again it changed back, and another bight came sweeping across the bottom, this time to catch in the fragment of the Paulding's bow. As it came across, it just happened to land across Mike's shoulders; had he been six feet forward or aft of where he was, it wouldn't have caught him. But it did, and pressed him down on the deck.

Mike said afterward that he didn't know at all what had happened to him. All he knew was that he was pulled down to the deck. But I think he was pushed down. Anyway, after he was down the yawing went on, and the turns were laid on top of him.

Mike wasn't to blame for getting foul. It was through no inattention of his. Nor was his tender to blame for his part, in giving the slack. It was the result of conditions on the surface, that's all.

I first tried to clear him. I saw one bight that was caught in an angle iron, down on the side of the boat, that was bent into a U-shape, and I realized that if the line could get into that U it could get out.

So I got down over the side. I couldn't see, even with the light, but I felt down below the angle iron, got hold the line, braced my foot and pulled. But with all my strength I couldn't get it out.

I wasn't talking to the topside much. I simply told them, "It's quite a mess here. Don't bother me."

I saw that if I started anywhere but where I was, I should get the snarl into a worse mess yet. Even the part on which I came down to where it was caught was underneath several other lengths, and it couldn't be freed till they were off. I never saw such a mess.

As soon as I had sized up the situation with the light, I realized that the wire cutters were absolutely useless. They couldn't cut the angle iron. I came to the conclusion that the best way would be to saw through the angle iron, through the bight of the U, and let Michels stand up on his feet. So I telephoned up for a hacksaw, and told them to shackle it onto my light wire; it would come down quicker than as though they sent it on my line, where it might hang up on hose connections. When I got it, I went over to Mike.

I hadn't spoken to him, for the topside had told him I was coming. I was close to him, and he knew I was there; he kept pointing to where he was foul, and I would make a motion that I understood. He was really only a dim outline in that muddy water.

But I wasn't paying any attention to him whatsoever. I wasn't concerned with him, but with what held him.

Even with these explanations it doesn't take long to tell all this; but I had been down fifteen or twenty minutes. The hacksaw came down very quickly after I asked for it, and I took the light over to Mike, put it in his hand, and put his hand so the light would be in the position where I needed it, and told him to hold it in that position. He was within five or six feet of that U-shaped iron, but he couldn't get over to it. He was so held down that he could not even get his hand to his air-control valve. Had it been shut off, for instance, to telephone, he would have suffocated. That was why they couldn't get his messages very well; he was in a position where he couldn't shut off his air, and you have to shut it off to use the telephone well.

He held my light, but in less than a minute it flared up in my eyes so I couldn't see a thing. He couldn't hold it, but I didn't know that. I got kind of angry, and shook him, and said, "Hold it there!"

Then it flared again. He had dropped it.

This time I realized that something was wrong with him. He would have helped me if he could. As a matter of fact, he was unconscious; his suit had become cut and was full of that ice-water, and he couldn't move to keep his circulation going.

So then I took the light and put it against the gun mount; Mike was lying in the wreckage forward of the gun, which is forward of the conning tower at least six feet. And finally I got to work sawing that angle iron.

It was a miserable job. The iron was loose, and I had to hold it with one hand and saw with the other. It was in an awkward place, near the edge of the superstructure, and I had to lie right down by Michels to work, in the wreckage. I had to go slow and carefully too, for a hack-saw blade is brittle, and, if I broke it, it would cost time to get new blades. And time was the breath of life. I could last only about so long, and Mike could live only about so long.

It took me forty to forty-five minutes to cut through that stout angle iron. Inside the boat they never made a sound; they undoubtedly thought that whatever we were doing was toward their rescue. It was very cold, and my hands were aching terribly.

Finally I got through, but here was a new misery. Lying down to cut it, a sharp angle in the wreckage had cut my own suit, and I was wet to the neck.

The bight I had freed, however, was the end nearest to Mike, and as soon as I had worked the slack back and forth and got some more, I stood him up. I still thought he was conscious, though he didn't help me when I pulled him up. As a matter of fact, he was out and I didn't know it. I could hardly see him at all; there was a lot of mud.

By this time I was taking the turns out of his lines, and telling the people on the topside to take it in slowly. I thought I had got it all clear, when I noticed a bight leading over the side and another on the port side.

Before I went over the side after it, I put my line and hose in Mike's hands, for him to hold me. Then I went over the side, and he let me go entirely. So I secured my life line round part of the wreckage, and started in to clear him down there. It was just hung up by the strain and didn't take long to clear.

I telephoned the surface. "Take in the slack on his life line and hose," I told them, "and tell Mike to follow me to the descending line."

As I was along toward the descending line, I felt myself becoming buoyant.

"Stop pulling me up," I said.

"We aren't pulling you," they answered, and I turned round quick and saw Mike's feet floating about level with my face plate. I grabbed them and pulled him down.

It was found afterward that one of us had taken a turn in the other's life line, and his buoyancy was pulling me off the deck. But at the moment, I merely tripped his spitcock to relieve his buoyancy. Then, realizing what must have caused it, I pulled down the lines till I saw the turn and passed him under the lines to clear him.

Even then I didn't realize that he was out. I simply wondered why he didn't work with me.

I closed his spitcock again; then I motioned to him to come toward the descending line, and held the line behind me to show him the way. In a moment I looked round, and again I couldn't find him.

"Where's Mike?" I called on the telephone.

They said, "He's all right." The reason they knew he was all right was that they now had all of his line except just enough to reach to the bottom, so they knew I had him clear.

We didn't know how bad things were. The Falcon had begun to drag anchor in the gale. She was drifting so badly that she had dragged her anchors four hundred and fifty feet, even though two other ships had their moorings out and had their lines on the Falcon trying to hold her up in position. The Falcon has anchors one thousand pounds heavier than ships of a like size, so you can see it was blowing some on the topside.

It meant that Mike and I were at the extreme end of our lines. Captain Hartley figured that in five to twenty minutes longer, if I hadn't got Mike clear, we should undoubtedly both have been left there. So time was even more precious than we had any idea.

When I got to the descending line and didn't see Mike, I told them on top that I couldn't.

"All right," they said, "stand by to come up."

"All right, haul me up—I'm wet to the neck," said I.

They would have hauled me anyway. Under the conditions and with the ship drifting they couldn't have me taking my decompression in the water.

I was still carrying the light, and when I got to the

surface the light of it showed Michels lying blown up, on the surface.

They didn't know he was on the surface. And that's how he reached the surface before me, and I got into the tank ahead of him!

They got the stage over, and got me aboard and rushed me into the tank. There were already three other men in there, waiting for us, to take care of us. The three of them took my suit off. They were still at it when Mike was passed in. It was just the same as you'd pass in a broom; he was as stiff as a board.

His eyes were rolled up into his head; he was frothing at the mouth and making a gurgling sound, and we had to cut his clothes off him, diving suit, underwear, and all. He had a pair of woolen gloves on, and, even though we cut them, his fists were clinched so tight that it took all the strength of two men to open his hands and make him let go of them.

According to the decompression tables, we should have been under a pressure of thirty pounds, but when I saw his condition I ordered the pressure run up to sixty pounds to relieve the bends—for it looked as if he might have a serious case of them, on top of the exposure. However, he didn't; it turned out to be only a bad case of exposure.

They took an hour to run the pressure down to thirty again. I said to the other fellows, "Men, you've got to work," for it looked as though we'd lost him after we thought we'd saved him. The three men and I massaged his body, slapped his face, and in general gave him a beating.

Cold as I was myself, I never felt it until I noticed that Mike was apparently coming round. Then I began to shiver. I lay down right into Mike, both of us naked and under blankets, to share the heat of our bodies.

It was 11:40 when we entered the tank; it wasn't until 3:30 that Mike regained consciousness and could recognize any one. The first man he recognized was Lieutenant-Commander Ellsberg, who had just come in. He had volunteered his services and had just arrived on the job. And ten minutes later we got down to atmospheric pressure.

I left then, and went down, turned in, and slept. They kept Mike in the tank. In the morning he sent for me and told me what he could remember. He could remember very little, and only for a short time after I came down. He had put his hand out for the hacksaw, he said, because he had the idea I wasn't working fast enough and he wanted to help. Well, he'd have gone at it so bull-headed he'd have lost time.

He was still very weak in the morning, and it was thought that to save his life he ought to be taken to a hospital. The only safe way to get him there was in a decompression chamber, and as the Falcon was the only ship that had a decompression chamber, she had to be used. That was the reason she left the scene, and I think it was a thing worth while doing; it saved Mike's life, and the conditions at the wreck were so bad that diving was impossible. This was Monday morning, and we had one more signal from the submarine before the Falcon left.

All through the storm, the only line the Falcon had on the submarine was the descending line. As the ship yawed or dragged, this line had to be tended by hand. Before the Falcon left for Boston, she buoyed the line and let it go. This was the buoy that carried away and lost the S-4's position for us.

The Falcon transferred Michels at the navy yard at Charlestown to an ambulance from the Naval Hospital, and stayed only long enough to take aboard supplies that were urgently needed, and that had been ordered to the wharf by radio. I managed to get out on the pier and find a telegraph messenger, and I sent Mrs. Michels a telegram to say that Michels was taken to the hospital as a precaution, that he was perfectly all right, and that she was not to worry.

*The Laurentic Yields Her Gold**

by Edward Ellsberg

A foremost authority on diving, submarines, and salvage, EDWARD ELLSBERG *has directed many of the submarine salvage operations for the U. S. Navy. He has only recently returned from war duty with the Navy abroad where, among other accomplishments, he restored to working order a smashed Red Sea port. This chapter on salvaging the Laurentic's gold is part of his* Men Under the Sea, *an account of men who have dared the ocean depths for treasure or for lives.*

* "The Laurentic Yields Her Gold" from *Men Under the Sea,* reprinted by permission of Dodd, Mead and Company.

THE YEAR 1917 had just dawned. For thirty months the war had raged in Europe, and German submarines had taken heavy toll of British commerce. And now, to cap all, Germany had just announced an unrestricted submarine campaign with every ship, neutral or belligerent, approaching the British Isles to be sunk without warning. In the offices of the Admiralty at Whitehall strained faces looked at the mounting curves of tonnage sunk by U-boats and knew that the threat was no idle boast—Germany had enough submarines in operation to bring England to her knees in a few more months if sinkings continued at the current rate. Regardless of what happened on the Western Front or on the Eastern Front, the war would be lost at sea unless a curb on U-boats' successes was soon found.

For hard-pressed Britain, with her man-power drawn away from farm and factory to hold back the German hordes pressing across France, was vitally dependent now upon the steady flow across the seas to her of those supplies she could neither raise nor manufacture in sufficient quantity—American wheat and cotton, American steel and powder. But the getting of them to Britain was as much a headache in the Exchequer as it was in the Admiralty, for somehow those purchases in neutral America had to be financed or they would never become reality enough for Britain's sea lords to have to worry themselves over in safe transportation through submarine-infested waters.

Every device known to finance in London had already been used—British balances in the United States had been exhausted; the maximum that Britain could borrow in America had been raised; American securities owned by British investors had been mobilized in London and shipped to New York to be sold to provide further credits—but still all this was not enough. If the pound sterling was not to drop against the dollar in New York to the point where it would sadly cripple further purchases, gold must be shipped in huge quantities to bolster up the pound.

For some time for this purpose, the tide of gold had been flowing westward. Now, in January, 1917, another huge shipment was to start, and the Lords of the Admiralty were confronted with a major problem. How should they route that priceless gold shipment to escape having it sunk at sea by hidden U-boats?

To start with, they chose R.M.S. *Laurentic,* a large White Star liner, as the carrier, a vessel fast enough to outrun any submarine which sought to chase her, a vessel already converted into an auxiliary naval cruiser and heavily enough armed with naval guns to fight off any submarine which might attack her, a vessel already manned by a naval crew as skilled as any in detecting lurking periscopes among the waves.

Next they sought the safest route westward. The seas to the north of Ireland were not so much traveled and were usually too boisterous in winter time for U-boat commanders to lie in wait for victims—the chart of sinkings, emphasized by the point of loss of the *Lusitania,* indicated that the waters south of Ireland and in the Channel were the favorite hunting grounds for lurking submarines. So for the course of the *Laurentic* they chose the route around North Ireland.

From London to Liverpool ran a special train with 3,211 ingots of gold carefully boxed up for shipment on the naval auxiliary cruiser *Laurentic;* 3,211 ingots of gold then valued at £5,000,000 or $25,000,000—in present dollar value, about $44,000,000. In boxes weighing 140 pounds each, the gold was carried aboard the *Laurentic* through one of the entry ports low down in her heavy steel hull, carted athwartship to the second class baggage room, and there locked up, 43 tons of gold. In secrecy such as surrounded the movements of every naval vessel, the *Laurentic* sailed from Liverpool with her precious freight and little else aboard other than her crew.

A short run to the northward through the protected Irish Sea, and the *Laurentic* pointed her bow westward through a wintry January gale, plunging heavily into head seas as she fought her way into the Atlantic with the near-by north coast of Ireland looming up on her port hand across the tumbling seas. The *Laurentic's* captain had good cause to congratulate himself on his luck; in that weather no submarine, even if present, could hope to make a successful torpedo attack, and he would shortly be out on the deep Atlantic where submarines rarely went.

Then off Lough Swilly came disaster. A terrific explosion rocked the ship. No submarines were near, but one had been in better weather beforehand, planting mines beneath the surface. The unfortunate *Laurentic* struck a hidden mine which inflicted damage far worse than any torpedo might have done, and, heeling over, started to sink rapidly. As best they might in the freezing weather, the crew struggled to launch the boats from their foundering vessel. Between the icy water, the driving seas, and the heavy list of the stricken liner, they were none too successful in getting away, and when the *Laurentic* disappeared, over half her crew, several hundreds of seamen, went with her.

When from the frozen survivors who finally made shore in the ice-coated lifeboats the news of the loss of the *Laurentic* was radioed in code to London, deep despair struck the Exchequer and cold fury reigned in Whitehall. The Lords of the Treasury looked in anguish toward the Admiralty—£5,000,000 in gold gone, the largest sum in all history to be lost at sea. But it was worse than the mere loss of £5,000,000. The loss was in gold, and gold above all else was needed in New York to bolster up the tottering pound sterling and keep the stream of food and steel flowing toward Britain. Could the Admiralty do anything?

If it was humanly possible, the Admiralty would and could. The gold had been lost while in the hands of the Navy; it was the Navy's obligation to recover it.

To Commander G. C. C. Damant, R.N., the British Navy's premier diving authority, was given the task, with orders to start immediately. He was not to regard his task as a salvage job but as a military undertaking of the utmost urgency. It was wintertime, it was wartime, but, in spite of the weather, in spite of the war, Damant was turned to at once with the best divers the British Navy could muster under his command.

Minesweepers soon located the wreck. They found the hulk not far off the mouth of Lough Swilly in a depth of 132 feet of water, or 22 fathoms, and buoyed the spot for Damant. It was a terrible place to work. Unsheltered by any land, the *Laurentic* lay in the open sea, exposed to the full sweep of every northerly or westerly Atlantic gale, and with Lough Swilly to the southward to allow a stiff sea built up by any southerly gale to strike full force over the wreck. Racing tides sweeping back and forth along the coast meant fierce currents to be encountered by the divers. To top off all, January in that latitude meant freezing spray on deck to hamper the workers and icy cold in the depths below to numb the divers.

Then there were the Germans. It was unduly optimistic to hope that the loss of the *Laurentic* and her fabulous cargo could long be kept secret from Prussia's prying intelligence agents. What the prize they had struck from Britain's grasp meant in the way of munitions would be as well realized in Berlin as in London; the military value of frustrating recovery of the gold would be immense; and Damant could expect, if Germany found out what he was about, to have submarines sent north for the specific purpose of blowing his little diving ship, a perfect anchored target for a torpedo, completely out of the water, with himself and his men sure to be killed by the explosion without chance of escape.

With all that in the back of his mind, Damant went at the job. His first diver down found the *Laurentic* lying in the sand on her port bilge, heeled over about 60°, so that walking on the deck was wholly impossible and even clinging to the sloping starboard side was out of question except where the diver could grip a porthole, a padeye, or some other protruding fitting. But nevertheless with lead-soled boots braced against rivet heads on the shell, and freezing fingers clutching at what they could grasp, the divers crawled over the badly listed side, looking for the entry port through which the gold had been loaded. Amidships in the second class baggage room, down what would now be a steeply inclined passageway leading from that sealed entry port, they would find the gold.

Long ocean swells left by the last storm were sweeping in steady succession over the *Laurentic's* tomb, each wave, even in the depths below, setting up a strong surge as its crest passed. The divers, searching in the dim depths for the entry port, found themselves nearly swept from their precarious perches on the *Laurentic's* side by each surge, and were forced to cling tightly most of the time to the nearest fitting, scrambling along a few feet only between pulsations. To make matters worse, the *Laurentic's* crew in abandoning ship had of course lowered all the boats they could, and the boatfalls now hung down the ship's side to what had once been her waterline, with the heavy blocks at the lower ends of the falls swishing erratically with every surge like huge pendulums from the davits overhead.

To see, as the first diver clinging by his fingernails to the side did, one of those massive boat blocks go flying through the water within inches of his faceplate, nearly braining him, was a sight to chill any man's blood and give an impressive demonstration (if any had been needed) of the wave action going on below. Damant had first of all to cut loose those death-dealing boat blocks before his men could proceed in such reasonable safety as even divers are entitled to.

Another diver soon found the entry port and tied a buoyline to it. The mooring buoys of the diving ship were then immediately relaid about this marker as a center, so that the diving ship might plumb the hatch below and minimize the danger of fouling a diver's lines.

Damant (who was himself as fine a diver as any of his men, and as a lieutenant had taken a leading part in developing the theory of stage decompression), having checked all to his satisfaction, now went further. A charge of guncotton was placed against the heavy steel entry port doors and exploded electrically from above. His next diver found the doors torn loose as expected. As was not expected, the doors were found resting a few feet inside the ship against something, still a total obstruction to entrance. Only with some difficulty were the doors torn out of the ship and removed, to expose behind them a heavy latticed iron gate across the passage, against which they had been resting. Another charge of guncotton took this gate off its hinges, but it required two more dives to remove some heavy packing cases in order to clear the passage inboard to the strong room.

So far, in ordinary weather, what had been done by the divers might easily have been done in a couple of days, but Damant had been struggling to cling to his moorings in a continuous series of midwinter gales punctuated by snow squalls, and two weeks had gone by during which diving was possible only for brief intervals and even then under conditions when normally it would not have been attempted. But each time the wind and sea lulled enough to make it seem probable that the moorings would hold his ship even for an hour, down went a diver into the freezing water, and so, bit by bit, over a fortnight, Damant had managed to get done two whole days' work and he began to breathe a little more freely.

He had not yet been torpedoed, his men were doing well in that cold water, and the backbone of his job was broken—the way to the treasure room was cleared. It was a difficult way, down a passage sloping at an angle of

60° and around several corners, but Damant had often seen worse. It looked now as if a few weeks' work would see the 40 odd tons of gold in the *Laurentic's* strong room lifted box by box to the surface and shipped safely back to the vaults of the Bank of England—two weeks' time if he were favored by the weather, somewhat longer if he were not, but at any rate long before an inkling of what he was about got back to Berlin to bring a U-boat to the spot.

In the late afternoon of his fourteenth day over the wreck, the last obstruction in the passage was removed. To Diver E. C. Miller, one of his best men, Damant gave the task of getting into the strong room. With a chisel and a short-handled sledge hammer lashed to his belt, Miller in the gathering darkness of a brief February day went over the side of the salvage ship, slid 63 feet down the descending line to the opened entry port on the high side of the listed *Laurentic,* and crawled into the ship. With his tenders carefully paying his lines out foot by foot, Miller half slipped, half dropped down the now nearly vertical deck going inboard, groped his way in the utter blackness of the water-filled passage around several bulkheads, and then felt out the steel door leading to the strong room. With sledge and chisel he smashed his way through the nearly horizontal door, to slide immediately into the black water inside the strong room and bring up sharply with his lead boots clattering on a pile of bullion boxes jumbled in a huge heap against the port side bulkhead of what had been the second cabin baggage room.

Never before or since in history has it been given to any diver to land on such a hoard of gold. Forty-three tons of it in 3,211 bars lay in a scrambled heap against the bulkhead where it had been tossed when the crazily heeled *Laurentic* hit bottom. Everywhere Miller reached out a canvas-clad arm through the black water he felt stout boxes of gold—$40,000 worth of it in each box, $25,000,000 of it altogether. Excitedly Miller telephoned to Damant that he was in the bullion room and that, except for the smashed door, the bullion room was intact and the treasure all there! He was more entitled than he then knew to his excitement, for Miller unfortunately was the only man who ever saw (or rather felt) that bullion all together in the sunken *Laurentic*.

Miller's task, forcing open the strong room, had taken all his diving time. He had been down an hour already; it was dark on deck; the sea was none too good for holding on. Sharply they signaled him to come up so the ship could unmoor. But with all that gold about him, Miller was not going to come up empty-handed. He seized the nearest box of gold, a small box about a foot square and six inches deep, and got, as everyone gets when first he grabs a golden ingot, an incredible shock at its weight. The little box weighed 140 pounds, no easy load even for a strong man to carry under the best of circumstances, and Miller's circumstances for carrying anything were atrocious. But he refused to let go the gold; he had first found it, he would be first to bring some up. So vertically up through the strong room door, around the bulkhead corners he struggled in the water-filled passages with his golden ballast, little help possible from his tenders above on the salvage ship because of the many turns and twists his lifelines took inside the wreck on their way down to him. Pushing the five ingots in that box ahead of him, he wormed his way up the steeply sloping decks with superhuman strength and agility, till finally in the clear his tenders got a straight pull and heaved him up to the entry port where at last he was able to lash his precious burden and send it up on a line. He himself spent the next half hour dangling at various stages in the icy water while he was hauled up in a much-shortened decompression.

So after only two weeks' work in the *Laurentic,* Miller sent the first gold up, but the strain and the excitement must have been too much for his circulation; he had soaked up so much nitrogen that within an hour he was being jammed into the recompression chamber for treatment for "the bends." Bubbles of air had gathered in his joints, doubling him into knots with pain. It was remarkable to note, however, when, inside the tank, the pressure had been run up on Miller to 20 pounds, how suddenly his pain disappeared, after which he was gradually decompressed for several hours down to atmosphere and then emerged from the tank feeling quite all right in his joints and much elated over his success.

When morning dawned again on the gray sea tumbling over the *Laurentic,* the barometer was falling. Commander Damant, eying it uneasily, concluded that with luck he might get in one more dive before he had to let go his moorings and run before the rising storm. That meant that if any more gold was to be recovered, only Miller, who already knew the way, had a chance of getting into the strong room quickly enough to have time remaining for any useful work; so overboard, in spite of his bout of the night before with "the bends," went Miller again.

Miller quickly demonstrated that he had learned the tortuous way into the bowels of the badly listed ship and profited by his experience of the previous evening, for in one dive of only 60 minutes, he managed to mule three more boxes of gold up out of the strong room and send them to the surface, a feat which to some degree took the sting off the imperative necessity of letting go the moorings immediately upon his coming up. With four boxes of gold, about $160,000 worth, in his hold, Damant ran for shelter into Lough Swilly before a mounting northerly gale, with every expectation of coming back to finish lifting out the rest of that $25,000,000 within a few more weeks. Had anyone then told him that he was to be at it yet for seven more years, Damant would have been completely incredulous. But so it was.

For a solid week a fierce winter gale blew from the north with ever-heightening storm waves sweeping in never-ending succession over the grave of the *Laurentic,* 22 fathoms down. Long before that storm blew itself out, the north coast of Ireland for miles around was strewn with wreckage from the sunken *Laurentic,* much of it easily identifiable as having come from the inside of the ship, an ominous portent to Damant and his men of what those waves were doing on the bottom to their wreck.

In deep trepidation when the storm finally moderated and diving could be resumed, Damant watched as the first diver went overboard to secure a new buoy line to the entry port. And his heart sank as he noted that the pressure on the diver at that entry port now showed it at a depth of 103 feet, whereas before it had been but 62 feet from the surface. Somehow the side of the *Laurentic* was now 40 feet lower than it had been before the storm; he soon enough found out why. The diver going through the entry port into the passage below could get but a few feet; the deckplates forming the ceiling of that passage were squeezed down to within 18 inches of its floor, and buckled bulkhead plates jammed in between completely sealed off what little space was left. Under the endless pounding of the storm waves beating against her tilted sides and decks as she lay far over on her port bilge, the *Laurentic* had folded up like an accordion, and in way of the entry port, even an eel could no longer squeeze through that flattened-out passage to the strong room!

To Damant and his divers, that was a body blow, but they had to get through again to that strong room in the wreckage of the *Laurentic,* and they set out to do it. With successive small charges of guncotton exploded in the crumpled passage, they forced apart the steel plates, shoring up as they went inboard to make a tunnel through which a diver might crawl. It was a terrible job, with the broken plating overhead, five decks of it, groaning and creaking and working like a thing alive as the surging waves beat down through the depths; and the diver, alone and in darkness, stretched out in that quivering mass of steel supported by nothing in particular, well knew, as he wormed his way along with guncotton or with shores, that if those plates should fold up on him no one could ever get him out.

That it could ever have been done had not Commander Damant been himself a diver, I very much doubt. But where the leader will go, the men will follow, and the tunnel advanced till at last the way was cleared to the strong room and once more on deck they prepared to hoist out the gold.

For the third time, Miller slid down into the strong room, reaching it now at a depth of 120 feet, right down on the sea floor where the collapse of the *Laurentic* had dropped it. But this time as he slid into the inclined room, Miller brought up against the far bulkhead with a metallic clatter as his lead-soled boots landed directly on the steel and no heap of stout wood bullion boxes broke his fall. Anxiously he felt about him but it was useless—the bullion room was completely empty!

In a daze, Miller groped through the water, his numbed fingers traveling over deck, bulkheads, and ceiling, searching for that pile of gold, but he found none. Instead, gaping rents in the steel deckplates and in the lower bulkhead showed only where it had gone. In the widespread collapse and flattening out of the *Laurentic,* the strong room plating had given way under the load of that 43 tons of gold and had torn wide open, spilling the precious bars downward somewhere into the general tangle of wreckage of the ship to port.

For Damant and his salvagers that was a heart-breaking discovery. Gone now was every hope of quick recovery of that treasure which a few weeks before had indeed been within their grasp—the relentless sea seemed to have taunted them with the feel of it only to snatch it then abruptly far beyond their reach and bury it beneath thousands and thousands of tons of broken steel down in the sands of the ocean floor.

On the surface, Damant gloomily recast his plans. He had to recover that gold as his bit in backing up his shipmates of the Grand Fleet and his khaki-clad countrymen struggling to hold their own in the trenches on the Western Front. His enemy was as powerful and as ruthless as any they faced; but his weapons were slight in comparison, simply the weak bodies of a few men struggling with him under the sea, held to their task by no hope that any share in the *Laurentic's* gold would ever be theirs for their efforts.

It was obvious that the tunnel driven from the entry port in the starboard side of the ship down to the strong room was too dangerous for use in the gigantic task that lay ahead, and that, in spite of the peril and the labor spent in clearing that tunnel, it must now be abandoned.

Nothing remained except on the bottom of the sea to tear the *Laurentic* to pieces, plate by plate and beam by beam, working vertically downward from her upper deck into her hold, till they came on the spot in the port bilge into which the gold must have been spilled when the strong room gave way.

With explosive charges, Damant began to blast his way down through the collapsed wreckage on the port side. To his despair, he quickly discovered that the loosely lying steel plates failed to break under the action of his explosives in the normal manner. With no strain any longer on those steel plates, they simply flopped loosely up or down under the impact of the exploding guncotton like flags waving in the wind, without ever parting. To sever the plates he found he had to seize each plate with clamps, heave taut on the clamps with a line to the boom on his salvage ship until the plate was strained hard out, and then fire a charge under it to cut it free at its lower edge. Thus the work went slowly ahead as, one after another, the *Laurentic's* plates were blasted out and dumped well clear of the ship. But not wholly without mishap.

Blachford, veteran diver, was working below. Twenty fathoms down, clutching gingerly a charge of guncotton with its detonator imbedded inside, Blachford crawled on hands and knees over torn steel through the water to get beneath a steel plate swaying, at its outboard end, from a line to the salvage ship—a plate which his immediate predecessor on the job, Diver Clear, had hooked with a shackle, and which at one end was now being held up, stretched taut by the straining wire line to the winch on deck. Getting in first on all fours under that ton of steel undulating like a blanket in the water, Blachford next stretched out on his stomach and wiggled along as far beneath it as he could get, then thrust the guncotton ahead to the limit of his extended fingers, jamming it hard between the lower end of the wobbling plate above and the wreckage on which he lay. Carefully he felt out the lead of the firing wires to make sure they still ran unbroken past him to the detonator, and then telephoned up:

"Take in the slack on the firing circuit."

On the surface, a tender hauled in gently on the electric circuit. At that instant, the wire rope holding up the plate over Blachford suddenly shot up in loose bights out of the sea like a broken fishline and fell back in a tangle of slack coils onto the deck of the diving ship. Startled, Damant looked at the writhing wire. Something had let go below, the heavy plate it had been holding up had dropped, and Blachford was right under it!

In anguish Damant pressed Blachford's telephone to his lips, feverishly calling his diver. After several very long seconds he got a welcome reply, in strained and measured syllables slowly calling out:

"Give—me—all—the—air—you—can—sir."

Thankful that Blachford, with the crushing load of that steel plate on his back, was still at least alive enough to talk, Damant signaled hastily to raise the air pressure on Blachford's diving line. Immediately the additional air started down the hose, came another call from the agonized diver buried beneath the steel:

"That's right! Give me more yet! And get another diver down here quick!"

As for the last request, that was wholly unnecessary, for already the previous diver, Clear, who had just come aboard after his decompression and was then still in his wet suit, partly undressed, was in hot haste having his weights replaced and his helmet screwed back on, while other seamen hurriedly were reeving off a fresh hoisting wire and some new slings to lift that plate again. But at the request for still more air, Commander Damant paused. The pressure gauge on Blachford's air line already showed a huge excess over what he needed to balance the water at the depth at which he lay; unquestionably under that pressure his suit must be completely ballooned out, and to increase the pressure further meant grave danger of bursting the canvas suit and drowning Blachford immediately. On the other hand, his suit might already be torn somewhere and partly flooded, so that he badly needed the extra air to hold the water from his face as he lay there unable to move under the crushing load of that steel plate on his back.

Should the air pressure be increased or not? Damant was in a terrible dilemma, with Blachford's very life depending on his decision and no help from the telephone in resolving it, for the air roaring now through Blachford's helmet all but drowned out the diver's voice, and very evidently he could not hear Damant's. When carefully the air was throttled down a little to improve the hearing, before Damant ever could get in a word, he heard over and over, slowly articulated by the trapped diver, the anguished plea:

"Give—me—more—air!"

But balancing all the risks, it seemed to Damant unwise to raise the pressure any further, and thus matters stood when Clear, on whom everything now depended, was dropped overboard with the new hoisting sling, to slide directly down Blachford's air hose as a quick guide to the spot where he lay trapped.

Clear landed 20 fathoms down, in the crater of wreckage already blasted through the *Laurentic,* and followed the air hose through the dark water to where it disappeared beneath a twisted steel plate with some loose wire tangled about one end. There was no sign of Blachford save a mass of air bubbles rising in fine clusters from all about that sheet of steel.

Hastily Clear dragged up the fresh wire sling held by a marline lanyard to his wrist, carefully slipped the clamps of a new wire bridle over the edges of the steel near (but not too near) the free end of the plate. Swiftly but gently he secured the clamps, trying not to jar the plate, working all the time with the knowledge that, aside from Blachford, jammed in under the other end of that sheet of steel was a fulminate detonator buried in guncotton, and that sometimes even more stable explosives than fulminate did queer things. Should his jarring of the wreckage set off that cap, he as well as the trapped Blachford would be blown to bits.

Clear finished securing the new sling, stepped back a little, and shouted into his telephone:

"On deck! Heave round!"

The wire line in the water above him stretched taut, the end of the plate lifted slowly and evenly, exposing Blachford's feet, then his body, soon his helmet. Queerly, in that topsy-turvy world of water, as the distorted steel sheet rose up, Blachford, still nearly horizontal, rose with it, pressing against its under side as if glued there, for with his rig bulging like an overstuffed sausage, he had tremendous buoyancy and could not stay down.

Now a new danger entered. Should Blachford slide out from beneath the steel with that inflated rig, he would "blow up" instantly. And Blachford was helpless to do anything himself to prevent it, for spread-eagled as he was, he could not get his fingers onto his control valves. But Clear could. Seizing his helpless shipmate by one bulging leg to hold him beneath that restraining steel plate lest he float away and suddenly go shooting skyward, Clear reached in, opened the exhaust valve in his helmet wide, and bled the excess air from his suit till Blachford shrank to more normal proportions. Becoming heavy once more, he dropped away from the overhanging plate and thankfully crawled free of it after having been a prisoner for nine minutes.

Fortunately Blachford's copper helmet had protected

his head when the plate dropped, or his skull would unquestionably have been crushed by the blow. As it was, the load pressing on him was in a fair way momentarily to break his back, and only the excess air expanding his suit like a pneumatic tire had taken weight enough off him to make the pain bearable till the plate was lifted. Naturally, all he wanted was all the pressure he could possibly get. Damant, solicitously examining Blachford when finally he came up, was not surprised to learn that it had never occurred to his diver, in imminent danger of being crushed to death, that overmuch pressure would rupture the canvas fabric of his suit and drown him.

For two months the blasting went ahead, as monotonously they tore the *Laurentic* apart, with their major excitement the activities of German submarines in that vicinity. Strangely enough no torpedoes came Damant's way, but his divers had ample reason to know that U-boats were working near, for British minesweepers, steaming by them in pairs with long wire sweeps dragging between their sterns, occasionally exploded freshly planted submarine mines. One such went off two miles away, with a detonation coming through the water that struck a diver like a triphammer, giving him a violent and a dangerous shock. After that, whenever the minesweepers got within five miles of his ship, Damant hastily dragged his divers out of the water; but even so, a detonation six miles off soon gave another unlucky diver a severe jar.

However, nothing could be done about it; Damant dared not still further extend his margin or he would have been forced to quit diving altogether, what with the endless forays of U-boats planting mines and the continuous counter-activities of trawlers sweeping them up.

But after two months of blasting, they suddenly forgot all about U-boats. Miller, with a scent unequaled by any of his mates, ran across the gold again! Delving amidst the rubbish sandwiched in between the now uncovered lower deck wreckage lying to port of the flattened-out strong room, he spotted a yellow ingot! Like a hound on a fresh scent he was off, burrowing through the wreckage for more. His time on the bottom soon ran out; Damant signaled him to come up, but nothing could tear him from the job till, having been down 90 minutes and by strenuous exertions having dug out 10 bars altogether, he was satisfied at last and cleared his lifelines of the wreck, so he could be lifted with $80,000 in gold to accompany him.

Here was welcome news for London! Promptly Commander Damant slid into a diving rig and dropped to the bottom to spend a long hour in the depths in that crater they had blasted in the *Laurentic,* checking, in the crushed and crumpled steel all about him, his directions from the remnants of the strong room and what next to tear away to expose more gold. Finally, with a picture of the wreckage vividly impressed on his memory, he started up, taking only a relatively short decompression on his rise.

On coming to the surface, he was somewhat dismayed to find that Miller, between his overlong stay on the bottom, his exertions there, and the excitement attendant on his rediscovery of the gold, had developed another case of "the bends" and had had to be shoved into the recompression chamber for treatment, where he then was, under air pressure again to overcome his torments. Damant peered through a glass port at him. Miller, inside the little single-chambered tank (which was all they could accommodate on their small diving ship) seemed to be already relieved of his pains and resting comfortably, so Damant left him to direct the next diver where best to look for more gold.

But within an hour after emerging from the sea, Commander Damant himself was no longer concerned over gold. He soon found himself in difficulties with one of the rarer manifestations of compressed air disease—his eyeballs began to diverge radically and he began to see double. Then, to top off his troubles, the air bubbles developing in his forehead began to pain him excruciatingly.

Unfortunately for him the only recompression tank they had on board was already occupied by Miller, who would not be out from under pressure for 40 minutes yet, and unless the pressure in that little single chamber were completely released, no one else could enter. With his eyes diverging more and more each minute and the top of his head feeling as if it were about to explode, Damant could hardly wait 40 minutes. Fortunately for him, Miller, inside the tank looking out of the port and glimpsing the most cock-eyed set of optics he had even seen looking longingly in at him, immediately sensed the situation. Chivalrously he blew down the pressure in the tank at once so that the door could be opened to admit his commander, with the result that his own torments promptly returned to double him up in pains worse than ever.

When the door had slammed tight behind him, Damant opened the air valve and started to raise the pressure once more. With gratification he noted as the air roared in and the pressure rose, compressing the bubbles in his head, that the two entirely distinct figures of Miller he saw before him gradually began to approach each other till finally, at 10 pounds pressure, the two Millers coalesced into one only, while at the same time the tortures in his head magically disappeared. However, he had to run the pressure up to double that amount before Miller himself got any relief.

Unfortunately, as the pressure was thereafter gradually reduced, while Damant's troubles was gone for good, Miller's were not. At 4 pounds pressure, Miller again began to suffer the tortures of the damned and there was nothing for it except to jump the pressure up again till his pains vanished and then to try releasing the air at a slower rate. But nothing helped; each time the pressure dropped "the bends" doubled Miller up again. Finally after six and a half hours in the tank (it being then 1:30 A.M.), the temptations of a warm meal and a bed as compared to the chilly interior of that iron chamber overcame the restraints of reason and the two divers at last took a chance and blew down the few remaining pounds of air so they could emerge. But Miller paid for it, for he was soon back in the tank, to suffer all the rest of the night and most of the next day before finally he could rid his system of the nitrogen he had soaked up in his excited grubbing for gold.

So on through the spring and the summer and the early fall, taking the iron wreckage at the bottom of their crater apart bit by bit, and searching amongst the jumble of smashed furniture, bedding, waterlogged provisions, and wooden paneling thus gradually exposed, the divers recovered 542 gold bars, to a total value of about $4,000,000, all of which went promptly back to Britain's hungry Treasury.

After September, wintry weather hit the salvagers once more. It was now apparent there could never be any quick recovery, and something else had meanwhile occurred to put a new complexion on the whole affair. On April 6, 1917, a few months after the sinking of the *Laurentic,* the United States had entered the World War on the side of the Allies. Within a few months of that time arrangements were completed between London and Washington whereby America undertook to finance Britain's purchases in the United States, with the promise of reimbursement later. Britain no longer had to support the pound sterling in New York; while the war lasted, there was no longer any necessity of shipping another ounce of gold westward; and, so far as its effect on the conduct of the war was concerned, the pressure to recover the *Laurentic's* treasure was completely gone.

As a result of this, when winter set in, the Admiralty withdrew its divers from the *Laurentic,* and, while the war lasted, they never came back. Not that Damant and his divers were given any rest even during that winter—quite the contrary—for during the next fourteen months they were kept busy searching the smashed wrecks of sunken U-boats for codes and other useful wartime information.

In the spring of 1919, having been away eighteen months, Damant and his divers returned, a little easier in their minds than formerly as they resumed the job, for they had under them at last a properly equipped salvage ship, the *Racer,* and their fears of submarine attacks were gone.

The *Laurentic,* to their surprise, had changed but little. Apparently the sea had already battered her so flat that not much more crushing was possible, and the divers took up where they had left off, promptly beginning to find more ingots in the wreckage.

But soon a new danger began to threaten. They had been working in way of what had originally been a well deck aft, with forward of them, rising a sheer two deck heights, the after end of the superstructure carrying the first class cabins, and abaft them a similar superstructure carrying the second class accommodations. Oddly enough while the heavy hull plating had given way and folded up, these lighter superstructures had remained fairly well intact, rising like two islands fore and aft of the crushed hull where the divers worked.

With increasing dread, Damant noted that these two superstructures leaned more and more toward each other as he undermined their foundations by tearing away the hull between, but so long as he was finding gold, he was exceedingly reluctant to take his men away from treasure recovery to dismantle the adjacent hull. So, daily keeping an eye on these threatening leaning towers, he kept on delving in the wreckage between, recovering that season some $2,350,000 more. But as the summer drew along, ingots became scarcer and scarcer, and he could only conclude, as has many another miner before him, that his vein of gold was pinching out. Damant decided that in the collapse of the strong room, the gold must have separated into two parts—one part (which he had apparently retrieved) having shot to port through the ruptured bulkhead, while the major part, some $18,000,000 worth, had disappeared through the torn floor of the strong room and must be somewhere buried in the hold underneath everything. With this deduction he was forced to be content when no more bars could be found and winter came to end his labors for 1919.

1920 and 1921 were heartbreakers. The salvagers returned in the spring of 1920 to find that the winter storms had finally torn away the toppling superstructures, spilling them in a mass of twisted steel into their excavation, and filling in the chinks with mattresses, springs, broken china, smashed chairs and tables, tiles and cement from bathrooms, and every conceivable kind of rubbish. To make a complete job of it, the profile of the wrecked hull had been further flattened out so that sand and stones from the sea floor now swept over the broken sides to settle in amongst the wreckage, there to be pounded by the tidal currents and the surging waves into a compact caked mass of conglomerate for which the metallic remains of broken mattress springs formed excellent reinforcements and binders.

For two years, during which very little gold was recovered to encourage anybody, the divers struggled in the sea to remove this debris. Against the sand and the rubbish covering everything, explosives were worthless. Powerful pumps brought in to suck away the sand were equally ineffective; and grabs and clamshell dredging buckets got nowhere, partly because of the short periods during which the *Racer* could be held steady over the wreck, partly because of the obstructions below. Nothing showed any effectiveness against this refractory mixture except streams of water from hose nozzles which the divers used to break up the hard-packed sand, after which they hastily filled bags with what sand they had washed loose, and tore away any more substantial wreckage exposed during the washing.

But it was disheartening work, with storms continually washing in fresh sands so that for months it was questionable whether success would ever be possible. In fine weather, the divers gained, and in bad weather, the sand. The discouraged divers found themselves, as storm succeeded storm, beginning to believe that they would never make way against the overpowering forces of the sea. Fortunately, a few scattered bars of gold turned up now and then to revive the drooping divers when defeat seemed inevitable, and finally Damant's ingenuity saved the day.

After every possible mechanical contrivance had folded up in the face of that mixture burying the *Laurentic's* treasure, and it was evident that the bare hands of men alone were all that was left, Damant pulled the job to success by making a hotly contested competition out of the amount of sand each man could dig out in a 30-minute dive under standardized conditions. For 12 minutes with a hose he could wash sand; for 13 minutes thereafter he could pack the sand he had washed free into a near-by sack; and his last 5 minutes he had left to get his bag of sand over to the hoisting bucket to be weighed on deck when he came up.

Scores were carefully kept on what each man brought up; the ingenuity of the divers in fabricating scoops and scrapers to help their speed in digging was amazing; and for the next twenty days the amount of sand brought up per man daily increased as brains came to the aid of brawn and the competition to dig up sand waxed keener. It soon became evident to all that Balson, the strongest diver on the job, was unbeatable, after which interest somewhat declined; but by that time a high standard had been set, below which no diver's pride in the contents of his bag of sand would allow him to fall, and the salvagers started to gain on the sea.

1920 and 1921 dragged wearily away, with very little gold to encourage anybody, and only mountains of worthless sand and an occasional steel plate blasted loose as signs of progress. Still, the hole in the *Laurentic* was continuously getting deeper, and when in 1921 the winter storms arrived to chase the salvagers off, they had at last exposed the shaft tunnel and some of the inner bottom plating near by, so they knew that they had worked their way completely through the ship's hull from top to bottom, and now had before them mainly the sand-filled hold to search.

1922 saw the *Racer* and her crew back again as soon as spring allowed, full of eagerness now that the shell of the ship was near. The first diver down got the surprise of his life when he landed on the bottom of the crater in the *Laurentic's* hulk actually to *see* bars of gold sticking out of the sand! For once the currents had worked on the side of the divers, and during the winter had washed out some two feet of sand which previously had silted in. With a glad cry, the diver started to pluck golden ingots from the sand; before that day was over, 19 bars had been recovered. "They gave themselves up like lambs," the divers reported to Damant.

From that lucky spot the trail of gold led away through the sand toward the port bilge. Daily scraping and digging unearthed more gold nestling in the sand against the shell of the ship, usually one bar at a time buried in hard-packed grit. But the divers nearly went delirious when they came across one nest of 90 ingots surrounded by the broken remnants of the boxes in which originally they had been packed. $750,000 worth of gold went up that day!

That happened only once. The other bars they had to dig for one at a time, completely uncovering the steel skin of the *Laurentic,* section by section, till some 440 square feet had been scraped. By this time the divers found themselves out to the turn of the bilge with the shell there covered by overhanging deck plating that had been pressed down to within a foot or two of the outer skin, and somewhere between those two layers lay the rest of the gold, millions and millions of dollars of it yet.

To blast away the overhanging plating meant delay and the removal of a shield which was partly holding out the sand. As long as the divers could in any manner squeeze in beneath the wreckage overhead, Damant determined to keep on as he was. So, stretched out flat, head-first, the divers snaked themselves beneath the broken deckplates to wiggle along on their stomachs over the shell, searching in the deep corrugations (which the collapse of the hull had pressed in the flat shell plating) for gold bars which might have come to rest there.

The corrugations were, of course, all filled with sand, and the digging was hard. Diver after diver wore away his fingernails grubbing through hard-packed sand in these corrugations feeling for ingots. They might have worn gloves, but inside gloves a man lost his sense of touch and wasted time digging out rocks and broken crockery; whereas with his finger tips a man might soon become expert enough in the feel of gold to pass over without loss of time the rubbish he encountered and save his precious minutes under water for digging out the gold alone.

The divers now had a tough time of it. To avoid having the strong sweep of the current on the long stretch of lifeline and air hose in the water tear them away from their work or perhaps foul the swaying hoses in the wreckage overhead, they tied their lines, when they reached bottom, to a convenient plate, leaving themselves some 30 or 40 feet of slack line to get to their job. Then headfirst they slid in between the waterlogged plates and started burrowing, but it was a ticklish business. As a man's feet were higher than his head, in that position air started to work up from the helmet into the canvas legs of the suit, gradually inflating them so they became lighter and tended to float in spite of heavily weighted shoes. When that happened, there was nothing for a diver to do except on all fours to crawl out backward and stand erect a moment till the water about him had pressed all the air upward again into his helmet, when once more he could slip back into his hole and resume digging for gold with his finger nails.

In this wise, one of the divers, Light by name, was working away trying to dig free an ingot which he could barely feel through the sand with the tips of his outstretched fingers. Tantalizingly his fingers traveled over it, but the refractory bar was so solidly imbedded in the sand it refused to tear free, and so absorbed did Light become in getting a better grip on that $8,000 bar of gold that he completely forgot his own precarious state till suddenly his legs floated upward to touch the overhanging plates, leaving only his helmet bearing on the steel below.

That brought Light back to the realities of his situation, and immediately he attempted to crawl out backward, but with his helmet in the sand and his legs floating up at a fair angle, he no longer was in any position where crawling was a physical possibility.

With his buoyant legs starting to pull him upward, Light hastily took a fresh grip on the ingot (which had gotten him in trouble) to anchor himself down, and shouted desperately into his telephone:

"On deck! Shut off my air!"

On the *Racer,* strange though the request sounded, a tender rushed to comply, but it was too late. Light was light indeed now. Despite his frantic efforts to hang on to that buried gold bar, the pull of his inflated legs was too much for his fingers and tore him loose, to send him shooting up the slope beneath the plating overhead and then, with increasing buoyancy, to float him upside down through the water till he brought up with a jerk on the end of his slack lifeline 40 feet from the bottom, pulling hard against the lashing which held his lines to the wreckage below. There, helmet down, arms stiffly outstretched, feet up, he hung spread-eagled with his rig ballooned out to the uttermost, streaming in the tidal current like an anchored kite balloon.

To make matters worse, Damant, who at Light's first request to shut off his air, had seized his telephone to learn what was wrong, now heard from Light that there was some water in his helmet and he could not tell where it was coming in.

That was bad; every diving suit usually leaks a little, but, except for wetting the diver, the quantity of water entering is of no great moment. However, in Light's case, even a little water was now dangerous. Upside down as he was, a quart of water inside his helmet might well drown him.

It so happened that Blachford, the diver who had preceded Light on the bottom, was still in the water not far below the *Racer's* hull, being decompressed on his way up. Damant promptly had him dragged over by the tenders till he could clutch the air hose running down to Light, then ordered him to slide down that hose to the bottom, cut the lashing that held it there, and ease out on Light's lifeline till he came to the surface.

Down like lead through the sea went Blachford, who, having been once himself in a tight spot on that wreck, knew well enough the need for haste. In less than a minute he was on the bottom, and there at his feet was the lanyard holding his shipmate's air hose, while stretched taut from it, running up to the invisible Light floating somewhere above midway in the depths, was the rest of his air hose.

Blachford drew his diving knife. Getting a good grip with one hand on the hose leading upward to Light, with the other hand he slashed savagely at the lashing and cut it in one stroke. And then things happened fast. In a twinkling, Blachford felt himself shooting upward through the water. So great was Light's buoyancy that, the instant the lanyard was cut, the straining lifeline which Blachford was clutching dragged him surfaceward, with poor Blachford no more able to hold Light down than if he had hold of a stratosphere balloon.

Before the astounded Blachford could let go his grip, he had been jerked so high himself that the air in his own suit expanded enough to spread-eagle him also, and there were both divers, Blachford and Light, with tremendous buoyancy, helplessly racing surfaceward!

A few seconds later in quick succession they shot from the sea and splashed back to float horizontally in their distended rigs on top of the waves, fortunately both of them having missed killing themselves by colliding with the *Racer*. Hurriedly their tenders reeled them in alongside, where Light was hastily taken aboard and jammed immediately into the recompression chamber to get him back under pressure again. Blachford, after enough air had been bled out of his suit to get him vertical once more, was sent down under water to complete his decompression in the normal manner.

Meanwhile the astonished Damant, deeply thankful that neither man had been injured, concluded he had made a mistake. He realized that he should have known that Blachford, none too heavy himself, could never have held Light down. Instead of having him cut the lashing, he decided that he should have ordered Blachford to climb up the line to where Light was floating upside down, grab Light by both feet, and, by making himself as heavy as he could, capsize Light. After that, he might have deflated Light's rig enough so that both would have sunk gradually to the bottom again and all might have been well.

However, since both men had come through anyway without mishap, Damant could only chalk his conclusions up as something to be remembered next time, and soon the grubbing after gold bars was going on again as if nothing had happened.

By October, 1922, when stormy weather again stopped the job, the season's work had yielded 895 more gold bars to a total value of $7,500,000 and matters were looking better. Still further to brighten up the picture, 1923 was nearly a repetition of the year before, only better, with 1,255 additional ingots, valued at nearly $10,000,000, recovered from the depths in that one season. By 1924, all except 154 bars, worth about $1,200,000, had been retrieved, and so thoroughly had the divers scavenged the wreckage inside the now exposed shell of the *Laurentic* that it was hopeless to expect to find anything further inside the wreck. Still, $1,200,000 in real gold, the leavings so to speak of six years' work in picking the *Laurentic's* bones, was in itself a substantial prize, more than many a salvage expedition can look forward to as a reward for the whole job.

But where was the rest of that gold? It wasn't inside the shell, so all Damant and his divers could do, when they came back for their seventh year's struggle with the *Laurentic,* was to start digging beneath the shell plating through the rents and openings like portholes in it, into the clay bottom of the sea beneath, in the hope that the missing bars had fallen through the openings and there they might find them.

So down on the shell plating went the divers again, 10 feet now below the level of the adjacent sea floor, fighting to hold back the inflowing flood of sand the while they probed every tear and hole in the steel carpeting the bottom, for ingots beneath. Once in a while they found one, and whenever a diver came to a gap large enough to let him slide through, he started to excavate underneath, with the surprising result that some ingots were discovered under the shell several feet away from the nearest edge of the opening through which they had fallen.

The only possible explanation of this odd phenomenon was that, in the years that had gone by since the gold fell through the holes, the entire shell plating of the wreck must have slipped a few feet, covering the ingots.

Excavating wholesale beneath the shell to recover the lost bars was both slow and dangerous, so Damant decided instead to cut the last layer of the *Laurentic's* bottom up piecemeal, searching the uncovered ocean floor beneath as he went along.

With explosive charges in long strings to do the cutting, the thick steel skin of the *Laurentic* was plate by plate taken apart and the sea floor beneath carefully combed, till an area of over 2,000 square feet had been thus searched. The result of months of this was that 129 out of the last 154 bars had been found buried in the clay when winter finally came to end the search in 1924, leaving still missing only 25 bars out of the 3,211 which eight years before had gone down in the *Laurentic*.

Where to look for those last 25 bars no one could tell, but with 99.2% of all the gold recovered, it appeared that searching another year for the few remaining ingots would not repay the cost of holding back the sand. Accordingly in the autumn of 1924 the job was concluded, eight years after it had started and with seven years actually spent in salvage. The total cost of the work was between 2 and 3% of the bullion recovered.

The recovery of that $24,800,000 in gold from the *Laurentic* stands unique in salvage annals. Over 5,000 dives were made and a large ocean liner was cut to pieces by divers from top to bottom under the worst working conditions imaginable. Work has been done before and since at greater depths, but no submarine job approaching in magnitude and recovery the *Laurentic* salvage has ever been attempted. That no diver was killed nor any even permanently injured, is a tribute to the technical skill with which Damant managed his job, and that such a heartbreaking task was ever successful in the face of practically insuperable obstacles is due only to the extraordinary leadership both on deck and under the sea exhibited by Commander (now Captain) G. C. C. Damant, R.N.

*Kitchener's Gold**

by Charles Courtney

An admirer and friend of Houdini, CHARLES COURTNEY *has rivalled the great master in his knowledge of locks and keys. From boyhood and his first job at nine as apprentice to a locksmith he has been intrigued by such devices. Now he is known all over the world for his skill with them. Whenever a safe or a vault must be opened, the call goes out for Charles Courtney, master locksmith. On the face of it a locksmith's life might seem an unexciting one but when the locksmith is also a diver and a man with the heart for adventure, adventure and danger seek him out. Such chapters as this one from his own story* Unlocking Adventure *prove his profession an active one.*

* "Kitchener's Gold" from *Unlocking Adventure* by Charles Courtney, reprinted by permission of McGraw-Hill Book Company.

SPRING OF 1933 came, bright and raw and gusty. The two deep-sea divers who were working out preliminary plans for the "Hampshire" expedition had spent several weeks in New York checking every final detail of equipment. They were outstanding in their profession: Costello, a lanky Australian who had brought up gold from many a famous wreck, and Mansfield from Norfolk, one of the best divers on the eastern coast, like his father before him. Early in the new year, they sailed to fit out the mother ship and gather a crew.

There was nothing to do but wait and try to keep my mind on the shop. Finally, one Wednesday afternoon in late March, my secretary called me from the cutting machine.

"London on the phone."

It had come. Sir Basil Zaharoff's voice, as clear as if he had been speaking in Manhattan, instructed me to take the "Bremen" on Friday for Southampton, where I would receive further instructions. With scarcely time to eat or sleep, I made final arrangements at the shop, bade my wife and daughter good-by, and fell into my berth on the "Bremen," too tired to think. On that voyage across the Atlantic, as I looked over the rail into the deep water, realizing that I was soon going down 400 feet, there were several moments when I would have turned back if there had been an opportunity.

Mansfield was on the pier in Southampton. After a hurried day in London where I took out a $100,000 life policy, we left for Stromness where we were to join our salvaging boat lying about sixteen miles offshore. Everything had been done with the greatest secrecy, because no salvager has a claim to a wreck unless his ship is actually tied to the hulk.

A small boat took us out to the "K.S.R.," a stout snub-nosed vessel lying at anchor in a choppy sea. Captain Brandt, a tightly knit, gray-haired German with a competent air, met us at the ladder. He saw me examining the boat, noting the sand- and mud-sucking pumps, the winches and grips.

"Yes," he said with a smile that deepened the furrows in his eroded face, "she's equipped with everything you ever heard of. Finest salvaging ship afloat." He took me below to a cabin in which Costello was sitting over a game of solitaire. We three had barely settled ourselves over a glass of beer when we felt the boat heading out to sea. As we bounced about in the cabin, we checked over final plans for the work.

"We three, and the skipper of course, and the representatives of the syndicate, are the only ones who know what we're after," said Costello. "The skipper has told the crew that we are a German outfit fishing for submarines, but he must think they are cross-eyed if they don't recognize the British flag. Most of them may suspect that we are after bigger fish but they don't know what. In addition to us, there are several experienced deep-sea divers. The rest are a gang of about fifty ordinary divers, Greeks from the mainland and Crete and Italians from the Mediterranean."

"Won't they be a job to handle?" I asked, remembering the crew of the "Artiglio II."

"Yes," Mansfield grinned, "but the captain and crew are German and they're tough."

That evening an engineer who was in charge of the armored suits gave us a talk on proper breathing under water, and Max Weissfelt, a stout middle-aged German who said he represented the syndicate, impressed upon us the necessity for speed and secrecy.

The sea continued to run high. Off the Orkneys we were pitched about by a gale. Cursing, the skipper put back to Stromness, but before the storm had blown over, we were out again, impatiently skirting the coast, turning out to sea when the waters were too rough.

Then the sun came out and the wind died. All night we rocked gently on a placid sea. In the morning the boat began to cruise around in circles, darting this way and that like a pointer on a scent. Costello paced the cabin, nervous as a cat.

"The 'Hampshire' should be just about under us. When we found her last year, I went down and fastened a buoy to her. She's so heavily armored that we're going to have a tough job. We can't use dynamite, and we'll have to be very careful with the torch or we'll explode the ammunition and send ourselves to kingdom come."

We felt the engines stop. The next moment the captain stuck in his head.

"All right, boys. We've dropped anchor."

Mansfield leaped up and we all followed Captain Brandt along the companionway. We helped Costello pull on a couple of woolen undersuits and pushed him into his diving armor. When his feet were on the stage, we bowed our heads while the captain muttered a prayer. Then we lowered the stage as the captain and engineer payed out the taut guy lines.

We kept our eyes on the rope, listening to the steady throbbing of the pumps. The captain looked at his watch.

"How long has he been down?" asked the mate, coming on deck. From his post by the loud-speaker, Weissfelt answered, "Half an hour." Even as he spoke, Costello's voice came through the telephone.

"Here she is, buried in the sand. Buoy still fast." Slowly we pulled him up and helped him out of the armor.

"Well," asked the captain, "what's the job?"

"The stern has settled," Costello told us. "She is three fathoms deeper than she was last summer. There's a mountain of sand to be got away."

Then began a week of concentrated preparation, drills, instructions. First, the divers had to be broken in, as most of them had never been deeper than 100 feet. The engineer took six or seven at a time, put them on a stage and lowered them gradually in their heavy rubber suits. When they reached the total blackness of 250 feet, the mental and physical depression that seized them threw them into a panic. They shouted on the phone that they were sick, dying, anything to get to the surface. The engineer called soothing words to them, all the time lowering the stage. When they had reached the bottom and found themselves in the more cheerful twilight made by the reflection of the water on the sand, they felt better. If they did not recover from the panic and the physical discomfort, they were brought up and given work aboard ship, but most of them stuck it out.

They were a hardy, reckless lot. The bare maintenance that they received as wages made them take any risk to win their percentage of the find. I had seen their breed on the "Artiglio II." During the last frantic week, they stayed down so long after their allotted hour that several dropped dead with the bends when they were brought to the surface. When they were within reach of gold, they took the chance of torn tissues, ruptured nerves, and frightful muscular pains.

Soon the salvage boat was tied firmly to each end of the wreck and the divers were working with sand suckers and grabs, clearing a way to the breach that Costello had located the year before. When they were on the salvage ship, they lightened their boredom by endless fights and quarrels below decks. The captain was a driver, but just. He and the engineer kept a vigilant watch and were careful to separate the Italians from the Cretans, the Cretans from the men of Samos. They were never sent down on the same stage, nor were men who had quarreled; it was too easy to cut an enemy's life line.

In the meantime we were busy above, checking our equipment. On the largest space of deck, we drew our chart. Costello outlined the "Hampshire" as she lay, showing the two holes that pierced her armor, the large jagged one through which we could not gain entrance and the small one on the bottom, aft of the first bulkhead, which he had found open on their initial trip.

Were they torpedo or mine holes? Costello could not be sure. The larger one was undoubtedly a mine hole, but the small one might have been made by a torpedo that hit on a slant and tore a jagged opening instead of the usual round hole. Of one thing he was positive: there had been no explosion from within as had been rumored in England, because the edges of the holes were bent in, not out. When the divers cleared the opening and worked into the first bulkhead, it was our job to break through the door, and so from bulkhead to bulkhead, until we reached the captain's cabin and the gold.

When the sand and debris were cleaned from the breach, Mansfield, Costello, and I went down to inspect. The day was unusually calm and the sink plates that we had lowered to test the underwater currents, indicated no crosscurrents.

To go over the side on a bright day when the sun is irradiating the water is always intoxicating. The fish darting about in the upper layers, their fins gleaming in the blue light, give one a sense of well-being. The black-out zone lost most of its terrors in the armored suits that withstood pressure.

We kept on going down. In the great depths the diver, no matter what kind of suit he wears, is shut in with a terrible loneliness—with the feeling that there is nobody in the world but him and God. And in this dark wilderness of sea, it is a sharp personal encounter. I have talked to hundreds of divers and have never met one who has not had this experience.

At 385 feet, there was light enough to see our way around. The fine sand that our boots stirred made the water thick and murky, like fog. On the sandy bottom under the "Egypt," I remembered, we kicked up a white dust as if we were walking in the desert.

The hulk was slippery, but at that depth our suits seemed to have no weight. Exploring aft, below the poop deck, we stumbled over skeletons. Where they were dislodged by our feet, we saw a ghastly thing—arms, hands, parts of legs on which the flesh had been preserved by their casing of sand.

The port side of the gun deck had been fairly cleared of wreckage. Each gun was loaded and beside it was a mound of skeletons with earphones on their heads, lying by shells that were never fired. These men had not deserted their stations. They must have believed that they had been hit by a submarine, for they went down standing by their guns, looking for revenge. In the forward hatchway, we stumbled over hundreds of skeletons, sailors who had tried to come up from below decks when the order was given to abandon ship.

At the small breach, luck was against us. A great mass of debris had blocked it from the inside, so we were pulled up and each took a stiff drink of Scotch to help us forget those poor fellows down below. At the end of the day, there was always plenty of Scotch for the Americans and English, beer for the Germans, and wine for the Italians and Greeks.

For the next few days, we stayed on deck while the divers worked into the hull. Then we went down to attack the first bulkhead, accompanied by several other divers to keep our lines clear. We were using a new method to drop off the armor plates. Where water had seeped in around the rivet heads and rusted them, we broke them off with pneumatic chisels, then pushed the rivets out with a pneumatic hammer. When the plates didn't fall clear of the wreckage, they were dropped to the bottom by the grab. The progress was slow, as we reckon work on land, but every day the hammers came nearer to the gold. Point by point, the advance was recorded by the chief engineer. At night the sand pumps thumped and in the morning the sand was spread over the ocean as far as we could see.

For those of us on deck the time dragged. On Easter Sunday, after our dinner of roast pig with an apple in his mouth and all the trimmings, I borrowed two pieces of paper from Weissfelt, whose pad, brought from a hotel in

Berlin, was the only writing paper on board. I sat staring at the crest of the Eden Hotel, trying to make the most of the space to write my wife and daughter and hoping to have the letter mailed by one of the engineers who was going ashore for supplies. It was early April, the wind was raw, and I suspected that the treacherous crosscurrents were making hell for the men below. But the work went on. Every once in a while, we heard a dull plop as a piece of armor fell to the bottom.

By night the wind had risen to a gale and the captain's face was as angry as the sea. There was nothing for it but to run to Stromness harbor.

We were not encouraged to go ashore. Those four days cooped up on the idle ship, listening to the wind and watching the whitecaps foaming on the savage black waves that rushed the harbor, were enough to wear down any man's nerves. I remember how Weissfelt snapped at the first mate when he said that the North Sea could be as calm and beautiful as the Mediterranean.

Chiefly we talked about the "Hampshire," not about our hopes for the gold—they were too intense for comfort—but about the fate of the cruiser and the men aboard. The long controversy about the manner of the sinking we fought again. Was the cruiser destroyed by a U-boat as the Admiralty had reported, or by a mine? How it happened that the War Minister of England and her greatest hero, not to mention the Bank of England's $10,000,000 in gold, had been risked in the North Sea without certainty of a clear channel was a matter of endless speculation.

Sitting over our games of pinochle, we contributed what we knew and pieced together a fairly accurate picture of the catastrophe. A year earlier, in 1932, I had heard that the police in New York had picked up Captain Fritz Duquesne, the same Duquesne who was convicted at the beginning of the Second World War as the head of a German spy ring. He was not a stranger to them; a versatile, prankish, enormously conceited fellow, he had escaped from the prison ward at Bellevue by faking paralysis and was not above twitting the police about it. This time, Scotland Yard was looking for him. He had been boasting that he was the man who had killed Kitchener. Disguised as a Russian officer and furnished with the proper papers by the German Intelligence Service, he was supposed to have sailed with the English mission aboard the "Hampshire." Off the Orkneys, he signaled a U-boat and escaped in it as the ship went down.

One of the officers told us a likelier story. He had known a German officer stationed with the code department at Neumünster. This young code expert's account was so credible that it appeared in a leading German weekly.

On the evening of June 1, 1916, this young officer was sitting in the code room with the lights dimmed, on the alert because he was expecting a big action by the German fleet. Spread out on the table were messages waiting to be decoded. The urgent one on which he was working interested the officer because of the two English words, "Orkney Islands." While he was puzzling over it, two other messages were picked up from English boats in the North Sea, identical messages: "Proceeding according to orders." Decoded, the first message was an Admiralty order to take a course west of the Orkneys, south to north, as the route was free of mines. Evidently two boats were following these orders. What boats, he wondered. Perhaps a torpedo boat escorting an important transport or a munitions ship. As these waters were usually clear of mines, the Admiralty must be sending a very important ship to take such precautions.

On June 2, the officer knew that Captain Kurt Beiten was ordered to proceed to the Orkneys as fast as possible in the underseas mine layer "U-57." He laid thirty-four mines in the northerly course off the Orkneys and on the third, was back at his base in Helgoland.

On the evening of the sixth, the code officer at Neumünster heard an SOS directed to a special station in the north of England, saying that a ship had struck a mine and was sinking near the Orkneys. This was followed two hours later by several messages from English ships that were evidently searching for something more important than a torpedo boat. It was not until weeks afterward that the world knew about the sinking of the "Hampshire," which drowned Lord Kitchener and 650 men.

Costello was inclined to credit this story because it

fitted in with what he had been able to learn. Since his salvaging trip the preceding summer, he had become so interested in the fate of the "Hampshire" that he had spent some time digging up all the facts and surmises that he could find. He had discovered that the lonely watcher on the north coast who had received the SOS was so incoherent with horror that by the time he had stumbled to a telegraph station and wakened the sleepy operator, it took his message two hours to reach the Admiralty.

On that shore also was landed the handful of survivors. The only eyewitness that Costello could find was a sailor named Rogerson. At the first explosion, about seven-thirty in the evening, the commander ordered all hands on deck and sent an officer to launch the captain's boat. Lord Kitchener came on deck with the other officers. As the ship was already listing badly to starboard, the commander shouted to Kitchener to come onto the bridge while the boat was being lowered. The war lord went to the bridge and stood by the commander. As the sailors tried to lower the longboat, four officers came forward to take Kitchener to it, but the Minister of War would not budge. One of the officers seized him by the arm and attempted to drag him forward, shouting to the officers and men, "Make way for Lord Kitchener!" At that moment there was a second explosion, and the cruiser sank with no boats lowered.

Costello also had verified the rumors about the gold. It was true that in the government archives, at least so far as a private citizen could discover, there was no record of the $10,000,000 in gold for the Russian government, but there was a record that this amount had been withdrawn from the Bank of England. Not even a wartime government draws $10,000,000 secretly and makes no record of it unless it is intended for a very important mission.

All these stories were secondhand, but there was one man with our expedition who was more closely related to the event. He was Lieutenant Weissfelt. Max had been a German sailor during the First World War and had served on the mine layer "A-10" off the coast of Helgoland. The boat had covered a certain territory, laying mines and checking up every now and then to see that they were in their right places, especially after storms when they were likely to break loose or drag anchorage.

The day after the "Hampshire" sank, the "A-10" found that five of the mines in that part of her territory were missing. Max remembered them when he heard about Kitchener's death and checked in the little record book in which he entered the longitude and latitude of every mine in his territory.

After the war he wanted to forget everything connected with it, so he stuck the notebook away somewhere at home with his uniform. Perhaps he would never have looked at it again if he had not met Henry Row. Row was an Englishman, who was in Germany looking up every German sailor who had served with mine layers in that part of the North Sea. After he had followed many false clues, he met Weissfelt and learned about the little black notebook with the record and position of all the mines that had been laid off the Orkneys. Weissfelt was not at all sure that the book was still in existence. The two went to Max's old home in Stettin and searched through all his books and papers until they discovered it in an old trunk in the attic.

With these records to guide them, the two chartered a fishing boat and spent three years dragging the waters off Marwickhead Bank. When they had almost given up hope, they found the wreck. There could be no mistake, because Weissfelt went down in a diving suit and brought up a piece of the vessel that was lettered "H.M.S. Hampshire."

"Then what did you do?" we asked.

Costello answered for Max. "You can be sure that he didn't sell his information to the British Admiralty, although he and Row tried hard enough. The Admiralty flatly denied that there was any gold aboard. Consequently, he formed his own syndicate. The gold's there, all right. All we've got to do is to haul it up when we get a break in this filthy weather."

The next day we chugged out of the harbor in the face of a dying wind. We were a gloomy bunch, in spite of our relief at getting started. Suppose the storm had loosened a rack of the "Hampshire's" bombs. She was full of ammunition and torpedoes. We might find her scattered all over the floor of the North Sea with her gold buried in slime.

Costello and Mansfield went down, although the crosscurrents were so strong that they had to crawl. In a few moments they pulled the signal rope. They didn't even wait to telephone. We who were hovering around the loud-speaker knew that something was wrong.

That evening in the captain's cabin, we held a consultation. The whole ship was buried anew in sand, they told us, and it would take weeks to clear another opening. Again the divers made their way toward the captain's cabin. For seventeen days they worked, going down twice and sometimes three times a day in weather that was often so foul that they were risking their lives every time they went over the rail. The deck above the captain's cabin was dragged away by grabs, powerful ones that could lift fifty tons.

On the next trip I went down with Costello and Mansfield to open what we believed was the door to the gold. It was a still, bright Sunday morning, a perfect day, and we descended immediately after church, with the prayers still on our lips. Climbing over the wreckage, we unscrewed the dogs, the small levers that stop the bolt, attached the hoist-chain tackle to the airtight door, and slowly pulled it open. There in the sealed room were two perfectly preserved officers staring at us. The water flowed in gently and the countercurrent lifted the officers from their chairs and swept them past us. Reaching out my hook, I caught a hand. It came loose from the arm and I was left holding it while the rest of the officer floated by. On one of the fingers was a gold signet ring. I dropped it into my bag, thinking it would identify him, and threw away the ghostly hand. Glancing around for Mansfield and Costello in the dim flame of the submarine lamp, I saw that they were making for the door. Mansfield I heard calling for the emergency stage. When we reached the surface, we were all three so shaky that we couldn't stand.

"I thought they were chasing us," muttered Costello, taking a long swig of whisky.

The next day we were so jittery that we didn't go down but lay in our bunks steadying our nerves with Scotch. Weissfelt and a German diver, Gruber, put on the armor to bring up the papers from the captain's cabin. Gruber was a good diver, but a gloomy soul and not afraid to express himself. They had not been down twenty minutes when he called the emergency. The two officers were floating about in the ship, pursuing them. It was fully a week before we were at normal work again.

We found the safes not in the captain's cabin but in the little anteroom beyond, six enormous strongboxes and a smaller one that was evidently the ship's own chest. The grabs could not reach these strongboxes without dynamiting, so they had to be opened where they were. I began on the smallest one, working for three days to cut the bar that engaged the lock. When the door gave, Weissfelt and Costello pressed forward so eagerly that the floodlights were too near to give a proper light. I raised my right hand to say O.K. and stepped back. The light fell on rows of splintered boxes disgorging gold coins dull and green with tarnish.

Costello pushed forward a canvas bag with a lead bottom and I dropped into it the coins, which were several times as heavy as lead. Costello dragged the bag back to Mansfield, who gave him an empty one and passed the loaded one on to the next diver. Bagful by bagful, the gold was passed back through several hands until the man at the breach loaded it on the bucket of the hoist. With the last bag we packed the ship's papers. They had not been kept watertight, but some of them might be legible.

Gold at last. On board the "K.S.R." the diving gang went mad. Everyone had gold in his hands and was shouting what he would do with it when the job was done.

In the captain's cabin we tried to decipher the ship's papers and code books. The outer sheets were hopeless, but the inner ones had been pressed so tightly by the weight of the sea that they could be pulled apart and read. Yes, there they were, in precise military language, the orders for this expedition that was to bolster Russia with England's greatest soldier and her gold.

After working steadily for a week, we checked our salvage and found that, in addition to paper money, we had brought up £60,000 in gold. As supplies were running low, we heaved anchor and made for Stavanger. It had been arranged that the first gold would be deposited in England, but on the way the captain asked that it be taken to Germany. When the argument grew heated, I was elected referee. As this money was only a small part of the salvage and much of our success depended on the good will of our German crew, I decided for Berlin. Delegated to take the gold, I was landed with it and did not draw a normal breath until it was safe in the vaults of the Reichsbank.

It was April 29. Hjalmar Schacht himself thanked me and gave me an invitation to attend the great May Day celebration at which Adolph Hitler was to speak. I had heard that it was to be a mighty gathering and it looked as if everybody in Germany was there. My seat in the Tribune was so close to Hitler that I could easily have stuck a knife into him, but I was not impressed with the bare-headed little man in the shabby brown raincoat who spoke Low German and shouted in a high rasping voice.

On the third day we were back at Stavanger, but our luck had run out. All the time we had been away the "K.S.R." had been hounded by such a storm that the crew were fuming and cursing. The captain was so glum that he would barely speak and the men kept out of his way.

Next day we put to sea again. Scarcely had the boat tied up to the wreck than Costello and Mansfield were over the side, only to find that once more the hulk was buried, inside and out, in seaweed and sand. That meant days of work to clear the passage again. Grimly the divers dug a new entrance, heartbreaking work in competition with the currents. All night and part of the day, the pumps spewed the sand upon the dirty sea. The weather was foul and our tempers were short.

Many a day the divers went down when the crosscurrents were so strong that they were flirting with death. Costello and Mansfield kept at it too, directing the job of forcing the bulkhead where the rest of the bullion was stored, reserving for me the final work of opening the safes. I was afraid that their nerves were stretching to the breaking point. When a diver loses his coolness and judgment, he is in grave danger. Kruger, one of the best German divers, was nearly killed when his line was fouled, and from that time on, Gruber was full of black forebodings. Between the liquor, the fog and rain, we were all as restless as a cage of wildcats.

One morning when the sink plates warned that to go over was a plain invitation to death, the captain ordered me to go with the other two on an inspection trip. Unless the current had washed in more sand, the strongboxes were uncovered. I looked at Costello. He was so exhausted that his hands twitched, and his face was flushed with anger, although I could see that he was trying his best to hold his tongue. Mansfield looked as if he had seen a ghost. They had done the gruelling work; I could afford to stand up to the captain.

"No," I said, "I won't go down in this weather. Look at your plates. It's suicide."

The wrinkles in the captain's face grew taut. His watery eyes blazed.

"What, yellow?"

"Call it that if you want. Your gold is no use to me when I'm dead. I won't go down until it's decent weather."

"Then you go down without him, Costello. You and Mansfield."

"No," snapped the lank Australian, "I want to live too."

The captain glared at us, his thin lips quivering. He walked to the door and back again. Then he stepped up to me and thrust out his hand.

"I'm sorry. It's this damned North Sea. It's getting me down."

We shook hands but there was no warmth in his voice.

All that day we sat in the cabin and played pinochle. We were miserable and self-conscious, thinking about the $500 that each day cost, dollars that would be subtracted from the crew's percentage, and imagining that we could feel the Greeks hating us the way the captain did, cursing us under their breath because we were practically stealing their gold.

The next morning was little better, but Mansfield decided to go down and see if the boxes were clear. His line fouled and he was slammed against the walls of the hulk and pulled up unconscious, but by night was well again except for a dizzy head.

Next morning the weather was still foul but we decided to risk it. Costello, Mansfield, Weissfelt, and I went first in the armored suits, each on a separate stage, after the captain had said his prayers. Half an hour later, the rubber suit divers followed. The current was so strong that they could not stand up and looked like horrible deep-sea monsters crawling toward us.

Forcing the bulkhead door farther back, we crawled into the bullion room where we found chest after chest of gold coins, twenty-ruble pieces. The boxes of gold were too heavy to drag out, so Costello and I broke them open, filling our bags with as many as we could manage and passing them back to Mansfield and Weissfelt, who started them down the line to the hoist. We had been working for two hours and should have gone up for new air, but the excitement of handling the gold kept us below.

Suddenly the water began to move to and fro. A crosscurrent snatched us. The bulkhead door was pushed almost shut, leaving us in total darkness. I was hurled against the wall so violently that I thought I was being torn apart. My left wrist broke and something crashed into my right side, stabbing me with agonizing pain. Hot blood ran down my right leg and a noise like Big Ben began to thunder in my ears, telling me that the air supply was giving out. Through the water, I could hear the screams of Weissfelt and Costello.

For one hour we were trapped, waiting to die. The horror of that hour is so vivid that even today, nine years later, the memory of it gives me a collapsed feeling in the pit of my stomach. The one image that tormented me was the grave of my son. Fiercely I prayed God that I might go back to it, not be left on this wreck, a skeleton to be kicked and trampled by other hunters for Kitchener's gold.

Then the current shifted. With all our strength, we forced back the door and inched toward the breach.

Suddenly I felt the horrible fear that I was going to go mad for lack of air. Detaching the cable inside the suit, I reached the top deck, blew the ballast water out of the suit and popped to the surface of the water, hoping that Martin, the quartermaster who was on the lookout, would see me before the tide carried me away.

For about twenty minutes I floated, slapped about by the waves. Then I heard the sound of rowing coming closer and closer, every stroke vibrating through the water like a hammer blow. My iron coffin was too heavy to lift into the boat, so the crew tied a rope to an eyebolt in the helmet and towed me to the ship where the winch dragged me aboard. When my helmet was pulled off, I collapsed beside Costello who lay on deck with a crushed chest. Weissfelt had a broken spine, Mansfield was injured, and Kruger dead.

We heaved anchor and raced to an English port where Sir Basil Zaharoff swore us to secrecy and rushed us to hospitals. For three days I lay on my back, living over in my delirium that hour of agony. On the fourth day the strength began to flow back into me and I asked for a barber. When he had finished shaving me he held up a mirror. I did not recognize the man who stared back at me; his hair was completely white.

*Escape Artist and Master Magician**

by Harold Kellock

Although he died in 1926, Harry Houdini's name is still a synonym for escape artist. No man has ever rivalled his incredible escapes from handcuffs, strait jackets, prisons, metal-lined boxes. Because his feats were dependent upon skill, muscular coordination, and complete freedom from fear, his career is as much one of dangerous adventure as that of Akeley or Eadie or Ditmars. HAROLD KELLOCK *has here told something of Houdini's boyhood and youth and something of his greatest tricks.*

* "Escape Artist and Master Magician" from *Houdini: His Life-Story* by Harold Kellock, reprinted by permission of Harcourt Brace and Company, Inc.

HOUDINI BEGAN his career with a traveling circus at the age of nine, in the Middle West, and his first trick, which he had perfected laboriously in secret in the family woodshed, was to pick up needles with his eyelids while suspended by the heels, head downward. From this humble early beginning it was a far cry and for many years a laborious struggle to the rôle of the master magician who thrilled and amazed great audiences everywhere with his daredevil feats, his unsurpassed dexterity, his almost superhuman physical endurance, his mystifying escapes from manacles, strait-jackets, prison cells, sealed chambers, chests and casks of every kind, from his famous Chinese water-torture cell, from a living grave six feet in the earth, and from a heavy packing case, carefully nailed together by experts, weighted, and tossed into the sea. When he died, in Detroit, October 31, 1926, at the age of fifty-two, he had been a public performer for forty-three years.

Hundreds of thousands of persons in various cities have seen Houdini, stripped and securely handcuffed by police experts, leap from some bridge or boat into a stream or harbor, on some occasions in weather so cold that a hole had to be cut in the ice before he could jump, and have seen him emerge again, within two minutes, free and smiling. Other hundreds of thousands have seen him encased in a police strait-jacket, and thus securely trussed, suspended, head downward, by a block and tackle outside some public building, and have watched him free himself within a few minutes. Scores of thousands more have observed him, on the stage of the New York Hippodrome, perform the most ambitious vanishing stunt ever undertaken by any conjurer. Before them on the stage, directly over the big Hippodrome tank containing a quarter of a million gallons of water, stood a five-ton elephant, swaying heavily in the spotlight, and almost in an instant, behold! that huge mass of living flesh had disappeared and the big stage was empty, save only for the smiling, nonchalant showman. Finally, in all the larger cities in America and in many of the principal European capitals Houdini mystified the public authorities by his jail-breaking demonstrations. After permitting the police to strip him, cover him with manacles, and lock him in their securest cell in their best-ordered jail, in a few minutes he would walk into the office of the warden or police chief, free and fully clothed, the elaborate shackles dangling loose in his hands.

What was the secret of these feats of wonder? His art really included manifold secrets, and very largely the details of these must rest in the grave with him. Only one person, his wife, was in his confidence, and in certain matters she was pledged to secrecy. In a general way, however, Houdini on occasion would frankly discuss his methods with his few intimates. His great secret, in fact, had a double key.

"My chief task has been to conquer fear," he said. "When I am stripped and manacled, nailed securely within a weighted packing case and thrown into the sea, or when I am buried alive under six feet of earth, it is necessary to preserve absolute serenity of spirit. I have to work with great delicacy and lightning speed. If I grow panicky I am lost. And if something goes wrong, if there is some little accident or mishap, some slight miscalculation, I am lost unless all my faculties are working on high, free from mental tension or strain. The public sees only the thrill of the accomplished trick; they have no conception of the tortuous preliminary self-training that was necessary to conquer fear.

"My second secret has been, by equally vigorous self-training to enable me to do remarkable things with my body, to make not one muscle or a group of muscles, but *every* muscle, a responsive worker, quick and sure for its part, to make my fingers super-fingers in dexterity, and to train my toes to do the work of fingers."

This double spiritual and physical training was the foundation of his art. In his case, also, genius consisted of an infinite capacity for taking pains.

Intimate visitors to Houdini's home had glimpses of this infinite capacity. Seated conversing with friends, he would absently take a pack of cards from his pocket and for half an hour or an hour would exercise his fingers in manipulation, making certain cards appear at the top of the pack when they seemed hopelessly shuffled, all the time conversing on a wide range of subjects and paying not the least attention to the cards or his sensitive and agile fingers. "I have to keep in practice to do things like this mechanically, like walking or breathing," he explained once to a friend who inquired the reason for this intermittent exercise. On other occasions he would take a length of string from his pocket, tie it in various sorts of knots, and drop it on the floor. Presently his visitor might observe that Houdini had unobtrusively slipped off his shoes and socks and was untying and retying the knots with his toes, meanwhile never so much as glancing at his own remarkable manipulations.

His training for his various immersion stunts and for feats such as remaining encased in a sealed casket under water for an hour and a half was peculiarly arduous. For months on end, several times a day, he would practice going under water in his own bathtub, holding a stop-watch to test his endurance, lengthening the period of immersion each day until he could stay under for more than four minutes without grave discomfort. His high record was four minutes, sixteen seconds, in a public test. For hours at a time he would practice slow-breathing exercises, accustoming himself to get along with a minimum of oxygen, so that he could feed his lungs sparingly with the few cubic feet of air in a little casket and endure for an almost unbelievable time. It is safe to say that no human being could compete with Houdini in keeping himself alive, on occasion, with hardly enough oxygen to suffice a mouse.

On tour, with cold weather approaching, he would take matutinal cold baths, a little icier each morning, to prepare himself for his stunt of being pushed overboard handcuffed in chilling waters and freeing himself on the bottom. His diaries record the stages of this Spartan preparation. Typical are the successive entries in January, 1907. They run: "*Jan. 7.* Gee whiz! Another ice-bath. They want to see me earn my money.—*Jan. 9.* Took cold bath, 49 deg. *Jan. 10.* Took cold bath, 48 deg. Doctor stops ice bath.—*Jan. 16.* Cold bath, 40 deg. Gee, it's cold.—*Jan. 18.* Taking icy baths to get ready for bridge jump. Water about 36 deg."

On more than one occasion his training in complete mental serenity under the most critical circumstances saved his life.

One conspicuous instance occurred in Detroit, where he had a fortnight's engagement at the beginning of the winter of 1906. In accordance with his usual custom of giving a free public thriller to excite interest in his show, he arranged to be hurled, handcuffed, into the Detroit River from the Belle Isle bridge during one of the first days of his engagement. When the morning arrived the manager of the theater called him up to report that the river was frozen solid, and the stunt, therefore, could not be performed.

"The public will think you were four-flushing," he said. "Can't you do something else that will go just as big?"

"What's the matter with the river stunt?" Houdini came back. "Can't you get some one to saw a hole in the ice under the bridge? That will be all right with me."

Accordingly a large open space was cleared in the river ice, and at the appointed time Houdini made his way through the throng of thousands that had gathered on bridge and shore in the bitter north wind. Mrs. Houdini was not with him that day, though almost invariably she accompanied him to the scene of his public thrillers. She had a bad cold, was running a temperature, and was forbidden to leave her bed in the hotel. There she fretted, in great discomfort of mind, listening to the north wind whining across the roofs and thinking of Houdini in the icy river. The water stunts were the bane of her life anyway, for she more than any one except Houdini himself knew the risks he was taking. Moreover, she had to conceal her terror over these daredevil performances, because she knew she must do nothing to damage his morale. She remembers kissing him gayly as he went off to the bridge, though her heart ached with fear.

At the bridge he stripped to bathing trunks, was carefully manacled by policemen, exchanged a little banter with newspaper friends, and, by his own instructions, was pushed off the parapet of the bridge and vanished with a splash into the icy water.

On such occasions Houdini always had with him in the crowd a skilled under-water man as a sort of aqueous life insurance. This man had a rope with him, and his instructions were, if Houdini did not appear by the end of the third minute, to make the rope fast, toss over the free end, and go down and get him. Of course the presence of this emergency man was not generally advertised.

Usually, on such occasions, Houdini reappeared in a little over a minute. This time two minutes passed, then three. The rope man was slow with his rope. It took a lot of courage deliberately to let oneself down into that black hole in the ice. Possibly his hands were already numbed with cold and he had difficulty in getting his rope ready.

The time went on. At the end of four minutes the police surgeons and other physicians who had been invited to witness the performance expressed the opinion that some mishap had occurred and Houdini had done his last stunt. The newspaper men began sending off messengers with hasty bulletins to their papers. They and the doctors, with occasional glances at their watches, kept their eyes glued on that black hole in the ice, and in the big crowd, in which a low murmur of dimay was growing, thousands of eyes were fixed on that spot.

Finally the rope splashed into the water. A terribly frightened diver started to climb down. But before he got under way Houdini's head and arm flashed out of the water, and the next instant he was supporting himself by the rope on the surface of the stream. He had been under water eight minutes!

Back in the hotel Mrs. Houdini was lying uneasily in bed when she heard newsboys crying in the street.

"Quick, open the window wide," she said to her attendant, and suddenly the cries became clear: "Extree! Extree! Houdini dead!" "Extree! Houdini drowned in river."

She hurried the woman out to get a paper, and the next few minutes were the most desolate of her experience. But when the woman returned, Houdini himself burst in close behind her. His head was still dripping, and he was blue with cold, but he was alive.

After he had a hot bath and rub-down, and some steaming tea he told his wife the story.

"I reached the bottom and freed myself quickly as usual," he said, "but there must have been more current than I calculated, for when I came up there was solid ice above me, and I couldn't locate the hole. I went down again and looked, and I swam about under water a little, that confounded hole had vanished as if it had suddenly frozen over—and after a little, I began to need air. That bothered me, but I got an idea. I let myself come up gently, and sure enough my idea was a good one. Between the surface of the water and the under surface of the ice was a little air space, about half an inch wide. By lying on my back and poking my nose into this gently, I could fill my lungs.

"Of course this wasn't too easy. If I drew in water with the air I'd take to choking, and then—well, I didn't think about it. I'd get a little air, and then navigate around a bit looking for that damned hole, and then I'd have to get another breath. I couldn't see much anyway, and it wasn't so warm down there.

"After what seemed about an hour, I saw the rope flash into the water, not very far away, and you bet I made for it. That was that."

Sometimes, in rare moments of confidence, Houdini would give an intimate friend a fleeting glimpse of his technique. Late one afternoon, at the office of his attorney, some months before Houdini's last illness, in the interval of waiting for some legal papers, the talk turned on the opening of safes, and the lawyer asked if it was really true that Houdini could open any safe. "Yes," said Houdini. "If every one knew what I know about safes, safes wouldn't be worth very much. I sometimes wonder at the possible consequences if a clever hypnotist should get hold of me, and dig out my secrets about safes, and pass them on to persons in the underworld. But it is a remote danger. I don't believe they would know how to apply the secrets, even if they heard them.

"When I was a youngster in petticoats locks had a fascination for me. As I grew up I worked with various locksmiths. The study of locks led to the study of all sorts of locking appliances. In this connection I took up physics, even dipped into chemistry a bit. You know five hours is a full night's sleep for me. I can do with less. It's remarkable what a lot of work a fellow can get done during those three extra hours while the rest of the world is in bed. It's nearly eleven hundred extra hours a year. Maybe that's one of the reasons I am the Great Houdini instead of a sideshow piker."

"Can you open our office safe?" asked the lawyer presently.

"If you give me three minutes alone with it, I'll try," said Houdini. "But first let's make sure it's locked. It isn't any trick to open a safe that isn't locked."

The safe was a large Herring-Hall-Marvin affair, such as is used as a repository for wills and other precious papers in a large law office. It had been locked for the night. The lawyer left Houdini in front of it, and retired to his private office. In a few minutes Houdini summoned him. He walked up to the safe, without hesitation turned the knob to the proper combination, and the big steel door swung open.

Back in the inner office, Houdini, on a sudden impulse, said: "I'll show you the secret. No one has seen it before."

He took from his waistcoat pocket something that resembled the case of a watch, save that within was a single sensitive dial instead of the two fixed hands.

"I made this myself," he said. "It is the only one in the world. If you knew what it meant, and how to use it, it would give you the combination of any safe anywhere."

He slipped it back into his pocket.

The two men left the office together. It was in a large building stretching to two streets, with entrances on both, the rear entrance being closed after 6:30 at night. Absent-mindedly, after they left the elevator, the lawyer led the way toward the rear entrance, but as they reached it he saw that the heavy, buglar-proof locking apparatus had been set and the doors were closed for the night.

"I'm sorry," he said, turning. "We'll have to use the other exit."

He took a few paces, continuing the conversation, when suddenly he noticed that Houdini was no longer by his side. He turned back just as Houdini was starting to call him.

Houdini stood holding the "burglar-proof" door open, grinning like an urchin.

"What's the matter with this exit?" he asked naively. "It opens all right."

They passed into the street, and then Houdini stooped over the lock a minute.

"I'd better leave this the way I found it, or your office might be robbed in the night," he remarked. A few turns of his wrist, and the lock was adjusted again.

By a curious irony of fate, after Houdini died no record could be found of the combination of his own private safe in his home, and no one could open it. On a certain day it became necessary, rather unexpectedly, to secure immediately certain papers locked in that enigmatic safe. It was Election Day, a holiday, and the office of the makers of the safe did not respond to the telephone when an attempt was made to get them to send professional aid. Finally, through some roundabout inquiries, a retired expert cracksman was secured. He labored for half a day over a problem which Houdini could have solved, in the case of a strange safe, on the instant. Finally he had to blow the thing open. If Houdini were looking down on the sweating cracksman, he surely had a full appreciation of the situation . . .

Magic is almost as old, apparently, as man. In primitive times the sleight-of-hand artist found a credulous audience, and easily preyed on the wonder and fear of his tribal mates for his own elevation. He pretended to control both good and evil spirits and thus secured for himself the prerogatives and emoluments of a supernatural being. Up to fairly recent times the most reputable magicians did not disdain to permit the humble folk to believe that they had supernatural aid, or even that they occasionally received counsel from Beelzebub himself. The elaborate gimcrack apparatus, the peaked hat, and the decorative flowing robes affected by the old-time magicians lent color to this common belief, and the robes were also useful for making objects appear or vanish unexpectedly.

For hundreds of years crowds gaped at performers who could swallow fire, glass, or swords, who could walk on red-hot coals, sit serenely in a burning cage, tread unharmed on broken glass, or mount a ladder of swords. These things sound like marvels; in fact they are very simple, quite in the elementary grades of magic. No supernatural aid is needed for such feats. In one of his books, *Miracle Mongers and Their Methods,* Houdini gave comprehensive descriptions of the various methods of accomplishing these seeming miracles. Some of them are not without risk, but they are normally safe enough for the seasoned performer.

During the past century the higher-grade magicians have steadily shown a tendency to disavow all claims to supernatural aid and to stand on their own feet as artists. The flowing robes and the superfluous hocus-pocus have been discarded. The profession has gained correspondingly in dignity and public favor. Houdini was surely the most explicit and painstaking of magicians in explaining that his magic had no supernatural attachments.

Mrs. Houdini writes:

"When Houdini made a five-ton elephant vanish from the stage of the Hippodrome, that was a trick and only a trick. I know how it was done, and I saw every step of the arduous months of planning and preparation that made it possible. No demons or angels whisked the elephant away, and, I may add, there was no trap door, nor was the trap door possible with a huge tank of water just beneath the stage floor.

"When, on the same stage, Houdini would swallow, or seem to swallow, a large spoolful of thread and a dozen packages of needles and would subsequently draw the thread out of his mouth with the needles strung on it at intervals, until two hundred threaded needles from his mouth were stretched on a hundred feet of thread across the stage—that also was a trick and only a trick. I know how it was done, and I was with Houdini when he discovered the germ of it in an old book of magic picked up in a second-hand bookshop in London. No visitor from the other world imparted the knowledge.

"When Houdini escaped from every sort of manacling device, from every sort of prison cell, from every sort of cask and chest and packing case devised by experts and nailed up and sealed by them, these things were tricks and tricks only. They were performed as the result of long forethought and skill, and persistent, arduous training, by a man of steel nerves, but there was no supernatural agency involved." . . .

Had Houdini put his abilities to evil uses he would undoubtedly have been the gravest individual menace ever known to organized society. He could enter or leave any building or chamber at will, leaving no trace of breakage behind him, and he could open the strongest steel vault as easily as a skilled second-story man could pry loose a bedroom window. No cell or jail could hold him, for he could solve any lock system in a few minutes and pass through the most elaborate door. Had he chosen the crooked path, society would have been compelled to have him put to death for its own protection, for nothing short of the capital penalty would have served.

Doubtless Houdini would have wrought even greater havoc in human society had he perverted his genius for illusion to make himself the central figure of a new religious cult. He could have done this without difficulty.

Moreover, he was aware of what he could accomplish in setting himself up as the inspired prophet of a new mystical religion, and the full implications, in wealth and power and position, of such an adventure. Those of his friends who were privileged to witness the occasional "séances," usually of a wholly impromptu character, which he sometimes had for their edification during his later years, can understand his possibilities in this field. The effects he would produce in the course of an evening at a friend's home where he happened to be making a social visit would make the ordinary mediumistic phenomena seem quite childish. Spectators would be awed in spite of repeated assurances from Houdini that he was merely tricking them. On Hallowe'en, 1922, while he was a guest at the home of Sophie Irene Loeb at Harmon-on-Hudson, Houdini gave a mock séance including a spirit message from Jack London, and the effects he produced were so weird that after he returned home he was impelled to write in his diary, "I must put on record that it was done wholly by dexterity."

Had Houdini posed as one supernaturally inspired, one who could escape even into another world and return with messages and mandates and commands, and had he chosen to substantiate his claim by achieving seeming miracles for which a normal physical explanation could hardly be found, he could easily have established a formidable army of worshipers among millions of simple and credulous persons eager to be lifted out of a humdrum existence by messages from the skies. The pseudo-prophet would have been a more terrible portent than the supercracksman, because of his power to sway the minds and souls of men.

Fortunately neither crime nor black magic had any lure for Houdini. He was a healthy-minded human being, apparently with no abnormal rift in his psychological structure. It was natural for him to play straight, and so he lived and died as a great showman.

Yet that description falls short of doing Houdini justice. Quite aside from his professional genius, he was a rabbinical puritan, with much sentimentalism in his make-up, and a streak of mysticism. While he devoted his life largely to devising methods for the breaking of physical bonds, he was also interested in breaking psychic bonds and communicating with friends who had passed through a door for which he had no picklock. After the death of his mother this curiousity developed into a passion. His experiences with mediums led him to a warfare on frauds who strove to palm off phenomena of trickery and sleight of hand as manifestations from the dead. During the last few years of his life all his energy and skill and showmanship were enlisted in this crusade.

On Safari[*]

by Theodore J. Waldeck

As a boy THEODORE WALDECK *determined to be a big game hunter and go "on safari." Despite the protests of his father who had a more conservative profession in mind for his son, Theodore at eighteen gained permission to join an expedition to Africa organized by a family friend. Although he did eventually become a successful hunter and a writer of authentic animal stories, Theodore had much to learn about safaris —including the lesson which he describes in these chapters from his* On Safari.

* "On Safari" from *On Safari* by Theodore J. Waldeck, reprinted by permission of The Viking Press, Inc.

WHEN I WAS YOUNG, I delighted in reading the tales told by travelers to far places. I knew the story of Stanley and Doctor Livingstone. I devoured the tales of Sven Hedin. I knew the life histories of the explorers of my time and before, and a dream came into being. Some day when I was old enough, I promised myself, I would go exploring. I would go to India, or to Africa. I saw myself as the owner of a great plantation in some wild, craggy place of my own imagining, with hundreds of black servitors.

I didn't often speak of this, even to my grandfather, with whom I lived after the death of my parents, for he had no patience with wanderers, with spinners of tales, with young folk who dreamed too much. Rolling stones, he insisted solemnly, gather no moss. How often he recited platitudes to me; how often I reserved opinion. For did I not know that he had had his dreams too?

How could I help knowing? Was not the Duke of Mecklenburg a close friend of my grandfather, visiting him often? This man, it seemed to me, had been every place in the world I had always dreamed of seeing. If my grandfather did not hold with travel, why did his eyes glisten when he listened to the tales the Duke told of an evening, and why did he ask questions and keep the Duke long past the time he had intended to stay, in order to hear more of the marvelous tales the Duke could tell so well? I had read the Arabian Nights. The Duke of Mecklenburg had lived them all. I steeped myself in his tales, keeping very quiet and out of the way, lest I be sent to bed before he had finished some account or other.

By the time I was eighteen my dream had crystallized. It had not dimmed with the years, as so many dreams do. It had not changed. Its outlines had simply grown sharper. My determination to follow my star grew with the passing years.

My grandfather wanted me to be a lawyer or a doctor, a good lawyer or a good doctor. He insisted that my education should prepare me for a career that definitely precluded castles in Spain, or camel routes through High Tatary, or treks through India's fabulous Terai, where cobra de capello awaited the unwary. I absorbed the education. In fact I enjoyed it. But to me it seemed, then, that the world held too many doctors, too many lawyers. Even if I made good in either profession, there would be hundreds who were just as good or better.

But when it came to exploration . . .

Couldn't my grandfather see that the Duke of Mecklenburg was a man who stood alone, head and shoulders above other men? Not because he was a duke, but because he was a frequent visitor to the little-known places of the earth. He was planning a new expedition to Africa, and I was determined almost from the moment he told my grandfather about it to go with him. I took him aside at the first opportunity and told him so. He smiled at me.

"I've expected this," he said. "I haven't missed your big ears!"

"Big ears?" I repeated, lifting my hands to cover ears that weren't big at all.

"Not actually big," he said, "but always listening to things. I've known you would ask from the moment I realized that you listened to the wild tales I told your grandfather."

"Wild tales? You mean they were not true?"

"Tales, my young friend, can be wild and still true. My stories were both. Just what have you in mind, anyhow?"

I blurted out my dream. He didn't laugh at me, nor did he upbraid me or try to talk me out of it. He probably remembered his own dreams, and how they had come true because he made them come true. I could not have found a man who understood better than the Duke of Mecklenburg. Dreams that sounded foolish even to me, when I confessed them to my grandfather, sounded grand and fine when I retailed them to the Duke.

"I simply want to go with you," I said. "No matter where."

"I could probably find a place for you," he said, while my heart soared with hope. "But you'll have to talk to your grandfather about it. He has strong convictions on the subject."

"I had hoped that you would ask him for me," I said.

He smiled again. "Yes, I rather thought you might have hoped that; but you'll have to do your own pleading. And I don't think it will be easy."

Neither did I. But the Duke had said he could use me, and that was a wedge. At least I had something on which to base my request for a chance to try my wings in far places. The Duke had scarcely left when I went to my grandfather. I had to go to him before I lost my nerve.

"The Duke of Mecklenburg," I said to my grandfather, "would like to have me on his expedition!"

My grandfather looked at me. The room became very still. His piercing old eyes searched my face.

"Just like that, eh?" he said, after a long pause. "He simply told you out of a clear sky that he would like to have you on his expedition. Funny he didn't mention it to me."

"Well, he didn't exactly mention it first . . ."

"I rather imagined not," said Grandfather dryly. "You deviled him into a sort of half-promise, I'll be bound."

"Then I can go?"

"Not so fast, not so fast. Who said anything about your going?"

"Well, the Duke and I . . ."

"The answer is no. You can't go. There is school. Your career after you have finished college, university."

"A doctor or a lawyer!" I cried. "Dozens of doctors to every sick person, dozens of lawyers to every courtroom!"

"But if you are as good a doctor or lawyer as I plan for you to be, you will stand alone."

"But I don't want to be a doctor or a lawyer!" Since I had started this thing he might as well know exactly how I felt about it. I told him my dream all over again. I embroidered it, embellished it. I added new corners, extended the boundaries of my imagination. I was, perhaps, more eloquent than I had ever been before, or became thereafter. And he heard me through.

"This is very close to your heart, isn't it?" said Grandfather.

"It's the one thing I want to do."

"I doubt," he said gravely, "that you know what you want to do. You are eighteen. The steps you take now will affect your whole future life."

"I want them to! I want them to lead me to the life I am sure will make me happy!"

"But when you are twenty-five will you still want what you want now? The man you are at eighteen is not the man you will be at twenty-five. But if, at twenty-five, you have made a mistake, it may be too late to change it, pick up where you leave off with your schooling, and go on to what I now think is right for you."

"But wouldn't that apply even if I decided to be a doctor or a lawyer?"

He agreed that it might. He was very fair, my grandfather was, and he was probably right, though now, after all the years I have spent as an explorer, I do not think he was right where I was concerned, for I have never had regrets.

"I'll make a deal with you," my grandfather said. "I'll permit you to accompany the Duke, since it probably won't be for very long, on one condition . . ."

Relief flooded me. I'd have agreed to any condition. I held my breath, however, to hear what this one would be.

"On condition," he went on, "that when you return you'll go on with your schooling. It's just a precaution against the time when the man of twenty-five may be different from the boy of eighteen. Agreed?"

I don't believe I slept through any night after that, until the day came when I actually did join the expedition of the Duke of Mecklenburg. African names kept running through my head. They didn't have to be the names of places I was destined to visit this time. Just names, strange names, of places, of people, of rivers and lakes. Dar-es-Salaam, where we would begin our trek into the interior. Nairobi—I rolled it over my tongue with delight. Tanganyika. Uganda. Kenya Colony. Tanaland. Ukamba. Buganda, Ruanda, Urundi. I could have written music to fit those names, because they were music in my ears. They had been music when I had heard them pronounced by the Duke of Mecklenburg. They had always been music. They are music today, twenty-eight years later.

And this is the tale of those twenty-eight years.

I had little to do with the organizing of that first expedition to Africa in 1912. I wasn't a principal in it. I was just going along to make myself useful, to learn what I could. But to myself I was Sven Hedin or Stanley, or Marco Polo up to date, or any one of the famous men who had opened the globe's dark places to the light of civilization.

The voyage? The boat was to me something out of a fairy tale. It might have been only a tub to people who knew much about boats. But it carried me away from civilization for the first time, and I would never forget it.

It carried me to Dar-es-Salaam, and plunged me head foremost into my first contact with Africa, the Dark Continent.

Dar-es-Salaam was simply a collection of buildings on the flat African coast. The houses had galvanized iron roofs which turned them into furnaces during the heat of the day. The nights were cold. There was nothing in the town really worth seeing. It was only a place from which to start the trek into the interior. I wanted to get started right away. I think I was afraid, the moment we landed, that something would happen to keep me from going inland. I was in a fever of impatience to get away. Right then I learned something that always proved true on later expeditions: you are never ready to leave on the date you plan, and never have all the paraphernalia you really need. The Duke, seasoned traveler though he was, found himself in need of additional equipment. It seemed that he would not be able to leave Dar-es-Salaam for some weeks to come. Equipment had to be sent on from England, and he couldn't leave without it.

I soon exhausted the sights of the town, but I did not venture outside it for fear something would happen that I might miss. That boat, coming from Europe, was ominous to me. It would be so easy for Grandfather to order me home.

Catastrophe fell heavily, just before the safari started. I became seriously ill and had to go to the hospital. I fought off my fever with all my will power because I knew what it meant: I would be left behind, to take the next boat home. Nobody can ever guess how I suffered, quite aside from sickness that turned my skin the color of lemons or old parchment. I had done considerable bragging at home. I had promised lion skins to many of my friends, great elephant tusks to others. Now I would be going home, back to my books—a failure! It was just too much to bear. So I tried hard to fight off the sickness.

The Duke came to see me one day.

"I'm sorry, young fellow," he said, "but we're going on. We can't wait. You understand that, don't you?"

I understood all right. I'd been expecting it. But the blow hit just as hard for all that. I confess that I pleaded with him to hold off until I was well enough to join them. It was foolish of me to expect him to accede, and he didn't. He had his job to do, already too long delayed. So with some three hundred porters the expedition set out. I could have wept, had this helped any.

"I've cabled your grandfather," the Duke told me, "and you'll go back home when you are well."

I couldn't say anything. I could only see myself returning, with no lion skins, no elephant tusks, without even stories to tell of anything that had happened to me—except that I had got sick and been left behind. Fate was good to me in one way. When the next boat came in, I was still too sick to be moved. But soon after, I began getting well, only to realize that the expedition had been gone too long for me to do anything about it. My grandfather cabled money for my return. It came after the departure of the Duke, who, not knowing for sure what my grandfather would do, had also left a considerable amount for me.

I left the hospital, realizing that I must go back home. As the days passed it became increasingly difficult to face the inevitable. I felt that I simply could not face it. Go home and admit that I wasn't a great explorer after all? While waiting for the next boat I walked around Dar-es-Salaam. I went into the depot where the Duke had arranged for his supplies of food and additional equipment and asked a lot of questions. The man who ran the place knew who I was, and sympathized with me for having been sick.

"Africa is a bad place," he said. "One day you are well, next day you are sick enough to die."

We talked at length of the interests of Africa and what one might expect to encounter in the interior. And as we talked my eagerness to see all of this grew. A few days later, I walked outside the town and saw the veldt stretching away to infinity. I walked out into it farther and farther, until I got tired. Then I looked on ahead and said to myself:

"Since it stretches on and on, until it comes to the Duke's safari, why couldn't I follow?" What was to keep me from going into the interior, which was just a continuation of what I had already seen? With this question stirring in my mind, I went back to the supply depot and talked with the owner.

"How would I go about starting a safari of my own?" I asked him. I looked right at him as I asked, mutely daring him to laugh at me. He actually did start to laugh when he saw I was in earnest.

"It's impossible," he said. "You're still weak from the fever. Africa is bad for you, you can see that. Moreover, a safari is dreadfully expensive."

"I have plenty of money," I said.

"But aren't you supposed to spend it to get back home?"

"I'll still have enough left. The boat won't come for another two weeks, and I can at least use that time in looking over the veldt to the north."

The Duke had left no word about me with the authorities. If he had asked them to make sure that I caught the boat, I'd have been beaten. But he had told nobody. He had simply taken it for granted that I would return home; so nobody had a right to stop me.

The depot man became interested. Of course there was

a chance for him to make a profitable deal, and expeditions did not leave every day. I had an idea that I needed a regular arsenal on my trip. I fancied myself with a big belt all studded with revolvers, and with a big gun draped over each shoulder. I fancied myself a Nimrod, shooting at elephants in front of me, lions to the left, and zebras to the right. There would have to be, of course, a different sort of gun for each kind of big game.

"You might make it at that," said the trader slowly. "First, though, let me plan it for you. I'll outfit you if you'll let me hire the head man. I know one who will be just right. He lives in a village not far from here, and has been head porter for many expeditions. If he's available we'll start from there."

I went back to the hotel in deathly fear that the boat would come before I got away, and that something would happen to make me go back. I was in terror that the head porter would not be available, and the trader would refuse to outfit me. But the next day he proved as good as his word. The head porter was available and would be glad to go. He left the hiring of ten additional porters to the head porter.

I told the trader what I wanted in the way of guns, and he manfully refrained from laughing at me.

"You'll need a heavy double-barreled rifle," he said, "for big game; a smaller rifle for smaller game, and just one revolver. To have more firearms than that would be dangerous." I listened to him, though none too sure he knew what he was talking about!

"I'll only need one blanket," I told him. "Why would a strong fellow like me need more than that?"

"Pardon," he said. "You'll need three. One to sleep on, two to cover you. The nights get very cold."

I left the rest of the outfitting to him, knowing that I could depend on his experience in outfitting expeditions. While I was getting ready, I talked with the head porter. He knew the dialects of many of the tribes through whose country we would pass. Few safaris left Dar-es-Salaam, so he would be able to follow the Duke without difficulty. If the spoor were not still visible, he would find out from the native villages along the way, all of whom would know all about it.

Surely no grander or more imposing "expedition" had ever left Dar-es-Salaam! Imagine it! I had a head man and ten porters. The Duke had a mere three hundred. What did he have that I didn't have? I'd overtake him in no time at all!

And so we started. I was togged out now in tropical clothing, complete from boots to pith helmet. The revolver on my belt was the real thing! My two rifles were perfect—not enough of them, but enough to do. The barrels of the rifles would probably get hot, I'd have to kill so many elephants, lions, and leopards. Of course the veldt was alive with them, and I'd have to shoot fast and often, to keep them from charging and pulling me down. My spoor would be marked by great piles of tusks, worth a fortune, and my porters would be loaded down with the skins of big game. I was sure of it!

We set out into the African sun. Our water supply was limited from the start, but it was up to Bimbo, the head porter, to see that the water supply was maintained. Every few miles I drank. The water was warm and didn't slake my thirst at all. It filled me up. Then I perspired freely and had to drink again.

Bimbo—almost all head porters are called Bimbo, which is Swahili for "big man"—finally ventured to remonstrate with me, and my education as an explorer began.

"You must not drink too much, Bwana," he said. "It do no good, for when you drink, you drink right away some more. Tea, hot, for breakfast, for dinner, for supper, is better. It will make you lively and not so thirsty."

Hot tea, under a sun so hot? Why, the man was crazy! But I listened and obeyed, and he was right. It is cooling and refreshing, just as a rag dipped in hot water to wipe off perspiration is more cooling and refreshing than if dipped in cold water.

I started right out to walk the porters into the ground. Loaded down as they all were, it should be easy, I thought.

It was hard going when the sun was right overhead. It became so hard—what with those new boots of mine that were like walking in a pair of heated chimneys—that I forgot all about the charging elephants and lions, and concentrated upon keeping on my feet and not staggering too much, or drinking more water than was good for me.

If the porters noticed that I was losing ground, they

gave no sign. Not even Bimbo said anything, but very gravely, at four o'clock, when I felt that I couldn't have taken ten more steps, he said:

"Is enough for the first day. Now we camp, pitch tent, fix cot, you bathe and drink tea."

I managed to stand until the tent was up and the cot inside. Then I shut myself in, sat down on the cot, and pulled off my boots to find my feet covered with blisters. As I look back, I feel a little sorry for that "explorer." No man of eighteen ever wept, of course. But *that* eighteen-year-old "explorer" did—silently, so that Bimbo and his men would not hear. What a fool I had been! How grand and cool and nice the house of my grandfather, and what did I care, after all, if my schoolmates laughed at me? At that moment I thought: "There is really no place like home."

I slept. Next morning I could not put on my boots. My feet were terrible to look at. I actually suffered. But I was now some distance from Dar-es-Salaam, and it was just as nearly impossible to return—unless Bimbo and his men carried me—as it was to go on. I couldn't do either, until my feet were well.

And as I stayed on, waiting for them to heal so I could get my boots on once more, pride came to my aid. I could certainly go just as far ahead as I could go back. I didn't go back to Dar-es-Salaam. To this day I have never gone back to Dar-es-Salaam. But I always long for Africa once more—no matter what hardships she may have in store for me. She showed me the star I had always wanted to follow, and taught me one thing I have never forgotten: when you go to bed at night, sure that you can't possibly go on tomorrow, forget it. You *can* go on, if your pride, ambition, and perseverance are what they should be.

Even blistered feet will heal. The time came when I could put those boots back on—and push ahead. No great animals had been seen anywhere near camp. There weren't great herds of elephants, as I had expected; nor vast numbers of lions or leopards. I didn't learn until later that I wouldn't have known if a leopard or lion had been within a few yards of the camp. My education hadn't then progressed that far!

The second day—with a week or two separating us from the first day's safari—we kept going until four-thirty. I had learned by now to live in rough camps. We were far out of touch with Dar-es-Salaam, as though I were actually in the heart of Africa. And I was afraid! Not of Africa itself, or of any wild animals, but of Bimbo and the ten porters. They were utterly alien to anything I knew. I was one white man among them. "Not so long ago their people were primitive savages," I thought. Even the fathers of these might have been. My fear, then, was twofold: that the Negroes would leave me in the night and I wouldn't be able to find my way back to civilization or ahead to the camp of the Duke, and that the blacks would destroy me for my possessions. In my imagination I saw Bimbo regard my rifles with desire. In fancy I saw him stealing them at night, and sneaking away into the veldt, never to return.

It was all nonsense, of course, but many times I wakened in the night and peered through the flaps of the tent to make sure that my porters were still with me.

Bimbo began to lengthen the day's march. I learned something else, then: to start early in the morning, before the sun is up, and get in your best licks before the heat of the day. Then rest, and start again when the sun is going down. When the trek is afoot, it isn't wise to travel by moonlight, for tufts of the bush may hide the carnivores. However, years later, when I used cars on my expeditions, we did some of our traveling at night.

Days passed, and weeks, and Bimbo assured me that we were coming closer and closer to the Duke. He was sure, from the spoor, and from what he had picked up from the native villages.

I shot no big game. I didn't even see any. I didn't look, for that matter. I simply couldn't spare the time for hunting, while covering the distance between us and the Duke's safari.

But as we hurried on through lengthening days, I began to look ahead and visualize the reception the Duke would surely give me. Wouldn't *he* be surprised! He'd forgotten all about me by now, but I was fooling him, wasn't I? He'd stand aghast when I walked into camp at the head of my own safari!

And surely he would welcome me into the fold with

dignity and appreciation—for hadn't I crossed miles of African veldt to reach him! Many times, as we hurried forward, I pictured my welcome by the Duke.

Nine weeks after we started out, we actually reached the Duke's camp. He was away, and would not be back for several hours. I was tired out. I wanted a place to sleep. I couldn't wait for my tent to be pitched.

I told the blacks in camp to inform the Duke of my arrival, then boldly went into the Duke's tent, took off my upper garments, flung myself down on his cot, and slept. The "old campaigner" had completed what he had set out to do; now he had but to wait for the return of the Duke himself to receive the welcome he deserved! I knew all there was to know about safaris, for had I not successfully completed one of my own? If I hadn't felt so sure of myself, I wouldn't, naturally, have helped myself to the tent and the cot of the Duke.

I was awakened by the sound of shouts. The blacks in camp were hailing the return of the old man, the Duke himself. I could have gone out to meet him, but I preferred for him to hear of my arrival from Bimbo. Bimbo would tell him where I was. He would come to me, as I awaited his homage in the tent, and would tell me how well I had done! I'd heard the words in my imagination hundreds of times—the words with which he would greet me.

The flap of the tent snapped back. I sat up, trying to look nonchalant, and stared at the Duke. For the first time I didn't feel so cocky about things! I might be wrong, at that. Maybe there would be no welcome, after all. Maybe I shouldn't have been so brash as to use the Duke's tent, and his cot.

When I saw his face I had certain doubts, which crystallized a lot faster than my dreams had. I was probably in for something or other. I began to feel very young, the way I felt when my grandfather stared at me, and muttered "dumb-head" under his breath—and not always under his breath, either.

The explosion didn't come. The Duke was going to tell me how well I had done, after all. He leaned back. He put his fists on his hips as he stared at me. Then he said: "For the love of Pete!"

My doubt of my own smartness in traveling for nine weeks through the African veldt grew as the Duke kept staring at me. His face was suffused with wrath. It began to dawn on me that the only reason he had spoken just one sentence was that he was too choked with anger to say anything else. Just the same, I still felt a bit proud of myself. So I set off the explosion by saying:

"Well, Sir, I made it!"

"Yes," he snapped, "you made it! You made a fool of yourself, a dolt!"

"But, Sir . . ."

"Shut your mouth while I'm talking! I said you made a fool of yourself. If I had better or bigger words of condemnation I would use them. You are a selfish, ungrateful, thoughtless . . ."

"But, Sir, I succeeded . . ."

"Shut your mouth! I've already told you what you succeeded in doing. Stop for a moment and think what sorrow you would have caused your grandfather if you had never been heard of again! Far older men, far better and more experienced men, have been destroyed by Africa in a lot less time than you spent on the veldt. How you escaped, only those who look after drunkards and fools can possibly say. Do you realize that if anything had happened to you I would have been held responsible? You might as well get it through your head right now that the leader of an expedition is just as much master of everybody connected with it as the general who commands an army. Moreover, his responsibility, if only in his own mind, is just as great. If he bosses people around he also looks out for them, and must answer at a court of justice and to his own conscience if anything happens to them. I made an error in judgment when I thought you would behave yourself if I left you in Dar-es-Salaam. You betrayed my trust in you!"

"But, Sir . . ."

"See, you're not even listening! I tell you the responsibility of the leader of an expedition, and you keep saying: 'But, Sir, but, Sir,' like a phonograph with a faulty record that keeps repeating itself."

It finally came home to me that the Duke was dreadfully angry. My grandfather would have been sad, maybe, if anything had happened to me, as the Duke had said, but nothing *had* happened. Why should he complain so much when nothing had happened to me? However, I had finally got it through my head that I must hold my tongue, until he gave me permission to speak.

"Well," he went on, "now that you're here, I guess you'll have to stay. I can't spare the men to send you back."

"I've got my own men," I said, my own anger rising, "and I can get back myself."

"You could do nothing of the sort, even if I did not need the men you brought with you. You could not, and will not leave the camp without my permission. You still don't seem to understand that you are entirely responsible to me for everything that happens to you, from now on. I'll take your Bimbo and use him as a head porter for some of my own group. The other men will be pushed in with my porters. And as for you, yourself . . ."

He paused, as though to think up a punishment for me that would be fitting and proper. I was shaking like a leaf. My grandfather had talked to me like this, but he had always loved me. But that the Duke, who was no relative at all, should talk to me so, made me feel as though he were literally stripping off my hide. But what he told me was true, and I deserved it all.

"As for you, yourself," he repeated, "you are not, under any circumstances, to leave the camp without my permission. You will stay in camp and read books, or sleep, or do anything you like, as long as you keep out of the way of the important people in the expedition. Now get out of my tent! Don't ever enter it again without permission. Inform some of the men that I have issued instructions that a tent is to be erected for you."

"I have my own tent, Sir," I said, forgetting again that I must not interrupt him.

"It's a pup tent," he said contemptuously. "I might add the obvious statement that a pup tent is for a young pup. But you must retain the prestige of the white men, and have a tent of the proper size. There is one for you. So, see to it!"

Crestfallen, but inwardly furious, I quitted the tent of the Duke, intent upon showing him that he was wrong about me, that I was just as much a man as anybody else with the expedition. I issued orders—and I didn't tell the blacks that they came from the Duke! All the time I was burning up with shame and almost wished that I had never tried to join the expedition.

When suppertime came that night, of course all the white men had heard my story. They explored into laughter, which I thought was complimentary. I expanded under their talk like a toy balloon filled with hot air—which is, at that, an apt simile, now that I look back on that first night with the expedition. How the men roared when I told of my blistered heels! How they roared when, with becoming modesty, I told of sneaking to the flap of my tent, and making sure that my porters had not run off and left me. Yes, Sir, I was quite a fellow!

How humiliated I would have felt had I guessed that they were laughing at me, instead of with me. I thought I was so smart, so big, so just right! Only one man, a British Major, took my part in the laughter and badinage. I blush even now when I recall how I boasted and tried to look modest when I got across to them what a fellow I was. But the British Major was actually the only one there who was the sort of friend I needed at the time.

I felt pretty good when I went to bed that night. I thought that when the Duke found what a big hit I had made with the men that night, he would relent, and allow me to take active part in the work they were doing.

But next day I was doomed to disappointment; he curtly told me to stay in camp and read a book. Read a book! Read a book! Why should I *read* books of adventure—the only kind I cared about anyhow—when I was living adventure beyond any writer's imagination, or soon would be?

With mixed feelings, I watched the men go to their duties. That I would remain in camp indefinitely I did not believe for a moment. If the Duke didn't relent I'd go on my own again.

The Duke sent certain men out into sections of the vicinity to gather specimens. When the collections of plants, insects, minerals, etc., had been made, they were then classified, catalogued, and preserved. A large number of men and porters were sent hunting. I watched these various men go out with envy in my heart.

It didn't help a bit when they came back that evening, and one of them had shot a large rhino. He had brought back the complete skin and head, for the scientist to preserve. The talk, that evening, was of the kill, and how dangerous a rhino was, and what a good shot it had been that had brought the monster down. I was being utterly ignored, whereas yesterday I had been the hero of the expedition, according to my own mind. And I knew that I could shoot a rhino as well as anybody else. But I did't get a chance. Nobody asked me to go with the hunters.

One evening a group came in to report that a huge lion they had been trying to bag all week had escaped them again, though one of the men had had a good shot at him. The lion, it appeared, had a charmed life. There was a lot of talk directed at the hunter who had missed, in which I joined immoderately, showing by the manner of my laughter that I felt sure I wouldn't have missed my aim! Someone spoke up:

"I'll bet Ted would have got him, first shot! That's what we should do, send Ted out for the big game. I'll bet *he'd* bring home the bacon, the rhino, and the lion!"

What a roar of laughter went up! And for the first time it came to me: every one of those men, with the exception of Major Fisher, thought me as much a fool as did the Duke. I hadn't been a hero, but a fool. They'd been laughing at me all the time. When I finally understood what they were doing, I could not eat. I rose from the table and ran out into the night. My cheeks burned with shame and resentment. I would show those men. I didn't learn right away, as young men must, that I must be able to "take it." I had to learn this lesson slowly—which probably made it more valuable—because I had to take more before I began to understand.

"I'll show them! I'll show them!" I kept telling myself. "And right away, tomorrow!"

For that the laughter at my expense would continue from now on, I was sure, and the first thing I knew I would be fighting with everybody—and probably getting whipped!

"I'll go out myself and shoot a rhino," I whispered. "I'll shoot a lion, and maybe even an elephant, all in the same day. Won't their eyes pop out when I come back and throw all those animals in their laps!"

Considering the size and weight of the animals mentioned, and the size and weight of this writer, I'm sure their eyes would have popped! I slept on the resolution that I would go rhino-hunting the next day—of course after the Duke had gone out on his regular work. I was lulled to sleep by the laughter of the men from the great canvas tent where the white men ate. And every sound of laughter was laughter at me! At least I felt that it was.

Next morning, bright and early, after the Duke had left and I was the only white man in camp, without the slightest desire to read books, I set my plans of the previous night into motion. I picked out two boys, a trekker and a gun-bearer. I had watched the behavior of all the whites toward the blacks, and pretended to be just as tough as the toughest of them.

"Here, you!" I snapped, glad that I had just passed the age when my voice had started in the lower registers and zoomed to calliope shrillness. "Get some food ready! We're going hunting!"

The two boys were surprised and perturbed, as well they might be. But I was white and must be obeyed, even though they knew I didn't know what I was doing.

"Get my rifles!" I snapped at my gun-bearer.

He got the biggest rifle I had, and gave it to me. Then he dared what he would not have dared with any other white member of the expedition; he criticized my choice of a rifle.

"Bwana," he said, respectfully enough, "this rifle no big enough, happen we find somethin' big."

He was right, of course, I decided immediately. But this was the biggest rifle I had, so what should I do? For, though I hadn't yet told the gun-bearer, I was going to bag a rhinoceros. Maybe he had guessed! Where would I get a rifle big enough? I'd take my own, of course, but I'd need two, as every hunter should—more if I got the whim. You might guess what I did. In spite of the Duke's instructions that I keep out of his tent, I went into it and looked at his personal rifle rack. Boy, some of his guns were monsters! One of them was a double-barreled elephant gun, firing a cartridge fully four inches long, with a two-hundred-and-eighty-milligram bullet, backed by three hundred and eighty milligrams of powder. A cannon to be carried in the hand! But you've no idea how invincible I thought myself when I found cartridges to fit that monster, and took it out to the gun-bearer. His face was an enigma as he took the rifle.

The other boy was ready with water in a canteen and food in a basket. We set out—and when we were well away from the camp, I told the boys what we were hunting. I wanted a rhino, if possible bigger than the one brought into camp recently. The boys didn't even shrug. Maybe they thought that the chances of encountering a rhino were slim indeed.

I didn't. I'd find a rhino, or know the reason why.

The sun rose higher and higher, and got hotter and hotter, and we encountered no rhinos, large or small. We found no lions, no giraffe, no anything. Far off I saw some antelope, but they were small game, for children to stalk and shoot. Why, the gun that was commensurate with my size would have blown one of those antelope into nothingness. So, I wasn't interested in antelope—then.

The hours passed. We were making a wide circle, back to camp. I was intent on reaching it before the Duke got back, so that if I did not kill a rhino before I reached camp, I could return the rifle to his rack, swear the boys to secrecy, and nobody would be the wiser. Then next day, or the day after, I'd try again—and keep on trying until I got my rhino. Hadn't my grandfather often told me that if at first I did not succeed, I must try, try again? Of course!

But it was almost four in the afternoon, I was more tired than I had ever been, and we had found exactly nothing. I had never seen such empty country! I didn't see why the boys had to be so careful, one walking ahead of me a couple of paces, the other to my right rear—that was the gun-bearer—ready to slip the rifle into my hand when I reached back for it, which would of course be when the rhino was in full charge.

Nothing. . . .

We came to a large group of boulders covering many acres. I'd resigned myself to failure for this day at least, when all at once the boy in advance of me halted, stood stock still. He whispered and pointed:

"Look, Bwana! Look!"

I looked and looked. I looked everywhere, and all around, and couldn't see anything whatever—except more rocks. I'd been seeing rocks all day, interspersed with patches of dry grass, thickets of brush, and sand into which my feet sank almost to the ankles. This was simply more of the same. The gun-bearer moved silently up to stand beside the first boy. He, too, pointed and whispered:

"Look, Bwana, look!" Again I looked, and looked again, but all I saw was rocks. The gun-bearer dropped behind me, pushed the big double-barreled rifle into my hands. But why? I couldn't see anything to shoot at. Of course I knew that the eyes of natives are far keener than mine, but I certainly ought to be able to see anything big enough to merit the big rifle. I must not let them know I could not see whatever it was they saw, or I would dim the prestige of all white men. And I still could see nothing. Nothing but rocks. . . .

Then, one of the rocks began to move, to rise up—and it was as big as a mountain! Moreover, it had a pair of nasty-looking horns on its snout! A rhino, by all that was unholy and hideous. I hadn't been able to see it because it blended so well with the surrounding territory. It had been lying beside another rock, which was why I had missed seeing it. Then—the *other* rock began to move, to rise up!

Those two big rhinos were not more than fifty feet away. And I'd heard how rhinos behaved. If they had our scent they'd charge as soon as they were on their feet. Fortunately we were downwind, and rhinos have poor eyes. Just the same, fifty feet was much too close for me to be to any rhino, to say nothing of two.

"Shoot, Bwana! Shoot!" said the gun-bearer urgently. I brought the rifle to my shoulder. It was suddenly so heavy I had to bend almost backward to keep the muzzle elevated. Then it came to me—what a terrific noise that big rifle would make, and how it would kick me. I was more afraid of the rifle now than I was of any rhino. For was I holding a rhino to my shoulder? No, the nearer one was fifty feet away; but the rifle was right against my shoulder.

"Shoot, Bwana! Shoot!"

I knew that I had to shoot. I puffed out my chest. I held my breath. I lowered the rifle in spite of myself—and noted that the rhinos were facing us, and sniffing and snorting. They saw nothing, smelled nothing, but were suspicious. I lifted the rifle again, aimed it in the general direction of the two rhinos, shut my eyes, yanked the trigger—and the sky fell right on top of me. The ground rose and slugged me. The crack o' doom sounded o'er all Africa. I had never been hit so hard by anything, nor listened to such an explosion so close at hand. I knew I was lying down. I was sure that one of the rhinos had hit me broadside on. Nothing else could have hit so hard. Strange that I hadn't seen the rhino charging. They must travel faster than the eye could follow them. The rifle was gone from my hands. My jaw had been hit so hard I couldn't even feel it. My shoulder felt as though I had fallen down a mountain and landed on it.

Then I was conscious that the two boys were lifting me up. They tried to hand me the rifle again, but I wouldn't have it, now that I realized that it had knocked me over, not the charging rhinos.

In my excitement, my shaking terror, I had not placed the butt squarely against my shoulder, had only engaged the toe of the butt with the top of my shoulder. That I didn't have any broken bones was a miracle.

"Where's the dead rhino?" I finally managed to gasp, in a voice that must have been mine, though it sounded like that of a badly shaken stranger.

The boys pointed. Their faces had not changed expression. I looked. The two rhinos were trotting away, at right angles to the direction I faced, wagging their ridiculous tails behind them. Sadder and much, much wiser, I returned to camp.

The
*Cave of the Bats**

by Ivan T. Sanderson

Born after the museums of the world were well stocked with animals and would no longer finance big-game hunting, IVAN SANDERSON *proved that there is always a career in his chosen field for the man who uses his head. Determined to be a scientist-explorer, he investigated the real lacks in museum collections; he discovered a few gaps to be filled and saw the need for observation of animals in their native habitat. And so he got museum backing for his scientific expedition to the coast of West Africa to find specific information and specific specimens. He found a few moments of danger, too, as he tells in his* Animal Treasure.

* "The Cave of the Bats" from *Animal Treasure* by Ivan T. Sanderson, reprinted by permission of The Viking Press, Inc., and the Author.

AFTER SEVERAL WEEKS' intensive trapping around the camp, we appeared to have more or less cleared up or frightened away all the animals. Trap lines were thus being moved to another locality, because, with that particular method of collecting, a practice known as "completing a circle" is employed. This means that one selects a circle and works inwards from it to the camp, so that all animals, to get away, must either pass through the ring of traps, or congregate in the end around the camp. When the traps reach the borders of the camp, a final swarm of animals appears. After they are collected or have escaped, the whole area is played out.

With a view to selecting a new ground I left camp for a day's outing by myself, in order to cover a wide area and quietly investigate its possibilities to the best of my knowledge and ability. These days alone were most profitable, as we had discovered, not because we wanted in any way to be away from each other, but because the absence of conversation and freedom to wander wherever the spirit moved one brought to one's notice an extraordinary number of new facts and phenomena.

On this particular occasion I set out towards a large "lake" of grass that had been reported to me as existing to the south-east of the camp. I chose this as a starting point, since I was rather keen not to get lost in the forest again as I had done only a short time before.

Entering the dense forest beyond this open grass area, I was rather surprised to find that the ground descended very abruptly. Before I had gone far, I saw at a distance below me the glimmer of sun reflected from water. By some exigencies of local geological structure, the Mainyu River that we knew so well elsewhere had got twisted up into a knot and meandered off into the jungle, to appear here flowing in an exactly contrary direction to its main course. This we discovered later by following it downstream. I at once decided that this was to be our future happy hunting ground and the site of our next camp.

The whole structure of this gorge will one day prove of the greatest interest to geologists. It is a natural model of the great Rift Valley of East Africa. Following a subsidence or a great release of pressure, the land surface has simply collapsed along a central line now occupied by the river. The "country" rock, as it is called, has fractured all along into gargantuan cubes which, with the general subsidence, have shifted about so that they may be likened to the lumps of sugar in a bowl. Between them and under them are almost endless narrow clefts and passages leading into the side of the gorge, along its face, and out again into the open air.

The whole area was covered with dense forest. As I began exploring the level, sandy floors of the street-like passageways between the great chunks of rock, the light became fainter and fainter. There was practically no bare rock at all, every inch of its surface where there was any light being covered with smooth, soft, bright-green moss. The place was like a buried city, silent, mysterious, and eerie.

Turning an abrupt corner, I came upon a wide sunken arena overhung by a tall cliff. In the very dim light under this natural arch I saw an endless stream of bats passing to and fro from the mouth of a cave at one end to a monstrous horizontal crack at the other. The whole roof of this archway was a dense mass of sleeping bats, suspended upside down in serried ranks. The ground below was covered to a depth of more than a foot with their excrement, which had distintegrated under the influence of the weather and resulted in a mass of broken remains of uncountable millions of insects.

In this stratum of bat guano, I found a number of peculiar insects and a small bright-red millepede that I have never seen anywhere else.

By a mere fluke I had a torch in my collecting bag; with its aid I entered the cave. Though the mouth was just wide enough to permit my squeezing through, it expanded somewhat within and rose to a great height above. On both walls, as far as the light of the torch penetrated, bats were hanging or crawling about. The air was literally filled with them. The floor here was covered with guano to such a depth that I could not reach the earth below even by digging with a trapper's friend!

I was so amazed at the whole place and its denizens that I forgot all time and scrambled onwards into the depths, following the endless streams of bats that hurried along and round the corners just as busy traffic does in the streets of a great city.

Turning a corner, I was confronted by a blank wall. The bats were all passing upwards and disappearing over the top of a miniature cliff. I clambered up with some difficulty, to find that I was on top of one of the great blocks of rock. The next one above it was held away by a third block's edge far to the right. This left a horizontal gallery that stretched far ahead, beyond which I could see a large chamber. Into this I eventually emerged complete with gun and all other equipment, after a few uncomfortable minutes of wriggling through, all the time obsessed with that ridiculous but persistent impression that the roof would suddenly cave in and pin me in a not quite dead condition where nobody would ever in any circumstances find me.

The place I now found myself in was much larger than any that I had previously passed through. It was nearly the size of one whole block and almost exactly cubic in shape. The air was as dry as a desert sandstorm; whether it was due to this or the pungent smell of the bats I do not know, but my lips became hard and cracked in a surprisingly short time and my eyes began to water. The roof was altogether free from resting bats, but on the walls were what I at first supposed to be a great number of them. Some being very low down, I put down my collecting bag and gun, and advanced with the torch and a net only, to try to effect a capture.

As I approached the side, however, these things that I had supposed to be bats vanished as if by magic. One minute they were there; the next they were gone. By the time that I was close enough to the rock face to be able to see what they were, had they still been there, there was not one in sight. This was most perplexing.

Deciding that the light must disturb them, if they were not mere shadows, I put out the torch and crept forward to another wall. When I judged that I was close enough, I suddenly flashed on the torch again. A perfectly horrible vision met my eyes. The whole wall was covered with enormous whip-scorpions, crouching and leering at me. Only for a second did they remain, then, like a flash, they all shot out and away in all directions, disappearing into paper-thick crevices with a loathsome rustle.

Their behavior and appearance are, as I have remarked before, revolting in the extreme, but they were of such unusual size and color that for the sake of science I steeled myself to a systematic hunt with all the low cunning of a cave man in search of food. Eventually I captured a few after many misses, once being subjected to the nerve-shattering odiousness of having one of them scuttle over my bare arm in escaping from the net.

After this experience I deemed science had sufficient

material to gloat over, and I devoted my attention to an examination of the ground for other invertebrates. The bats were entering by the same route as I had done. After crossing the gallery diagonally, they disappeared through one of three vertical fissures, though most of them streamed into and out of the left-hand one, which was the widest. Across the floor below the line of their flight stretched a ridge of their droppings, showing that they excrete while on the wing. Elsewhere the floor was covered with silver sand and spotlessly clean. Only in one corner of the room, remote from the bat highway, was there a pile of small, pellet-like dung.

Examining this, I at once noticed that it was not composed of the crushed remains of insects as was that of the other bats. It resembled more the droppings of a rabbit, although there seemed to be a few small bones projecting from it. This prompted me to search the ceiling above to ascertain where this might be descending from. All I could see, however, was a small cleft above; so, taking the shotgun, I managed by degrees to lever myself up the sharp angle of the corner and eventually peered over the brink into the cleft.

As I switched on the torch, I went cold all over and felt as if my skin were wrinkling up everywhere preparatory to splitting and falling off in one piece. The only alternative to looking into the crevice a second time was falling down backwards. Therefore, after summoning up courage, I switched on the torch again and took a second look. The result was just as bad.

In the mouth of the hole not eighteen inches from my face, four large greenish-yellow eyes stared unblinkingly at me. They were so large that I thought unvoluntarily of some dead human thing, but the face that projected in front of them soon dispelled this impression. That face is indescribable, and I resort to a detailed reproduction of it alongside. In addition there were clammy groping fingers all muddled up with endless flaps of wrinkled naked skin. I pushed in the net and made a random scoop; then I slipped and crashed to the bottom of the cave.

The gun, luckily, fell in the soft sand, and I retained hold of the net in which a huge hammer-headed bat (*Hypsignathus monstrosus*) was struggling. My left leg was emitting piercing pains and both wrists were quite numbed. There followed an awful period during which I tried to kill the bat in the net and nursed my leg and arms, making, I am afraid, a great deal of noise about it. At last I got the animal under control and chloroformed in the "killer," and then set about gathering together the wreckage. When I came to the gun, my wrists were still numb, but being anxious to make sure that there was no sand choking the barrel, I foolishly tried to open the breech. I am not exactly certain what happened; anyway, both barrels went off almost at once and the gun shot partly out of my hand.

At the same moment the light went out.

There was a period of tremendous echoing, then the whole of this eerie subterranean world seemed to give way, starting with a gentle "swussssh" and culminating in a rattling roar. Things fell down on all sides; choking dust filled the air; while I groped for the torch, hundreds of bats wheeled around my head screaming and twittering.

The torch would not light; for some maddening reason it was not forming a proper contact. I had to sit down and take the batteries out in the dark. I pulled out the metal strips on the ends and procured a flash of light by holding on the screw cap at the back of the container. In my excitement I could not for the life of me get this screw onto the thread. Finally I had to light a match, but before I could see anything, the flame went greenish-blue and quickly died. Other matches did the same.

I had just discovered that they burnt better at a higher level when, with an awful crash, a shower of earth cascaded down from my right side and covered my feet and most of my equipment, which was lying on the floor. There was a wild scramble to retrieve all my possessions and move to a bit of clearer ground, but every time I bent down, the match went out. There was obviously some gas or lack of gas that killed a flame near the floor. I therefore concentrated on fixing the torch. At long last it lit up.

It was less use than a car headlight in a dense mist, because the air was filled with clouds of billowing dust from which a very much startled bat periodically emerged. Groping forward, festooned with gun, collecting bag, net, and torch, I tried to locate the wall with the cleft through which I had gained an entrance, but I soon lost my sense of direction. Then I stumbled across the ridge of bats' dung. This I followed up until it disappeared under a great scree of fine dry earth which was still being added to from above. After further fumbling I found the cleft; the dust was so dense that I could not see more than a few feet into it. This was, however, quite sufficient really to disturb me.

The cleft was choked with earth and rubble. Slowly it dawned on me that the percussion of the shots had released all kinds of pent-up things and perhaps even shifted the roof, as I had imagined might happen through natural causes.

By this time the dust had begun to clear considerably and the rumblings and droppings had ceased. I trekked back to the other side of the cave and tried each of the three exists. The largest, upon which I based my hopes, narrowed quickly, then plunged downward into a low, uninviting crevice. One of the others was too narrow to permit the passage of my head, while the third, although very small, seemed to continue endlessly. Its floor descended rapidly, however, and I soon discovered that the air was very bad a few feet down—matches hardly lit at all. I had therefore to return to the central cave from which I felt almost certain there were no other exits. As the dust was by now less thick, I determined to go all round and make certain.

There proved to be a hopeful-looking chimney in one corner, but try as I would, my left leg steadfastly refused to assist me to climb! This was rendered even more exasperating by the fact that a piece of burning paper thrown upwards to its mouth was instantly sucked up out of sight never to return, which all went to show that the passage had some connection with the outer world. Burning bits of note-book were then applied to the three exits. In one the flame promptly went out, in another it just wilted, and only in the narrowest one did it sail away into the distance, burning merrily. Such a result might, of course, have been predicted!

It then struck me that the choked entrance might not be all choked, so, scrambling along the ledge formed by the long horizontal mouth of this, I peered among the piles of earth that now clogged it, pushing small pieces of burning paper into any gaps or hole that remained. About two-thirds of the way down to the right the paper left my hand and blew straight into my face. I could feel a small draught. The hole was very low and descended towards the right, whereas the part of this gigantic crack through which I had come further up had distinctly sloped upwards out of the square chamber. There was fresh air coming in, so, provided it was not too small, it seemed the only feasible exit. I accordingly packed everything into the collecting bag, including the stock of the gun, wrapped the gun-barrel in the muslin bag of the net to prevent its getting scratched, crammed my felt hat onto my head for the same reason, and, holding the torch in my right hand, committed myself to the depths and the will of Allah.

Progress was slow and at one period extremely painful, for the ceiling—being the flat underside of a giant tilted cube—gradually descended until there was room for me to squeeze through only with the greatest difficulty. This effort I had to make, because I could reach for and feel the angular edge of the ceiling cube just beyond. This edge was as sharp as the angle on a small pack of cigarettes, though the block of rock above must have weighed thousands of tons. Through this slit I must get, and it was a struggle in no way made easier by having a now more or less useless left leg and also having to get the collecting bag over my head in order to push it through before me. How I envied those beastly *Amblypygi!*

Once through, I found myself in a long wide corridor again immaculately carpeted with silver sand. Having by now lost all sense of direction, I set off to the left, where I was soon involved in a tumbled mass of immense angular boulders. To climb over them was a little more than I felt prepared to attempt, so I dived in and tried to find a way through. This led me into a tunnel that smelt strongly and vaguely familiar. Before I had time to think what the cause of it could be, a rasping grunt echoed out from its depths; realizing at once that I had walked voluntarily into a leopard's private quarters, I lost absolutely no time at all in passing back through those boulders as if I were a sandworm brought up to perform such feats. The only course now was to try the other way, as I had no desire to meet a leopard, and even less to fire at one with a shotgun in the depths of the earth, considering what had occurred after the last cannonade.

The other end was a perfectly smooth blank wall. I

began to feel rather desperate, a thing one should not do in well-regulated adventures. The feeling was nevertheless sufficiently insistent to call for a cigarette. How I thanked everything, not least myself, that I had cigarettes!

While seated on the sand smoking, feeling sorry for myself, and recounting a lot of things I should like to have done, I played my torch hither and thither over the opposite wall. It was only after a long time that it dawned on me that I was gazing at great patches of green moss. Even after this it was a long time, during which I repacked my equipment, bandaged a knee, and smoked another cigarette, before my idiot brain put two and two together and arrived at the simple fact that green moss meant sunlight. Then all at once this fact penetrated my silly head and I realized that I had never yet looked at the roof. I flashed my torch upwards and saw a line of green branches dangling down into the cleft. During my subterranean meanderings night had come—I was actually standing in the open air.

Putting the gun together and loading it against a chance encounter with the inhabitant of the boulders, I advanced on his domain. After some exertion I managed to climb up over the boulders to arrive among the roots of the trees near the bottom of the gorge.

Two hours later I was back in camp, sore, temporarily crippled, and very thirsty.

*Elephant**

by Carl Akeley
and Mary L. Jobe Akeley

More than any other one man CARL AKELEY *is responsible for the magnificent animal groups in the Museum of Natural History in New York City. From boyhood his love of animals and keen observation of nature drove him to seek methods of taxidermy which would preserve the life-likeness of museum specimens. He gave an entirely new aspect to museum exhibits; and through his expeditions into Africa and his insistence upon putting animals into native settings he produced some of the most complete and authentic exhibits in the world. His books are full of nature lore, admiration for wild life, and incidents where only Akeley's quick wit and courage brought him out alive. This account of elephants he has met or heard of is taken from his* Adventures In The African Jungle *which he wrote with his wife* MARY L. JOBE AKELEY.

* "Elephant" from *Adventures in the African Jungle* by Carl Akeley and Mary L. Jobe Akeley, reprinted by permission of Dodd, Mead & Company, Inc.

HUGE GRAY SHADOWS are creeping through the forest but there is not even an echo of a footfall. The feathery foliage is stirring overhead. But there is no sound. You are only dimly conscious that something is happening in the great mysterious jungle. Something is living, breathing, moving vaguely, in the awesome gloom. A faint whisper—"Tembo!" The black gun boy has seen! His eyes are a hundred times keener than a white man's will ever be. Cold steel—your heavy gun barrel—is slipping through your cold fingers. They shake a little as you grasp your rifle and bring it to your shoulder. Suddenly you are face to face with the greatest mammal in the world. The elephant! Free and fearless, quick and powerful almost beyond comprehension, he fixes his small wicked-looking eyes upon those who have dared to cross his trail. With ease and grace his long, prehensile trunk, so near and so menacing, may reach out and smite, finishing an earthly career forever. The herd has been disturbed; it stands tensely silent, while the scales of life and death balance and a coin spins at the feet of the gods.

Now, with scarcely a murmur, the great elephant herd

shifts and ebbs and flows. It has seen you, but the dawn breeze has been favorable. Tembo has not smelled you. He glides noiselessly into the inner recesses of the great dark forest. The lord of the land has spoken and his word is "peace."

The sun breaks through a piled up cloud, its rays filtering through the tree tops to the trail beneath. A tiny bird twitters—bursts into song high up on a moss-draped bough. The silence is shattered. Something relaxes the whole length and breadth of your nervous system. Tembo has retreated to the remote feeding grounds of his jungle home.

* * * * *

The elephant always may be trusted to provide the hunter with plenty of excitement. His great size, colossal strength and magnificent courage are qualities that make him stand out as one of the most interesting as well as one of the most dangerous of beasts. Often he appears when least expected and frequently does the totally unexpected. Walking unprepared into his presence is like stepping out of a quiet home into No Man's Land—it may be perfectly safe but the odds are considerably against it.

One day in Uganda we followed the trail of two old bull elephants for five hours. We were in a big feeding ground and the elephant tracks crossed, intermingled and circled in a bewildering maze. I had told Bill, my faithful Kikuyu gun bearer, to follow the trail, more to test his ability than in the hope that he would succeed in bringing me to the herd. But I underrate Bill. Suddenly the boy stopped short and held up his cane as a signal for caution. Not more than twenty feet from us stood the two old bulls. They had not heard our approach nor had they caught our scent, but as I studied them from the shelter of a dense bush I realized that we were in a very dangerous position.

I had no desire to kill an elephant, except one for my museum group—and that meant only an unusually fine specimen; but I had even less desire to be killed by an elephant. So, with two of them as close to me as if we had been in the same room, and with nothing between us but a flimsy screen of bushes, I could take no chances. I hesitated, trying to convince myself that the tusks were fine enough to justify a shot. Then, without warning, my decision was made for me. A great gray trunk was thrust inquiringly forward—forward until it nearly touched my gun barrel. The movement may have been an attempt to catch my scent. I do not know. I had one glimpse of angry eyes set in a solid wall-like head—and I fired. The animal, wounded in the neck, swung around and bolted. I could not watch him nor gauge the effect of my shot, as his companion was right in front of me. He paused for a moment; then, apparently familiar with the deadly language of the rifle, he made a quick retreat.

Bill and I followed for about a hundred yards. The wounded bull scented us, turned and charged. I took aim, but there was no need to press the trigger, for the giant had made his last stand. His column-like legs swayed, crumpled beneath his weight, and the tremendous body lay outstretched on the ground. My bullet had pierced the jugular vein—a quick death. It had been a chance shot but, fired from such a short distance, it was much more effective than such shots usually are.

I had luck that day. Not, however, until some years later, when I talked with other hunters in Nairobi, did I realize how good my luck really was. I talked with men there who had had experiences similar to my own but who had not had my good fortune in escaping without injury. Great hunters who had been tossed and trampled—and lived to tell the tale.

Outram by keeping cool in a great emergency saved himself from a most unpleasant death. He had shot an elephant and the beast had fallen. Believing it finished, Outram approached. "Suddenly," he said, "to my surprise and horror the *dead* elephant rose and rushed at me. He caught me with his trunk and I went spinning through the air. I don't know whether in that brief flight I thought at all, but by the time I landed rather hard in the grass, amazement had given way to fear and I was sure that something had to be done and done quickly.

"I could see the elephant coming after me to trample me into the ground. Fortunately he paused for a second to crush my helmet, which had fallen off during the attack. That second saved me. I got under the beast's tail and there I clung while he wheeled and circled in a vicious attempt to get me in reach of trunk or tusks or feet. After a few moments of this sport, my injuries began to tell on me. The unequal contest could not have lasted much longer. Fortunately at the crucial moment my companion arrived and killed the elephant."

Hutchinson's story was similar to Outram's. An elephant caught him in the same way, wiped up the ground with him and then threw him into the trampled vegetation; but he had presence of mind enough to mix himself up in the animal's legs until his gun boy could fire.

The angry beast that caught Alan Black more nearly carried his charge to a finish. The method of attack was the same; but when the elephant discarded him, Black landed in a bush that broke his fall. The elephant followed and stepped on him, returning two or three times to step on him again, but the bush into which Black had fallen served as a cushion and saved his life.

The elephant's trunk is the most remarkable organ any animal possesses. The arm of a man is notable because it may be swung about at any angle from the shoulder, but the elephant's trunk may be twisted and turned in any direction and at any point in its entire length. It is just as powerful in one position as in another. It is without bone—a great flexible cable of muscles and sinew, so tough that the sharpest knife will scarcely cut it. It is so delicate that the elephant may pluck the tenderest blade of grass, yet so strong that he may lift a tree weighing a ton and toss it about easily. With his great height and short, thick neck, the elephant would find it difficult indeed to feed if it were not for his trunk. However it enables him to secure the choicest morsels on the ground or in the tree tops and to strip a whole forest of bark and branches, if he feels like it. With his trunk he has a most extraordinary ability to detect the faintest scent and to punish or kill an enemy.

Since the elephant has something like a fair chance, elephant hunting, unlike a good deal of the shooting that is done in the name of sport, always seems to me a legitimate game. This splendid animal wields a pair of heavy weapons—his mighty tusks—each one of which may weigh as much as the average man; and they are backed by several tons of brute strength. With an agility and a sagacity not to be rivaled by any other beast of his size today, he is a worthy opponent for any sportsman. Elephant hunting is always a game full of interest and excitement, because the elephant is such a wise old fellow that the hunter never learns all of his tricks.

Swiftly and surely the white man and the white man's rifles are getting the better of old Tembo. Everywhere is he compelled to retreat before the advance of civilization. But occasionally the African elephant has his innings; and when he does, he winds up the episode with a dramatic flourish of trunk and tusks that the most spectacular handling of a gun cannot rival.

Every elephant hunter has known moments of nerve-torturing suspense—moments when his wits, his courage and his skill with a gun have stood between him and an open grave. His opponent is adroit, fearless, resourceful, and possessed of tremendous strength. Of course, no one can put himself in the elephant's place and imagine the animal's feelings when it faces a rifle, but I am convinced that this great beast's attitude is one of supreme confidence. A man is handicapped, when he confronts a charging elephant, by his own state of mind. He knows he has "picked the fight." He knows he is the intruder. And he has a guilty feeling that creates in him a demoralizing fear that could never affect one who enters a contest with an absolute conviction of right.

"Here's something about half as big as one of my legs," says Tembo to himself. "A dwarfed thing equally objectionable to my eyes and nose. He's trying to frighten me with that little stick he's carrying but I'll trample the runt and gore him and perhaps sit on him afterwards."

Then, when the "stick" emits a roar and a flash, if death is not instantaneous, the elephant is thoroughly angered and becomes more dangerous than before. To the hunter it is a different story. He is not overconfident, through ignorance of his antagonist's power. Instead, he is handicapped by the knowledge that if his gun or his wits or his nerves fail him he will be quickly finished by the charging beast.

If the man keeps his head, he has slightly more than half a chance in any combat with elephants; but if the elephant gets his man, it is fairly certain that there will be no need for the services of a doctor. There are exceptions to this rule—once in a while the victim survives—as I can testify.

I had been on a collecting expedition for the museum, and had obtained all the necessary specimens, when an old bull who tried the quiet waiting game "got" me. Descending from the ice fields of Mount Kenya, that snow-capped peak on the equator, we had made a temporary camp, intending to rest until our base camp could be portered to us. The interlude gave me an opportunity to make some pictures of the typical elephant country all about us. With a party of fifteen, including gun boys and a few porters, I went back up the mountain to an elevation of nine thousand feet at the edge of the dense bamboo forest.

Probably all would have gone well, and I might have obtained some valuable photographs, had we not run across the spoor of three large bulls. It was an old trail and I knew it would take time to follow it, but the tracks were so unusual in size that I could not resist the temptation. There was always the chance that the trail might be crossed by a fresher one made as the bulls circled about feeding, but instead it led us on from noon until sundown without bringing us to any new sign.

The night on the mountain was so bitterly cold that we were glad to be up and on the move again at daybreak. There was frost in the air and the morning was still misty when we entered a great elephant feeding ground. It was an open space where the rank growth attained eight or ten feet in height and where the animals milled about eating the vegetation and trampling it down until there was very little left. The place itself was a labyrinth of trails, and from it, as the spokes of a wheel radiate from a hub, were the clear and definite tracks of the departing elephants. Soon after we left this feeding ground I came upon the fresh tracks of my three old bulls, so fresh that they must have been in that very spot an hour before.

But the network of paths led nowhere. For some time we wandered about in an attempt to follow the elephants; then, growing impatient, I left the clearing, intending to circle about it in the hope of finding on its outskirts the trail which the tuskers had taken. I had gone but a short distance when I found more fresh tracks. I stopped to examine them, and, as did so, the crackling of bamboo not two hundred yards ahead caught my attention. The bulls were almost within rifle shot and were giving me the signal for the final stalk.

I waited while one of my trackers ran silently along the trail to a point about fifty yards away where it made an abrupt turn. He indicated the direction the animals had taken. Then I turned my attention to the porters, watching them select a place to lay down their loads in a clump of trees where they would be somewhat protected in case of a stampede. The second gun boy presented his rifle for inspection. I examined it, found everything in order, and sent the boy to a safe distance with the porters. The first gun boy presented his gun; I took it, handing him the rifle I had already examined. The second gun was now ready. I leaned it against my body and stood, my back to the wall of the forest, blowing upon my hands numbed by the cold and chafing them in order to have at a moment's notice a supple trigger finger. At the same time the first gun boy was taking the cartridges from his bandolier and holding them up so that I could be sure that each was a full steel-jacketed bullet—the only kind that will penetrate an elephant's head. There was no reason to suppose that the animals suspected our presence, and I prepared for the stalk with my customary caution and with more than my usual deliberation.

I was standing with my gun leaning against my hip, still warming my hands and still looking at the cartridges one after another. In a flash, one of the calmest moments of my hunting experience changed to the most profoundly intense moment of my entire life. I suddenly *knew* that an elephant was right behind me. Something must have warned me, but I have no idea what it was. I grabbed my gun, and as I wheeled around I tried to shove the safety catch forward. It would not budge. I wanted desperately to look at it, but there was no time. I remember thinking that I must pull the trigger hard enough to fire. Then something struck me a staggering blow. I saw the point of a tusk right at my chest. Instinctively I seized it in my left hand, reached out for the other tusk with my right, and went down to the ground between them as the great body bore down upon me. One merciless little eye gleamed savagely above me as the elephant drove his tusks into the ground on either side of me, his rolled-up trunk against my chest. I heard a wheezy grunt as the great bull plunged forward, and I realized vaguely that I was being crushed beneath him. Then the light went out.

It was evening before I recovered consciousness, in a

dazed sort of way. I was dimly aware of seeing a fire. I was lying where the old bull had left me, in a cold mountain rain, while my superstitious black boys, believing that I was dead, refused to touch me. I tried to shout, and I must have succeeded after a fashion, for a little later I felt myself being carried away by my legs and shoulders.

Later I had another lucid interval, in which I realized that I was in one of the porters' tents. Then I tried to piece together the events that had led to my accident. I supposed that my back was broken because I could not move. I felt no pain. I was miserably cold and numb, and that reminded me of a bottle of brandy, carried for emergencies. I ordered the boys to bring it to me and pour it down my throat. I also had them prepare for me some hot bovril, and gradually the numbness left me. Then I discovered that I could move my arm a little. I tried the same experiment with my leg and was successful. Though the effort brought pain, it told me that I had at least a chance for recovery.

When morning came, my mind was clear enough to inquire for my white companions at the camp below, and the boys told me that soon after the elephant knelt on me they had dispatched a messenger asking for help. At that rate, assistance should have been close at hand. Fearing that the rescue party was lost on the mountain, I ordered my heavy gun to be fired every fifteen minutes, and within an hour my boys heard an answering shot from a smaller rifle.

When relief arrived I was a sorry looking spectacle.

The blow from the elephant's trunk which had stunned me had also skinned my forehead, blackened and closed an eye, broken my nose and torn open one cheek so that my teeth were exposed. Several of my ribs were broken and my lungs were punctured. I was covered with mud and splashed with blood. But apparently it was my face that was the awful sight.

Just why I was not crushed completely, I shall never know. Beneath the old bull's weight, or even under the pressure of his enormous trunk, my body would have offered about as much resistance as a soda cracker. My only explanation—and I think it is the correct one—is that a root or rock under the surface of the ground must have stopped his tusks, and that seeing me unconscious he must have thought he had killed me. He had then left me and had charged about the clearing after the black boys.

My experience is just one more illustration of my idea that a combat between a man and an elephant is still a fairly equal contest. Even the express rifles of the twentieth century have not given the hunter an overwhelming advantage over this mighty beast.

There is no older game on earth than that of elephant hunting. Before the dawn of history, some twenty thousand years ago, the elephant's claim to aristocracy among the hunted things of the world was well established. At that time his ancestors, the mammoths, clad in heavy hair a foot long, were common in western Europe. Often their portraits were painted and carved in outline on cavern walls in southern France. Even then the contest had begun, as is clearly proved by charred and broken mammoth bones found among the relics of the cave men. Fifteen hundred years before the time of Christ, Egyptian kings recorded in hieroglyphics the number of tusks brought home from elephant hunts.

In the days of Alexander the Great and of Pyrrhus, Indian rajahs were training elephants for use as beasts of burden and as war steeds. In modern times the taming of the African elephant is in its beginning. A small herd of elephants, however, trained to work, is found in the Belgian Congo. This herd, now efficient in lifting and in hauling is a tribute to the patience and skill of its trainers as well as to those who conceived the plan.

The heavy work of timber hauling, as in India where elephant power is so valuable, is not everywhere a factor in Africa because of the scarcity of the forests. The great beast can be used only in areas where there is ample forage. His appetite is enormous and in Africa, the regions of plentiful feed are by no means abundant. From time immemorial brown-skinned natives have trapped old Tembo for his flesh and for his tusks, and ivory hunters of every nationality have followed his trail and even today are tracking him into the remote parts of Africa. For many years to come he will probably be considered more valuable for his ivory than as a beast of burden.

Man has not played this elephant hunting game for centuries without learning at least its elements. There are many white hunters in Africa who have gained great knowledge of elephants, and it was with one of these professionals, Cunninghame, that I did my first tracking. He was a real hunter, and he taught me everything that one man can teach another about the game; but even so it did not take me long to discover that my schooling had only begun. Most of the essentials in hunting an animal as intelligent as the elephant belong in the list of things that can be learned only by experience. He who can understand the elephant well enough to guess his next move—and then forestall it—will stand the best chance of success.

Moreover, there is much to learn about an elephant in addition to the best method of killing him; and learning it gives one many a thrill. An elephant alive is vastly more interesting than an elephant dead, and my object in going into Africa was not primarily to kill, but to make acquaintance—as intimate acquaintance as possible with the live, wild elephant in his jungle home. I have studied Tembo for months at a time under every possible condition; on the plains, in the forests, on the mountain sides, even above ten thousand feet—and I have reached the conclusion that the professional hunter has missed half the excitement, half the interest and half the sport of his own game. I firmly believe that of all the wild animals on this earth today, the African elephant is the most fascinating and the most difficult to understand.

The student of animal nature must know how to handle his elephant gun. Frequently when he least expects it he is forced to use it. The great expanse of hide of an African elephant would seem to make him as easy a mark as the proverbial barn door. But as a matter of fact there are only three vulnerable points in all his huge body. You can kill if you can hit an elephant's backbone and sever the spinal cord. You can kill by hitting his brain or his heart. A bullet anywhere else probably will not hurt him much; at least, not immediately. But the brain and the heart shots are the only safe bets. I say "safe" a bit doubtfully, for the brain is armored by an amazingly thick skull, and the heart in silhouette would cover only an approximate square foot of area; and, besides, it requires a good knowledge of elephant anatomy to locate it in the huge frame.

It might not be so difficult to place a shot in one of those three assailable spots if elephants were not so clever at playing hide-and-seek. Elephants in the jungle do not exhibit themselves from trunk to tail as they do in the circus. You are lucky if you realize that the little patch of gray hide showing through the foliage is not a section of granite boulder, and if you can distinguish an old cow's motionless trunk from the surrounding trees.

The elephant is so nearly the color of the shadows and the tree trunks and the boulders that he may be as invisible as a cotton-tail rabbit in a hedgerow. The point of a glistening tusk, a sparkling, wicked little eye, or the tip of a great scalloped ear, is not camouflaged as successfully as the trunk or a patch of hide; but even with such a starting point it is a picture puzzle. It will give you more serious thought than entertainment to figure out just how the beast is standing and where one should aim among the bushes to strike heart or brain. Failure to select a vital point may be fatal to the hunter.

A bullet from an express gun which hits an elephant in the head will not invariably stop and turn him. One time when I was coming down through Uganda I crossed the tracks of a herd of elephants. As we were down wind from them and as it was about noon, the quietest hour of the day, the chances appeared good for overtaking them with ease. It seemed an excellent opportunity to look them over and perhaps to find the big bull I needed for my museum group. Just as I expected, we approached unnoticed to within twenty-five yards. We examined them leisurely through the glasses, as they gathered in the shade for their usual siesta. I have never seen African elephants lie down. They come together to rest, mill lazily about under the trees, and only occasionally change position. We studied the slowly shifting herd, taking our time for it and finding it almost as difficult to select a particular elephant from the mass as to distinguish his outline behind a screen of shrubbery.

At last we picked out what seemed to us an exceptionally fine bull. One of the party took deliberate aim and fired. The elephant dropped, apparently dead. We could not rush in for the customary finishing shot, for, instead of making off with all speed as is usually the case, the herd lingered. To our great surprise when his companions finally got under way the bull struggled to his feet and continued after them. A volley of bullets from our guns appeared only to speed his departure.

We followed the elephant, taking his own trail because the vegetation was too dense to travel silently in any other way. We had been going for some time, hoping to reach a space sufficiently open for us to leave the trail and come alongside for a more effective shot. Suddenly I began to realize that the trail had been slowly turning so that the wind was from us to the injured bull. Hastily we moved out to the side, but we were too late. The bull already had our wind. I knew he had it, although I could not see him, for there was a crashing among the bushes as he wheeled. Then came the piercing scream of an angry elephant.

No one who has heard that scream ever forgets it. It is like a shrill locomotive whistle, intensified by the consciousness that the locomotive is after *you*—just *you*. It is the warning of a charge, and after it echoes through the forest a man who knows what it means needs plenty of self-control not to fire wildly. Snorting and grumbling our elephant now broke through the underbrush. Gun in hand, I waited. On he came, bursting into view, with his great ears outspread twelve feet from tip to tip and his trunk thrown high and furiously lashing the air. At thirty yards I shot. He stopped, but seemed puzzled rather than hurt. I emptied the other barrel of my rifle and signaled to my gun boy for the second. Shot after shot I pumped into him with as much effect as if I were firing so many bullets into a mountain wall.

Meanwhile my companion had been shooting also, and with equally unsatisfactory results. We were frantically wondering how to gain time to reload, when the old bull answered the question by retreating into the woods. Obviously he wanted a moment's breathing space away from the pelting rain of bullets. All the rules of elephant hunting seemed to have failed. We had fired numerous shots, several of them well placed brain shots. The first should have turned him; and, failing that, any of the others should have killed him. But he had taken them, and finally gone off seemingly unharmed, leaving us weak, bewildered and absolutely helpless.

Scarcely had we reloaded when we heard him coming on his second charge. Screaming, grunting, roaring, he rushed at us. Again the first shot stopped him. Again he took our fire standing and finally retreated, angry but apparently no worse for our barrage. It seemed we could not knock him down. What, then, if on his third charge we could not even stop him? I was sick of it and quite ready to quit, but we had started something that had to be finished. He now came at us so promptly that we had no choice but to stand our ground. For several seconds we could hear his onrush without seeing him. Then he came into view, headed some thirty feet to one side of us and thrashing the limb of a tree back and forth in his trunk.

Without stopping to wonder by what lucky chance his charge should have been so utterly misdirected, I fired once more. It was a good brain shot, this time from the side, and it took quick effect. The old fellow tottered and fell lifeless.

A second later a trembling native crawled out of the bushes in front of our dead bull. It was my tent boy, Ali, who at that moment was the whitest black boy I have ever seen. Without my knowledge he had followed to watch the sport and had experienced the supreme fright of his life when, luckily for us, he happened to draw the last charge. When I examined this elephant I found the thickest skull I have ever seen. Almost any of my shots would have killed an ordinary animal, but in his case all but the last—the one fired from the side—had been stopped by bone.

Another animal who tried to hunt the hunter by doubling on his own trail was the old bull which now forms the central figure in the group of African elephants which I mounted for the American Museum of Natural History in New York. He also proved to me most effectively that the elephant has another advantage over man in the hunting game—the ability to move through the forest as silently as a shadow. I had wounded the beast, but he was still leading me a long chase. I followed one hour, then another, and finally settled down for a good long trek in country where the going was rough and the forest too thick to see in any direction. Suddenly, with no warning whatsoever, the elephant charged directly across my path. I fired two hurried shots as he passed, and he disappeared in the growth on the other side of the trail. He was tired of being followed, and had come back after me, intending to wind up the affair in his own way. The inaccuracy of his charge probably was due to the fact that he was depending on sound to locate me rather than on sight or scent. It was a close call—the elephant was less than ten feet away when my shot stopped him, as I afterwards proved by placing the skull at the normal height and extending the line cut through the bone by my bullet to a point at the height from which my gun was fired.

High up on the Aberdare Range, where the slopes are so steep that a horse can travel only with the greatest difficulty, but where the elephants move along with an amazing ease and rapidity on age-old paths worn deep in the rocks, a herd of elephants, whose spoor I was following, again got my wind by redoubling on the trail. Realizing that they were passing me as they descended on a parallel trail, I gained on them by cutting across at my own level. And then I learned something more about the sagacity of elephants. They came to a place on the mountain where it was so steep that a landslide started beneath their feet. All around, the earth was soft and slippery. As each elephant reached this spot, he squatted, remaining motionless as the loose dirt gave way beneath his tremendous weight. One after another the tuskers tobogganed down the mountainside as if *glissading* on a snow field. One by one, as their respective mud sleds came to a standstill some two hundred yards below, they got up, shook themselves and proceeded on the downward trail, leaving me high and dry and safe above them.

Now that my elephant-hunting days are over, and my specimens of the grandest beast of the Bright Continent are mounted in two great museums of the Western World, I like to think of the elephant not as my enemy but rather as an honorable and worthy opponent who is so placed in the grim scheme of existence that at times he has sought my life as I have sought his. I have never killed except for scientific purposes or to save myself from death. The elephants I have seen in action require no apology—they have always been moved by the instinct of self-defense.

I like to think of the elephant as a member of a clan to which he is intensely loyal. I like to think of him as a creature of tremendously keen intelligence and of living sympathy for his kind. I like to recall the way the young and husky members of a herd form an outer defensive ring to protect the very small and the very old when danger threatens. I like to remember the efforts I have seen elephants make when lifting up and helping along a wounded comrade. I like to visualize the splendid struggle the elephant has carried on throughout the ages and the versatility he has shown as he has adapted himself to changing conditions and has defended himself against varying modes of attack, each more fatal than the one before. Finally, I like to think of the obstinacy with which he has survived, in the midst of circumstances which have caused the extermination of many of his early ancestors. Today the wild beasts of Africa are being driven back mile after mile into the strongholds of forest, hill, and mountain; but wherever animal rights still triumph over human invasion, old Tembo remains the jungle's overlord.

*Tapir on a Rampage**

by Frank Buck

FRANK BUCK *is known widely to zoos and circuses as the man who can furnish alive any specimen they need. His own account of animals he has hunted makes his* Bring 'Em Back Alive *as full of excitement as the unknown jungle itself. He has met on their own ground pythons, cobras, lions, tigers, and a dozen other dangers. Of all the animals he has faced, the tapir surprised him most because he took its lethargy so much for granted that he treated it like a domestic pet.*

* "Tapir on a Rampage" from *Bring 'Em Back Alive* by Frank Buck and Edward Anthony, reprinted by permission of Simon and Schuster, Inc.

ALMOST ANY ANIMAL is dangerous when aroused. In 1926 I came close to being killed by a tapir, the meekest of animals.

I was in Sumatra assembling a group of specimens that included some pythons, Sumatra hornbills, langur monkeys, civet cats, porcupines, a siamang gibbon and a tapir.

Normally it would have been safe to bet that the pythons would make more trouble for me than the rest of this collection put together. But this was not a normal situation. It was the tapir that won the Trouble Sweepstakes, breezing in with several lengths to spare.

The experience proved to me all over again how foolish it is to generalize about animals. I've seen two tigers, for instance, animals of the same sex and age and caught at the same time, display utterly different characteristics. One grew so tame that after a few weeks I was putting my hand inside its cage and stroking the back of its neck; the other became more and more vicious, until the process of feeding it involved real danger and required absolute caution.

It isn't much less intelligent to generalize about animals than it it to generalize about people. It's about as sensible to say, "Elephants are kind," or "elephants are mean," or "tapirs can be trusted," or "tapirs can't be trusted," as it is to say flatly that all human beings are noble, or the opposite of that proposition. One finds almost as much variety in animal character as one does in human character.

Of course, there are certain basic things that are true of animals just as there are certain fundamentals that apply to most people but this does not alter the fact that the minute a man starts generalizing about animals he displays his inexperience. Perhaps the nearest one can come to a generalization is to say that most animals are dangerous when they think they're in danger. And, after all, that is less a generalization about animals than it is a basic fact of life, involving human beings and the animal kingdom both.

The tiger that strikes at the man who is feeding him through the bars has decided that this man is an enemy with designs on his life; the gentler tiger has something in his make-up that resigns him to his captivity and tells him he has nothing to fear from the two-legged creature who is looking after him. Eventually the rougher specimen, when he discovers that his keeper is not someone he will one day have to fight for his life, tones down too and becomes manageable.

Of all the animals in the Malayan jungle the tapir is

probably the least dangerous. He is much less formidable, for instance, than the wild boar which has tusks that are capable of ripping open an unwary enemy in a fight.

The tapir in addition to having no tusks is also clawless. Each front foot has four hoof-like toes, each back foot three; and these are hardly weapons. He has big powerful teeth but since he is known to be a vegetarian these are feared by neither man nor beast. One is about as conscious of them as one is of the teeth, however capable, of the average horse, cow or deer.

The tapir is a strange creature, in a class by itself. It is the only animal on earth today that has come down the ages in its present form. Evolution has left it untouched. It was as it is today thousands and thousands of years ago when the camel was no bigger than a greyhound and the horse was a four-toed animal the size of a fox terrier. It has always been to my mind such a placid symbol of age and tradition, so perfect an embodiment of the quiet mellowness of the years, that I could have as easily imagined myself being suddenly attacked by the Sphinx as by a tapir.

I couldn't have given less thought to the troublesome possibilities of my specimen if he had been a jack rabbit. The only thing that made me at all conscious of him was the fact that he had a badly barked back.

He was a full grown Malayan tapir, weighing about six hundred pounds. I had secured him to fill an order from an animal dealer in Kansas City who supplies the zoos of the smaller cities. It hardly pays me to round up the scattering orders of the very small zoos and such transactions are usually made through a dealer.

For the full length of the back, along the spine, the skin of this animal was badly barked. He had walked into a trap that was a log-fenced enclosure with a gate that snapped to. (The inside of the trap and the approach to it had been baited with tapioca root, a favorite delicacy of the tapir tribe.) In his frantic efforts to escape he had plunged about blindly and succeeded in scraping whole patches of skin off his spine.

In terms of my business this meant that I had to do a job of dealing on that back, for, after all, I had an order for an animal with a whole skin. I wanted to apply some ointment when I first noticed the animal's condition in Sumatra but the conditions were not favorable there nor on the little Dutch boat on which I brought my collection back to Singapore.

On the outskirts of Singapore is the small town of Katong where I maintained a compound. There I instructed Dahlam Ali, the Malay who served me on expeditions in and around the Malayan district—(just as Lal Bahudar assisted me on collecting trips where a knowledge of Hindustani and Hindus was essential)—to build a small pen for the tapir. He and another boy in my employ built one about twenty feet square. They drove posts into the ground and with two-by-four planks built an enclosure about five fect high, a height which the animal could not jump. When three sides were up I drove the animal in from his cramped native cage, and with Ali hastily nailed up the opening while the other boy kept our captive cornered with a pole. Never had I seen a more harmless looking tapir. It seemed as I regarded him that it had been wholly unnecessary to keep him cornered while we nailed him in. He was completely absorbed in the business of contorting himself so that he could scratch his irritated back, which was itching, against the planks of the enclosure.

No gate was made in the pen as this seemed unnecessary labor. The spaces between the planks (through which the animal was fed) provided a good foot-hold and it was a simple matter to climb over. I did so, as casually as if I were entering a cow pasture. In my hand I carried a pound can of zinc ointment.

Ali was with the other boy feeding a great collection of birds which I had stored in a shelter 200 feet away, a collection that included a big cage of hill minas. These are coal black chattering birds with yellow wattles, some members of the species possessing the doubtful gift of gab even to a greater extent than parrots.

I scooped up a handful of the ointment, and, walking over to where this member of the animal kingdom's Oldest Family was scratching himself against a plank, slapped it over his back with as much detachment as if I were a bricklayer slapping some mortar on a brick. Bricks aren't very dangerous (unless heaved at one) and neither are tapirs . . . unless . . .

As I slapped that fistful of ointment over the tapir's spine he started running, I following as best I could, with my hand over his back like a bareback rider preparing to leap aboard his charger. Suddenly the animal whirled around, dropped back a few feet and charged straight at me, burying his head in my stomach and knocking the wind out of me as his six hundred pounds sent me sprawling on my back. I had hardly hit the ground when the Meekest of Animals jumped on me, his front feet bearing down on my chest, his hind feet on the ground.

I started swinging over on one side in an effort to get up. This inspired the jungle's Greatest Example of Humility to hoist his hind legs over my lower end, in the process dealing me a painful and weakening blow in a delicate region. It was a palpable foul but as there was no referee present this pacifist proceeded to stomp up and down all over me, bruising me in a dozen places.

I didn't exactly enjoy what was happening to me but neither did I become alarmed until the animal's six hundred pounds began to feel like a ton. It's hard to take a tapir seriously until something happens that forces you to do so. In all my previous dealings with the species it had lived up to its reputation for harmlessness, so it took me a few minutes to get it through my head that this tapir was more than nettled; that the infuriated creature had murder in his heart.

It's hard to figure out what happened inside that animal's sluggish brain when I applied that first big daub of ointment. The salve doubtless caused some irritation but this hardly could have been enough to convince the beast that he was in the presence of an enemy. . . .

The tapir had me painfully pinned down. I could feel his breath on my face. Not a sound came from him, except his heavy breathing. His eyes had a look that made my flesh creep. I had never seen such hate in a tapir's expression.

My first attempts to whirl around and free myself having failed, I poised myself for a great effort into which I put every ounce of strength I had. In swinging around I succeeded in partly freeing one shoulder, but this accomplished nothing, for the enraged beast pounded me flat again, moving up a few inches closer to my head in the process.

And then I had a moment of horror. Opening his big mouth, the animal bared his powerful teeth and reached to get hold of my face. It didn't take much computing to see that that awful mouth was capable of taking in the width of my head. Once he got my face between those jaws it would be an easy matter to pull the flesh off.

As I looked straight down the throat of this panting brute, I realized my danger and the next thing I knew I was yelling—yelling for all I was worth. I'm not ashamed to admit it. I had no desire to have the meat ripped off my face by this vegetarian on a rampage.

With all the lung power I could summon I fairly shrieked, "Ali! Ali!"—at the same time freeing one leg by a tremendous effort. As the animal strained forward, his teeth coming nearer and nearer, I got my right knee under his lower jaw, and reaching up, got hold of both his ears with my hands. He started furiously swinging his head right and left in an effort to shake me off but I held on for dear life, my knee keeping his teeth and my face apart.

. . . And then the demented creature started dragging me all over the enclosure, jumping off me to make it easier for him to take me for a ride. Every time I made an effort to get up he'd pound me flat against the turf with his front feet.

"Ali! Ali!" I yelled myself hoarse. Why didn't he come running over? Where the hell was he? . . . And then I answered my own question. I had sent Ali to care for my birds. He was in the bird shelter, looking after them. . . . With a sudden vehemence, I found myself cursing my collection of hill minas. These boisterous birds—(all other birds seem quiet by comparison)—were probably chattering away at such a rate that it was impossible for Ali to hear my cries.

I felt the power going out of my fingers and in desperation I strove to tighten my hold on the crazed creature's ears. And, with one of those unnatural bursts of strength that come when destruction is staring one out of countenance, I stiffened my knee against the tapir's chin. With renewed fury he started dragging me all around the lot, adding new lacerations to my sore and battered body.

"Ali! Ali! Ali!" I put everything I had into this final cry.

I was beginning to wonder how long I could hang on. My back was aching as it had never ached in all my days, and my chest was sore from the pounding of those hoofs. I would have to scramble to my feet somehow and get over that fence. Having survived encounters with tigers and leopards I had no intention of being wiped out by a damned tapir, an animal that had always seemed to me a sort of giant cockroach, with as much spirit and personality, under normal circumstances, as that loathsome bug.

My weakening fingers clutched the tapir's ears in a final frenzy of self-preservation and my knee, doing its best to seem a firm and determined knee, managed to maintain its wobbly intercession between me and the teeth of the four-legged lunatic that was trying to destroy me as Ali at last came running up, excitedly shouting, *"Apa ini, tuan? Apa ini?"* [What is this, master?]

It wasn't necessary for me to answer Ali's question. Screaming for the other boy to come over and help him, he grabbed a board,—one of the pieces of lumber left over after the pen had been built—and started beating the animal over the head with it. The other boy who was at the far end of the compound finally heard his screams and came tearing over.

With even more presence of mind than Ali,—(a real surprise to me, for over a period of years Ali had displayed more resourcefulness in emergencies than any native I had ever employed anywhere in Asia)—the newcomer grabbed a two-by-four scantling and shoved it into the open mouth of the would-be killer, the animal biting down on it. The surest way of saving my features was to put something besides my wornout knee between me and those vicious teeth, and the scantling did the trick.

The animal, one piece of lumber between his teeth and another being brought down on his head, backed away a few paces. As he did, Ali reached through the fence and grabbed my arm, pulling me further away from the maddened creature. At this point the other boy jumped over the fence, and, while Ali beat the animal off with his board, lifted me to my feet. Almost falling against it in my weakened condition, I grabbed the top of the fence, putting one foot in an open space between the boards about a foot from the ground. Then this boy who served as Ali's assistant—(although in this stirring operation *he* was really the leader and Ali the assistant)—gave me a great boost, which, combined with my own efforts, sent me toppling over the fence onto the ground on the other side where I landed in a limp heap. A mass of bruises, I lay there for half an hour before I could summon the strength to move.

When I stood up at last it was with the aid of Ali and the other Malay, who hustled me off to bed. The battering I had received left me black and blue from head to foot and it was three days before I could get up.

The day after I was laid up for repairs, Ali, who was looking after me, sat beside the open window of my room chewing betel nut and using for his cuspidor that portion of Katong which lay beneath my window. Ali was hardly ever without a good gob of this Eastern equivalent for chewing tobacco and he spat frequently. It seemed to help his thinking.

Ali was puzzled about that tapir. To him, as to me, the tapir was a perfect exemplification of the peaceful attitude toward life. The normal rôle of the animal was running away from fights instead of getting into them.

Ali had more to say about tapirs that day than he usually has to say about everything in the course of a whole week. Under normal circumstances he did most of his talking through the medium of gestures,—a shrug of the shoulders, a movement of the hand, a toss of the head. A few facial expressions rounded out his vocabulary.

Although he didn't bother selecting the right words, he spoke English understandably. But most of the time he was able to express himself without words.

Today, however, he needed words to unburden himself,—words supplemented by a wrinkling up of his nose, his favorite method of expressing displeasure. Normally if I asked him what he thought, let us say, of some animal that I was thinking of taking off a trader's hands, he would wrinkle up his nose if he thought the creature a poor specimen. If he thought it a good buy, he would beam all over. No words.

That nose of his was as wrinkled as an octogenarian prune as he started discussing that tapir. The animal had the devil in him, a whole tribe of devils. He spat vehemently to emphasize his point.

Ali seemed more picturesque to me than ever as he sat by that window speculating on how all those devils had got inside that tapir. He was dressed in an outfit that was standard for him unless he was at work on a dirty job. It consisted of an immaculate white starched *baja,* which is a shirt much like the top of a pajama jacket and worn over the *sarong* or skirt, which today was a red and blue affair, cut very full. On his head he wore a black velvet Mohammedan cap.

Ali wasn't in the habit of getting particularly excited about anything. His philosophy was the philosophy of "*Tidak apa?*" (Which in Malay means, "What does it matter?")

The soul of conscientiousness, he yet reserved the right to a resigned outlook. Things happened. That was life. Why examine anything too closely?

In considering the tapir that had tried to annihilate me, he made an exception to his "*Tidak apa?*" rule. It did matter. Tapirs had no business acting that way. One had enough problems in life with animals and people that were frankly one's enemies without having to face sudden attacks from what one had a right to regard as peaceful sources.

Over and over we discussed the whole race of tapirs, making many points, relevant and irrelevant.

The reader may be acquainted with the fact that tigers, leopards and other carnivora regard the tapir as a very choice dish. The tapir, needless to say, is familiar with his popularity in these quarters as a table delicacy; and he uses every resource at his command to keep out of the way of his enemies. Nature has come to his assistance in making it possible for him to stay under water for several minutes at a stretch. Consequently his normal habitat is near a river. When pursued by some killer ambitious to dine off his chops, he calmly steps into his convenient river, walking along its bottom and passing the time in the gentle pursuit of pulling up the roots of water lilies and other aquatic plants. He is as fond of these morsels as the tiger is of tapir meat.

After nibbling away for a few minutes, he comes to the surface, swimming off to some other point where there are more tasty roots to eat.

But when the jungle fruits are ripe, the tapir, unable to resist these dainties, forsakes his river. He makes for the higher ground where rambutan, checo, jack fruit and other jungle palate-ticklers fall to the ground.

Here in territory where he is easy prey for carnivora on the prowl, he vies with other herbivorous animals for his favorite delicacies. Cautiously emerging from the brush, he comes out into the more open spaces of the jungle where the fruit-bearing trees are found. In his movements is the accumulated timidity of thousands of generations of tapirs, all of them hunted animals.

Fear of attack is always uppermost in his mind. He isn't even free from it when he is near the water. More than one Dyak savage has made a meal off the remains of a tapir he has found buried in the mud along the margin of a river or swamp, the victim of an assault by a giant bull crocodile that seized its prey in the water, held it under until it was drowned and then tore it to pieces.

Practically everything Ali and I said on the subject—and our experience with tapirs had been wide—contributed to the point that it was unusual for a tapir, one of the least courageous of the perpetually hunted animals, to make an attack such as the one to which I had been subjected.

This being so, didn't the *tuan* believe that the animal was full of devils? How could a tapir act that way otherwise?

I tried to tell Ali, in simple language, that the animal's conduct represented the aggressiveness born of perpetual fear. The creature had got it into his head that I was trying to destroy him; so he tried to destroy me. If there had been a river to run to, the tapir would have headed for that instead of me. It was as simple as all that.

Ali wrinkled up his nose. He was displeased.

He kept after me until, to end the discussion, I told him that he was probably right. The creature must be full of devils.

Ali beamed. He knew all along that I would see his point. Of course the animal was full of devils!

But he wasn't finished yet.

Did the *tuan* think it wise to ship to America an animal so full of devils? Would it not make trouble for me?

This was carrying a joke too far. I finally convinced Ali that an animal so full of devils should be shipped out of Asia, which was already over-stocked with devils, with all possible haste.

For the good of my soul and that tapir's back, I was

determined to resume my operations with the zinc ointment. This I did, but I confess that I ministered to his skinned back from the outside of the pen. I wrapped some rags around the end of a long stick and tied them securely in place. Then I put some ointment on the rags and with this home-made apparatus succeeded in giving him a thorough smearing. A series of these treatments proved effective and before long the tapir's back was healed. A few months later I delivered him to the Kansas City dealer who had ordered him for a small mid-western zoo. There he proved as easy to handle as a kitten.

*Buying Dynamite**

by Raymond L. Ditmars

RAYMOND LEE DITMARS *was for years in charge of the Reptile Collection at the Bronx Zoo and afterwards became Curator of the Zoo. His trips rivalled Frank Buck's as did the specimens he brought back alive. Not only a foremost authority on snakes and the man who did much to develop anti-snake-bite serum, Ditmars was a storyteller of uncommon gusto. His accounts of snakes, monkeys, bats and other wild life are full of excitement frequently spiced with humor. "Buying Dynamite" is such an account from his* Strange Animals I Have Known.

* "Buying Dynamite" from *Strange Animals I Have Known* by Raymond L. Ditmars, reprinted by permission of Harcourt, Brace and Company, Inc.

AS THE READER may already have gathered, the purchase and shipment of our new specimens is one of the most fruitful sources of adventure in my strange business. My experiences in escorting an oriental shipment form a good example.

I received word to leave immediately for San Francisco where some big orang-utans had just arrived from Singapore. There was also, in addition, a series of assorted animals from which I was to buy what was practical. I was not surprised on arrival to find a number of rival purchasers from zoos and circuses who had come to meet the same ship.

I bought some reptiles, some pygmy Philippine cattle or anoas, a husky male orang-utan weighing close to a hundred and fifty pounds and a baby of the same species. I thought the latter would be an interesting little friend for the many children who know the Park and recognized their individual pets. The work of caring for this baby, with its finicky appetite and a snuffling cold, was a job in itself; but I took the risk as it was a particularly intelligent looking example. I brought the baby through all right, but it was the big male which gave me the real job. He acquired country-wide fame during the four days' overland trip to New York! Here are the pungent details of that unforgettable journey:

After the usual custom clearance a truck took my cases and the big orang-utan to a theatrical warehouse. It was necessary to leave them there for about two days, while I attended to formalities relating to government quarantine of the wild cattle I had bought. The cattle were to follow across in a month, cared for by express employees.

Unfortunately there was no place to put my big orang temporarily in a zoo as the local one was an open air collection. I found a good space near a sunny window at the warehouse. By nailing two strips of two by four timber to the floor and spiking these to the orang's cage, there was no danger of him walking it around the place by shaking the bars. A bright little Irishman, on duty during the day, said he would keep an eye on him. The understanding was that I would come morning, noon and early evening to inspect and feed the animal. Meanwhile my baby orang waited outside in a taxicab. When I had the old fellow settled I took the infant to the hotel and in deference to the management went skyward with him in the laundry elevator. After the management discovered what I had in my room the ensuing arguments about violations of rules were continuous, but as they could show nothing specifying orang-utans I managed to keep my baby with me. He soon yanked the telephone wire out by the roots and got me into lots of trouble by other similar tricks.

During the stay in San Francisco I arranged with a Chinese restaurant to cook some rice and dry some loaves of graham bread for my charges. Fresh bread is not good for animals. Going into the Chinaman's spotless kitchen I inspected a batch of rice that was just right. Every grain was separate, nicely puffed, not too moist or too dry. As no container except a fair-sized aluminum pot was at hand, one of the Chinamen stuttered his willingness to walk over to my place. I told him the rice was for an animal, a big monkey, but he didn't seem to have the faintest idea what I was talking about. He carried the pot of rice and I lugged the bread and some bananas.

I found the warehouse was dark and forbidding. A watchman admitted us. Inside, a single lamp burned high overhead on a suspended cord. It showed dim outlines of covered pianos and stacks of scenery. Among all this loomed the orang cage, showing only the bars and a black interior. The big fellow was in the shadow of its depths, wrapped in his tan blanket, of which he was very fond. As soon as it grew dark he threw this blanket over his head, clutched it under his chin and stretched out to doze.

The Chinaman stepped to the bars to peer in. He was holding the pot of rice. Fearing that he might be startled I grabbed him at the rear of the belt, but wasn't quite quick enough. The rice smelled good to the orang, and, even in the dim light, it looked good. Instantly a great, clay-colored face, surrounded with wisps of red hair appeared at the bars. The top of the head and shoulders were covered with the blanket. A hairy hand, of excessive length, clutched the blanket under the chin. Darting from this apparition was an arm, with hand nearly twelve inches long. This great member dove into the pot of rice and scooped up a tremendous fistful. There was a smacking of lips denoting an appetite in keeping with the picture. The Chinaman was horrified, but he made only a single sound; it was no louder than that of a little bird—just a sort of peep. The bowl of rice crashed to the floor. I felt the Chinaman's belt slip through my fingers as he fled.

My return to the East with my animals was routed by the fastest trains and best connection at Chicago. The matter of taking the orangs as excess baggage puzzled the railroad people, but was finally arranged. A carpenter built me a little travelling house for the baby and everything went aboard the baggage car of a crack train over the Union Pacific route. The passenger traffic manager gave me a letter to employees to extend all courtesies. Remembering past difficulties, I asked for a specific paragraph to dining-car stewards to give me anything which I might order and have it cooked under my personal direction. No food was put aboard except a dozen loaves of stale bread. Everything else could be obtained in the dining-cars.

The big orang's cage had a sliding panel of teakwood, with many holes bored in it. This provided protection when the cage was in open transportation. I didn't intend to keep the front in place while the animal was in the baggage car because he would not get enough air.

The baggage cars of the transcontinental fliers are just as long as the Pullmans. They have at their head end a steam turbine and a big dynamo, the former fed by a flexible pipe from the locomotive. The idea of this plant is to supply the elaborate lighting and fan equipment of the trains, where the ordinary belted generators on the Pullman trucks would be unable to keep the batteries charged. This apparatus keeps a man constantly on duty. With this man and the baggageman to keep an eye on the orang it seemed safe for me to remove the panel from the front of the cage. But, as an added precaution, I fastened the cage to the steam pipes.

My compartment was seven cars back, the only space I could get. But I promised the men in the baggage car that I would be up at least three times a day. Porters were instructed to quickly pass word back to me in case of emergency.

Around midnight of the first day's run there was a loud knocking at my compartment door. The porter apologized but said I was needed up in front. Staggering sleepily through the long avenue of swaying corridors and green curtains I came upon an irate Pullman conductor, a heavy man who had just cause for complaint. From what he told me, he had, from the first, felt little respect for an animal that wrapped itself in a blanket and looked like a tramp snoozing in the back of a big packing case.

It seemed that, though there was a desk at the head of the car, the conductor had absent-mindedly paused at the orang's cage to sort some of his car slips. Possibly the train struck a curve, awakening the orang, for when the conductor started away the animal was sitting up, still wrapped in his blanket. The conductor started by with no thought of evading the cage. Suddenly the orang shot out a hand completely enveloping the official's leg and brought him down flat! It was lucky the poor man hadn't broken both knee-caps. Now he indignantly demanded that the panel of the cage be locked in place to keep the beast from tripping up somebody else.

I argued that the car was very wide and that he had had ample room to pass, and now that he knew what might happen he could take precautions. But he was angrily obdurate. There was nothing to do but comply. Luckily it was cool in the car because we were coming down the slope of the Sierras. I put up the panel while the orang watched me with a lowering eye, though we were already on friendly terms.

When I visited my orang in the morning with cooked oatmeal, apples and bananas, the turbine mechanic pointed considerable wreckage out to me. What had happened was that as dawn had filtered into the car there had come a series of crashing sounds. The orang was rising and, wishing to open his bedroom shutter, began to smash it. He did a thorough job. The panel had been split into half a dozen pieces and hurled in all directions. After this he patted his blanket into a seat and patiently awaited breakfast.

I fed him the entire bowl of oatmeal from a tablespoon.

When he finished he lolled back with an inscrutable gleam in his crafty eyes while the morning's house-cleaning was performed in his and the baby's cage. Meanwhile the little fellow was coaxed to take proper nourishment and had some treatment for his cold.

We ran into Ogden, Utah, for a half-hour stop. It was good to get out and stretch and breathe the clean, dry air. But up ahead there soon arose a commotion. I heard shouts and yells and laughs. The train crew were changing engines, but this was never attended by anything more apparent than a bump and hiss of adjusted airbrakes. I gathered that the excitement was at the baggage car. Instantly I concluded that my orang had something to do with the rumpus.

It *was* the orang. I found the baggage car was so full of crumpled paper that it looked like a safe receptacle for loose china. Moreover, the bulk of paper kept growing. It expanded and rolled out as if a giant were whipping cream. What had happened was that a newsboy had boarded the head of the train with a large bundle of papers to sell. The orang had grabbed the bunch and uttered a deep-chested whoop. What a joy it must have been, with nothing for a spirited orang to do in a monotonous baggage car, to be thus provided with recreation! He rapidly dissected page after page, waving them violently and watching the mass fluff up into billowing mounds.

I unhesitatingly paid the boy for his whole bundle of newspapers.

The Ogden papers promptly published an account of the episode and it was wired ahead to Chicago that Number Two was carrying a very eccentric passenger. This story bore fruit as I progressed eastward.

That evening my anthropoid associate ate a hearty supper of fruit and stale bread. On leaving the car I was comforted to note that he had thrown the blanket over his shoulders as if preparing to retire at an early hour. However, around two in the morning there was another knocking at my compartment door. The porter didn't stop to apologize.

"Come right away, suh! Yo' big monkey have a long knife and walks all around fo' to cut baggage!"

I envied some of the peaceful snores sifting through green curtains.

This is what had happened: The heavy bread knife which I used to cut hard, stale bread into slices, had been slipped behind a protruding slat in the car. It was hanging there by the handle when the baggagemen started to shift trunks at Cheyenne. Fearing that the knife would be hidden behind some new baggage, he thoughtfully placed it on the top of the orang's cage. It was easy to surmise what followed. The ape had been awakened by the commotion in the car. He soon noted something had been laid on top of his cage. A careful squinting through crevices showed this something, and it looked interesting. The several openings in the top between the boards of teak were about half an inch wide. The night was long and the orang was refreshed from retiring at an early hour. Here was something to do! By sticking the end of his little finger through one crack, then the other, he worked the knife to the front. When it was near enough he made a curling reach upward through the bars and seized it.

In characteristic fashion the orang experimented with the shaft of shining steel, banging here and there until he discovered the end would stick in the wood. It was fun to do this and yank it out again. But the amusement was curtailed. The thing would only stick a little way into the hard teak of the cage, or in the stubborn floor outside. Across the car was an interesting pile of leather baggage. It looked as if it could be dug good and deep. How could it be reached? Why, by a mighty heaving at the bars which stood a chance of slipping the cage from the troublesome rope, restraining it at the rear. That heave was probably a herculean affair, but orangs have great power. The cage nearly upset backward but it also slipped the cords running over a cleat at the top and jumped forward.

The commotion attracted the man at the turbine. He saw the cage advancing in jumps. At short intervals between jumps a long arm stretched forth, waving a shining knife. It was at this point that word was passed to me. I saw at once that it was hazardous to go near the cage. The orang had no idea of stabbing anybody; in fact, he had not the remotest inkling that the knife was a weapon. He was simply delighted with our interest as we danced around, and he kept on shoving the blade through chinks in the sides and back in demonstration that it was a plaything of varied use. I finally got it from him, by offering him in exchange, a long-spouted brass oil-can, which was demonstrated by giving it a squeeze. Here, he instantly decided was something appearing to yield jets of nectar. He dropped the knife and stuck the spout of the oil-can in his mouth. The taste didn't appeal to him, but the new game was fun. I got the knife and we moved the cage into place, securely tied it and clinched a couple of nails over the cords.

This episode, possibly a bit elaborated, was also wired to Chicago, for as we stopped at Omaha there was considerable platform gossip during my rush around for strips and nails to repair the broken panel. It would be needed for the street transportation from one railroad station to the other, in Chicago.

As a result of all this advance publicity, a crowd of newspaper men awaited me and my Bornean protégé at Chicago when Number Two rolled into the terminal. The panel had to be temporarily removed and he was amply photographed. From Chicago to New York he rested and we reached our destination without further adventure.

I had another orang travelling companion that came into Philadelphia on a freighter. It was a smaller one, though not a baby. He was a pet of the captain, but had such a number of accumulated misdemeanors that the officer wanted to donate him to the Park. He telephoned New York and asked me to come down on the first train

I could get as he was leaving port. Custom clearance was quickly arranged, but when I asked the captain for the cage he said there wasn't any and he wanted to cast off in a quarter of an hour! The orang weighed about fifty pounds. When I spoke to him he threw long arms around my neck and I went ashore carrying the creature like an overgrown child. I hailed a taxi and drove to the Broad Street Station. It took only about two minutes at the terminal to gather a seething escort, but I went to the ticket office and asked whether I could take my "child" into the smoker on half fare—or what could I do? The ticket agent was so astonished he referred me to the station master. They sold me one ticket and sent a rocking chair into the baggage compartment for me.

One morning I received a telephone call from one of the older animal dealers whose disordered gloomy places are fast disappearing. The man was excited and urged me to hurry down, that he had two big king cobras loose. We wanted to buy a pair of these creatures but I didn't relish the job of capturing them. Nevertheless the head-keeper and I started down. We carried a large fibre satchel in which were two deep, burlap bags, and a staff with a noose at the end.

The king cobra holds the palm as the largest and most active of all poisonous serpents. It grows to be fifteen feet long and is built like a great whip. From its size and extremely deadly venom it is by far the most formidable of any serpent. But added to all this is its curiously alert mentality or intelligence, and its common habit of deliberately pursuing and attacking humans. It is Indo-Malayan and fortunately not generally common.

We found the dealer in a bad state of excitement. He had had a shipment of birds from India and among the cages was a large case of the usual Oriental teakwood with a few holes at the top. It was heavy and he had carried it up to a room where he broke up boxes and cages, intending to knock off the top and carry the "python" it appeared to contain to the downstairs snake cages. As he expected to find a twelve to fifteen footer, stupid on being exposed to the light after its long journey, he anticipated no trouble in two men carrying the beast—one at the head and another at the tail—leaving the box behind to be broken up.

He knocked off part of the cover and at the first glance was surprised to see so much space in the case. He expected to find the highly piled coils of the Indian python. The weight of the case had deceived him as teak is very heavy. Another look told the story. There were many loops of pale olive, no thicker than a man's wrist. As the dealer brandished the hammer in fright, an orange-colored head with glowing eyes rose straight up. He backed for the door and the apparition continued to rise directly upward until the cobra had reared to the level of the man's breast, giving him a fearless preparatory stare. By this time the man had retreated through the door, stepping on the feet of the assistant who had come to help him. They both fell backward against the balustrade in the dark hallway. Just as the dealer closed the door he caught the flash of a second cobra rearing beside the first, the two like great candlesticks. And they stared venomously at him!

I know only too well that curious stare of the king cobra. Its eyes are strangely brilliant—not luminous—but *alert.* The stare is piercing, as if to analyze and anticipate one's moves. The color of the reptile's eyes usually matches the hue of its throat and head which are of ruddy yellow like an orange skin, giving the anterior portion of the snake distinct character in contrast to the pale olive body.

The dealer was terrified that the snakes would escape. There were two windows in the room, but they were safe because the place had been used for transferring large birds and the sashes were covered with fine but strong mesh, cut in panels stapled over the entire casing from top to bottom. The room, however, was about eighteen feet square, and it was filled with trash, broken boxes and their covers, which were piled waist and shoulder high. There were rats in the old building and the floor of the room had not been examined for years, owing to the litter. The dealer feared that rats might have gnawed through the floor to make a meeting place of the room and to enlarge their travelling channels. If so, the cobras could escape into the building. He wrung his hands at the thought of king cobras at liberty in downtown New York and implored me to get busy. I'll confess, that right there I was somewhat apprehensive about going up to that room.

The first thing the dealer did was to take a key from his pocket and unlock the door. Then he backed off while we peeked in. There was nothing in sight. Fortunately, there was some cleared space on our side. The door swung inward and jammed on the floor when half way opened. I momentarily closed it to make more room. There was a stout piece of wooden strip loose on the floor which the head keeper appropriated as a staff. We had the two burlap bags and the stick with the noose.

Next we cautiously peered around, gently shoving a broken box here and there before we saw the first snake. A greenish fold protruded from beneath a case. The cobra was asleep. But I knew what he would do if we touched him: boil out from the shelter and rear in combat attitude, possibly come right at us. However, I figured we could handle him with the two sticks if the second cobra didn't join the party.

"Go around behind me and open the door so we have a getaway; I'm going to stir him up!" I cautioned the head keeper. He quietly moved behind me and grasped the handle. *The door was locked!*

My anger at the cowardly dealer for locking us in was hard to repress. But I had to grind my teeth and knock softly at the door. We didn't dare start any vibration by kicking it. There was no response. It was probable that the man was cowering downstairs.

We were in a fine mess! The door was too stout to be kicked through and the windows were covered with mesh. I told my companion not to hesitate, but swing hard and disable the cobra if he came at us. As there was nothing to do but start I poked the greenish coil.

Instantly there was a hiss like a muffled sneeze, deeper in tone than the characteristic sneezing hiss of the common Indian cobra—and out and up the serpent came, turning to us with his intent stare. His neck slowly expanded into the long narrow hood of his species, showing black and white spots between the scales.

That slow expanding of the hood was a favorable sign. The snake was hesitating between anger and surprise. I knew that here was the critical moment to get him. If the noose didn't work he would get one of us—or there would be a dead cobra.

My assistant slowly waggled his stick as I reached forward and upward with the noose. I saw the cobra's intent eyes give a flicking glance at the noose. There was also a slight movement of his head. But instantly the eyes gathered intensity in their gaze at me. Quickly the thin noose slipped over his head. But still he didn't move. A side swing of the pole tightened the noose and we pulled him down, the constricting cord narrowing his hood about three inches from the head.

The way that long body poured out from under the boxes was terrifying. There were fully twelve feet of him. He furiously chewed the stick, embedding his fangs again and again in it. When my assistant got his stick across the snake's head I grasped the brute by the neck. This is not so dangerous as it sounds if one knows how to do it. The idea was to back him into our bag. Meanwhile he was raising an awful rumpus in the room, throwing his body around and crashing over boxes right and left. I yanked my end toward a corner, the other man pulling the serpent hand over hand to the bag, then starting to shove the tail portion in.

We were successfully backing our first cobra in when we saw the other one. Impressions are sometimes instantaneous. I remember now that the throat markings were different and I realized the two were a pair. She gave us more of a shock than the first, being high on the boxes and rearing fully four feet besides. She looked balefully over the scene like an avenger about to descend.

"Swing for that one!" I shouted, gathering the bag around the first snake. He was helping, if anything, in backing into the bag in his effort to pull his head away. Catching the edge of the bag I waited for him to yank back hard—and when he did I let go. It was a fifty-fifty chance. He might have shot out like a rocket; but he didn't and he was not given an instant's handicap. There is a way of letting go such a bag with one hand and spinning it with the other that instantly seals the serpent inside. I learned this years before and had taught it to all the keepers of the Reptile Department. The trick caught His Majesty by surprise and gave us two or three minutes' leeway before he could push his head past the twists. All this was happening in less time than it takes to tell it.

At this moment there was an awful clatter beside me. It was my assistant trying to hold down the head and neck of the second snake. Now it was my turn to waggle the noose staff and stand ready. The lady pulled loose once and made a magnificent sweep at us, but missed by a couple of feet. We nearly climbed the wall in our scrambling jumps to duck that strike. A cobra doesn't strike like a viper, the latter being so quick there is a mere flash in the action. The king cobra sweeps forward in its strike and by a jump you can evade the movement if it isn't followed.

Now it was the cobra or ourselves and I was prepared to end it with a kill when the head keeper made a swing between a blow and a push and pinned the creature's neck against the top of a tilting case. The case lay fairly firm. I followed this by jamming the noosing staff nearer the head and holding with all my strength as she lashed and whipped her body all around the room.

"I have a good grip—pin the head!" I yelled. My man's stick advanced over the head. All at once we had her, grasped firmly by the neck like the first. Here was victory! By using his knee to lever the stick in down pressure, he pinioned her with one hand and grasped her with the other.

With my assistant now holding the snake's neck in a two-fisted grip and half squatting on the reptiles' anterior quarter, I tied the first bag. During the action with the lady cobra it had been rising and pitching from side to side like a drunken thing. We backed number two into a bag, which was a lively but not difficult act as there was nothing else to bother us. The next thing for us to do was to get the heaviest piece of wood in the room and batter down that infernal door. Here was a chance to vent our feelings. The racket we made in the job was satisfying to both of us. One panel was split in several places. A moment later we should have had splinters flying into the hall when the door opened and the owner peeked in. One look at his face was enough to still the thoughts of the verbal abuse which was ready on my lips. The dealer, who was an oldish man, was as pale as clay, perspiring and shaking. He gasped for a statement of results and I told him we had both cobras.

I have never seen a man recover his poise so quickly. He was keen for a dicker. Within five minutes he was rubbing his hands and telling us what a fine pair of cobras we had. The head keeper gave me a slow wink. We were also recovering our own poise and breath. King cobras were sold for about a hundred dollars apiece in those days before the war, a price that meant a good profit for the dealer. Such a price may seem ridiculous for a creature of the kind, but the truth of the matter was that daring native snake-catchers would occasionally trap or snare king cobras, bring them into the Chinese animal dealers' shops in Singapore and receive their price. Then the buyer, having a tremendous respect for the specimen, would get rid of it as quickly as he could. Such creatures were shipped along with other animals and there was an extremely small market for them. I had for some time been objecting to this indiscriminate shipping of deadly snakes and insisting that they should be transported only under the most responsible care. There was too much danger of their boxes being broken during careless handling or accident.

But to return to the action: "I'll give you a hundred dollars for the *two* snakes," I told the dealer.

He wouldn't listen to such a price, but was crafty enough to quote slightly lower than the average. I turned to the head keeper:

"Take them both upstairs and turn them loose where we found them."

That was enough. It closed the dicker. It was our revenge for the locked door.

There was some humor in the situation, but the really funny thing happened as we stopped for lunch. There was a restaurant on Park Row famous for its corned beef and much frequented by newspaper men along toward pay day when pocket money was getting short. We decided this place would be a good lunching spot where we could deposit our case while we ate. It wasn't far to lug the fibre receptacle in that direction and we shoved it under the table between us when we started the meal.

I had just sat down when someone slapped me on the back. It proved to be a veteran reporter of *The Times* staff whom I had always liked. Having an intense dislike for snakes he had in the past scolded me occasionally for leaving my satchel of lecture specimens in various parts of the editorial rooms when I went out on assignments. I now told him about our lively experience with the cobras and he was keenly interested, even breathing hard at some of the details.

"Those devils must be attracting a lot of interest at the Park!" he exclaimed.

"Not yet," was my answer. "I thought you understood. The thing happened only this morning. It's a long run uptown and we were hungry so we've just stopped in here on the way home. The cobras are right here with us! You've been kicking the satchel they're in for the past ten minutes!"

According to normal popular description, the fellow's knife and fork should have fallen with a clatter. But he only quietly laid his fork across an unfinished piece of pie—and walked out! He had a corking story in *The Times* the next morning and said nothing but complimentary things about both of us.

On another occasion I had gone to bring in two monster pythons—which, by the way, are still living. Each was in a teakwood case about four feet square. Such cases have rows of air-holes and a hinged top. You raise the lid and there is the big snake. There is no mesh covering.

The snakes had arrived from an Indian port and there was a custom examination. I told the officer what I had, but he was a bit grouchy. I don't know what he expected to see, but when he was greeted with the spectacle of two bodies as big around as furnace pipe, coiled in mounds, he nearly keeled over.

"Shut 'em down!" he yelled.

There is little danger of a python trying to escape when a case is first opened because the serpent is for the moment blinded and sleepy from its long fast and confinement. It may raise a head and look around, but that is all unless the case is left open ten minutes or more. Then it may decide to prowl. If so it would take a dozen men to put such a monster back again!

My two charges were soon on a fast train, carried as excess baggage as has been my custom whenever possible on such trips. As they required no further attention and were properly stowed, with locks securely snapped over the hasps, I was about to make my way back to the Pullman when the two conductors appeared, both train and Pullman conductors. They had heard about the big serpents and wanted to see them. As theirs was an entirely courteous request, I had no objection to throwing back the tops for a couple of minutes. The men drew in behind me. The locks were unsnapped and I simultaneously threw back both lids. A head six inches long rose inquiringly and a blue-black tongue as long as one's finger described an up-and-down arc, as forked tongues do when the owner is curious.

I told the conductors about the length of the respective serpents and gave them a few other points, but my audience remained silent. I turned around to tell them there was no danger. There was nobody there!

Locking the cases I went through the train and finally found the conductors. "Where did you fellows go?"

"You mean, *when* did we go," snapped the train conductor. "We thought those things were behind bars and got out as fast as we could on our toes, but the baggage-man jumped through the side door!"

Hoofed animals require more thought in shipment than the big snakes or carnivores. They are not so secure on their feet as the shorter-legged, soft-footed kinds of animals, and they spend the greater part of the time standing while in their travelling quarters.

This means that their crates must be carefully built in order to approximately "fit" them, or at least to fit their temperaments. In buying animals and selling duplicates I have crated and shipped large numbers of hoofed species all over the states and a number to foreign ports. But I never built a crate without first measuring the animal. This is easily done, no matter how wild the creature may be. I note some patch of ground on which it stands, observing a pebble in front of it or some other mark, and then something similar behind it. I then measure the spot. Sometimes I watch the animal as it stands near a fence and count the number of mesh panels or bars along its length. Its width of horns or breadth of shoulders, as well as its height, may thus be determined.

Crates may be divided into two classes: one is narrow so the animal cannot turn, yet is wide enough to enable it to lie down; the other is wide enough to enable the inmate to turn readily. It is highly important to keep away from anything between these extremes because an animal may struggle to turn and become jammed in a crate. No-turn crates are, of course, cheaper to ship and are really the best for nervous animals. They are also used, almost without exception, for extremely large specimens. Crates have a vertically sliding door at the rear for entrance of an animal and this is slightly raised for cleaning. There is also a vertically movable panel near the floor on the front for temporary insertion of the water pan and for serving of hay, or, in occasional instances, some grain. But grain is risky to use during shipment unless an expert animal man actually measures out each feeding and notes results, or the trip is to be an extremely long one. There is always the danger of overfeeding—and colic.

The biggest crate I ever handled came into New York on a ship from Africa and contained a practically adult giraffe. The vessel sent in a wireless when she was close to port announcing that the animal was aboard. We immediately queried the height of the crate. The answer indicated that the crate altitude added to the height of the lowest-slung truck obtainable produced a measurement that would never go through the vehicle runway of a ferry-boat—and the vessel was to dock at Staten Island!

When she arrived the profile of the crate looked like the side of a barn. I promptly ordered my truck to lie to in the city and await telephone advice. A power lighter was engaged and the captain said he knew a dock north of the Brooklyn Bridge where we could land the crate and the truck could continue up the easterly side of the city without coming in contact with the elevated except at Thirty-fourth Street, where it was high. Thus there would not be any trouble until we struck the overhead trolley wires of the Bronx, where we would have to look out.

All went well. The truck met me, the crate was transferred and we proceeded towards the distant Bronx, with me trailing the towering load in a Ford. When a repair shop came into view I gave the truck our prearranged signal to stop—three squawks on the horn. It was getting on toward dusk and there wasn't time for detailed explanation. I was afraid of the trolley wires and wanted to see what was going to happen if we didn't make the Park before dark.

An efficient looking mechanic, saturated in grease to the roots of his hair, crawled from beneath a dissected car where he had been swearing and doing something in the illumination of a greasy drop-lamp. I told him to bring his largest wrench and come out on the street. He appeared with a monkey wrench of proportions capable of taking a locomotive apart. I pointed to the truck and to my car, spoke about trolley wires and explained that we wanted light directed upward, to see if we had enough headroom. He was a man of few words but keen perception.

"I get'cha," he said, and opening the jaws of the wrench just wide enough to grasp the underpart of each searchlight bracket, put a large foot on the front axle of my Ford to prevent the car being lifted bodily. He bent one and then the other light upward at the precise angle to give the car the appearance of having severely bumped a preceding vehicle.

This was exactly what I wanted. It gave me a satisfactory analysis of our situation and the animal was delivered, after due caution but without trouble, that same night. And while the giraffe had been in its crate for weeks, without turning, it proved to be in the pink of condition. By morning it was airily swinging about its big corral as if it had been there for years!

There were so many experiences in chaperoning animals that I began to feel pretty well seasoned in this game. I was learning a great deal about animal psychology in skipping my experiences through buffaloes, giraffes, giant pythons and the like.

Once I was the escort from a big preserve in the Berkshires of "Apache," one of the finest bison ever to be exhibited and a flock of elk accompanying him. Apache was the type of buffalo that has made the American nickel look like real money. The only trouble with him was that he required a crate so big we could not get it through the ordinary freight car door. The elk, already stowed, moved off in a line of cars which were to be shunted and reassembled farther down the line.

I sent Keeper Gleason ahead with the elk. He had accompanied me to do the cleaning. It was up to me to stay with Apache—on a bleak and windy platform, waiting for a car with a higher door.

It wasn't long before a car rolled up, pushed by a switch engine. The freightmaster had no help. Apache's crate empty would have weighed close to four hundred pounds; this in turn was held down by the four-legged giant's two thousand pounds of beef and bone. As a result everybody in sight, including engineer and fireman of the switch engine, was called to give us a hand to start it moving. We levered it up with crowbars, got some pieces of pipe under it, rolled it into the car and threw in a couple of bales of hay.

I gave the big fellow some water while near a hydrant. Although his eyes showed a lot of the white edge and he snorted in a way to make the uninitiated jump, he drank more that half of the sixteen-quart pail and began to eat some hay which I had shaken in to him.

By this time I had become acquainted with the engineer, a kindly soul, whose name was Bill. Possibly he was a bit solicitous about me because he knew what I had in store—and I didn't. Bill had a moustache like a walrus and continually smoked a short pipe which sizzled like a leaky steam joint. He wore a peaked and thin cloth cap which at one time had been broadly stamped around its edge with some brand of goods or food, now but faintly suggested through its veneer of coal dust.

Bill asked me if I had eaten my supper. I told him there hadn't been a chance to get any, owing to the mix-up with the bull's crate. I asked him if there was time to run out to a coffee wagon at the edge of the yards, to get a bite and buy some pipe tobacco as I had run out of the latter.

He looked disturbed and sorry and said there wasn't time because he had orders to get my car out of the way. He had to take it out to a siding and leave it there for a string coming through which would pick me up and put me in contact with the cars which had gone out ahead. So that was that and Bill started for his engine.

Evidently deciding that I didn't look like a knockabout railroader and was peaked with the cold, he hesitated, then he invited me to ride in the engine. Its hissing, heat-radiating bulk looked so tremendously inviting that I climbed aboard. I still had visions that the car would be dropped not too far from a coffee wagon. But Bill completely shattered this illusion. He opened the throttle of his dumpy four-wheeler until I was soon dancing and jumping around the steel floor of the cab.

Presently Bill raised the hinged lid of his seat and drew forth a much rumpled paper grocery bag. He next rummaged around, found a newspaper and tore off a page. "I had a sandwich left from m'lunch," he said. "And y'might as well have it for supper. Here's some terbaccer, too," he added. He yanked a huge tinfoil package from his hip pocket, pouring a mixture as black as tea leaves into the newspage. "They'll pick y'up in a while," said Bill when I left him. "We gotta hop."

We shook hands when we parted. It was a kindly touch and I appreciated it. The engine pulled away. A lone switchman appeared from somewhere, threw over the ground-lock and climbed aboard. Then Bill streaked along the straightaway, his trail of smoke hinting at activities of his spidery fireman. Such are the chance acquaintances of an animal chaperone.

After some acrobatic manoeuvres I gained the floor of

the car and rejoined Apache. Once inside, I rolled the sliding doors shut against a bitter wind. There was still enough light to investigate the sandwich Bill had given me. It was of homemade bread with a fried egg and nothing from the hands of a professional chef ever tasted better.

The appreciation of Bill's tobacco was a different story. Three or four minutes' tussle with it in a pipe I had enjoyed for months convinced me that here was a brand few mortal men were strong enough to endure. Its effect on my tongue was similar to tabasco sauce.

The warming I had got from Bill's engine soon wore away. Apache's car was ghastly cold. I stamped and walked around and waited. Then I got out and ran up and down the track beside the solitary car—and finally climbed back into it. It was now pitch dark. Not knowing what on earth to do I listened to hear where Apache's breath was coming from. I was curious to see whether his head was high or low, and whether he was still standing or lying down. Right there I made a tremendously important discovery. He was lying down and radiating *heat!*

I felt like cheering. I rushed for the hay and shook one bale layer after another loose until it formed a high pile beside the crate. Then I burrowed right into that mound and within five minutes was comfortable and after a minute or so more was fast asleep.

I was awakened by the slam of a bumper and the car jumped, but this didn't bother me any as I had probably been sleeping for several hours. It was merely an incident of the night. Before I dropped off to sleep again there was the snorting of an engine somewhere ahead or behind. My only reaction was a very brief decision that the motion of a freight car was curiously different from that of a Pullman. I met the other animals the next morning and Gleason swung the batch into New York.

Today, whenever I look at a buffalo, I have a feeling of affection for it; and on seeing a switch engine I often think of homemade bread.

*Cap Ricardo Speaks**

by Courtney Ryley Cooper

❧❧❧❧

Maybe the heyday of the sawdust ring has passed now that the zoos are full of wild animals and motion pictures bring entertainment to every village. Still, it's a rare person even now who can resist the sights, sounds, and smells of a circus. Courtney Ryley Cooper *was a circus enthusiast from boyhood; as a man he spent much of his spare time chatting with circus folk and watching them practice. His* Lions 'N' Tigers 'N' Everything *is full of behind-the-scenes stories. One of the tense moments in any performance was the animal act with a cool trainer putting savage-looking lions, tigers and leopards through their paces. Here is Cooper's report of one old-timer's methods of animal training and some of his most exciting experiences.*

* "Cap Ricardo Speaks" from *Lions 'N' Tigers 'N' Everything* by Courtney Ryley Cooper, reprinted by permission of Little, Brown & Company.

PERHAPS the best way to realize how great a change has come about in animal training within the last few decades is to hear the story of a man who trained animals fifty years ago, and who continued to train them throughout half a century.

His name is Captain Richard (Dutch) Ricardo, a stocky man of iron-gray hair, deep-set eyes, and tight-lipped mouth, straight-lined beneath a closely cut mustache. I knew him twenty years—we were on the same show together and I already have mentioned him a number of times in this book.

Cap Ricardo—a captaincy among animal trainers is as necessary as a colonelcy to a Kentuckian—began as a runaway boy. But Cap's adventures shall not be told in the third person. True, I have set them down from notes. But I have striven faithfully to act merely as a reporter. And so, Ladies-s-s-s and Gentle—men, I take great pleasuah, in introducing to you, Captain Dutch Ricardo, animal trainer extraordinary, and his reminiscences of fifty years in the lion's den. For the rest of this chapter, Captain Dutch Ricardo will speak for himself.

I went into the arena as an animal trainer when I was a runaway boy, fifteen years old. The act consisted of five lions, three bears, two great Dane dogs and two bears, a "mixed group," as it is known. Albert Stadler, their regular trainer, had become ill. I was his helper, cage-cleaner and general assistant; I fell heir to the act. The danger of death for an inexperienced boy caused little concern either for the show or the audience. There was nothing extraordinary about my first performance. I wasn't frightened, and the audience's interest lay chiefly in the hope that I would be killed. But I wasn't and after that I substituted often. Also I continued to disappoint the audience. The greatest change of the last fifty years has been in the bloodthirsty attitude of the average human being.

Likewise the viewpoint toward animals has changed. Investigations have gone a long way toward proving that there isn't so much difference between the human being and the beast after all—that animals do think, and do reason, and do have the same primary emotions as the human. I'll give you an example of an animal's reasoning power:

A good many years ago in Baltimore, Md., I was working as a trainer at Bostock's Menagerie. There was one lion in the outfit, Spitfire, a female, who, as far as I was concerned, lived up to her name. She growled and hissed if I even came near the cage.

I didn't care about that. I wasn't her trainer. She belonged to an act trained by Madame Pianca, and with her she was a tractable beast, until she became the mother of several cubs and then, like any lioness with young, was hard to handle. One evening just as I was going to dinner Madame Pianca asked me to get the cubs out of Spitfire's cage for the night.

"You can do it better yourself," I said. "You know how she hates me."

However, the Madame persisted and I went to Spitfire's cage. As soon as I sighted the lioness, I noticed that she was extremely nervous, pacing her den with quick steps, or edging hastily along the bars as though in a fever of excitement. I spoke to her from a distance and she responded immediately—she seemed glad to see me. I purred to her and she answered. Then, with a bound, she hurried to an opposite side of the cage, caught a cub by the scruff of the neck, brought it to the bars and tried to push it through to me!

I saw now that there was no danger from the mother and went into the den. Spitfire continued to purr, and brought me her other cubs. Then, still surprised, I carried them away and went to my dinner. I had hardly seated myself in a restaurant across the street when a white faced cage-boy ran in with the reason for Spitfire's action. The menagerie was afire!

Spitfire's scent was naturally keener than that of a human. She had caught the smell of smoke and knew its threat of danger. Personal animosity had faded in the greater emotion of striving to save her young.

Fifty years ago, an occurrence like that would have been dismissed as a mere coincidence. Besides, the public didn't care. It wanted gore and thrills without much concern over how they were provided. A contest to the death between two animals to-day would result in wholesale arrests. Forty or fifty years ago they were commonplace affairs. I remember one that was held as late as thirty-five years ago, without more than local publicity attending it.

I was working then for a Colonel Boone in San Francisco. He had a menagerie in which were quartered a lion and a grizzly bear. Some gamblers stopped in front of the two cages one night and began an argument, as to whether the lion could whip the grizzly. Finally they asked me for an opinion. I said I thought the grizzly would win. Colonel Boone felt the same way, as did one or two of the gamblers. The others believed in the lion.

"Difference of opinion is what makes a hoss race," said one of the gamblers. "Let's try it out and see."

The lion was a bad one; it had torn up every trainer who had tried to work it and had a death record of two men. The grizzly had a mean temper also; soon the whole sporting element of San Francisco was betting on the result. The fight was to be held in San Francisco Bay, on a barge for which we offered $500 rental. When the owner discovered what was about to happen, he immediately canceled the contract, but not for humane reasons. He had a better idea; he'd let us have the barge free for the fight, with a $1,000 bonus if we'd give him the saloon and gambling privileges. Then other barges were hired, to group about the first one, and to take care of the spectators. As far as the battle was concerned, it was not even a contest. The lion swung into its usual three-foot fighting pose, lunging terrific blows with the fourth, which were disregarded by the grizzly, which closed in, caught the lion to him, and crushed the life out of him. This was in a time when humane societies already had done much work and children were being taught in the schools to pay their dues and wear a celluloid button proclaiming that they would work for kindness to dumb animals. One can judge from this what conditions must have been when I first went into the steel arena.

In those times, the average crowd attended a wild animal show to see fierce beasts attempt to kill a trainer, and the oftener the performance ended with the trainer carried away upon a stretcher, the better the crowd liked it.

The result was a brutal affair. Everything about an animal exhibition was brutal, in fact. Animals were cheap and trainers cheaper, cage conditions were bad for the beasts, there was practically no care for their infirmities and little thought given to anything save their ability to be fierce and intractable in the training den. Red fire was used at the finish of the act, filling the arena and the house with smoke and creating an atmosphere of excitement. Guns were fired incessantly, attendants beat upon Chinese gongs, presumably to excite the beasts, and a smoking brazier with its container of red-hot irons was a fixture beside the arena. However, these irons were not used, as the audience thought, to fend off murderous animals, but to force them from their pedestals and to their work! Trainers in those days did not know how to feed animals to give them the proper energy and ambition; besides, there was no incentive for a beast to work. All they got for their efforts were incessant cuttings from long bull and lunge whips, or blows from the lead-loaded butt ends. Every member of an animal act was bleeding when it came out of the arena.

Conditions were little better for the trainers. The red fire, the use of gongs and noisemakers, of hot irons and incessant firing from pistols, the fear that was in every animal's heart, made them undependable, treacherous, and often unmanageable. The audience wanted to see the trainer clawed up. Often it got what it desired. When it didn't, the management faked an injury. With the arena clouded by red fire smoke, the trainer would shout he had been hurt. Attendants would rush to the bars with hot irons to force the animals to the chutes. Then the trainer would reel from the arena, to be met at the door by an attendant who held either a cup of beef blood which he splattered over the animal man, or a beef liver which he slapped quickly across the trainer's face. After that, the "injured" and gory lion tamer would stagger forth to where the audience could get a good look at him, bow tragically—and collapse. Men would run forward with a piece of canvas, load him into it and carry him away, presumably to the hospital, while the press agent made the rounds of the papers with the announcement that at the next performance a new and more daring trainer would take his place. I have read my own obituary many times.

I didn't like this sort of thing. It all seemed so useless to me, especially when I could make friends with animals so easily. But I was surrounded by tutors who professed to know their business. They in turn had been taught by ignorant men, held to lines of cruelty by equally ignorant audiences. Naturally I followed my teachers.

Finally I broke an act or two of my own according to the rules then in use, and, by the time I was twenty I had taken my exhibition name of "Captain" Dutch Ricardo. Now and then I would find an animal that was unbroken and consequently amenable to kindness; I couldn't help a natural feeling of friendship for the beast. Finally I taught a lion to walk a "tightrope"—a board about six inches wide—by persuasion instead of by force. But he didn't walk fast enough to suit the owner of the show. He said he'd show me how it should be done.

Naturally, the lion did not understand. Instead of "forcing" he merely cowered, hissing and growling. The owner got a broomstick to which he attached an electric wire. He turned on the current and began to prod the beast with this. It failed to move the lion. Finally, as the beast opened its mouth to roar at its tormentor, the owner jammed the broomstick with its sizzling electric wire down the animal's throat. Not much chance for kindness in surroundings like that!

Fierceness was forced on animals, even when those beasts tried to be tame and tractable. I was working once with a fair in Toronto, Canada, at which was a Frenchman with a big Russian bear. The Frenchman was half-drunk, sitting in a chair near his bear and reading a newspaper. A newspaperman came along and asked the age of the animal.

"None of your business!" said the trainer.

The reporter laughed, and walking over to the bear, which was muzzled, began to pet him. The Frenchman jumped to his feet.

"Don't you know that's a dangerous bear?" he asked—his act thrived on its fierceness. The newspaperman continued his petting.

"Seems tame enough to me," he said.

The Frenchman became furious. He threw away his newspaper, and jerking the muzzle from the bear's head, tried to force the animal to attack the newspaperman. The bear refused. The trainer became more angry. He began to kick and beat the beast in an attempt to drive him on, and the bear obeyed. But he bit the man he really hated, the trainer, knocking him down and nearly cutting off one of his legs. Then as he broke to run, I caught the animal, jamming his head between the spokes of a wagon until I could restore his muzzle. The Frenchman was taken to a hospital where his leg was amputated and where he remained some months, while I included the bear as a part of my act and found him gentle, obedient and friendly. One day the Frenchman came back and wanted his bear.

"Why should you take him?" I said. "You don't know how to treat an animal." Then I offered him $150 for the beast. He wanted $500. I countered with a bill of $565 for taking care of the bear, and threatened to sue him for it. That was the end—the bear stayed with me until his death and never showed any more signs of viciousness.

That, of course, happened in later years, during the long weeding-out process and the struggle between old and new ideas. In the meantime, the audiences continued to call for fierceness. When the ordinary act wasn't strong enough, we tried the experiment of introducing fake victims into the lion's den. It was a great success. I forget how many times I have been married in the lion's den, with the supposed trainer on the outside, with the bride apparently scared to death—she could handle lions just as well as I could and had been my wife for years—and with the preacher reading the service between the bars. The first time I ever did it was at an outdoor carnival. The crowd was so great that spectators even climbed distant trees to see over the heads of the throngs in front of them. For several years it was the greatest kind of a drawing card, and the remarks of the audience regarding the status of the bride and groom—lewd jokes which would result in arrest in this supposedly loose age—were as big a part of the show as the marriage itself. Gradually, however, spectators who had watched one marriage after another in various parts of the country discovered a surprising lack of fatalities, and the thrill died out.

Then a greater one was introduced, that of a barber shaving a man in a den of lions or tigers. That went fine for a while too. But the barber was never killed and the barbee never got his throat cut, so this novelty went the way of the connubial one. It was about this time that I found a new thrill for the audience and at the same time played my part in the newer standard of living as experienced by the captured animal. I found out how to train animals without an atom of cruelty and at the same time give the audience the thrill it wanted—and still wants, if the truth be known.

I do not say that I was the first person in the world to train wild animals with nothing but a kitchen chair and a buggy whip. I believe that I was; I have been told that the method was used about the same time in Germany. But I do know that I discovered the system as far as I was concerned, and that for years I was the only person using it in America. An ordinary kitchen chair in one hand and an equally ordinary buggy whip in the other seem frail weapons with which to enter a den of lions, or tigers, or a mixed group. Confidentially, however, there is no greater training aid than that kitchen chair. The buggy whip is merely used to touch the animal, as it once touched the family horse, a guidance to his actions. As to my discovery—

About a quarter of a century ago I sat in a training den on the old Bostock Trained Wild Animal Show studying a bunch of lions. As I have said before, I had always been more or less rebellious against the straight ideas of cruelties and beatings. Now and then I had found animals tractable from the start; others, I had learned, could be more easily trained to tricks if I found out their natural talents. This I was doing on the discovery day—merely sitting in the arena with some six or eight lions, while they strolled about, or played, or quarreled among themselves. By this means, I could learn which ones were agile, which were evil-tempered, which were possessed of humor; recess time in a training den is the same as recess time in a kindergarten. One has an opportunity to learn individualities. There was one I had not counted on.

Years of old-time methods had made this particular lion crafty and hateful. After bullying the other animals, he climbed up on the arena and would not get down. I cracked my whip at him, intending to follow this with a fusillade of blank revolver shots, but I had no chance. The lion leaped; instinctively I whirled and grasped the heavy kitchen chair, pushing it in front of me for protection. The lion's jaws were open; one leg struck him on the roof of the mouth. Instantly he recoiled, only to leap again. This time I let him have the chair, breaking his charge with it and at the same time leaping to the other end of the arena. The lion tore into that chair with the same joy that he would have torn into me—but it didn't hurt the chair. After a time, apparently surprised at his inability to kill the thing or hurt it, he stopped his attack and went to his pedestal. I knew then that I had a new system of training.

The next day I tried it with a fresh group of lions. Other charges were made—the same thing happened as on the day before. If the attack was vicious, I poked that leg straight at the roof of the mouth, causing no injury but giving the same pain that one receives through a blow on the lips. But that pain meant kindness instead of the old cruelty. To explain:

If you should attempt to harm a policeman and he should hit you with his club in self-protection, you would have no recourse in law. The policeman was not harming you. He didn't force you to hit him, and you got what you deserved when he used his billy. The same thing applied to my animals. I treated them with the utmost kindness. I talked baby talk to them, and, laugh if you care to, the use of baby talk is a great factor in animal training. Try it yourself with a dog sometime; see which gets the greatest response, a harsh command or one given in a soothing voice, constantly complimentary.

Therefore, if during this coaxing process an animal did attempt fierceness, and received pain instead of giving it, he looked on it as his own fault. Do I make myself clear? By this system the animal learns that as long as he lets the trainer alone, the trainer will let him alone. But when he encroaches he learns that the trainer can protect himself and issue punishment at the same time—by making the animal hurt himself. Therefore he avoids doing the same thing again. It is the old story of the child and the hot stove: he doesn't touch it twice.

Now, countering this, is the incessant stream of coaxing talk, the pleading, "Come on, Old Fellow, be a good boy now! That's it, be a good boy, nice old fellow, good old King, good boy, just a little farther—just a little farther, King, old partner!" Is it plain now?

I hope that it really was my discovery. At any rate, it is the system in use by practically every trainer to-day. The old days are gone. New ones of kindness and understanding have come even for the most treacherous of all animals, the leopard. One of these animals, in particular, gave me the worst half-hour of my life.

I was on the old Gaskell and Mundy Shows and a new leopard had been received that morning. No one knew much about him. We did not know whether he was straight from the jungle or whether he had been worked before. I was doubly careful when I went into his cage, talking gently and purring. The leopard received me cordially.

At least he showed no signs of fight, and I put down the kitchen chair which I had poked ahead of me into the cage. Then I sat down and for a time merely talked to the beast. I purred to him and he purred in answer—he certainly acted like a friendly fellow. However, knowing leopard nature, I was still cautious. Finally, after a half-hour, I called for the hook-seats, and fastened them to the side of the cage. Then I touched the animal with my buggy whip and gave him the command of "seats." He obeyed, and I turned to the watchers outside.

"This cat's been worked before," I said.

I let him stay on that seat for a few minutes, sitting down myself and talking to him. I then sent him to the second seat and he obeyed readily. Again I seated myself to wait. But I was up again in an instant. The leopard had leaped!

He had me by the face and chest and torso and throat all in an instant, his teeth tearing into my cheeks, dangerously close to my eyes, his claws ripping my chest. I had dropped my whip now; it was a battle of muscle and of a fight to keep consciousness until I could fend the beast from me. My hands had become slippery with blood; my arms had been almost stripped of flesh, even the tendons being laid bare in places. We wrestled silently, fiercely, save for the noise of tearing flesh and the occasional snarl of the beast as I temporarily broke his hold and forced him for an instant from me.

Outside the cage, however, there was the shouting of men and the screams of women as a crowd gathered, show attendants striving vainly to hold back the throng. A policeman forced his way through the crowd, drawing his revolver.

"Turn this way!" he shouted. "I'll shoot him!"

"Put down that gun!" I answered. "You can't hit him without hitting me!"

Then I deliberately turned my back on him. A woman trainer had seized a broomstick and was poking it through the bars at the leopard. I edged toward her.

I was about done for. My face, neck and chest were badly cut. My body and stomach were slashed in a hundred places. My legs were deeply scored, even to my knees. I was losing a great amount of blood. I struggled closer to the bars; then as the woman struck again at the leopard with the broomstick, he turned slightly to roar a challenge at her. This was my chance. As he turned his head back to me, jaws widespread, I doubled my left arm, and with all my strength jammed my elbow down his throat, gagging him.

Hastily I backed to the door of the cage and opened it with my free hand. Then swiftly I edged through, holding the steel door tight against my body and literally scraping the leopard off as I did so. Volunteers leaped to catch me and to bolt the door again. Then I staggered away for a doctor, while the dancing girls on the ballyhoo platforms fainted, one after another, at the sight of me, strangely like tenpins in a bowling alley.

The claw and tooth marks ran into the hundreds; I don't know how many. It was as though I had been run through a chopping machine; muscles were stripped in places, the lower lid was torn from one eye, my scalp had been loosened, the backs of my hands laid as clean of flesh as though flesh never had existed there. But I did not lose consciousness, either while the doctor worked hour upon hour at stitching and bandaging, nor afterwards. I was the trainer of a new group of lions, and it is one of the rules of performing an animal act that there must be an unbroken continuity of performance. I had to work my act that night.

What the lions would do when they saw me, I could not guess. I only knew I had to work that act. I had found that I could move my right hand slightly. That would be enough, I felt, to hold my buggy whip and give the cues by which the beasts were sent to and from their pedestals.

I was bandaged from my knees to the top of my head.

My face was entirely covered except for two tiny eye-holes; my head was encased in a full cap-bandage, about which I wrapped a colored handkerchief, Spanish style, to conceal my injuries from the audience. There was little sense in that; my shirt could not close at the neck, and the sleeves had been cut from it, owing to the thickness of the arm bandages. As for my arms themselves, they were strapped to my sides; one hand completely useless, the other movable only from the wrist. I went into the arena.

For an instant the lions milled excitedly, and I waited at the arena entrance, hesitant about approach. They roared and bounded from their pedestals to the ground and back again; if lions believe in ghosts, I was mistaken for one, for a moment at least. Then, above the smell of medication, one of the older cats caught my scent and answered my purring, muffled from behind the bandages. Slowly, one after another, they went to their pedestals and awaited my commands. At last they swung into their routine as though there was nothing wrong with their master. After years, it seemed, the act was over, and I staggered out of the arena to take my bow. Is it any wonder I detest leopards?

Otherwise, however, animals come to depend upon their trainers to a large extent, in the same way that a clerk depends upon his boss. If the head of an office is upset, the whole organization soon becomes the same way. But while an office force may take it out in talk and mistakes, the result with animals is different. Teeth and claws are their only mode of expression. It is up to the trainer to keep them steady, no matter what the cause may be. I have held my animals calm in many a storm, with the canvas lashing overhead and the quarterpoles dancing so madly that the audience itself was on the verge of panic. But the animals held steady simply because I held steady; if I could keep my head, they could too.

Human beings often commit murder without a real desire to kill. The good trainer knows that the same rule applies to animals; no matter how well trained and friendly his beasts may be, an unusual incident may throw them off balance. Unless their boss's brain is agile enough to combat that incident, they may kill him.

With Colonel Boone's show, many years ago in San Francisco, was a trainer named Fritz Greenburg, who in addition to working an act consisting of seven lions and two great Dane dogs, possessed two other lions which he drove about the arena, hitched to a chariot. One of them, named Parnell, was inclined to fight at night, with the result that Greenburg put a collar and chain on him after each performance.

One night we all started to dinner, and Fritz said that he would join us in a few minutes, that he was going to put on Parnell's collar. He went on to his work and we went to dinner. Just as we sat down, the electric lights—they had a habit of winking in those days—went out for about five minutes. When they came on again and the restaurant resumed the serving of food, we ate without much thought of Fritz. He had not appeared, but that was nothing unusual. There might have been work to do around the menagerie, or he might have decided to go somewhere else for his meal. An hour or so passed, and we returned to the show. Fritz was not there. After a half-hour more in which he did not appear, we began to look for him. There was no evidence of disturbance in the cage; certainly he was not there. But at last we decided to make a closer investigation.

The lions were roaming their den as usual; only a slight flutter of something in a far corner attracted our attention as one of the great cats passed over it, rumpling it with his heavy foot. It was a piece of cloth; we hurried closer. Then something round seemed to evolve from the shadows—with black, staring eyes. It was a human skull.

We found the other bones, scattered and broken. Fritz had not kept his head when those lights went out. Evidently he had become panicky, and the animals had done likewise. They had attacked the strange thing which had bumped against them in the dark. The attack had continued until death, and with the salt taste of human blood they had reverted to primary instincts. The bones were licked clean when we found them.

Against this was an experience of my own some years later. I had evolved an act in which I sat at a table, the open drawer of which was toward me and filled with strips of beef. About me, upon their pedestals, were grouped five lions, three males and two females. I called the act "The Feast of Kings."

The performance was one of animal control. Starting at the right, I would feed the two lions strips of meat from my hand, making each wait until his turn came. Then I would switch to the left and feed the two beasts there. After I had done this, I would take a long strip of meat and place one end of it in the mouth of the lioness which faced me, taking the other end between my own teeth. Then, with only a few inches between us, the lioness and I would have a tug of war for possession of the food; first she would pull me half over the table, then I would retaliate by stretching her a foot or so in my direction. One night, I had fed the four other lions. I had placed the strip of meat between the teeth of the lioness and taken the other end in my own mouth. She was just pulling me across the table; the audience was applauding. Then the lights went out!

Immediately the audience began to fret; I could hear seats rattling as various groups rose; herd instinct applies both to humans and animals. I could hear ushers calling for order, and nearer, the anxious call of assistants:

"Cap! Cap! Are you all right?"

"Shut up!" I commanded between closed teeth. I had not released that strip of meat. Then I continued talking, as I had done every instant since those lights flickered out: "Major! Duke! Prince! Easy boys—e-a-s-y now! Hold it, boys! Hold it! Queen! Betsy! H-o-l-d it!" And at the same time, I continued to sway and pull on that strip of meat, the lioness opposite me doing the same. Only one move out of the ordinary did I make, and of that the lions knew nothing. Carefully—so carefully that I did not even display the motion to the lioness with whom I was playing a pitch-black tug of war—I had reached into my boot-top for my blank-cartridged revolver, carried there for emergency. I knew the position of the arena door; in the same tone that I was using to the lions, I called to an assistant to unstrap it and have it ready for quick opening.

"I've got her unstrapped!" the excited voice answered. "Want to make the run now? Don't know when the lights are coming on—they've sent for lanterns."

"Shut up! Stay by that door! Easy Prince! Duke, hold that seat—hold it Duke—!"

Then the lights came on again. An audience, scattered from the topmost row of seats down to the hippodrome track, turned and, still obeying the herd instinct, returned to its former position. And I, in the arena, finishing my tug of war with that strip of meat.

Flightiness in the training den is, in fact, a cardinal sin. On a show where I worked recently, I watched with a great deal of interest the vain attempts of a man to train a certain lion. The man was nervous, the lion was the same. They had constant brushes. One day the lion ran the trainer out of the arena. The man went to the manager.

"I can't go on!" he said. "That lion's bad. He'll get me if I try to do anything more with him."

"G'wan," I said, "that lion's not bad."

The manager laughed.

"I guess you think you could handle him?"

"I'll bet you a new suit of clothes that I can put him through the whole routine, and even put my head inside of his mouth in twenty-four hours and never get a scratch!"

The manager walked away, jeering over his shoulder: "I always thought you were crazy; now I know it."

"Is it a bet?" I asked.

"Sure it's a bet."

The next day I got my new suit of clothes and the manager threw a new hat into the bargain. I had sent that lion through his entire routine, not once but several times, and I had put my head in his mouth until both he and I were tired of the stunt. There wasn't any miracle about it. The trainer's nervousness had increased that of the lion until both were at fighting edge. I simply took things easy with the brute, coaxing him and petting him; baby talk with that lion did what forcing and rough commands could never accomplish. The lion was a sensitive beast, that was all.

The caged animal really wants to do his part, if you'll only give him a chance. I remember a lion named Julius which had experienced about everything in the world that could make a beast bad. After having been handled by inexperienced persons with a picture company, he was purchased by an equally inexperienced showman who believed that a lion act would take well in Old Mexico. He took the lion there and turned him over to a Mexican trainer whose sole knowledge of animals was what he had gotten from hearsay, coupled with the belief that one must have a hypnotic eye and a strong right arm to cow a wild beast. He tried it with this lion and got killed.

Then the owner conceived the idea that he could make the lion safe for handling by knocking out all his teeth. The poor brute was strapped and tied and his teeth were broken out one by one, as cruel a piece of human ignorance as I ever heard of; it accomplished nothing. The lion still had his claws, and even had the cheerful thought struck this man to pull these out by the roots, the beast would have continued to possess his muscles. A lion fights by striking, and the force of his blow is sufficient to disembowel animals even larger than he. Deprived of his claws his blow would not have the same tearing qualities, it is true, but it would possess the force sufficient to cause fatal internal injuries.

But the teeth were knocked out and the lion made "safe." He was so safe in fact that the next trainer, relying on the lion's reputation and believing that he must use force, was attacked, almost at the first command. His clothing was ripped from him and he was clawed into insensibility. The lion was sold as a cage beast, and its reputation traveled with it—that of being a "bad actor," an "untamable" and a "man-killer." At last he came to me, and I treated him as I treated all the rest. I stopped by his cage and talked to him. I called him pet names, and I treated him gently. One day I determined to see just how fierce he was and took him into the arena.

He didn't have many tricks, it is true—he'd never had time to learn many. But he responded and he learned. More than that, he seemed all the more willing to work because he had found someone who didn't beat him or force him. I worked that lion four years, and did not even get as much as a scratch. You'll find few humans with that much sense of forgiveness!

To tell the truth, it is usually the trainer's own fault when he gets torn up. I know that such has been my experience; even with that leopard which nearly ended my life. I took too much for granted; I gave the leopard qualities which I should have known he didn't have. Most of my accidents have been preventable. A lion tamer gets careless.

Once, while working for Colonel P. J. Mundy, I had a lion about which I boasted to everyone. He was the steadiest performer I ever had seen, and whenever an argument came up about animals, he was always my example of a good-tempered beast. But one afternoon as I started into his den to give him a workout, I had a hunch to stay out.

I forced the feeling aside and went in. The lion jumped to his pedestal, then refused to budge. I coaxed him a moment, in vain. Then I started to move closer, my kitchen chair before me, for I realized suddenly that the brute's temper had changed. He was looking for a fight. Even my kitchen chair wasn't enough when he leaped; it was knocked aside and the lion was upon me, sending me half across the arena with one sweeping blow of his forepaw.

In an instant he followed, striking me again, and breaking my left arm. Then he mauled me, first to one side, then the other, at last to leave me, walk across the arena, and there squat on his haunches, merely watching.

No assistant was near. For a time I lay still, wondering what the lion intended to do when I attempted to escape. There was only one way to find out, and at last I struggled to my feet; the beast made no attempt to follow me. He merely sat there; he neither growled nor snarled—he merely watched, and that was all, as I dragged myself to the door, unstrapped it, and went out of the arena.

That night in the hospital I still was thinking about it. As I looked back upon the attack, I saw that there was some reason for it all, as though the animal were angry about a specific thing and had expressed himself in the only way he knew. At last it came to me: for six years I had fed that lion promptly at five o'clock, and then, when his meal was done, had worked him. That explained my feeling of premonition as I entered the den—I had forgotten to feed him! The change in procedure had thrown the animal off balance. Besides that, he was grouchy because he had been asked to work without food. No wonder he had punished me, and then sat down and allowed me to think it over—which I did in the hospital! After my arm got well, I worked this lion consistently for years and never had another encounter with him.

The average person, of course, would reason that since an animal knows nothing about clocks, he would naturaly not know whether it was feeding time or not. That is entirely wrong. How they do it, I cannot understand, but an animal has a pretty exact knowledge of time. I have tested it often. I have often taken their word for it instead of bothering to look at my watch.

A good example of this came while I was acting as nurse to a number of orang-outangs for one of the big circuses. The shipment had started from Borneo with a total of twenty-two, eighteen of which had died through feeding problems. The remaining four were given into my care, for a system of dieting which must be exact and punctual. Meals were prepared for them at certain hours; after a time I noticed that the four orangs gathered at the cage netting at almost precisely the minute I should start my cooking. After they had become strengthy again, I decided to test them, and would deliberately forget to look at my watch. They did not fail once to remind me, and if I still hesitated, there would be a chorus of whimperings and pleadings which made the matter emphatic.

The dumbness of animals therefore is not their own ignorance, but ours. Because we don't know how to talk their languages, and because we don't understand their ways, we believe they don't know a number of things which are supposed to be wholly human. That is our own blindness. For years, we tried to teach animals to work, instead of to play! Recreation is in truth a fundamental of animal training to-day, especially for such stunts as the "untamable act" which the lion Duke and I did together so many years. It was the act in which Duke apparently tried to kill me and chased me from the cage at "each and every performance."

The explanation lay in the fact that Duke understood wholly the spirit of play—and as I have mentioned before, it is upon this that the supposedly fierce untamable act is founded. Perhaps I can explain better by telling just how that training is done.

Have you ever played with a dog and a stick, letting him pretend to attack it until you wanted him to stop? The untamable and chase acts are handled in the same manner. The first thing to do, of course, is to choose a levelheaded animal with plenty of spirit, so that he will enjoy the exercise. Then, with a broomstick, you go to the outside of the cage, pounding it on the floor in front of him and shouting until he becomes slightly irritated and makes a bound for it.

Immediately your whole attitude changes. You jerk the stick away. Your voice changes. The commands are soothing ones: "Easy, there! That's enough! Easy old boy! Easy now!" The lion naturally is puzzled. The thing is repeated. Again he attacks. Again he is halted and coaxed and soothed. Far sooner than one would expect, that lion begins to get the idea. This is a game of some sort, in which the stick isn't an enemy but a supposed one, and his part is not to be really mad, but to pretend it. So well do animals learn this that I can go to the cages of any beast under my control, particularly when photographs are to be taken, shake my fists and make faces and immediately have those animals apparently trying to break the very bars to get at me. Then I can change my tone and as quickly reach between those bars and ruffle the manes of those same animals, pat them on the head, and even pull their ears without the slightest danger. They know it's all pretense.

Since pretense forms the basis of the untamable act, in which the trainer pretends to try to force the animal into its tricks and the animal in turn pretends to become so infuriated that he finally drives the lion tamer out of the den, the whole affair is simply an amplification of that work with the broomstick.

After the trainer has firmly fixed in the animal's mind the fact that there is no danger in the stick, and to chase it only so far, he substitutes an animate object for the inanimate one, the same being himself. This step is to go into the cage, walk close to the lion, shout, stamp your feet and taunt the animal. He'll start for you at last. Then the switch of demeanor comes again, the command to halt, the soothing baby talk. Of course, this isn't recommended for a person who doesn't understand animals, or as a new Saturday night diversion; nevertheless, it is surprising how quickly the animal gets the idea. After the first few primary lessons, it is easy to enlarge upon the first steps—and to create a scene in which the animal and trainer are apparently fighting each other every inch of the way, but which is nothing but imitation, and which, for both, is a lot of fun.

Conditions have changed in the animal den. Where there was suffering there now is peace, where there was forcing there exists to-day a communion and understanding between the trainer and his beasts which accomplishes more than all the cruelty in the world. Just as I make no excuses for the old-time training methods, and just as I do not deny that there was bloodthirstiness in them, inhumanity and cruelty, so do I insist that in present days the average caged beast is much better off in captivity than in the wild state. To those who protest this statement I respectfully insist that they don't know animals. And there are many who fall in this category!

Thus ends Cap Ricardo's story. It must have been great fun while it lasted!

*The Great Climb**

by Edwin Muller, Jr.

Mountain climbing is one of the few adventures left to man where, in the last analysis, success depends squarely upon muscle coordination, physical skill, determination, and courage; no mechanical or scientific aids so far have given man the edge in conquering mountains. The golden age of climbing was the nineteenth century when men first challenged this last frontier in Europe. "The Great Climb," the story of the Matterhorn, is only one chapter in EDWIN MULLER'S *saga of Alpine climbing* They Climbed The Alps.

* "The Great Climb" from *They Climbed the Alps* by Edwin Muller, Jr., reprinted by permission of the author.

LATE ONE SUMMER afternoon a climber was slowly working his way down the rock face of an Alpine peak. He had not been to the top—no one had been to the top. In fact expert mountaineers all over Europe had called it a mountain that no one would ever climb. This man had been drawn by its legend of inaccessibility. His vacations were spent in tramping about its base, scanning its tremendous precipices for some way by which resolute climbers might haul themselves to the summit. Three or four times he had persuaded reluctant guides to try the ascent with him, but always the rock had repulsed them. It had been the same with other parties. Ice-glazed cliffs, avalanches, sudden storms, the terror with which the peak inspired the boldest guides—these had combined to defeat all comers.

On this particular afternoon the man had not tried for the summit. It was a reconnoitring trip, undertaken alone to spy out new routes. He had spent two days high up on the flank of the mountain, sleeping at night in a small tent set on a narrow shelf overhanging a thousand foot precipice. Now he was on the way back to his headquarters, a primitive inn whose roof he could pick out among the chalets of the little village six thousand feet below.

He lowered himself by rope down a "chimney," an almost perpendicular cleft in the face of the cliff. Then down a steep slope of ice by steps that he had cut the day before. Then across a rock face, clinging by hand and foot. All this was familiar ground to him, and he felt no uneasiness.

Then the unexpected happened. One more steep ice slope had to be descended, and below was another perpendicular "chimney" dropping sharply to a precipice hanging eight hundred feet, sheer above a crevassed glacier. Here the mid-day sun had almost obliterated his laboriously cut steps of the day before, and he had foolishly left behind in the high-level tent the ax with which he could have renewed them. Still there were only five or six steps to go. Placing each foot with painstaking care, he started down. The first was safely negotiated, his nails biting a precarious hold, the second, the third—but at the fourth he slipped, and the world turned over.

Let him tell it.

"The knapsack brought my head down first, and I pitched into some rocks about a dozen feet below; they caught something and tumbled me off the edge, head over heels into the gully; the baton was dashed from my hands, and I whirled downwards in a series of bounds, each longer than the last, now over ice, now into rocks; each striking my head four or five times, each time with increased force. The last bound sent me spinning through the air, in a leap of fifty or sixty feet, from one side of the gully to the other, and I struck the rocks, luckily, with the whole of my left side. They caught my clothes for a moment, and I fell back onto the snow with motion arrested. My head fortunately came the right side up and a few frantic catches brought me to a halt in the neck of the gully, and on the verge of the precipice. Baton, hat, and veil skimmed by and disappeared, and the crash of the rocks—which I had started—as they fell onto the glacier, told how narrow had been the escape from utter destruction. As it was, I fell nearly 200 feet in seven or eight bounds. Ten feet more would have taken me in one gigantic leap of 800 feet on to the glacier below.

"The situation was sufficiently serious. The rocks could not be let go for a moment, and the blood was spurting out of more than twenty cuts. The most serious ones were in the head, and I vainly tried to close them with one hand, whilst holding on with the other. It was useless; the blood jerked out in blinding jets at each pulsation. At last, in a moment of inspiration, I kicked out a big lump of snow, and stuck it as a plaster on my head. The idea was a happy one, and the flow of blood diminished. Then scrambling up, I got, not a moment too soon, to a place of safety, and fainted away."

He returned to consciousness as the sun was setting. Fortunately the five thousand feet of descent that remained was comparatively easy. He crept painfully down in the gathering darkness, in desperate fear lest he should faint again and lie out through a freezing night. Finally he reached his inn, submitted to the rude doctoring of the inn-keeper and was put to bed for a week.

The day after he was allowed out of bed he was high on the mountain again.

The man was Edward Whymper and the mountain was the Matterhorn. Looking back across the sixty years that have passed since that summer afternoon, the long struggle between these two antagonists takes on the aspect of a far-off battle between giants of a mythical age. The Matterhorn was guarded by the fates. Whymper finally climbed to its summit. But the day that he did it was one whose memory, throughout his life, brought him the keenest pangs of sorrow that a man can feel.

The approach to the Matterhorn is a masterpiece of dramatic effect. The main stream of tourist travel flows through Switzerland along the Rhone Valley, from the blue Lake of Geneva on the west to the great tunnel of the Simplon, sixty miles to the east. This flat valley, the floor of which is only three or four miles wide, is bordered on either side by shouldering mountain walls. These are pierced in several places by narrow entrances to subsidiary valleys which lead back ten to twenty miles into the heart of the snow peaks behind. One of these minor valleys, the Nikolai-thal, is entered at the little town of Visp, where one changes from the express train of the Rhone Valley to the rack and pinion road that climbs slowly up the eighteen miles to the famous mountaineering centre Zermatt. It takes three to four hours and one could wish it even more prolonged if one were not impatient for the climax at the end. The valley is cut so deep into the central chain of the Alps that, in some places, the sun only reaches its floor for a few hours of the day. Leaning from the broad windows of the observation car, one gets glimpses of boiling water-falls and lofty snow fields above. Finally the train swings around a rocky corner and the great mountain thrusts itself suddenly into view. Its unexpected height and overhanging mass are startling, one's face is raised sharply to look at it, it seems overhead.

The Matterhorn is one of those phenomena that infect with descriptive frenzy men who ordinarily speak and write like rational beings. Tyndall, a sober scientist, de Saussure, a traveller in the prim eighteenth century, others of equally undemonstrative nature, all break into a rash of superlative adjectives. If sophisticated cosmopolitans are so affected, it is easy to see why the peasants of neighboring valleys looked upon it with superstitious awe. They firmly believed it to be the highest mountain in the world. Around its upper slopes, they said, a line was drawn beyond which no man could go. "Within that invisible line gini and afreets did exist—the wandering Jew and the spirits of the damned." On its summit was a ruined city wherein the spirits dwelt.

Until about 1860 no one had considered the ascent of the Matterhorn as a serious possibility. For many years tourists had been drawn to its base, to Zermatt on the Swiss side and to the Valtournanche on its Italian slope.

Among them were mountaineers who had climbed most of the other major Alpine peaks. They examined the possible routes to the top, talked with the native guides and then went elsewhere to easier conquests.

The eighteen-sixties were the golden age of mountaineering. The British Alpine Club was founded by a group of adventurous spirits who were united in a passionate love for their sport. Every summer they set forth to the Alps, singly and in groups, and by the end of each season the number of virgin peaks was further reduced. Their Club Journal became a record of exciting adventure the reading of which is in itself a thrilling experience. The Germans, the French, and the Italians entered the competition. Climbing came into its own.

As the number of unclimbed peaks grew smaller with the conquest of the Weisshorn and other rugged giants, the bolder spirits turned again to the challenging riddle of the Matterhorn. They toiled up the Hörnli ridge and reconnoitred—this was long before the days of the rack and pinion—and re-examined the mountain. In Zermatt they were on familiar ground. With good reason it had become one of the great climbing centres of Europe. The town is set in the midst of a great amphitheatre of snow peaks and glaciers, Monte Rosa, the Weisshorn, the Dent Blanche of ethereal beauty, the huge massif of the Mischabel and a score of others. In Zermatt the climbers had consigned themselves to the hospitality of Herr Seiler, the founder of a famous line of inn-keepers. Establishing headquarters at his comfortable inn, they sallied forth and cut down the number of unclimbed peaks until only the Matterhorn remained. They accepted its challenge.

From the Zermatt side the mountain looked impossible. Facing them on that side was the great East Face which, starting at an apparent angle of 45°, soared up eight thousand feet, steeper and steeper, to the perpendicular and even beyond. Shaking their heads the climbers went off to observe the other faces, for they knew the mountain to be a pyramid with four faces and four corresponding ridges. They turned to the left, but a glance at that face seemed to show one smooth inaccessible cliff from base to summit. So they went around to the right to that face, which descends to the Z'mutt Glacier. But there a series of ghastly precipices equally forbade the attempt. (These reconnaissances, of course, extended over several years, and were the accumulated experiences of many climbers.) There was left only the Italian face, so some said good-bye to Herr Seiler, made a long day's journey across the main divide of the Alps by the glacier pass of the Theodule and established themselves in the tiny hamlet of Breuil. This was at the head of the Valtournanche, a picturesque valley leading down to join a larger one which continued to the flat plains of Lombardy.

This Italian face, as seen from Breuil, looked as if it might be climbed by a brave and skilful party. From this direction the mountain appeared to be broken up into a series of wedge-shaped pyramidal masses. This broken irregularity seemed to offer a chance to adept rock-climbers. Accordingly the early attempts were made on this side.

Those who came to make their climbing base in the Valtournanche found a community even more primitive than that of Zermatt. Breuil at the head of the valley in the shadow of the Matterhorn was a cluster of a dozen rude chalets with one unpretentious inn. The native peasants lived happily in filthy quarters, were ruled in most things by their Catholic pastors, and made a scant living by the manufacture of cheese. In the intervals of the latter they were open to engagement as guides, although this had by no means become the skilled profession that it is today. Among them was at least one great climber, Jean Antoine Carrel, the cock of the valley. He was a bronzed, resolute young fellow with a defiant air and a pugnacious nature. He differed from most of his neighbors in having not only physical courage and endurance, but a bold initiative as well. He had even dared to doubt the invulnerability of the Matterhorn, and had led several exploring parties high up on its slopes. Another distinctive figure was Luc Meynet, a bright-eyed little hunchback. He lived in a miserable hovel where he worked hard all day to support the children of his dead brother, but he carolled away at his labor as if he had never heard that we live in a world of trouble. In spite of his deformity he was a mighty man on the mountains and was the mainstay of many of the early climbing parties.

To supplement this local talent the Alpine Club men brought in guides from Zermatt and other parts of Switzerland. One of them, Bennen by name, sent by Professor Tyndall to reconnoitre the Italian face, came back with a discouraging report. "Herr, I have examined the mountain carefully, and find it more difficult and dangerous than I had imagined. There is no place upon it where we could well pass the night. We might do so on yonder col upon the snow, but there we should be almost frozen to death, and totally unfit for the work of the next day. On the rocks there is no ledge or cranny which could give us proper harborage; and starting from Breuil it is certainly impossible to reach the summit in a single day."

Nevertheless Professor Tyndall did try the ascent, retired beaten, came back for another effort, and then another. Kennedy, M'Donald, and other experts had no better success. In the years 1860–64 at least fifteen serious attempts were made, most of them on the Italian side. The experience gained by each party helped the strategy of the next, and the highest point reached was pushed further and further toward the summit. But, although the unclimbed portion shrank before successive attacks, the confidence of the climbers was not improved. The higher one climbed the more the difficulties increased, until the last few hundred feet seemed beyond human accomplishment. Tyndall was finally able to set foot 800 feet from the summit, but he came back utterly discouraged and, at last, ready to abandon the mountain forever. His party had included Carrel and three others of the best guides obtainable, all in perfect condition. Weather and snow conditions were ideal, as were the mental and physical equipment of the party. Yet, after standing almost within a stone's throw of the top they had to come down beaten. Can anyone blame the professor for having had enough?

And now another figure makes his entrance. Edward Whymper was an English artist who had waited until his late thirties to discover that climbing was to be the great passion of his life. Up to 1860 he had not even seen a real mountain. In that year he was commissioned by a London publisher to make sketches of some notable ascents that were scheduled in the Dauphiné Alps. The climbs were never completed, as the peaks proved too much for the attacking party, but Whymper had his first taste of mountaineering. The next year he returned with a companion and successfully accomplished the ascents of the Dauphiné peaks, then for the next five years he ranged up and down the Alps, seeking the difficult and untried.

He was a man of singularly mixed characteristics. He had the traditional British reticence, modesty and antipathy to display, combined with the highest degree of physical and moral courage. But, if "muddling through" be a British trait, there was none of it in Whymper. His mental habits were exact and thorough; he had the type of mind that insists on planning an action to its last detail before beginning its execution. He was an artist, a scientist, and a man of deeds; it is hard to say which of the three was uppermost.

Very early in his mountain career Whymper was drawn to Matterhorn. Here was a first-rate problem to be solved and, without broadcasting his determination, he decided that he was the man to solve it. Like the others, he concentrated his attention at first on the Italian side. He saw that the chief difficulty was in the unusual extent of the steep and dangerous part of the slope. Bennen was right —it was impossible for any party to climb from base to summit and back to base within twenty-four hours. Hence a night must be spent on the slopes and there was no spot where that could be done without danger and extreme hardship. One could find only a few inadequate little rock shelves where a tent might be anchored on the steep mountain side. Often the wind blew so hard that stones as large as a man's fist were blown away horizontally into space. Always at night the cold was intense. Great masses of rocks would split off far up the slope and come pouring down over the precipices in a thundering stream. It was hard to persuade guides, even those as brave as Carrel, to spend the night on such a mountain.

Between 1861 and 1865 Whymper made seven organized attempts to reach the summit. With him on each climb were two or three guides, the best obtainable. Jean Antoine Carrel was usually the first man on the rope, Luc Meynet was another standby, and on several occasions Valaisian guides were brought over from the Swiss side. On these ascents and on others that he made during the same period Whymper perfected his technique as a rock climber. Always the party went roped together on slopes that were difficult or dangerous, and that meant on nearly every foot of the Matterhorn after the high green Alps at the base were left behind. A regular routine was followed on steep rock. While the rest of the party remained clinging tightly to their handholds and footholds, the leader would work his way up, sometimes by footholds alone, sometimes by pulling up hand over hand while the iron-shod boots struggled to get a grip on the smallest irregularities of the rock surface. When he had ascended to the limit of the fifteen or twenty feet of rope that separated him from the second man, the latter would repeat the process, the leader, meanwhile, anchoring himself as firmly as he could. And so the process was repeated until all had made the distance, then up again went the leader. Often they were in positions where a slip by one would have pulled the whole party down to destruction. Then every step was made with the utmost care, and no hold for hand or foot was used until it had been tested. Never did two of the party move at the same time.

On each ascent it was necessary to spend a night on the mountain. This meant carrying a tent; otherwise they would hardly have survived the cold and exposure. As there were no ledges broad enough to support a tent in safety, they had to build up artificial platforms of loose stones. On this precarious flooring they lay huddled together under their canvas, waiting for the dawn to creep up over the distant Tyrolean Alps. From these lofty bivouacs on clear mornings they could overlook hundreds of square miles, wave after wave of mountain ranges rushing toward the far horizon. Sometimes they were battered all night long by storms that raged around the peak. These were desperate hours, for the wind blew so hard as to seem likely to wrench the tent from its anchorage and hurl it, with its occupants, five thousand feet down to the glacier below. Going out to strengthen the fastenings, they would see the great crags about them illumined in a terrifying way by continuous flashes of lightning.

Always they were forced back before the summit was actually threatened. Pessimistic mountaineers, watching the proceedings, were confirmed in their opinions on the folly of climbing the Matterhorn. Oxford dons, country rectors, and sundry others wrote to the Times commenting on the obvious impregnability of this mountain, and suggesting that sensible men would do well to direct their efforts elsewhere.

By 1865 Whymper began to examine routes other than those on the Italian side. He had the scientist's trait which makes one distrust both the appearances of things and the unproved opinions of men. He knew that other climbers had declared the eastern face to be utterly impossible. Walking around to Zermatt, he surveyed it again. Yes, it did look unclimbable, eight thousand feet of slope at an angle that seemed not far from perpendicular. But still he examined it. Then it occurred to him that his point of observation might have something to do with the apparent angle. From Zermatt and the slopes immediately above, the eastern face is seen neither in profile nor in full front, but from a point midway between. No one had considered the fact that, seen from such an angle, the apparent steepness of a slope is greatly exaggerated. Whymper began to suspect that the climbing fraternity had been deceived in this matter. In this he was confirmed by observing that on considerable portions of the eastern face snow lay all the year long. He knew that this was impossible on slopes that much exceeded 45°. To settle the question he made a day's expedition to the slopes above the Z'mutt Glacier, a spot rarely visited, from which he could see the eastern face exactly in profile. His analysis was confirmed; the angle of the slope was hardly more than 40°. Of course this is no small gradient when maintained over a great mountain slope, but it is by no means impossible.

But another difficulty that had been pointed out as to the eastern face was its well-nigh unbroken smoothness. Men despaired of finding anything to grasp. Whymper turned his analytic powers on this point and here his knowledge of geology helped him. He had observed that the rock strata of the Matterhorn rise toward the east and dip down toward the west. Therefore on the west or Italian side the fractured edges overhang, a constant difficulty to climbers. The same dip, however, made of the eastern face a natural rock staircase with steps inclining inwards. A two-inch foothold sloping inwards is worth more than one of twelve inches sloping out.

These considerations built up in his mind the conviction that, contrary to general opinion, the eastern face offered the easiest way to the summit.

Whymper spent the latter part of June, 1865, in the Valley of Chamonix where he made notable ascents among the difficult rocky needles that surround Mont Blanc. On these expeditions his chief guide was Michel

Croz, a native of the valley. Of all the guides with whom Whymper had travelled Croz was his favorite. He was endowed with strength and activity far beyond the average and was happiest when engaged in the hardest work on snow or rock. When Whymper, having finished his climbs in the Chamonix district, turned his face again toward the Matterhorn, he wished to take Croz along. But the latter was obliged to refuse; he had an engagement of long standing with another British alpinist, so the two parted. They were to meet again before long in unexpected circumstances.

Leaving the Mont Blanc region, Whymper, with two Swiss guides, made his way toward Zermatt, crossing the Italian ridges. He reached the Valtournanche where he sought out Jean Antoine Carrel to take part in the great effort. The latter was dubious about the eastern face and urged that the Italian ridge be tried again, but he finally consented to come and bring along his cousin Caesar. Accordingly Whymper dismissed the Swiss guides and busied himself with the collection of provisions and other preparations for the assault of the peak. This occupied two days, during which the Carrels were left to their own devices. On the third day Whymper happened to see Jean Antoine helping in the transport of supplies for an Italian gentleman who was en route to the head of the valley. When reminded that he was due to start the next day for the Swiss side of the mountain, Carrel made an evasive reply, and, being pressed for an explanation, at last came out with a startling and disheartening admission. He had engaged himself to Whymper with the full knowledge that he would not be able to fulfill his contract. He had been already pledged to guide the party of the Italian gentleman who was an agent of a high Italian official, Signor Sella. The latter had decided that he himself should have the credit for the first ascent of the Matterhorn, to which end he had engaged Jean Antoine, Caesar and the two or three other first rate guides of the Valtournanche. In this little conspiracy were the inn-keeper and most of the valley's inhabitants, they having the patriotic conviction that the great peak should be ascended by Italians on the Italian side.

For a moment Whymper was thoroughly discouraged. He had no guides, and, at this late date, it seemed unlikely that he could find any of the first rank. The rival party was well equipped and had an excellent chance of reaching its goal before he could organize a counter attack. He could not even procure porters to carry his supplies to the Swiss side, as the inn-keeper found plausible reasons why all of his men must be employed otherwise.

But Whymper was not one to let a contest go by default. He reconsidered his position. One point in his favor was that the Italians planned a reconnoitring climb before their final effort, as the noble Signors were anxious that the way should be smoothed for them. If he could contrive to transport his equipment to Zermatt he might yet find guides and ascend by the eastern face before his rivals could storm the opposite side.

Then a piece of good fortune came his way. On the

morning of July 11th a party dropped down over the Theodule Pass, coming from Zermatt, headed by a debonair young Englishman, Lord Francis Douglas. Although only twenty years old, he had had several seasons in the Alps where he had recently excited the admiration of the climbing fraternity by a first ascent of the Gabelhorn from Zinal. With him now were a seasoned Zermatt guide, Peter Taugwalder, and one of the latter's sons. The two Englishmen got into conversation and found that they had much in common. Lord Francis expressed a keen desire to make the attempt on the Matterhorn, and it was straightway decided that they should join forces. The next day the four of them recrossed the Theodule and deposited their tents, blankets, ropes, and other baggage in a little chapel at the Schwarzsee, a picturesque spot 5,000 feet above the valley near where the steep slope of the mountain begins. Then they descended to Zermatt where they took lodging for the night at Seiler's hotel, the Monte Rosa.

Here fortune served them again—the first person that Whymper saw on entering the hotel was his old guide Michel Croz. His Chamonix employer had been forced to return to England and Croz had been immediately engaged by the Rev. Charles Hudson who had brought him to Zermatt for no less a purpose than the ascent of the Matterhorn.

Hudson was considered by many to be the best amateur climber of his time. Long practice had made him as surefooted as a born mountaineer, and many of the notable first ascents had gone to his credit. He was the middle-aged vicar of a north-of-England living, a quiet unassuming man whom one would never have supposed capable of such great feats. With him on this expedition was a friend, Mr. Hadow, a young man on his first visit to the Alps.

This party had planned to start for the mountain early the following morning, coinciding with the intentions of Whymper and Douglas. The two parties went into consultation. It was agreed that it would be undesirable to have two independent expeditions on the mountain at the same time, so it was proposed that they join forces. Before committing himself to this, Whymper inquired closely as to the capabilities of Hadow. In many respects a climbing party is no stronger than its weakest member, and this was to be no training jaunt for a novice. But Hudson was reassuring. According to him, Hadow, although in Switzerland for the first time, had done notable work in the Mont Blanc region, and was a man to be depended upon. And so the party was made up—the amateurs, Whymper, Douglas, Hudson, and Hadow; the guides Croz and the Taugwalder father and son.

They started from Zermatt on July 13th, at half past five on a cloudless, brilliant morning. On this first day they did not intend to ascend to any great height, so they went at a leisurely pace, picking up the baggage which had been left at the Schwarzsee, and proceeding thence along the low Hörnli ridge.

"At half past eleven we arrived at the base of the actual

peak; then quitted the ridge, and clambered round some ledges on to the eastern face. We were now fairly upon the mountain, and were astonished to find that places which from the Riffel, or even from the Furggengletscher, looked entirely impracticable, were so easy that we could *run about.*"

By noon they had found a position for the tent, so there they stopped and made camp for the night. Croz and young Taugwalder went on ahead to spy out the work of the next day. They returned jubilant. "Not a difficulty, not a difficulty. We could have gone to the summit and returned today, easily." During the remaining hours of daylight they basked in the sunshine and rested for the strenuous work of the next day. As dusk came on they retired to their blanket bags in a jovial, confident mood.

Next morning they started as soon as it was light enough to see their way. For the first four or five hours they were steadily mounting the great natural staircase of the eastern face. It was not easy work, as most people would have viewed it, but there were no difficulties to give a moment's hesitation to trained mountaineers. Just before ten o'clock they encountered their first serious bit. They were then at a height of 14,000 feet, only 800 feet separating them from the summit. This is the part that from Zermatt appears to be perpendicular or overhanging, and, although that appearance is an illusion, the face at this point is, in fact, too steep to be practicable. They moved across, therefore, to the northern face, where the angle was slightly less formidable. The greatest caution was exercised, those leading who were least likely to slip and all being careful to keep the rope taut between them. The hand-and-foot-holds were small and, too often, were covered with a thin film of ice. Hadow was not accustomed to this kind of work and required continued assistance.

Fortunately this part was of no great extent as it required an hour and a half to ascend 600 feet. Then suddenly the slope eased off. With only 200 feet of easy snow remaining, the last doubt vanquished—the Matterhorn was conquered.

The last moments were full of tense excitement. Their joy of achievement was modified by the fear that they were not the first to reach the top. Four days had elapsed since the Italians had set forth on the opposite side of the mountain. Perhaps they had succeeded. All the way up false alarms had been raised: "Men on the summit!" At the end Whymper and Croz detached themselves from the rope and ran a dead heat to the actual summit. Victory! Not a footstep was to be seen.

But, as Whymper says, "It was not yet certain that we had not been beaten. The summit of the Matterhorn was formed of a rudely level ridge, about 350 feet long, and the Italians might have been at its farther extremity. I hastened to the southern end, scanning the snow right and left eagerly. Hurrah again—it was untrodden! Where were the men? I peered over the cliff, half doubting, half expectant, and saw them immediately—mere dots on the ridge, at an immense distance below. Up went my arms and my hat. 'Croz! Croz! come here!' 'Where are they, Monsieur?' 'There—don't you see them—down there!' 'Ah! the *coquins,* they are low down.' 'Croz, we must make those fellows hear us.' We yelled until we were hoarse. The Italians seemed to regard us—we could not be certain. 'Croz, we *must* make them hear us; they *shall* hear us!' "

Presently the Italians did hear them, looked up in astonishment, then turned and fled. Still, Whymper's triumph was mixed with the desire to have Jean Antoine standing on the summit by his side, enjoying the fulfilment of a lifetime's ambition. But the Italian had played the game in his own way and had lost.

Now the party gathered around the summit rocks. Croz had been so sure of success that he had brought along one of the tentpoles to serve as a marker. To this he attached his blouse, making a flag that was seen by the watchers in Zermatt below. Then all sat down for an hour's rest, and paid homage to the view. It was one of those superlatively clear days that usually precede bad weather. Mountains a hundred miles off stood out sharp and clear, all their details visible. Near at hand, seemingly close enough to toss a biscuit across, were the Dent Blanche and Monte Rosa; further away the giants of the Bernese Oberland dominated by the Finsteraarhorn; and to the east the Disgrazia and the Ortler; toward the south Monte Viso and the flat plain of Piedmont; and in the west, glowing in full sunlight Mont Blanc. Not one of the principal peaks of the Alps was hidden. Happy memories of by-gone climbers came to mind as the familiar forms were scanned. Ten thousand feet beneath were the green fields of Zermatt, dotted with chalets from which blue smoke rose lazily. There was every combination that man could desire.

For a fleeting hour life was a glorious crescendo of joy. Then they prepared to descend.

It was agreed that the safest arrangement for the descent was for Croz to go first, then Hadow, then Hudson, Douglas next and after him the elder Taugwalder with young Taugwalder and Whymper in the rear. The latter two had lingered behind a few moments to inscribe a record of the ascent and leave it in a bottle. They rejoined the others and tied themselves on the rope just at the beginning of the descent of the most difficult stretch of rock. Great care was being taken. Only one man was moving at a time; when he was firmly planted the next advanced, and so on.

"Michel Croz had laid aside his ax, and in order to give Mr. Hadow greater security, was absolutely taking hold of his legs, and putting his feet, one by one, into their proper positions. So far as I know, no one was actually descending. I cannot speak with certainty, because the two leading men were partially hidden from my sight by an intervening mass of rock, but it is my belief, from the movements of their shoulders, that Croz, having done as I have said, was in the act of turning round, to go down a step or two himself; at this moment Mr. Hadow was seen flying downwards; in another moment Hudson was dragged from his steps, and Lord F. Douglas immediately after him. All this was the work of a moment. Immediately we heard Croz's exclamation, old Peter and I planted ourselves as firmly as the rocks would permit: the rope was taut between us, and the jerk came on us both as on one man. We held; but the rope broke midway between Taugwalder and Lord Francis Douglas. For a few seconds we saw our unfortunate companions sliding downwards on their backs, and spreading their hands, endeavoring to save themselves. They passed from our sight uninjured, disappeared one by one, and fell from precipice to precipice on to the Matterhorn-gletscher below, a distance of nearly 4,000 feet in height. From the moment the rope broke it was impossible to help them."

For half an hour Whymper and the two Taugwalders remained on the spot, unable to move. Father and son were paralysed by terror. For a time it seemed certain that they too would suffer the fate of the others, but at last Whymper was able to inspire them with the resolution to continue the descent.

"For more than two hours afterwards I thought almost every moment that the next would be my last; for the Taugwalders, utterly unnerved, were not only incapable of giving assistance, but were in such a state that a slip might have been expected from them at any moment. After a time we were able to do that which should have been done at first, and fixed rope to firm rocks, in addition to being tied together. These ropes were cut from time to time, and were left behind. Even with their assurance the men were afraid to proceed, and several times old Peter turned with ashy face and faltering limbs, and said, with terrible emphasis, *"I cannot!"*

About 6 P.M. they reached the snow upon the ridge descending toward Zermatt and all peril was over. It was impossible to reach the spot where their comrades had fallen, and it was, of course, beyond hope that any had survived. Night overtook them and, for a time, they continued the descent in the dark. Then a resting place was found on a wretched slab, barely large enough to hold the three, and there, huddled together, they passed six miserable hours. At daybreak the descent was resumed and before noon they reached Zermatt. Seiler met them at the door, and, on hearing their news, burst into tears. Immediately the village was aroused and a search party was organized. In spite of his exhaustion Whymper insisted on going with them. Making their way through the ice-falls of the Matterhorn Glacier, they reached the plateau at the top and within sight of the corner in which they knew the bodies must be.

"As we saw one weather-beaten man after another raise the telescope, turn deadly pale, and pass it on without a word to the next, we knew that all hope was gone. We approached. They had fallen below as they had fallen above—Croz a little in advance, Hadow near him, and Hudson some distance behind; but of Lord Francis Douglas we could see nothing. We left them where they fell, buried in snow at the base of the grandest cliff of the most majestic mountain of the Alps."

Later the bodies were recovered, all save that of Lord Francis Douglas, of whom no trace was ever found.

Today, sixty years later, all of the actors in this drama have long since made their exits. As you walk down the principal street of Zermatt a foot-path leads off to the left. If you follow it you reach a tiny English church, surrounded by an overgrown churchyard. Here, under simple tombstones, surrounded by others, rest the bodies of the climbers. Far above them is the towering mass of the Matterhorn.

Summit of the World: The Fight for Everest[*]

by James Ramsey Ullman

No one who knew of James Ullman's *own skill as a mountain climber could be surprised at the absolute reality of the climbing episodes in his novel* White Tower. *Only a man who had known the treachery of ice and snow or the joy in mastering a rocky needle could keep arm-chair travellers on the edge of their seats with the conviction that they, too, were inching up from toe-hold to toe-hold or clinging to bare rock by their finger-nails. It is this combination of experience and vivid description which gives vitality to Ullman's account of men's assaults on mountains from the Alpine conquests to the Everest attempts. His "Fight for Everest" is a chapter from his broad history of mountain-climbing* High Conquest.

* "Summit of the World: The Fight for Everest" from *High Conquest* by James Ramsey Ullman, reprinted by permission of the author.

IN THE EARLY AFTERNOON of June 8, 1924, a man stood on a crag in the freezing sub-stratosphere, 26,-000 feet above the sea, raised his eyes and stared. On a ridge high overhead he saw two human figures, black and tiny against the sky. Less than 800 feet above them was the snow-plumed summit of the highest mountain on earth.—A minute, two minutes the watcher gazed, while the climbers crept upward. Then clouds swept in upon the mountain-top, blotting them from view.

They were never seen again.

So ended the most splendid and tragic of many attempts to conquer Everest, king of mountains. To this day no one knows whether George Leigh-Mallory and Andrew Irvine reached the top before death overtook them. No one, probably will ever know. One thing is certain: no man has ever reached the summit and returned to tell the tale.

The story of Mount Everest begins in 1852, when a clerk in the office of the Indian Trigonometrical Survey looked up excitedly from a page of figures and cried to his superior, "Sir, I have discovered the highest mountain in the world!" A careful checking of his calculations proved him right. The remote Himalayan summit listed prosaically on the charts as "Peak XV" was found to be 29,002 feet high—almost a thousand feet higher than its closest rival. Later observers corrected its altitude to 29,141 feet and named it for Sir George Everest, first Surveyor-General of India. But its supremacy remained, and remains today, unchallenged.

What began as an exercise in higher mathematics was to become, as years passed, one of the great adventures of the human spirit.

For a half century after its discovery Everest was a mountain of mystery. Tibet and Nepal, on whose frontiers it rises, were both rigorously closed to outsiders, and, far from climbing it, men of the West were unable even to approach it or learn anything about it. All they knew were the tantalizing figures of the Trigonometrical Survey. All they could see was a remote pinnacle of rock and ice, one of thousands in the great sea of peaks to the north of the Indian plain. The mountain itself—its structure and appearance, its surroundings and approaches—was as unknown as if it stood upon another planet.

Then, in the late 1890's, as we have seen, the full tide of mountaineering interest and activity turned toward the Himalayas. Soon a thin trickle of pioneers began to penetrate into the great passes and gorges where no white man had ever been before; adventurous spirits crossed the frontiers into forbidden Tibet and Nepal, disguised as Hindu or Mohammedan traders; men like Freshfield, Kellas and Longstaff turned their attention from the Sikkim and Garhwal foothills to the greater peaks that lay beyond. Slowly the net closed in about the remote, secret place where rose the highest mountain in the world. Mountaineers had heard the siren call of the mysterious and the unknown, and all the obstacles of man and nature were not going to stop them in their quest.

A lone traveler might slip into Tibet without official sanction; not so a large expedition equipped to tackle Everest. The permission of the Tibetan government was essential, and for long years this permission was not forthcoming. At last, in 1913, it appeared that the way was clear, and an exploring party was about to be organized by Freshfield; but the project was ended before it began by the outbreak of the First World War. It was not until seven years later that men were again able to turn their eyes and thoughts to the greatest mountain.

Early in 1920 the Royal Geographical Society of London and the British Alpine Club joined forces to form the Mount Everest Committee and after prolonged negotiations secured permission for an all-English party to approach and, if possible, ascend the mountain. Preparations were immediately begun on an elaborate scale. It was planned to send out two expeditions, a year apart, the first to explore and reconnoitre, the second to climb. As it eventually turned out, there was a third, and it was this final attack that was to end, a scant few hundred feet from triumph, in mystery and tragedy.

But to begin at the beginning:

The 1921 reconnaissance expedition to Everest was composed of the flower of English mountaineers and explorers. The leader was Colonel C. K. Howard-Bury, who had traveled widely in Tibet and knew that mysterious land as well as any white man living. Next in command were Dr. Kellas, and A. F. R. Wollaston, who had won fame on Ruwenzori and many another far-flung mountain range. Others were Harold Raeburn, a veteran Himalayan climber, Dr. A. M. Heron, a geologist, and Major Morshead and Captain Wheeler, army surveyors who had known and traveled among the great Asiatic peaks for years. To these mature and experienced hands were added two younger men with brilliant, if briefer, mountaineering records: G. H. Bullock, of the Consular Service, and George Leigh-Mallory, master at Charterhouse College, Cambridge.

It was Mallory who was to become the foremost of the "Everesters" and the most famous mountaineer of his day. He was the only man to participate in all three of the great expeditions between 1921 and 1924, and although never the official leader (He was only thirty-eight when he died), his marvellous climbing accomplishments and his flaming spirit made him the outstanding figure in every one of them. Everest became *his* mountain, as completely as the Matterhorn, sixty years before, had been Whymper's. His climbing companions, to a man. believed that if any one of them was to achieve conquest of the highest summit on earth Mallory would be the one, and many of them, in later days, clung staunchly to the belief that he attained his goal before death overtook him in the clouds.

There was nothing of the conventional athlete about Mallory. Slight and slim, with a round boyish face, he was anything but the popular conception of a rugged outdoor man. Again like Whymper, climbing was to him not exercise or amusement, but passionate devotion, and, like all great mountaineers, less a physical than a spiritual adventure. His explanation of why men climb remains today the simplest, and at the same time perhaps the most profound, that has ever been given.

"But *why?*" a friend asked him as he set out for a renewed assault on Everest. "Why do you try to climb this mountain?"

Mallory's answer consisted of four words:

"Because it is there."

"There," however, was a remote, unknown corner of the earth, and it required an arduous journey of many weeks before the Everesters of the 1921 reconnoitering party came even within sight of their goal. Beginning at Darjeeling in the middle of May their march carried them first through the steaming tropical jungles of Sikkim, then up through great mountain passes onto the desolate, windswept wilderness of the Tibetan plateau. In a straight line the distance from Darjeeling to Everest is only a hundred miles, but they had to journey more than three hundred, threading their way among the great peaks and gorges of the eastern Himalayas.

These were days of endless toil and hardship, and they took their toll in sudden and tragic fashion. Dr. Kellas, whose health was no longer robust, strained his heart while crossing the high passes and died in the Tibetan village of Kampa Dzong. Soon after, Raeburn became seriously ill and had to return to India, with Wollaston accompanying him. These two were not able to rejoin the expedition until the middle of the summer. Everest had begun to claim her victims even before they had had so much as a glimpse of her.

The others struggled on, saddened but resolute. There were only six white men now, at the head of a vast cavalcade of Sherpa porters, Tibetan guides and helpers, ponies, donkeys, bullocks and yaks. Day after day they pushed northward and westward across as savage country as exists anywhere on the earth's surface—through sandstorms and raging, glacial torrents, across vast boulder-strewn plains and passes 20,000 feet above the sea. At night they camped under the stars or enjoyed the primitive hospitality of Buddhist monasteries and village headmen. Their passports from the Tibetan authorities in Lhassa assured them kindly and courteous treatment, but the announcement of the purpose of their journey elicited only a dubious shaking of heads and a solemn turning of prayer wheels. To these devout and superstitious orientals, Everest was more than a mountain. Chomolungma, they called it—Goddess-Mother-of-the-World. It was sacrilege, they believed, for mere mortals even to approach it.

At last, late in June, the expedition arrived at the great Rongbuk Monastery, where an isolated colony of priests and hermits dwelt, some twenty miles due north of Everest. And from here, at last, they saw their mountain head on, in its titanic majesty—the first white men ever to have a close-up view of the summit of the world. "We paused," wrote Mallory, "in sheer astonishment. The sight of it banished every thought; we asked no questions and made no comment, but simply looked. . . . At the end of the valley and above the glacier Everest rises, not so much a peak as a prodigious mountain-mass. There is no complication for the eye. The highest of the world's mountains, it seems, has to make but a single gesture of magnificence to be the lord of all, vast in unchallenged and isolated supremacy. To the discerning eye other mountains are visible, giants between 23,000 and 26,000 feet high. Not one of their slenderer heads even reaches their chief's shoulder; beside Everest they escape notice—such is the pre-eminence of the greatest."

The explorers set themselves at once to their tasks, reconnoitering, surveying, studying the colossal rock-and-ice mass that towered before them and probing the possible routes to its summit. They were already at an altitude of 18,000 feet—far higher than the highest summit in the Alps or Rockies—and the slightest exertion set their lungs to heaving and their hearts to pounding. The world around them was a trackless wilderness of peaks, ridges and glaciers, and wind and snow roared down from the heights with hurricane fury. And still there remained two vertical miles of mountain soaring above them into the sky.

Working slowly around its base Mallory and Bullock discovered that Everest was constructed as an almost perfect pyramid, with three great faces and three main ridges sweeping downward from the summit like vast buttresses. The faces were all built up in tiers of precipices which no man could even dream of scaling, and the south and northwest ridges, miles in length and flanked by vertical ice-walls, appeared almost equally hopeless. In addition, the whole southern half of the mountain lay in Nepal and was therefore politically closed to them.

Only on the northeast did Mallory detect any possibilities whatever. Here bordering the ten-thousand-foot precipice of the north face, a jagged arête descended from a great rocky shoulder near the summit to a high snow saddle on the east of the Rongbuk Glacier. The angle of the arête was steep, but not so steep that experienced mountaineers could not ascend it, and from the shoulder upward the main east ridge and the wedge-like summit pyramid seemed to present no insuperable obstacles. The first great question mark was whether a way could be found to reach the saddle.

A way was found, but the finding required two long months of planning and toil. The saddle—or North Col, as it came to be known—rose from the Rongbuk Glacier as an almost perpendicular ice-wall 4000 feet high, and even the dauntless Mallory realized that it could never be scaled from that side. His only hope was that the far, or eastern, side might prove more feasible. The next and greatest job was to get there.

The Rongbuk Glacier was a narrow avenue of ice walled in by tremendous mountains in which no break appeared to exist. Actually there was a break, and if Mallory had found it he would have been able to reach the far side of the col in a day or two. But it was so tiny and obscure a passage that he missed it. The result was a circuitous journey of more than a hundred miles, back across the plateaus and passes which they had traversed before, and then south and west again toward the base of Everest.

This last stage of their journey took them through a mountain wonderland such as no man had ever been privileged to look upon before. The Kama and Kharta valleys, up which they pushed, were great gashes in the earth, so deep at their lower ends that their floors were covered with lush, tropical vegetation, so lofty at their apexes that the explorers found themselves struggling in snow up to their armpits. At their head loomed the mighty upper slopes of Everest, flanked by the pinnacles of Makalu, Chomolönzo and Lhotse, themselves among the highest summits in the world.

At last, after innumerable delays and hardships, the climbers reached the apex of the Kharta Valley—a wild blizzard-racked pass known as the Lhakpa La, 22,000 feet above the sea. From here they could see the long-sought eastern approach to the North Col, and it was indeed as Mallory had hoped: the great saddle of snow and ice rose on this side to a height of only 1500 feet above the glacier floor, as against 4000 feet on the Rongbuk side. It appeared not impossible to scale. A cheer went up from the lips of the frozen, exhausted men, for they knew they had found the key to the mountain.

By this time it was late August and the brief Himalayan summer was almost over. The work of the expedition, however, would not be done until they had reached the col, and so the three strongest climbers, Mallory, Bullock and Wheeler, pushed on over the Lhakpa La, down its far side and across the glacier below. On their way they made a second important discovery: that there was, after all, a passage from the Rongbuk Glacier to the eastern side of the col. It was of course too late now for it to be of any help to them that year, but the narrow defile was used by all subsequent Everest expeditions.

Once found, the eastern wall of the North Col did not prove a particularly formidable obstacle—at least not in 1921. The outer surface of the wall was composed of frozen avalanche snow, and up it the three climbers hacked their way, slanting carefully to right and left to avoid the gaping blue abysses with which it was scarred. At noon on the twenty-fourth of August they stood upon the top, at an altitude of 23,000 feet—higher than any mountain-top in the world outside of the Himalayas.

The pinnacle of Everest, however, was still 6000 feet above them and two and a half miles away. Scanning the northeast ridge, the shoulder and the summit pyramid, they saw that Mallory's earlier surmise had been right:

the upper mountain slanted upward in a fairly easy gradient of rock and snow, seeming to present neither difficulty nor great danger. The temptation was strong to venture still higher, but they were almost done in from their exertions as it was and realized they could not hope to match their strength against the wild wind and blizzards of the exposed heights. After taking as complete observations as they could they descended from the col, rejoined their companions on the Lhakpa La and began the long return journey to India.

The members of the 1921 expedition had never once actually set foot on Everest itself; their highest point on the North Col was where subsequent expeditions would begin their real work. Yet, except for the untimely death of Dr. Kellas, the venture had been a complete and distinguished success. The trail to the mountain had been blazed, the weakness in its armor found. Everyone was agreed that, as far as actual climbing problems were concerned, the greatest mountain *might* be climbed. That "might" was all the Everesters needed. No sooner had the reconnaissance party returned to England than preparations for the real assault began.

On May 1, 1922, the first Mount Everest climbing expedition pitched its base camp within sight of the great lamasery near the snout of the Rongbuk Glacier. It was composed of thirteen Englishmen, sixty hillmen from Nepal and northern India, a hundred-odd Tibetan helpers and more than three hundred pack animals—a veritable army in miniature. Remote and isolated Tibet had not witnessed such a sight in the thousands of years of its history.

In the preceding year the purpose had been to explore, reconnoitre and learn. Now, however, all else was to be subordinated to one great purpose: to reach the top of Everest. To this end, the personnel of the party had been almost completely changed, with only Mallory and Morshead remaining from the original group. The new leader was Brigadier-General Charles G. Bruce, a veteran of the British army in India and a far-ranging Himalayan explorer over a period of many years. Colonel E. T. Strutt, another noted mountaineer, was second in command, and Dr. T. E. Longstaff, although now too old for the highest climbing, was on hand to lend the benefit of his wide experience. The others included Lieutenant-Colonel E. F. Norton, Dr. T. Howard Somervell and Dr. Wakefield; Captains Geoffrey Bruce, George Finch and C. G. Morris; C. G. Crawford, of the India Civil Service; and, as official photographer, Captain John Noel. Of these, Norton, Somervell and Finch were climbers in the prime of their careers and were expected, together with Mallory, to make the final bid for the summit.

As we have repeatedly seen, the climbing of a great mountain is far more than a matter of putting one foot in front of the other and moving uphill. Indeed, in the case of a giant like Everest, climbing in itself may be said to be of merely secondary importance. Two-thirds of the 1922 expedition's battles had to be fought before a single man set foot on the mountain proper.

First, there was the all-important problem of weather. No man, to be sure, could hope to prophesy the day-by-day variations of calm and storm in those wild Himalayan uplands, but the observations of the previous year had convinced everyone concerned that Everest was climbable, if at all, only during a very brief period of the year. Until early May the whole region was locked in savage, blizzard-driven winter; after the middle of June the eastern Himalayas received the full brunt of the Indian monsoon and remained through the summer a death-trap of snow and sleet and rotten, melting ice. A period of only some six weeks intervened in which the climbers might hope for reasonably clear skies, a minimum of wind and at least a fighting chance for success. It was therefore not accident, but careful planning, that brought the 1922 expedition to the skirts of Everest on May first. Their next great task was to get onto the mountain itself as quickly as possible. The race with the monsoon was on.

For two long weeks climbers and porters crept back and forth along the vast northern glaciers, transporting food, supplies and equipment. Mallory, in an analysis of the problems of Everest, had likened a climbing expedition to a ladder, in which the higher rungs were useless unless the rungs below were dependable and strong. It was these lower rungs which now had to be fashioned—a chain of camps, not more than an easy day's march apart, extending as high as human strength could take them. Camp I was pitched between the Rongbuk and East Rongbuk Glaciers, in the narrow defile which Mallory had missed the previous year. Camp II was established halfway up the East Rongbuk Glacier, and Camp III near its head, close by the eastern wall of the North Col. The older and less acclimatized members of the party were left behind to staff and maintain communication between these lower stations, while the stronger climbers and porters proceeded to the establishment of Camp IV on top of the col.

This in itself was a feat more difficult than the ascent to the summit of a lesser mountain. Mallory and Somervell led the way, chopping countless steps in the glaring ice-cliffs, edging their way around bottomless, dark crevasses and snow-masses as vast as toppled buildings. The porters followed, straining on the ropes, scarcely more than creeping under their heavy loads. On their return to civilization the Everesters were unanimous in declaring that without these sturdy Sherpas from the hill country of northern India their assault on the mountain would have bogged down before it even began. Unlike the Tibetans, who refused even to set foot on Chomolungma, the haunted mountain, these men climbed doggedly and cheerfully to heights where no men had ever stood before and in 1924 achieved the almost incredible feat of carrying packs and establishing a camp at an altitude of more than 27,000 feet. "Tigers," the Englishmen called them, and they richly deserved the name.

With a huddle of tiny green tents established on the

col, the assault on Everest proper was at last at hand. Mallory, Somervell, Norton and Morshead were selected for the first attempt, and at dawn on May twentieth, accompanied by a group of the strongest porters, they set out for the unknown, untrodden heights. The cold was almost unendurable; the wild west wind roared down upon them like an invisible avalanche; and their goal was still a mile above them, remote and tantalizing in the sky. But their hopes and hearts were high. "No end," wrote Mallory, "was visible or even conceivable to this kingdom of adventure!"

Hour after hour the climbers toiled up the northeast ridge. The going underfoot was not technically difficult, but constant care was necessary to guard against a slip on the steep, ice-coated slabs. The wind tore at them relentlessly, and, worse yet, as they ascended it grew more difficult to breathe. Later expeditions were to learn an important lesson from their ordeal and allow themselves more time for acclimatization before storming the almost oxygen-less heights.

They had hoped to pitch their highest camp close under the northeast shoulder, but at 25,000 feet cold and exhaustion forced a halt. Sending their faithful "tigers" down to Camp IV they pitched their two tiny tents in as sheltered a spot as they could find and crawled into their sleeping bags. All night they lay there, while the wind howled and the mercury in their thermometers dropped to seven degrees above zero.

At first daylight they were moving upward again through thick mist and gusts of windblown snow. After an hour's climbing Morshead reached the limit of his endurance and had to turn back, but Mallory, Somervell and Norton still struggled on. Their progress consisted of fifteen or twenty minutes' slow, painful climbing, a long rest, another period of climbing, another rest. Before long their hands and feet grew numb and their mouths hung wide open, gasping for air. Even their minds and senses, they reported later, were affected by oxygen starvation: ambition, judgment and will disappeared, and they moved forward mechanically, like men in a trance.

By mid-afternoon they had reached a height of 27,000 feet. They had ascended two-thirds of the vertical distance between the North Col and the summit and were a full 2400 feet higher than any man had ever stood before. Physically they could have gone even farther, but to have done so at that late hour, without food or shelter, would have been suicidal. Too exhausted to feel disappointment, or any other emotion, they turned their backs on their goal and began the descent.

As it was they were lucky to return to their companions alive. At Camp V they found Morshead so crippled by frostbite that he had almost to be carried down to the col. Then, crossing a steep snow-slope lower down, one of them slipped, and the four were carried to the very brink of the precipitous north face before Mallory succeeded in jamming his ax into the snow and holding the rope fast.

As a crowning misfortune, night overtook them before they reached the col, and it was past midnight when at last they groped their way into their tents.

The same day that the first attempt ended in heroic failure, the second was launched. The climbers now were Finch, Geoffrey Bruce and Tejbir Bura, a Gurkha corporal who had proved himself a first-class mountaineer. Captain Noel ascended with them to the North Col camp, where he remained in reserve, and twelve porters set up a fifth camp for them at 25,500 feet—a full 500 feet higher than where Mallory and his companions had bivouacked a few nights before. This headstart for the final dash, added to the advantage that they were supplied with tanks of oxygen to aid their breathing, gave the second party high hopes of success.

They were hopes, however, that were to be quickly shattered. No sooner had Finch, Bruce and Tejbir crawled into their tent for the night than a blizzard swooped down upon the mountain. For more than twenty-four hours the wind shrieked, the snow drove down in an almost solid mass, and the climbers struggled desperately with ripping canvas and breaking guy-ropes. It was little less than a miracle that men, tent and all were not blown bodily off the mountain into the mile-deep gulfs below.

After two nights and a day the weather at last cleared, and the climbers made their delayed start in a still, frozen dawn. At 26,000 feet Tejbir collapsed and had to return to the tent, Finch and Bruce continuing. The oxygen which they carried spared them the tortures which their predecessors had endured, but this advantage was more than nullified by the thirty pounds of tank and apparatus which each carried on his back. Worse than this, Bruce's apparatus was almost the cause of his death, for without warning, at an altitude of about 26,500 feet, something went wrong with it and the flow of oxygen stopped. Accustomed by then to artificial breathing, Bruce would have been able to live for only a few minutes without it. Finch however, quickly connected Bruce's mouthpiece to his own tank, and betwen them they were able to make the necessary repairs.

Hoping to escape the full brunt of the wind, they left the northeast ridge a few hundred feet below the shoulder and headed diagonally upward across the smooth slabs and powdered snow of Everest's north face. They made remarkable progress and by midday had gained a point only half a mile from the summit and a scant 1900 feet below it. But here they reached the end of their tether. Their bodies and brains were numb; their limbs were ceasing to function and their eyes to focus; each additional foot upward would probably be a foot that they could never return. They turned back defeated, like their companions before them, but in defeat they had set a new world's climbing record of 27,235 feet.

One more attempt the expedition of 1922 was to make. It was doomed to be the most short-lived and disastrous one that has ever been made against the king of mountains.

The dreaded monsoon came early that year, and already

in the first days of June dark banks of clouds appeared above the mountains to the south and the snow fell in billowing drifts on the upper slopes of Everest. A final thrust, if it were to be made at all, must be made quickly.

The main base, at which the whole expedition now gathered, resembled a field hospital more than a mountaineers' camp; of the high climbers only Mallory and Somervell were fit for further work. Resolved on a last try, however, they again pushed up the glaciers and, with Crawford, Wakefield and a squad of porters helping, resumed the laborious task of packing supplies up to the North Col. A night of sub-zero temperature had apparently solidified the fresh snow on the great wall, and they had reason to believe the going would be comparatively easy.

Starting early one morning from Camp III, Mallory, Somervell, Crawford and fourteen heavily loaded porters began the ascent. The Englishmen were on one rope, cutting steps and leading the way; three roped groups of porters followed. All went well until they had reached a point some 600 feet below the summit of the col. Then suddenly they were startled by a deep, rumbling sound beneath them. An instant later there was a dull, ominous explosion, and the rampart of snow and ice to which they clung seemed to shudder along its entire face. An ocean of soft, billowing snow poured down upon them, knocked them from their feet and swept them away.

By miraculous good fortune, Mallory, Somervell and Crawford were not in the direct path of the avalanche.

Caught by its flank, they were carried down a distance of some fifty feet; but by striking out like swimmers they were at last able to struggle to the surface and gain a secure foothold. Not so the unfortunate porters. Struck by the full force of the snowslide, they were catapulted down the steep slope to the lip of a sheer ice-wall below. A moment before there had been a gaping crevasse beneath the wall; now it was filled by the avalanche. Hurtling over the brink, the porters plunged into the soft, hissing sea of snow, disappearing from sight one by one as thousands of more tons poured down after them.

Grim and heroic work was carried out on the ice-wall that day. Hour after hour the climbers floundered through the great drifts, burrowing, straining at ropes, expending their last reserve of strength to find and rescue the buried porters. One or two they found almost uninjured. A few more, who at first appeared dead from suffocation, they were able to revive. But seven were beyond help. To this day their bodies lie emtombed in the snow and ice beneath the North Col, tragic victims of the wrath of the greatest mountain.

So the 1922 attack on Everest ended, not only in defeat but in disaster. Any further attempt on the peak that year was unthinkable, and it was a silent, saddened band of mountaineers who, a few days later, began the long trek across Tibet toward India and home. Behind them the summit of the greatest mountain loomed white and lonely in the sky, its snow-plume streaming in the wild west wind.

The curtain drops for two years on Chomolungma, Goddess-Mother-of-the-World. No expedition was sent out in 1923, but the struggle was by no means at an end. The Mount Everest Committee continued with its work —planning, financing, organizing—and in late March of 1924 a third expedition set out from Darjeeling on the high, wild trail to the heart of the Himalayas. Before it returned it was destined to write the most famous chapter in the history of mountaineering.

Several of the old Everesters were back again in harness: the indefatigable Mallory, of course; Somervell, Norton and Geoffrey Bruce; Noel with his cameras. General Bruce had again been appointed leader, but early in the march through Tibet he was stricken with malaria and had to return to India while Norton carried on as first-in-command. New recruits included N. E. Odell, the geologist, who twelve years later was to reach the top of Nanda Devi; E. O. Shebbeare, of the Indian Forest Service, as transport officer; Major R. W. G. Hingston as physician; Beetham and Hazard, both experienced mountaineers, and Andrew Irvine, young and powerful Oxford oarsman. In addition to these were the usual retinue of native porters and helpers, among them many of the veteran "tigers" from the 1922 attempt. Almost three hundred men, all told, were in the party when at the end of April it set up its base camp beside the great moraines of the now familiar Rongbuk Glacier.

The preliminary moves of the campaign were carried out according to the same plan as before—but more methodically and rapidly. The first three advance camps were established a day's march apart on the glaciers, and within two weeks the advance guard was ready to tackle the North Col. The whole organization was functioning like an oiled machine; there were no accidents or illness, and the weather was fine. According to their schedule they would be on the northeast ridge by the middle of May and have almost a full month for climbing before the arrival of the monsoon. Even the most sceptical among them, staring eagerly at the heights above, could not but believe that Everest at last was theirs.

This time, however, misfortune struck even before they reached the mountain.

Scarcely had Camp III been set up below the col than a blizzard swept down from the north, wrecking everything in its path, turning camps and communication lines into a shambles. The porters, many of them caught unprepared and without adequate clothing or shelter, suffered terribly from exposure and exhaustion. Two of them died. The climbers, who were supposed to be conserving their energies for the great effort higher up, wore themselves out in their efforts to save men and supplies. Two weeks after the vanguard had left the base camp, full of strength and optimism, they were back again where they started, frostbitten, battered and fagged out.

A major blow had been dealt their chance for success, but the Everesters pulled in their belts and went at it again. The porters' drooping spirits were raised by a blessing from the Holy Lama of the Rongbuk Monastery, and a few days later a second assault was begun. At the beginning all went well, and the three glacier camps were reestablished and provisioned in short order. But trouble began again on the great ice-wall beneath the North Col. The storms and avalanches of two years had transformed the thousand-foot face into a wild slanting chaos of cliffs and chasms. No vestige of their former route remained.

Then followed days of killing labor. Thousands of steps had to be chopped in the ice and snow. An almost perpendicular chimney, a hundred feet high, had to be negotiated. Ladders and ropes had to be installed so that the porters could come up with their loads. There were many narrow escapes from disaster, notably on one occasion when Mallory, descending the wall alone, plunged through a snow-bridge into a gaping hole beneath. Luckily his ice-ax jammed against the sides of the crevasse after he had fallen only ten feet, for below him was only blue-black space. As it was, his companions were all too far away to hear his shouts for help and he was barely able to claw his way upward to the surface snow and safety.

At last, however, the route up the wall was completed. The body of climbers retired to Camp III, at its foot, for a much-needed rest, leaving Hazard and twelve porters in the newly established camp on the col. During the night the mercury fell to twenty-four below zero and at dawn a heavy snowfall began; but Geoffrey Bruce and Odell nevertheless decided to ascend to the col. They did not get far. Halfway up they encountered Hazard and eight of the porters coming down. They were near collapse after the night of frightful cold and wind on the exposed col. Worse yet, four of the porters were still up above, having absolutely refused to budge downward over the treacherous fresh snow of the chimney.

A sombre council of war ensued at Camp III. Snow and wind were now driving down the mountain in wild blasts, and it was obvious that the marooned men could not survive for long. All plans had to be set aside and every effort devoted to getting them down.

What follows constitutes one of the most remarkable and courageous rescues in mountaineering annals. Mallory, Norton and Somervell, the three outstanding climbers of the expedition, fought their way up the ice-wall and came out at last upon a steep snow-slope a short distance below the top and immediately above a gaping crevasse. At the top of the slope the porters huddled, half-dead from exposure, but afraid to move. The snow between them and the rescuing party was loose and powdery, liable to crumble away at any moment.

At this point Somervell insisted on taking the lead. Roping up, he crept toward the porters along the upper lip of the crevasse, while Mallory and Norton payed out behind him. But the rope's two hundred feet were not enough; when he had reached its end he was still ten yards short of the men. There was nothing for it but that they must risk the unbridged stretch on their own. After long persuasion two of them began edging across. And made it. Somervell passed them along the rope to Mallory and Norton. Then the other two started over, but at their first step the snow gave way and they began sliding toward the abyss below. Only a patch of solid snow saved them. They brought up at the very edge of the crevasse, gasping, shaken, unable to move an inch.

Now Somervell called into action all his superb talents as a mountaineer. He jammed his ice-ax into the snow and, untying the rope from his waist, passed it around the ax and strained it to its fullest length. Then he lowered himself down the slope until he was clinging to its last strands with one hand. With the other he reached out and, while the snow shuddered ominously underfoot, seized each porter in turn by the scruff of the neck and hauled him up to safety. Within a few hours climbers and porters were back in Camp III, all of them still alive, but little more.

After this harrowing experience a few days' rest at lower altitudes was absolutely necessary, and for the second time in two weeks the Everesters found themselves driven back to the base camp. Their situation could scarcely have been more discouraging. They had planned to be on the northeast ridge by the middle of May, and now it was already June and no man had yet set foot on the mountain proper. In another ten days, at most, the monsoon would blow in and all hope of success would be gone. They must strike hard and strike fast, or go down again to defeat.

The next week witnessed climbing such as the world had never seen before.

The plan called for an assault in continuous waves,

each climbing party consisting of two men, each attempt to begin the day after the preceding one. The base of operations was to be Camp IV on the North Col. Camp V was to be set up on the ridge, near the site of the 1922 bivouac, and a sixth camp higher yet—as near to the summit as the porters could possibly take it. The climbers believed that the establishment of Camp VI was the key to the ascent; the experiences of the previous expedition had convinced them that the top could be reached only if the final "dash" were reduced to not more than 2000 feet. In the first fine weather they had experienced in weeks the band of determined men struggled back up the glaciers.

Mallory and Geoffrey Bruce were chosen for the first attack. With Odell, Irvine and nine porters they reached the North Col safely, spent the night there, and the next morning struck out up the ridge, accompanied by eight of the "tigers." Odell, Irvine and one helper remained on the col in support. The climbers made good progress the first day and set up their tents at 25,300 feet—a mere 200 feet lower than the highest camp of 1922. A night of zero cold and shrieking wind, however, was too much for the porters, and the next morning no amount of persuasion would induce them to go higher. Seething with frustration, Mallory and Bruce were forced to descend with them.

Meanwhile the second team of Norton and Somervell, had started up from the col, according to plan. They passed the first party on its way down, reached Camp V and spent the night there. In the morning their porters, too, refused at first to go on, but after four solid hours of urging three of them at least agreed to make a try. The work they subsequently did that day has seldom been matched anywhere for endurance, courage and loyalty. Step by gasping step they struggled upward with their packs—freezing, leaden-footed, choking for air—until at last Camp VI was pitched at the amazing altitude of 26,-800 feet. Their task completed, they then descended to the North Col, to be hailed as heroes by all below: Lhakpa Chede, Napoo Yishay and Semchumbi, greatest of all "tigers."

That night Norton and Somervell slept in a single tiny tent, higher than men had ever slept before. Their hearts now were pounding with more than the mere physical strain of their exertions: the long-dreamed summit loomed in the darkness only 2300 feet above them; victory was at last within their reach. Carefully, for the hundredth time, they reviewed their plans for the final day. There were two opinions in the expedition as to the best route to be followed. Mallory and some of the others were in favor of ascending straight to the northeast shoulder and then following the crest of the main east ridge to the base of the summit pyramid. Norton and Somervell, however, believed that by keeping a few hundred feet below the ridge they would not only find easier climbing, but also escape the full fury of the west wind; and it was this route that they now determined to take.

Dawn of the next day broke clear and still. By full sunrise they were on their way, creeping upward and to the west over steeply tilted, snow-powdered slabs. As they had hoped, they were protected from the wind, but the cold was bitter and both men coughed and gasped in the thin, freezing air. They could take only a dozen steps in succession before pausing to rest. While moving, they were forced to take from four to ten breaths for each single step. Yet they kept going for five hours: to 27,000 feet—27,500—28,000—

At noon Somervell succumbed. His throat was a throbbing knot of pain and it was only by the most violent effort that he was able to breathe at all. Another few minutes of the ordeal would have been the end of him. Sinking down on a small ledge in a paroxysm of coughing, he gestured to his companion to go on alone.

With the last ounce of his strength Norton tried. An hour's climbing brought him to a great couloir, or gully, which cuts the upper slopes of Everest between the summit pyramid and the precipices of the north face below. The couloir was filled with soft, loose snow, and a slip would have meant a 10,000-foot plunge to the Rongbuk Glacier. Norton crossed it safely, but, clinging feebly to the ledges on the far side, he knew that the game was up. His head and heart were pounding as if any moment they might literally explode. In addition, he had begun to see double, and his leaden feet would no longer move where his will directed them. In his clouded consciousness he was just able to realize that to climb farther would be to die.

For a few moments Norton stood motionless. He was at an altitude of 28,126 feet—higher than any man had ever stood before; so high that the greatest mountain range on earth, spreading endlessly to the horizon, seemed flattened out beneath him. Only a few yards above him began the culminating pyramid of Everest. To his aching eyes it seemed to present an easy slope—a mere thousand feet of almost snow-free slanting rock beckoning him upward to the shining goal. If only his body possessed the strength of his will; if only he were more than human—

Somehow Norton and Somervell got down the terrible slopes of Everest. By nine-thirty that night they were back in the North Col camp in the ministering hands of their companions, safe, but more dead than alive. Somervell was a seriously sick man. Norton was suffering the tortures of snow-blindness and did not regain his sight for several days. Both had given all they had. That it was not enough is surely no reflection on two of the most determined and courageous mountaineers who ever lived.

Norton and Somervell's assault was the next-to-last in the adventure of 1924. One more was to come—and, with it, mystery and tragedy.

Bitterly chagrined at the failure of his first effort, Mallory was determined to have one last fling before the monsoon struck. Everest was *his* mountain, more than any other man's. He had pioneered the way to it and blazed the trail to its heights; his flaming spirit had been the principal driving force behind each assault; the conquest of the summit was the great dream of his life. His companions, watching him now, realized that he was preparing for his mightiest effort.

Mallory moved with characteristic speed. With young Andrew Irvine as a partner he started upward from the col the day after Norton and Somervell had descended. They spent the first night at Camp V and the second at Camp VI, at 26,800 feet. Unlike Norton and Somervell, they planned to use oxygen on the final dash and to follow the crest of the northeast ridge instead of traversing the north face to the couloir. The ridge appeared to present more formidable climbing difficulties than the lower route, particularly near the base of the summit pyramid where it buckled upward in two great rock-towers which the Everesters called the First and Second Steps. Mallory, however, was all for the frontal attack and had frequently expressed the belief that the steps could be surmounted. The last "tigers" descending that night from the highest camp to the col brought word that both climbers were in good condition and full of hope for success.

One man only was to have another glimpse of Mallory and Irvine.

On the morning of June eighth—the day set for the assault on the summit—Odell, the geologist, who had spent the night alone at Camp V, set out for Camp VI with a rucksack of food. The day was as warm and windless as any the expedition had experienced, but a thin gray mist clung to the upper reaches of the mountain, and Odell could see little of what lay above him. Presently, however, he scaled the top of a small crag at about

26,000 feet, and, standing there, he stopped and stared. For a moment the mist cleared. The whole summit ridge and final pyramid of Everest were unveiled, and high above him, on the very crest of the ridge, he saw two tiny figures outlined against the sky. They appeared to be at the base of one of the great steps, not more than seven or eight hundred feet below the final pinnacle. As Odell watched, the figures moved slowly upward. Then, as suddenly as it had parted, the mist closed in again, and they were gone.

The feats of endurance that Odell performed during the next forty-eight hours are unsurpassed by those of any mountaineer. That same day he went to Camp VI with his load of provisions, and then even higher, watching and waiting. But the mountain-top remained veiled in mist and there was no sign of the climbers returning. As night came on, he descended all the way to the col, only to start off again the following dawn. Camp V was empty. He spent a solitary night there in sub-zero cold and the next morning ascended again to Camp VI. It was empty too. With sinking heart he struggled upward for another thousand feet, searching and shouting, to the very limit of human endurance. The only answering sound was the deep moaning of the wind. The great peak above him loomed bleakly in the sky, wrapped in the loneliness and desolation of the ages. All hope was gone. Odell descended to the highest camp and signalled the tidings of tragedy to the watchers far below.

So ended the second attempt on Everest—and, with it,

the lives of two brave men. The bodies of George Mallory and Andrew Irvine lie somewhere in the vast wilderness of rock and ice that guards the summit of the world. Where and how death overtook them no one knows. And whether victory came before the end no one knows either. Our last glimpse of them is through Odell's eyes—two tiny specks against the sky, fighting upward.

The rest is mystery.

The story of Everest from 1924 onward continues as it began. The greatest mountain still works its magic on the imaginations of men, and the fight for its conquest goes on. Again and again, through the 'thirties, bands of brave and determined climbers have come to challenge it, struggling through the passes and gorges of the Himalayas, penetrating its inner fastnesses along the great glaciers, storming the North Col, creeping doggedly upward through wind and blizzard and avalanche. Each successive expedition has added something to the store of man's knowledge. Some have performed feats of unexcelled skill and endurance. But every one has failed of its goal. All the determination of the human spirit, all the ingenuity of science, have not yet been able to get a man up the final thousand feet of that gleaming, snow-plumed summit—and down.

For nine years after the 1924 assault no climbers approached Everest. Tibet again closed its gates rigidly to white men, and it was not until 1933 that permission was once more granted for an expedition to try its luck. By this time most of the veterans of the previous attempts were too old for another ordeal on the mountain, but a capable team of younger climbers was assembled by the Mount Everest Committee. The new leader was Hugh Ruttledge, an experienced Himalayan climber. Among the others were Frank S. Smythe, Eric Shipton and Captain Birnie, whom we have met on Kamet, Kanchenjunga and elsewhere; Wyn Harris, L. R. Wager, J. L. Longland and T. A. Brocklebank—most of them still in their twenties, but all among the most capable mountaineers of their generation.

Following the by now traditional route, the 1933 party battled its way along the glaciers, up the ice-wall to the North Col, and established its higher camps close to the northeast ridge. From Camp VI, at 27,400 feet—600 feet above the highest previous bivouac—two successive assaults were made on the summit. The first, by Harris and Wager, carried across the brow of the north face to the far side of the great couloir and ended, with both men near collapse, at almost the identical spot at which Norton had turned back nine years before. The second, by Shipton and Smythe, got no farther. Shipton succumbed to the effects of altitude soon after leaving Camp VI, and was forced to descend, while Smythe, struggling on alone, reached the end of his endurance just beyond the couloir, as had the others before him. It seemed almost as if Everest were ringed by a magic wall a thousand feet beneath the summit, beyond which no man could venture and live.

A dramatic discovery was made by Harris and Wager

an hour's climb above Camp VI. On the tilted slabs just below the summit ridge they came suddenly upon a solitary, rusted ice-ax. The name of the Swiss maker, still plainly stamped on its head, left no possibility of doubt as to how it had come there: it was either Mallory's or Irvine's. Some mountaineers have claimed this to be an indication that Mallory and Irvine reached the top. Odell, they argue, saw them at a point much farther along the ridge, neither climber, presumably, would have attempted to go on without his ax, and the logical supposition, therefore, is that it was dropped in an accident on the way down. Others merely shrug their shoulders. Whatever one chooses to believe, there is no proof. The ax is no more than a tantalizing hint at the fate of the lost climbers.

The 1933 Everesters were favored by no better weather than their predecessors. Immediately after Smythe and Shipton's "all out" attempt, the monsoon struck in a fury of blizzards and all further climbing was out of the question. The expedition had accomplished notable work and suffered not a single fatality or serious accident. But the world's climbing record was still 28,126 feet, and Everest was still 29,141 feet high.

For many years men had looked longingly upward at the summit of the highest mountain. Now, in the same year as the third climbing expedition, men were to look *down* upon it.

Almost since the beginning of aviation airmen had been

considering the possibilities of a flight over Everest, and in April of 1933 the first attempt was made. It was completely successful. Under the leadership of the Marquis of Clydesdale (now the Duke of Hamilton) and Air-commodore Fellowes of the Royal Air Force two specially designed planes took off from Purnea, in northern India, and reached the peak in a mere hour. A treacherous down-current of wind almost crashed them against the slopes of the summit pyramid, but at the last moment they succeeded in gaining sufficient altitude to clear it. Then, fortunately, the weather improved, and they spent the next fifteen minutes circling the pinnacle, making observations and taking close-range photographs. In another hour they were safely back at their airport.

A remarkable flying achievement in itself, the flight was of importance to mountaineers chiefly in that it confirmed their belief that the topmost thousand feet of Everest did not present impossible climbing difficulties—provided a human being could reach them with any strength or breath left in his body. The highest pinnacle, viewed from above, was a gentle crest of white, wind-blown snow. No human relic could be seen.

The year 1934 saw only one short-lived attempt on the mountain—an attempt so foolhardy and hopeless that it appears less an actual climbing venture than an elaborate suicide. The would-be climber was Maurice Wilson, an English aviator who had never been on a high peak in his life. Like the ill-fated Farmer on Kanchenjunga, he smuggled himself into the forbidden regions of the Himalayas, hired a handful of natives to pack his supplies and launched a one-man assault on the mountain. Somehow he succeeded in struggling up the glaciers, but cold and exhaustion caught up with him below the ice-cliffs of the North Col. His body was discovered and buried the following spring.

In 1935 and 1936 the real Everesters returned to the wars. Because of long delays in gaining the sanction of the Tibetan government only a reconnaissance was undertaken the first year,* but in late April of '36 a full-fledged climbing party was once more at the Rongbuk base camp, ready for battle. Ruttledge was again the leader, and the climbing personnel was virtually the same as in 1933.

The earlier expeditions had had bad luck with the weather; this one had no luck at all. Wind-storms, blizzards and avalanches thundered down upon them from the first day on, and—crowning blow—the monsoon blew up from the south a full month earlier than expected. After a few hairbreadth escapes on the crumbling death-trap of the North Col, the climbers were forced to withdraw without having even set foot on the mountain itself.

In 1938 came still another expedition—the seventh and, to date, the last. The leadership had passed on to H. W. Tilman, of Nanda Devi fame, but several of the old guard were again on hand—notably Smythe, Shipton

* The 1935 expedition, however, performed many remarkable feats, among them the ascent of more peaks of over 22,000 feet than had ever been climbed before.

and the veteran Odell, now well on into middle age yet back for another try after fourteen years.

The venture was favored by slightly better weather than its predecessors. The North Col was reached in short order, the northeast ridge ascended, and Camp VI pitched at 27,000 feet. Beyond it, however, the climbers came up against the same invincible defenses that had defeated every previous effort; and with the same result. Two summit assaults were launched—the first by the old team of Smythe and Shipton, the second by Tilman and young Peter Lloyd, who had climbed with him on Nanda Devi. In each case, however, the climbers were turned back short of the final pyramid by exhaustion, oncoming darkness and the slanting, snow-powdered slabs of the north face. Then before they could reorganize their forces for still another try, the monsoon struck, putting an end to their hopes.

So stands the fight for Everest up to the present time. Seven great expeditions have come and challenged, struggled and failed. Many brave men, white and brown, have lost their lives. And the summit of the greatest mountain still soars into the sky, untouched and unconquered.

What will happen in the years to come, no man knows. Much has been learned from experience; still many "ifs" and "buts" remain. In general, however, future expeditions will be confronted with the same factors and problems as those of the past. Briefly these are:

1. *Weather*—Except for a few weeks in the late spring

and early fall Everest is unapproachable. Any attempt during a spring in which the monsoon arrives early will be doomed to failure. Some mountaineers believe that an attempt should be made in the fall, after the monsoon and before winter sets in, but this has not yet been tried.

2. *Transport and supplies*—The climbers must obviously be well fed, sheltered and equipped. This involves the packing of vast quantities of supplies over hundreds of miles of wild, mountainous country, and an elaborate and effective transportation system is essential. It has been suggested that a system of pulleys and conveyors might be established on the ice-wall below the North Col, to hoist loads up this particularly difficult stretch. Most mountaineers, however, are opposed on principle to artificial aids of this sort.

3. *Porters*—The most ingenious system of transport is useless without the proper quantity and quality of man power. Thanks to the earlier expeditions, a corps of first-class, trained "tigers" is now available, and less difficulty should be experienced with porters in the future than has been the case in the past. All Everesters agree that the higher the advanced camps are pitched, the better the chances for success. The establishment of these camps depends almost entirely on the spirit and endurance of the porters.

4. *Climbing personnel*—The conquest of Everest cannot be achieved by any individual, however skilled and daring. An expedition must function harmoniously, as a unit, with the ambitions and wishes of each man subordi-

nated to the welfare of the whole. The party should be neither so large as to be unwieldy, nor so small that the illness or injury of one or two members would ruin the entire undertaking.

5. *Acclimatization*—Experience has shown that men can live and move at a height of more than 28,000 feet. Before they can do this, however, they must have a period for acclimatization, in which their lungs and hearts become accustomed to functioning at increasingly higher altitudes. On the other hand, it has been found that if a man spends too long a period at high altitudes severe bodily deterioration sets in. Individuals vary greatly in the degree and speed of acclimatization.

6. *Oxygen*—Some Everesters have found oxygen a great help to them on the heights, others consider it worse than useless. All agree that no satisfactory apparatus—sufficiently light and yet dependable—has yet been devised. The conquest of the summit will be a more noteworthy triumph if it can be made without artificial aids.

7. *Route*—Every Everest expedition to date has attacked the peak by way of the East Rongbuk Glacier, the North Col and the northeast ridge. On the basis of present knowledge, this still appears to be the only practicable approach. On the upper mountain, most mountaineers favor Norton's route across the north face to the great couloir as against Mallory's route along the summit edge.

8. *Political considerations*—Last but not least, there is the problem of even gaining *permission* to attack Everest. To date, the Tibetan government has granted permission

infrequently, and then only to expeditions of all-English personnel. It is to be hoped that in the future these restrictions will be modified, so that climbers of other nations may have their chance at the mountain.

A formidable array of problems and obstacles! Yet, in spite of all of them and a hundred more, the fight for Everest will go on. When and how the mountain will be climbed is the secret of the future, but that it *will* be climbed is sure—as sure as that the oceans have been crossed, the continents spanned, the poles discovered. Perhaps the victory will be won on the next attempt, perhaps not for generations. But still men will come, and more men, and at last the day will come when the weather is right and the mountain is right and the men are right, and those men will get to the top.

Meanwhile, there is something better than victory—something that should make us almost thankful that the summit of the world has not yet been trodden by the foot of man. For until that happens Everest is more than the highest mountain. It is one of the great unfinished adventures of mankind.

*Knapsack of Salvation**

by Wolfgang Langewiesche

WOLFGANG LANGEWIESCHE *was one of those men born to fly. Although his pay as a teacher was small, he saved every penny for flying lessons and knew no joy like that of his first solo flight. It was in pursuit of money for flying time that he made his first parachute jump, the experience he describes with vividness and humor. Probably the days of such rash jumps are over since mass training and jumping in the past war have given to men the skill and knowledge which make the parachute an instrument rather than an unknown quantity. However, no matter how careful his training, every man has to jump the first time. Langewiesche has captured here both for the person who hasn't jumped and the one who has the sensations of a first jump out into the blue with only a frail canopy of cloth between life and death. "Knapsack of Salvation" is from his* I'll Take the High Road.

ONE DAY that summer, the Airport grapevine had news for me. A fellow named Barnes was making certain inquiries around the field. He was an operator and did a small business in sight-seeing hops on Sundays at some small flying field in the Sunday motoring country. It seemed that he wanted to have a parachute jump every Sunday. He hoped a parachute jump would help to attract a crowd to which his barker could then sell rides. As payment he was offering the jumper a block of Time on one of his ships.

"I wonder if it would open?" I thought.

Remember, this was several years ago. Mass parachute jumps were still in the future. It didn't seem likely that things would come to an end, but it seemed possible.

I went to George. George said no, he wouldn't touch the thing; in an emergency, perhaps; but he thought even then he would probably prefer to ride his ship down and take his chances. He guessed that it would open all right; what worried him, he said, was the landing. You might come down into a river or a high tension wire and even if you didn't you were as likely as not to break a leg or a hip bone. A proposition for circus men, he said, but altogether too risky for a pilot. He was in no way advising me to do it.

I cornered Barnes. Barnes kept his ships in Hangar 3. He had the usual equipment, a biplane trainer and a cabin ship; the latter was a six-seater. He turned out to be the fellow who always wore a get-up halfway between a yachtsman and an airline pilot; blue pants and jacket and a cap. His cabin ship bore a large inscription: "Barnes Airways, Los Angeles—Chicago—New York," which was meaningless except that it allowed back country yokels to think they were riding in a Giant Airliner.

Barnes proved amenable enough.

At that time, parachute jumps were no longer worth much. In cash they were worth perhaps fifteen dollars a jump, with perhaps a ten-dollar bonus for landing exactly in front of the spectators. Usually, in fact, they were worth whatever the jumper could afterwards collect in his hat. But Barnes, just like everybody around the Airport, was short of cash; I believe he was a little shorter of it than most of us. The only thing he had plenty of was Time.

As I have already explained, the flying rates we students paid included a large share of clear profit and/or reserve against accidents. Beyond that, when you looked into airport economics, you found that a big part of the costs of operating an airplane fell due only after several hundred hours of flight, at the time when ship and engine must be "majored," i.e., more or less completely rebuilt. The actual, immediate cash expenses of taking a fifteen-dollar-an-hour ship into the air were only about three dollars an hour.

Thus, I made a good agreement: three hours of ship Time per jump, and two hours extra if I landed in front of the spectators. But there was one condition. Barnes had recently been in trouble with the Government inspectors for overloading his ship with passengers. He was afraid he might get into trouble again in case something went wrong with one of my jumps. I was to make a practice jump in some other way first, so that I could technically be rated as experienced.

He who says A, must also say B. If I wanted to do cross-country flying, the thing to do was to learn how to handle a parachute.

Parachutes are special stuff—in a class with sharks, snakes, poisons, drugs.

Miller and Johnson, Parachute Service, lived inconspicuously in the rear of Hangar 3 in a small workshop. When one wanted to practice tail spins or acrobatics, air law prescribed that 'chutes must be worn and one rented a 'chute from Miller and Johnson at a dollar an hour. It was understood that in case one should actually use it, one would owe them ten dollars additional for inspection, repairs, and repacking. Air law also prescribed that a parachute must have been opened, inspected, and repacked by a licensed rigger within at least sixty days "prior to being worn in flight"—which provided them with a steady stream of jobs of repacking such 'chutes as were privately owned.

Their advertising notices were posted in every hangar:

> If given the proper care, parachutes will last for many years, but it has been our experience that many parachutes have been ruined through neglect, due to being stored in damp places, not being aired out at regular intervals, or allowed to remain in pack over sixty days. If they are neglected, the silk as well as harness will deteriorate rapidly and as your life may depend on the complete functioning of your parachute as regards both material and packing, surely you cannot afford to take a chance on a parachute failure due to your negligence.

And it warned of certain highly technical faults possible in parachute packing, known as "twisted lines" or "thrown lines," which would prevent the 'chute from properly opening even after the pack had been ripped open and the silk was stringing out behind the jumper; an event which, according to Miller and Johnson's restrained language, created embarrassment for the user.

One of the peculiar things about parachutes was that whether one bought them or rented them, one always had to buy a pig in a poke. The working depended entirely upon their having been properly packed, but if you had opened them to look, you would have undone the whole job and would have had to pay three dollars for repacking, and then, unless you had opened them again, you would again not have been quite sure. That is why in American airport lore there was the story of a pilot who bought a parachute secondhand and sat on it during many hours and trusted it, and then after sixty days opened it and found that its inside was not a silk canopy, but a batch of old newspapers.

But not Miller and Johnson's parachutes. Miller and Johnson were reputed to be good honest people. I went to talk to them, in confidence.

At their workshop, only their old assistant was in. Miller and Johnson themselves were out in the country on a jump, whatever that meant. He took down my request and promised not to talk about it at the Airport, for I had to think of my reputation as a steady and reasonable pilot of good judgment. He said they would write me an offer, and the next morning in my mail, it came.

It was a glimpse into a side of flying which I had not known existed at all, let alone at our modernistic Metropolitan Airport; only two hangars away from George, cold-blooded, reasonable George Adams: the world of the air circus.

The letter was three-quarters advertising. At the top and on both margins was crowded the following copy:

MILLER & JOHNSON PARACHUTE CO.

Balloons, parachutes, harness, safety belts, rope ladders, aerial apparatus for performers.

Special parachutes for the landing of freight, express, mail.

Experimental work, drop testing.

Reliable service men and performers from the far north to the tropics, from coast to coast.

Parachute leaps furnished from airplanes and balloons.

Fair Secretaries, Park Managers, Airport Operators, Carnivals, Celebration Committees, Lodges, and Campaign Managers consult us for prices on this 100% Crowd-Pulling Feature. A real treat to Young America. Operating in compliance with Air Commerce Laws of the U. S. A.

The letter itself said:

DEAR SIR:

Replying to your enquiry, advise that we frequently break in new men on parachute jumping, and if you are physically fit, will give you your first jump for $30 and $20 per jump thereafter, at the local airport here, Dept. of Commerce approved type parachute for the pilot, his service, airplane, and our service truck with licensed rigger in charge.

Two or three days' notice is necessary and the jump would be held in private, just before sundown, as we do not commercialize on jumps of this nature.

Awaiting your further reaction, and hoping you will get in touch with us, remain

Yours truly

MILLER & JOHNSON.

P.S. This proposition is subject to cancellation after we look you over, but from the information given to our rigger, believe we can O.K. your case.

Then a final burst of advertising:

SUPER SPECIAL. DIAVOLO: *braving death in its most horrible form;* allows himself to be ejected from a roaring cannon suspended from an especially constructed monster balloon—returning to earth with a parachute—leaving the spectators breathless at the sight of his recklessness. DIAVOLO also leaps from airplanes at dizzy heights, using bat wings and two parachutes.

Death in its most horrible form, I thought; you mean if it doesn't open, you pancake. Or rather, you burst. People are supposed to turn out practically liquid; except the skull. But you needn't be so outspoken about it. You are saying the right thing to the wrong party. I am not the looking kind of customer, but the jumping kind. You ought to have two different letterheads.

My further reaction? I got in touch.

Miller and Johnson turned out to be two grizzled men in their fifties. There was nothing in their appearance to connect them with the circus, or with airmanship, for that matter; if was more like being measured for a new suit at the tailor's. We fixed the third day from then for the jump, weather permitting, and they went to work immediately selecting the 'chute and fitting the shoulder straps and leg straps and chest straps of the harness. The 'chute itself was not the usual seat pack type, but was worn knapsackwise; that was to make it easier for the jumper to climb out of the ship deliberately without doing damage. Carried that way, it was heavy, and that was reassuring; it made you feel that at least you wouldn't have to jump off there defenseless.

"Now, when you pull the ripcord," began Miller, "don't be gentle about it."

"Give it all you've got," said Johnson. "Yank the— ——— right out."

"You bet I will," said I.

The ripcord ring was painted red; it looked much like the emergency brake in continental railroad cars and, under the circumstances, that carried a pleasant suggestion.

When your inner man complains and wants to put his trust in something, there is nothing quite as suitable as a gadget. The gadget will presumably work, while the same thing cannot always be said of one's intelligence or of one's own nerve, or of the grace of God.

Then came the second 'chute. Air law says two 'chutes must be worn on "intentional jumps." The second one was only a small one, eighteen feet in diameter. If I should have to use it, Johnson said, it would bring me down "awful fast." It was worn on the stomach, buckled onto the harness of the first one. When it hung, it acted as a counterweight to the first one, and made you feel like a pack horse.

But all to the good; as far as I was concerned, the more gadgets, the better.

"Now when you take off—" said Miller (what an elegant circumlocution, I thought, for letting yourself fall from an airplane) "now when you take off, the main thing to remember is not to pull too soon. It is as much as your life is worth." And he explained how the 'chute might get fouled in the ship's tail and throw the ship out of control; the pilot, he said, was going to wear a 'chute himself, that being another legal requirement and would jump. But I would get killed.

Johnson had a story to reinforce that. Some years ago,

some dizzy heiress had tried to jump and had caught in the ship's tail. By the grace of God, her 'chute had caught in such a manner that the ship was not thrown out of control, and it had plenty of fuel; but she had dangled there under the ship's tail for two hours. One had heard her from the ground, crying out pitifully above the ship's noise. Men had tried to reach her by rope ladder from another airplane and to let a knife down to her by rope, but to no avail. The pilot had tried to shake her loose by stunting, but with her weight and resistance on the tail, he hadn't been able to shake the ship much. They had considered landing the ship on water, but decided that it wouldn't improve her chances. And when it finally seemed that she must surely be killed as soon as the ship ran out of fuel, her 'chute had by pure chance come loose, and she had come down O.K.

Miller said I was to take off in a shallow dive, away from the ship—"the way you dive into a swimming pool." That way, he said, I would fall face downward, and would pull the cord in that position, and the canopy would be free to string out nicely behind me. That was a new one. Wouldn't a parachute open in any position? Johnson said yes, absolutely in any position, but smoothest that way. But he thought if I pulled in any other position, it would be just as well to keep my legs together and pulled up against the body in a crouching position, so the 'chute wouldn't get caught between them. Miller started to emphasize again how important it was to wait and clear the tail of the ship. "Don't worry, though," said Johnson, "the pilot has done this job many times; he will kick the tail out of your way."

I asked how long I should count before pulling. Miller said not to count at all. "A man can count so goddam fast." He said it was better to use my own judgment and to wait until I had fallen clear.

"After all," said Johnson, "you are a pilot, you are used to the air; you won't be nervous."

"Not much!" I thought.

Johnson advised me to have my hand on the ripcord before I even jumped. Miller had some parachute lore to cover that point. Some fellows got excited and couldn't find the ripcord, and went clutching for it all over themselves in a panic before they could find it. "Like this," said Johnson and started emitting guttural sounds of horror and clutching at the air, with a facial expression that was most convincing. Both of them laughed heartily.

Johnson had a companion story of a case where a newspaper writer had tried a jump. He hadn't trusted himself to keep his wits about him, and so his rigger had tied a long string to the ripcord, and had gone up with him in the ship to do the pulling himself after the writer would have fallen deep enough—which was, said Miller, more or less the system of parachute that had been in use before 1919 and the invention of the self-pulled ripcord: a line connecting the jumper and the aircraft and jerking out the 'chute. But it had often failed to work. Instead, the man had got tangled up in the string, and jerked it out of the rigger's hand, and being entangled, had then been unable to pull the cord himself; he had fallen straight down like a stone.

Between them they discussed an expedient sometimes used for breaking-in new jumpers: tie one corner of a handkerchief around the ripcord, tie the other corner into a knot, and have the jumper hold the knot with his teeth. A man always knows where his mouth is, said Miller. But it sometimes happened, said Johnson, that the jumper in his excitement pulled out all his front teeth before he pulled out his ripcord.

"Now when you land," said Johnson, "just go limp. Never mind if it rolls you over a few times. Just go limp."

Miller said, "Now don't worry about the landing. If you come down on the field we will be under you anyway."

It had been decided that I should jump into an abandoned flying field, near the state fair grounds, five miles from the Metropolitan Airport.

"But, of course, it is hard to judge," said Johnson. This year they had bad luck—their last man had fallen into a canal, and the man before him had landed on the roof of the grandstand and had broken a leg.

The three days before the jump were like the last days of a school vacation when one's forward perspective in time used to be completely shut off. The third day was fine; there was no storm; there was no high wind. At five I went to the Airport.

Miller and Johnson were waiting. First of all there

was a little thing to sign, all typed out for me. I, my heirs, executors, administrators, and assigns would make no fuss, whatever happened.

Then there was a long pause while we waited for their pilot. Miller sat on the workbench, and Johnson just stood around, watching the sun come down. I looked over the ships in this hangar. I didn't feel like talking. If the thing worked, there would be lots of time to talk afterwards; if it didn't, talking would be pointless.

The pilot came, looked me over in passing but said nothing. He grabbed a 'chute from the shelf, went out and started his engine. And they began to dress me up, goggles and 'chutes.

We filed out of the hangar, Miller ahead, Johnson behind me, not unlike a condemned man's walk to the chair.

At this moment, my whole past life flashed through my mind—it really did. This way: was there any evidence of mental disorder? There was the time when I wanted to quit school; there was the matter of the forgotten address; there was the fact that at parties I get moody and contrary; but all that wasn't convincing. Had it perhaps broken out suddenly? Rapidly, I ran through uncles and aunts; no insanity in the family.

I seemed to be sane.

"Just a moment," Johnson said, and took me aside. "Want to pay us now?" I couldn't get at my pocket past all the harness. We went in again. He unbuckled me, and we settled. He buckled me up again, and we went out.

Miller and the old assistant started up the truck to drive to the fair grounds and be under me when I landed.

Johnson thought of another thing: "Now that ripcord, you better hold onto it; don't throw it away in your excitement. It costs five dollars."

I said, "I'll do my best." He said: "You pay for it if you don't."

I climbed into the ship and climbed out again on the wing, by way of rehearsal. What, I said to myself, if when we get upstairs all I do is shiver and finally shake my head and climb back into the ship and sit down. I could picture quite clearly their polite smiles as we came down again and they helped me out of the ship; certainly, they would say, you're damn right, it is really not worth the risk.

Was I sure that wouldn't happen? I was not.

I climbed in again.

He took off.

We rose across the familiar fields, swung around and climbed over the open country. A phrase went through my head: "I earnestly hope."

At a thousand feet, the silliness of the enterprise had faded: now in the air, it was simply an aeronautical job to be done, and to be done with the usual aeronautical attitude—judgment, deliberation, control. At two thousand feet, that attitude had taken full possession of me; so much so that now if anything had seemed wrong, I would no longer have minded even calling the whole thing off and returning to the Airport, the way a good flier sometimes will.

But nothing did seem wrong.

At three thousand feet, we crossed over the state fair grounds, headed into the wind. The pilot poked me in the back and throttled back, to slacken the propeller blast and make it easier for me to climb out. I was glad I had rehearsed the job. It went smoothly, and I had attention to spare for easing my two 'chutes past all sorts of hazards without having the ripcords catch and rip open.

He put on the power again, and I had to hold on tightly, for the wind was pushing me heavily from behind and threatened to throw me off.

I looked down; half a mile down . . .

I should like now to report hair-raising sensations. But actually I was cool—or perhaps the better word is dead. While I stood out there and looked down, my heart stopped pounding. It was the factor X again, coming in handy; I could feel no animalic fear of falling, because I could get no animal sense of the depth. Looking back into the front cockpit, I could see the altimeter registering 2500 feet; we had lost altitude while I had climbed out. But the position of a needle on a dial was evidence too thin and intellectual to give you a good scare. It was different when I looked at the pilot. He was tense and worried, thinking probably about the job ahead and the chance that something might miscarry and he might have to jump. I preferred not to watch him; for fear can be induced the sympathetic way from man to man.

He throttled back again and nodded. I felt no reluctance. I let go of my hold, took hold of the ripcord ring over my heart, and with one long step walked out into the farms below.

The fall was violent. I fell and fell. I fell face downward, my left hand clawing at a cornfield, right hand on my heart, holding the ripcord. I fell so hard that I couldn't even be afraid; I was all filled out by one feeling, a feeling which, translated into colloquial language, was: "Oh, boy, oh, boy, here I go."

Falling is falling, from old habit, whether you do it in an optic vacuum or not. No factor X deadened that sensation. I held my breath, or rather my nerves did; they expected me presently to hit with terrific force, and to get hurt; because they had never known me to fall and then not hit and get hurt. I remember hearing myself gasp, which shows that I must have fallen quite deep below the airplane and its noise. I waited as long as I could. Then it seemed horribly urgent to find out whether or not the contraption would work.

Then I pulled the handle.

I gave it all I'd got. It came out with hardly any resistance, and went slack in my hand. I pulled it all the way out and stretched out my arm and held it far away from me, and grasped it hard; I must not lose it: point of aeronautical honor. Even while falling, I held it stretched out with my right, the way Marshal Bluecher holds his saber, in the pictures, riding an attack; even while falling,

I thought that was funny. And I waited with some impatience to be caught up.

Nothing happened.

Then there was a vision of laundry fluttering on a line. That was the silk, stringing out behind me. A gentle force seemed to lift me by the shoulders and pull me upright, much as one might pick up a child who had fallen, and I had just time to think, "Is that all?"

Then the canopy opened. The harness grabbed me around the thighs, jerking my legs apart. A bolt of energy struck down on my head, traveled down along my spine, my legs, and my feet, just as a crack travels along a whip, until I thought my feet were going to snap off. Something jerked me upward with a huge lift—a fish would feel that way when he is hooked. And I remember hearing myself groan—against that peculiar stillness. Then the forces subsided, and I was afloat.

Of all the sensations of air-faring, that is the most dreamlike—floating under a parachute. It begins with a wave of triumphal emotion which is standard accompaniment of everyone's first parachute jump and is unlike any other experience—there is in it the sudden deliverance from danger, also release from perhaps the most concentrated bit of waiting there is, and also exultation of being high up in the air, flying for once in silence, for once almost without a machine.

I looked up at my 'chute; the simplest of all aircraft

It quivered, high above me, the merest handkerchief in size; it seemed incredible that so small a bit of silk should have so much holding power. In the stillness it gave out a thin sound, like a peanut whistle. That was the air, escaping through its center vent hole. It was a warning, though I didn't understand it: an indication of the speed with which I was actually coming down.

For the time being, I was well afloat with my magic carpet. The harness was holding up my weight so evenly that I was hardly conscious of it. It is like flying in dreams, flying simply because you are light. My feet were limp under me hanging into a cornfield. The view was the usual one from an airplane, the green plain, the distant horizon. But there was no wind; when I moved my hand, the air felt thin.

I experimented with steering the 'chute by pulling the lines so as to set the canopy askew; it let me slide off sidewise obediently enough. But it also set me to swinging, pendulum fashion, and I had to stabilize myself by throwing my weight about the way a child stops its own oscillations on a swing. When I looked down again, I found myself bearing down on the race course. There was the landing to think of now.

My descent had become more noticeable. I watched for a while, with an eye practiced by so many approaches, and it seemed to me that I was undershooting the intended.

The race track seemed the probable point of contact and within the race track, the corner where the stables were and that grandstand. If so, I should get hurt. Beyond it, there was the abandoned flying field. I grabbed the two forward ones of the lines and hung onto them. It helped a lot; the wind combined with the 'chute to carry me forward beautifully. I flew across the roof of the grandstand, across the race track itself, sliding along weightless, without footing, like a ghost.

But again the maneuver threw me into violent swinging. I worked hurriedly to stop it. The grass was beginning to dilate under me as if pulled up by a magnifying glass. Only one hazard was now still before me: the fence of the fair area. Beyond it was the clear field. There was little time left. The wind was drifting me toward the fence, but not fast enough. And I was too low now to do any more maneuvering. I had to take whatever was coming, and it began to look like a 50-50 shot. I could already distinguish the individual strands of barbed wire.

I was floating down steeply now, the sinking much more visible than the forward drift. I saw that I was going to light exactly on the fence, but in my innocence, I was not much worried. I decided I would simply step lightly on the top wire, kick myself off from it, and step down, still borne by the 'chute, still weightless, from the fence into the grass, on the airport side. As it was coming up against me, I stretched my right foot down to meet it; and I missed. The wind had carried me forward by about two feet or so, and I was across. Then the grass took a lunge. There was just time to go limp.

It came up through my legs and my whole body as if they had been unsubstantive as a ghost's, went right at my chin, and swatted the living daylights out of me. And that was only the beginning. For a long time thereafter, though I thought I was down, legs and arms kept falling all around me and kept me wondering where it all came from. Then the bombardment subsided and it was quiet.

I looked up. The 'chute was standing upright in the grass, tugging at me with the force of a sail. I pulled in one of the lines and made it collapse and unbuckled my harness, working with a breathless haste for which there was no other reason than that my whole system was still timed for fast airwork. From the distance, people were running across the field, old Johnson doing his best to keep up with them. And the ship was coming in for a landing. I looked at my hand, and my ripcord was gone. Just before everybody arrived, I found it lying in the grass: a piece of wire rope, one yard long, attached to the ring. I also found a deep hollow scooped out of the soft ground, of the kind which in skiing is called a bathtub. That was the place where I had hit. My shirt was torn, and my trouser legs were torn. My cheek was bleeding; despite the goggles, my spectacles were bent.

There was a great deal of excited talk. I had been lucky. The fence was nine feet high, with steel posts and very tight wires, not an ordinary farm fence at all, but more like a burglar-proof factory fence. If I had landed on it, on this fence, with that force—I would have been cut in two. We stood around the 'chute. It lay there flat and dead on the grass. I felt as if I had landed some monster fish.

A NOTE ON THE TYPE

The text of this book was set on the Linotype in Baskerville. Linotype Baskerville is a facsimile cutting from type cast from the original matrices of a face designed by John Baskerville. The original face was the forerunner of the "modern" group of type faces.

John Baskerville (1706-75), of Birmingham, England, a writing-master, with a special renown for cutting inscriptions in stone, began experimenting about 1750 with punch-cutting and making typographical material. It was not until 1757 that he published his first work. His types, at first criticized, in time were recognized as both distinct and elegant, and his types as well as his printing were greatly admired.